Latin American Constitutions

Latin American Constitutions provides a comprehensive historical study of constitutionalism in Latin America from the independence period to the present, focusing on the Constitution of Cádiz, a foundational document in Latin American constitutionalism. Although drafted in Spain, it was applied in many regions of Latin America, and deputies from America formed a significant part of the drafting body. The politicization of constitutionalism reflected in Latin America's first moments proved to be a lasting legacy evident in the legal and constitutional world of the region today: many of Latin America's present challenges to establishing effective constitutionalism can be traced to the debates, ideas, structures, and assumptions of this text. This book explores the region's attempts to create effective constitutional texts and regimes in light of an established practice of linking constitutions to political goals and places important constitutional thinkers and regional constitutions, such as the Mexican Constitution of 1917, into their legal and historical context.

M. C. Mirow is a professor of law at Florida International University.

Latin American Constitutions

The Constitution of Cádiz and its Legacy in Spanish America

M. C. MIROW

Florida International University College of Law

CAMBRIDGE UNIVERSITY PRESS

CAMBRIDGE
UNIVERSITY PRESS

University Printing House, Cambridge CB2 8BS, United Kingdom

One Liberty Plaza, 20th Floor, New York, NY 10006, USA

477 Williamstown Road, Port Melbourne, VIC 3207, Australia

314-321, 3rd Floor, Plot 3, Splendor Forum, Jasola District Centre, New Delhi - 110025, India

79 Anson Road, #06-04/06, Singapore 079906

Cambridge University Press is part of the University of Cambridge.

It furthers the University's mission by disseminating knowledge in the pursuit of
education, learning and research at the highest international levels of excellence.

www.cambridge.org
Information on this title: www.cambridge.org/9781107618558

© M. C. Mirow 2015

First published 2015
First paperback edition 2019

A catalogue record for this publication is available from the British Library

Library of Congress Cataloging in Publication data
Mirow, M. C. (Matthew Campbell), 1962– author
Latin American constitutions: The constitution of Cádiz and its
legacy in Spanish America / M. C. Mirow, Florida International
University College of Law
pages cm
Includes bibliographical references and index.
ISBN 978-1-107-02559-2 (hardback)
1. Constitutional history – Latin America. 2. Law – Latin America –
Spanish influences. 3. Spain. Constitución (1812) I. Title.
KG545.M57 2015
342.802´9–dc23 2015016110

ISBN 978-1-107-02559-2 Hardback
ISBN 978-1-107-61855-8 Paperback

To Angela, Camila, and Andrea,
my Calliope, Thalia, and Clio

Contents

Acknowledgments

"One's second book is always the most difficult to write" observed David Brading when reviewing his contributions to the field of Mexican history over the past decades.[1] These words rang horribly true during the writing of this book and yet gave me the strength to complete it. Although I have participated in and written other books in the decade that separates this work from my study of Latin American private law, this work is in many ways my second book. It has certainly been my most difficult. Family, personal, and professional demands had at one time or another nearly conspired to convince me to abandon the work. The expansive and relatively uncharted nature of the topic and my increasingly keen awareness of its scope also led to moments of great doubt. Nonetheless, Brading's words and support from so many family members, friends, colleagues, and institutions gave me enough encouragement to see the work through.

I thank Dean Alex Acosta of the Florida International University College of Law and Professor Alejandro Guzmán Brito of the Escuela de Derecho of the Pontificia Universidad Católica de Valparaíso, Chile, for their support of this project. Essential research for this project was conducted at both institutions and at the Latin American Collection of the Smathers Library, University of Florida, Gainesville, and the Escuela de Estudios Hispano-Americanos, Seville, Spain. I am grateful to the University of Florida's Center for Latin American Studies for a research travel grant and to Richard Phillips who assisted my work there. Dr. Marisol Floren-Romero of the Florida International University College of Law Library provided excellent bibliographic support and advice.

[1] Brading, "A Recusant Abroad," 23.

Special thanks are due Julie Beineke, Assistant Director of International and Graduate Studies at Florida International University College of Law. She ran the daily administration of our Office of International and Graduate Studies so competently, thoughtfully, and skillfully that I knew everything was under control.

The following individuals have been academically or personally helpful at one stage or another in this project: Carlos Alejano, Sir John Baker, Thomas Baker, Lauren Benton, David Brading, Patricio Carvajal, Elizabeth Dale, Juan Javier del Granado, Antonio Dougnac, Thomas Duve, Scott Eastman, Stanley Fish, Carlos Garriga, Michael Grossberg, Felicity Heal, Clive Holmes, David Hook, Fr. Daniel Houde, O.SS.T., David Ibbetson, Graciela Iglesias, Robert Jarvis, Sherry Johnson, Charles Jones, Fr. Joseph Landauer, Abelardo Levaggi, Marta Lorente, Ian Magedera, Aniceto Masferrer, Eduardo Martiré, Alejandro Mayagoitia, Fernando Mayorga, Fr. Adelson Moreira, O.SS.T., Juan Pablo Pampillo, Eduardo Posada, Marci Rosenthal, Bernard Rudden, Austin Sarat, Frank Sicius, Natalia Sobrevilla, Jonathan Thacker, Kerri Stone, Victor Tau, Consuelo Varela, Howard Wasserman, and Alain Wijffels. Renzo Honores and Victor Uribe-Urán were selfless in their willingness to review nearly the entire work or large chunks of it at the final stages of writing. Any mistakes are mine.

Portions of this book have been presented at various conferences. I thank the following institutions for their hospitality and for their members' comments: the American Society for Legal History, Cambridge University, the European Society for Comparative Legal History, Fordham Law School, Ghent University, George Washington University, the Instituto Internacional de Historia del Derecho Indiano, the Instituto Riva-Agüero, the Max Planck Institute for European Legal History, Oxford University, the Pontificia Universidad Católica de Chile, the Pontificia Universidad Católica de Perú, the Pontificia Universidad Católica de Valparaíso, the Senate of Mexico, the University of Cambridge, and the University of Buenos Aires. In addition to these institutions, I thank the Centre Georges Chevrier (UMR 5605 – Université de Bourgogne/CNRS) (Dijon), the Escuela Libre de Derecho (Mexico City), the Fulbright Commissions of Chile, Peru, and the United States; Gonville and Caius College (Cambridge), the MECESUP2 program of the Chilean Ministry of Education, the Latin American Studies Association, the Mellon Foundation, and Merton College (Oxford).

At Cambridge University Press, I thank Deborah Gershenowitz for her wonderful and understanding encouragement, Diane Aronson and David Morris guided the book to completion. I also thank Theresa Kornak and

Nishanthini Vetrivel for their editing and preparation of the manuscript for publication. This work was also substantially improved by the corrections, comments, and suggestions made by anonymous reviewers for the press at various stages of writing. I owe these readers my many thanks.

Finally, I am grateful to my family for their support. My Colombian parents, Nelly Franco and Antonio Mesa, died shortly before I finished this book. They helped me in many ways, and I miss them greatly. I am blessed with many family members who lovingly refrained from asking too many questions about my progress. Shirley, Gregory, Jock, Joyce, Jake, Isabel, Trevor, Pedro, Norm, Cherene, and Amy, thank you.

Portions of Chapters 2, 3, 6, and 7 and the conclusion are derived from or republished from the article "Visions of Cádiz: The Constitution of 1812 in Historical and Constitutional Thought," *Studies in Law, Politics, and Society* 53 (2010): 59–88. Unless otherwise noted, translations to English are mine. I thank Carolina Academic Press for permitting me to reprint selected provisions of the Constitution of Cádiz in the Appendix.

Introduction

The central historic square of Saint Augustine, Florida, is called the Plaza de la Constitución, but it is not named for the United States Constitution. Instead, it commemorates America's other first constitution, the Constitution of Cádiz of 1812. Near the center of the square, a monument records the Constitution's promulgation in October, 1812, in the province of East Florida, then part of the Spanish Empire.

This Spanish Constitution, however, did not last long as a document guiding the political structure of Spain and its many possessions around the world. The Constitution was the product of the power vacuum resulting from Napoleon's invasion of Spain in 1808 and the ouster of Fernando VII. European and American Spaniards did not know where to swear their allegiance. Many turned to a revitalized representative body, the Cortes, which met in Cádiz, Spain, and ultimately promulgated the Constitution in the name of Fernando VII. He was restored to the Spanish throne in 1814 and was not interested in ruling as the first constitutional monarch. On restoration, he repudiated the document but the city of Saint Augustine never took down its monument. The monument stands today as one of the only squares and monuments dedicated to the Constitution left in all the Americas.

This mostly forgotten monument to a mostly forgotten document fails to portray the importance of the Constitution of Cádiz in the development of constitutions and constitutional law in the world. The Constitution of Cádiz had a dramatic impact on constitutionalism throughout the Western world, particularly in the former Spanish colonies. It was not only transatlantic in its effect; it was born of a transatlantic effort. Deputies representing many areas of the New World with deputies of peninsular

Spain debated, drafted, and promulgated a document that created equal Spanish subjects on both sides of the Atlantic Ocean. The Constitution moved into and out of effect three times before 1840 with the changing political dynamics of Spain and the king. Its provisions never fully took root in Latin America or Spain as an effective constitutional order, but the Spanish Empire experienced brief moments of constitutional life under its provisions in the Americas and on the peninsula.

The events and texts surrounding the promulgation and ultimate rejection of the Constitution of Cádiz will be one of the lenses through which this book examines Latin American constitutional development to the present day. In sum, this work views the Constitution not only as the first Latin American constitution and a liberal political turning point in American and European history, but also as a moment of lost opportunity and of lasting constitutional injury to the region. The Constitution of Cádiz heralded liberal constitutionalism in Europe and the Americas. Indeed, many newly independent nations looked to its provisions, as they did to the provisions of the United States Constitution, in drafting their own first constitutions. The document is about forty pages in length and provides for sovereignty in the nation, rather than in the king. Although maintaining Roman Catholicism as the official state religion, the Constitution incorporated various liberal ideas and institutions including representative electoral bodies at various levels of government, restrictions on the power of the king, codes of law applicable to everyone, rights for the criminally accused, freedom of contract, and individual property rights. With interesting content and demonstrated influence on the history of constitutionalism in Spain and in the world, the Constitution has been the subject of many studies and analyses, including polemical studies by liberals and non-liberals alike.[1]

The historiography of the Constitution in the past fifty years has been summarized well by Estrada, who sees in these works at least three "Cadices." The first group of works addressing the Constitution, anti-liberal in their tone, seeks to undermine the legitimacy of Cádiz by underscoring its inconsistency with Spain's ancient constitution. A second group of works emphasizes the Constitution's Spanish and national character without fully appreciating the geographical diversity reflected in its creation, text, and institutions. The third group discovers special relevance in Cádiz in light of the creation of a modern Spanish

---

[1] Breña, *El imperio*, 147–175; García Laguardia, "Las Cortes," 12–16; Rodriguez, *The Cádiz Experiment*, 75.

constitutional monarchy under the Spanish Constitution of 1976. This group finds inspiration in Cádiz's apparent ability to combine various territories within a single nation, an enduring constitutional and political question in Spain.[2]

As scholars unearthed the substantial Latin American contribution to the drafting of the document in Spain, they also revealed that Latin American deputies developed skills in constitutional thought and drafting that were transferred to independence movements in former colonies. Thus, the Constitution of Cádiz has been properly linked to the Age of Democratic Revolutions that flourished in Europe and the Americas.[3] It has similarly been linked to both an Age of Constitutions and an Age of Codifications.[4] It was a busy time for ages.

The relative newness of its electoral process and institutions has also been properly associated with the rise of modernity.[5] Intellectual and legal historians have debated at length the way the Cortes and the Constitution signaled a shift from the world of the *ancien régime* to the modern age, noting the liminal quality of these events and documents.[6] Indeed, some have linked the process of constitutionalization as a key component of modernization, defining modernity as "the process of constitutionalization of a society of individuals with a state power."[7] Related to this discussion, questions of the Constitution's incorporation or rejection of the *ancien régime*'s jurisdictional structures that served as a foundation of preconstitutional imperial government have been analyzed and debated.[8]

Despite the many liberal and modern aspects this early document in constitutional history brought to political thought, the almost immediate suspension and lack of long-standing force of the Constitution left fundamental fissures in Latin American constitutionalism from which the region still suffers. The suspension of the Constitution of Cádiz linked constitutions to political change and thus politicized constitutional law and constitutionalism. In other words, constitutions became part of the

---

[2] Estrada, *Monarquía y nación*, xviii–xix, xliv, xlvi. For the historiography of the Constitution see Breña; *El primer liberalismo*; Chust, "De rebeliones," 465–491; and Estrada, "Los reinos," 213–226 (addressing questions of territory).

[3] Rodríguez, *The Independence of Spanish America*.

[4] Mirow, "The Age of Constitutions," 229–235.

[5] Guerra, "El Soberano," 1–2; Guerra, *Modernidad*, 177–225; Lorente, "Esencia," 293–314; Van Young, "El momento," 221–292.

[6] Annino, *La Revolución*, 12–15; Garriga, "Orden Jurídico," 37–41.

[7] Garriga, "Orden Jurídico," 41.

[8] Garriga and Lorente, *Cádiz*; Rojas, "De reino," 212–216.

tool box employed by politicians to work political change, reform, or restoration. This hindered the ability of constitutions to transcend the political sphere in Latin America. In contrast, the United States Constitution, dating from the same period, has been able to govern above various political parties, policies, and movements. The result of the politically instrumental use of constitutions can be seen in the present lack of constitutional entrenchment and in the high frequency of new constitutions from which Latin America suffers today. These results can be traced to the region's experience with its first written constitution, the Constitution of Cádiz.

The Constitution of Cádiz is as much a constitution of empire as it is a foundational text of liberalism. The successes of European and Latin American liberalism have obscured the Constitution's place in the history of the Spanish Empire. The Constitution of Cádiz was a scramble to maintain the existence of the Spanish Empire and to maintain peninsular control of that empire through novel legal processes and institutions. It was an imperial bargain with liberalism in which established imperial beneficiaries – the church, the military, traders, and American élites – jealously and closely negotiated many liberal reforms. Those drafting and promulgating the Constitution cautiously balanced the internal conflicts in constitutional aspects now sometimes viewed as inevitably triumphant. These aspects included rights to liberty and property; the representative quality of the new government under the Constitution; the status of Indians, free blacks, and slaves; and national sovereignty.

This book seeks to inform the literature on comparative constitutionalism that is developing around the world. Some works, including some of my previous writings, argue that the United States Constitution should be viewed as an export product throughout the world and specifically in Latin America. The influence of the Constitution of Cádiz has been underestimated in the migration of constitutional ideas. While scholars have pointed out the essential contribution of the Constitution of Cádiz to the development of political ideas of independence and self-rule for the new republics of Latin America, this book focuses on its *legal* and *constitutional* legacy. Viewed from this perspective, the Constitution and its legacy have a multifaceted quality with successes and failures for legal and constitutional development in the region.

If the Constitution of Cádiz led the way into the realm of Latin American constitutionalism slightly more than 200 years ago, perhaps the next most important landmark constitution in the region is the Mexican Constitution of 1917, now approaching its hundredth anniversary. The Constitution of Cádiz was Latin America's first written constitution, and many have argued that the Mexican Constitution of 1917 was Latin America's first truly Latin American constitution. Each played a pivotal role in the nature, style, and ideology of constitutions in the region that would follow them. While the Constitution of Cádiz shaped nineteenth-century constitutional thought and practice in Latin America, the Mexican Constitution of 1917 was a turning point for the twentieth century, particularly through its advancement of social welfare rights related to work and its radical turn away from liberal notions of property. Since the Constitution of 1917, redefining the role of property and establishing constitutional regimes of agrarian reform have been core elements of attempts to deal with economic, political, and power imbalances in the region.

Constitutional law and meaningful, effective constitutional adjudication in Latin America have blossomed in recent decades as countries of the region have tried to shed dictatorships and autocracies for effective democratic governance and the rule of law. Substantial academic effort has been trained on present problems and challenges to an effective constitutional order in the region. By placing some of these challenges in historical context, this book reexamines the nature of these challenges and may tacitly provide some ideas about ways to move forward.

Scholars have arrived at different structures for the periods of Latin American constitutionalization. For example, Bernardino Bravo Lira has seen the region locked into a cycle of constitutionalism, anarchy, and militarism; failed democratic constitutional experiments led to anarchy that led to military dictatorships that led to new democratic periods.[9] Roberto Gargarella has recently divided Latin America's 200 years of constitutional history into the following periods: a first period from approximately 1810 to 1850; a second "foundational period" from approximately 1850 to 1900 dedicated to notions of "order and progress"; a third shorter period of crisis when the ideas of "order and progress" no longer functioned; a fourth period of social constitutionalism beginning in the 1930s; and a fifth period from the end of the twentieth century into the present as one of "new Latin American constitutionalism."[10]

Gargarella's periodization is useful in its broad strokes. This book similarly follows a chronological structure but ascribes the foundational period to the constitutionalism arising from the Constitution of Cádiz in

---

[9] Bravo Lira, *El estado constitucional*, 3, 196.
[10] Gargarella, *Latin American Constitutionalism*, ix.

1812, a document mentioned just a handful of times in his study. The present study finds foundational fissures from this period that have affected the region's constitutional development to this day. These include, for example, not only the clumsy juxtaposition of liberal and conservative ideas and hyperpresidentialism noted by Gargarella, but also the immediate politicization of constitutions and their lack of social entrenchment and political transcendence. We observe and report in different ways many of the same phenomena, and this book sees their origins stemming from a more distant foundational moment. And if Gargarella emphasizes change in the path of constitutionalism in Latin America, this work emphasizes continuity.

Chapter 1 discusses the crucible of the Constitution of Cádiz, mostly from an American perspective. The years leading up to the Constitution were politically unstable for the American parts of the Spanish Empire and the French invasion of Spain led to a rupture of the well-established and highly complex unwritten constitutions of colonial administration. This was a moment of constitutional limbo in Spanish America, with periods of unrest accompanied by nascent independence movements, often contradictorily grounded in direct loyalty to Fernando VII. As Latin American countries search for the "big bang" of their independence, they are often chagrined to find that there was no big bang at all, but rather a mixture of interests and assertions of loyalty to an exiled king marking the very first inklings of regional autonomy. Chapter 1 studies these moments from a constitutional standpoint, particularly in relationship to the appeal of the Cortes of Cádiz as a unifying representative body.

Chapter 2 shifts our focus to Spain. The Constitution of Cádiz can only be understood in its Spanish and European context as well. From 1808 to 1812, Spain was ravaged by war and political uncertainty. The Cortes of Cádiz met, debated, drafted, and acted against this backdrop. It was, of course, a highly interesting intellectual moment in European history. While cannon shots were heard as the deputies debated, the Cortes considered widely divergent views of what should be done with and for the Spanish Empire. This chapter explores the main issues that were at stake, the intellectual influences and political perspectives that guided the debate, and how the final text of the Constitution reflected and resolved these varied viewpoints.

Chapter 3 reveals the work of Americans in Cádiz. "The American question" involved issues of the representation of American populations and the citizenship of indigenous populations. Whether various populations counted for purposes of representation was debated with concern and passion. Just as the United States Constitution was forced to consider issues of slaves, slavery, and the slave trade, so too we find these issues at the forefront of the American question in Cádiz, Spain. The Americas were too powerful, too economically important, and too essential to Spain's funding of the war against France to be disregarded. Americans were not peripheral considerations; they often steered the agenda, led the debate, and greatly influenced the final text of the Constitution. They brought expertise, along with vocal expressions of national, regional, and local concerns. They continued to assert these interests in the Cortes that followed the Constitution in 1813 and 1814, and in the Cortes that were held again in the 1820s under the Constitution. This chapter also examines the constitutional ideas and experiences many returning deputies brought back to their countries, many of which were already well on the path to complete independence.

Chapter 4 considers the failures and successes of the Constitution of Cádiz. Here the furtive applications of the Constitution in Spain and in those areas that remained loyal to the Spanish crown or Cortes during these uncertain decades are examined. The chapter also consider the way the Constitution played into Latin American independence and to what extent the text and ideas behind the Constitution were influential in the constitutions of the early republics.

Chapter 5 traces what happened in Latin American constitutionalism as countries moved beyond the independence period after the 1820s and into the later nineteenth and twentieth centuries. Constitutions became tools in internal political squabbles and major political battles. Countries struggled with creating and enforcing constitutional rights through new procedural tools and courts.

The legacy of the Constitution of Cádiz as it is reflected in Latin American constitutionalism in the twentieth century is the topic of Chapter 6. The Constitution established certain patterns in the region, producing what I call the "Cádiz effect." Present-day constitutional intransigence and the frequency with which new constitutions are promulgated are part of this pattern. Indeed, the Constitution of Cádiz and its subsequent treatment by Fernando VII established a practice of the politicization of constitutionalism leading to a lack of entrenchment in legal and societal terms. This helped create a culture of constitutional noncompliance exacerbated by continued difficulties of effective constitutional enforcement mechanisms. The Cádiz effect even touches some of the theoretical problems of constitutional decision making in the region today. The Mexican Constitution of 1917, a document many consider to be the first truly autochthonous constitutional product of Spanish America, is a pivotal point in this chapter.

Nonetheless, Chapter 7 addresses more recent developments and suggests that the Cádiz effect can be overcome. Constitutionalism and courts enforcing constitutions are uncovering useful language in the new constitutions of the region. European and international models of constitutional practice and interpretation are informing new constitutional courts and tribunals. The region has witnessed brave constitutional judges and bold holdings directed toward the executive, legislative, and military branches, indicating that the Cádiz effect is not necessarily a permanent fixture of Latin American constitutionalism. Challenges, however, remain, and this brief assessment of current constitutional practices in the region also reports on hindrances to effective constitutional rule.

The recent bicentennial of the Constitution of Cádiz provides an apt moment to consider and to reconsider the document's creation, influence, and legacy. The text and those implementing it struggled with questions of sovereignty; electoral representation; the place and incorporation of various peoples within the Americas; limits on the executive branch's exercise of power; the role of the church, religion, and the military in politics and society; the place of the judiciary in these questions; and how to effect a lasting, meaningful, and entrenched constitutional regime that governed well and protected citizens. In many ways, the questions presented by the Constitution of Cádiz and its deputies are the same questions put to Latin American constitutionalism today.

Although the Constitution of Cádiz has been widely praised as a liberal document establishing a constitutional monarchy, it must be properly considered in the historical context of empire. There is also a negative side to the story. The Constitution of Cádiz represents a failed founding constitutional moment from which constitutional regimes in Latin America continue to recover with great effort and, at times, with great success. The constitutions of Latin American countries today must also be considered in their political contexts and in light of the interests that constructed them and administer them.

I

Constitutional Limbo in Early Nineteenth-Century Latin America

The years leading up to the Constitution of Cádiz were politically unstable for the American parts of the Spanish Empire, and the French invasion of Spain led to a rupture of the well-established and highly complex unwritten constitutions of colonial administration. This was a moment of constitutional limbo in Spanish America, with periods of political unrest and the development of nascent independence movements. Assertions of independence from the peninsula and its provisional government were contradictorily grounded in direct loyalty to Fernando VII, then in exile. As Latin American countries searched for the "big bang" of their independence, they were often chagrined to find that there was no big bang at all, but rather a mixture of interests and assertions of loyalty to an exiled king marking the first inklings of regional autonomy.[1]

These moments can be studied from a constitutional standpoint, particularly when recognizing the appeal of the Cortes of Cádiz as a unifying representative body offering imperial continuity. Two primary aspects shaped constitutional thought in the Spanish world as deputies assembled in Cádiz. These were, first, the unwritten constitution of the Spanish Empire, Spain's "ancient constitution," on the eve of the Napoleonic occupation and, second, the constitutional documents in circulation at the time of the Cortes, including early American constitutions of independence, often in their own wording, loyal and monarchical in tone. The Constitution of Cádiz in the Americas was prefigured by significant recent institutional changes from the 1760s onward that came from the Bourbon Reforms and by the surprisingly numerous written

[1] Similarly, Rodríguez, "We Are Now," 3.

9

constitutions that came before it in Europe and the Americas. Though officially banned, Enlightenment thought and writings were widely available. A member of the Spanish colonial élite, Antonio Nariño, obtained a copy of the French Declaration of the Rights of Man and published a translation of it that circulated widely. He was sentenced but escaped during his transportation to prison.[2]

Although to think in terms of a clear and inevitable transition of sovereignty from empire to nation may create a neat line of transformation, recent historians have reminded us that there was little or nothing that was core or fixed in either form of sovereignty, and that resulting nations, and underlying notions of nation, were only one direction of many possible directions. These paths toward the nation might include movement backwards, false starts, shifting views, and even moments of profound confusion and uncertainty. Recent investigations of sovereignty in the period reveal that it operated on various levels and that assumptions about territoriality, duality between metropole and periphery, and uniformity within empire must be discarded in favor of a more complex conception incorporating continually negotiated arrangements of internal and external power, jurisdiction, and even geographic formations.[3] Similarly, the legally pluralistic nature of empires has been uncovered and analyzed; different legal systems, components, and jurisdictions clashed with each other and with the centers of empire.[4] The constitutions of this period unwittingly battled with these complex legal models of empire as they sought to standardize and to make uniform the rules of law and government, rules that, in turn, became additional factors in the legal and governmental terrain.

In keeping with this newer appreciation of empire, Jeremy Adelman writes of the "elasticity" of "polymorphous sovereignties" in the period and warns us that "narratives of empire need not collapse repeatedly into familiar dichotomies of empire *or* nation, empire *versus* nation."[5] In fact, recent historians of Latin American independence have abandoned the theme of "the birth of the nation" and shifted their focus away from the search for national identity and sovereignty.[6] Nonetheless, when considering constitutional development and change, questions of sovereignty are central. Indeed, constitutions are essentially implementations

---

[2] Bushnell, *The Making*, 32–34, 38; Safford and Palacios, *Colombia*, 70–72.
[3] Adelman, "An Age of Imperial Revolutions," 320–334; Benton, *A Search for Sovereignty*; Benton, *Law and Colonial Cultures*, 1–30; Benton, "The Legal Regime."
[4] Benton and Ross, "Empires," 1–9.
[5] Adelman, "An Age of Imperial Revolutions," 336, 337 (Adelman's emphasis).
[6] Adelman, "What's in a Revolution?" 188–189.

of sovereignty. The documents and practices of unwritten constitutions and the texts of written constitutions reflect the same process of shifting agreements, compromises, and notions that constructed sovereignty in the period. Sovereignty was implemented in legal texts and constitutional documents as the region, not inevitably, wobbled toward independence.

Unwritten Constitutions of Colonial Administration

The unwritten Spanish constitution presents many challenges for constitutional historians. On the most basic level, a general sketch of the general contours of the unwritten Spanish imperial constitution will be useful as a basis for later written constitutions. This includes the way unwritten constitutional practices distribute political power and function in government and what obligations and expectations they place on particular members of society. One must take care to avoid ahistorical readings of such terms as "rights," "liberty," or "sovereignty." Indeed, tracing the development of the meaning of such terms is an important part of the puzzle of constitutional development.

As part of a debate about when the Spanish nation was first conceived, either at the time of the Constitution of Cádiz or at some earlier time in the 1700s, historians have probed sources to determine what the content of the unwritten constitution of Spain might have been or at least what the content of an *imagined* constitution from a period before the Constitution of Cádiz might have been in the construction of Spain's first written constitution. In drafting the Constitution it was politically useful to create a memory of lost liberties that were being recovered in the process of drafting a written constitution.[7] Similarly, Chiaramonte notes that the "ancient constitution" in this context can mean a set of legal rules delineating constitutional practices and structures or a "discursive weapon" engaged to undermine what are considered to be illegitimate innovations.[8]

An exploration of Spain's unwritten imperial constitution serves a dual purpose. The first is to describe the actual content of the unwritten constitution that governed Spain and its empire, particularly in relationship to its American colonies. The second purpose is to lay the groundwork for the rhetorical use of that material in the construction of a new constitutional order based on these pre-Cádiz materials and understandings.

---

[7] Lorente, *La nación*, 29–30. The topic is explored in Portillo, *Revolución de nación*.
[8] Chiaramonte, "The 'Ancient Constitution,'" 459.

By the late eighteenth century, Castile and the other medieval king-doms of Iberia had established complex and sophisticated institutions and sources for structuring and running their governmental and legal machineries. As regions of the peninsula were conquered and Muslim rule overthrown, law and government ran together, and the king and his royal courts and judges participated in a method of rule that centered on an adjudicatory framework in which the provision of justice provided the glue of royal power. *Fueros*, or special privileges, were attained by some regions, and Castile gathered its rule into an effective set of institutions and laws.[9]

With lasting impact on the Spanish Empire and the newly formed republics of Latin America, the thirteenth-century collection of laws known as the *Siete Partidas* not only spelled out, in great detail, par-ticular rules of private law, but also addressed essential elements of the ancient constitution. The *Siete Partidas* established important principles concerning the crown, the nobility, judges, and the church.[10] Royal coun-cils and *audiencias* were initially established in the fourteenth century. The *audiencias* served a variety of judicial and administrative functions under legally trained personnel.[11]

The church served as an additional, and highly successful, structure of administration and unification, and its theology and canon legal theory of natural rights served as fundamental ideas that guided later construc-tions of property and the treatment of human beings.[12] The association of the Royal Patronage (*Real Patronato*) of the church with its evange-lizing the Americas and financing these activities gave the crown signif-icantly more power over religious affairs in the Americas than on the peninsula. The king served effectively as the vicar of the pope through a series of papal bulls from the late fifteenth and early sixteenth centuries. Rights conferred on the Spanish crown in the Americas included the pre-sentment of ecclesiastical offices, including bishops; the administration of tithes; the creation and elimination of dioceses; and the resolution of conflicts between secular and regular clergy. In the role of the protector of the church, the crown wielded vast power over the nonspiritual aspects of the church in the Americas. The crown had the right to control the circulation and publication of church documents; to inspect communica-tions to the Holy See; to empower secular courts to review ecclesiastical

[9] Haley, "Foundations of Governance," 184–186.
[10] Ibid., 187.
[11] Mirow, *Latin American Law*, 22–25.
[12] Haley, "Foundations of Governance," 187–190.

judgments (a jurisdiction known as *recurso de fuerza*); to tax accumulations of property held by ecclesiastical corporations; to execute financial obligations on church members; and to veto, within the conclave, candidates for pope. Similar approaches to the administration of the church and cooperation with royal authority were found at the level of archbishops in the Americas.[13]

These structures, sources, and ideas were adapted to the Americas. The body of law specifically directed to these areas, *derecho indiano*, developed into a massive, complex, and functional set of royal legislation, rules, and institutions, all dependent on Castile and their peninsular counterparts under the crown.[14] The *Nueva Compilación de Castilla* (1567) applied directly in the Americas and the *Recopilación de Leyes de las Indias* (1680) set out a great amount of Spain's ancient constitution as it applied in the Americas. New American constitutional organs were created on the peninsula. The Council of the Indies was the chief body overseeing everything dealing with the Americas, and the Board of Trade managed the royal monopoly over American commerce, trade, travel, the flotilla system of ships, the precious riches dug from American soil, and slavery.[15] These institutions were known for their close scrutiny and precise system of record keeping and accounting. Generally, very little went on in these areas without a report; a letter; or a communiqué; and a signed, sworn, and notarized statement.

The most important cities, Mexico and Lima, and later Bogotá and Buenos Aires, were apexes of the highest administrative unit in the Americas, the viceroyalty. *Audiencias* were established in these and other important cities throughout the sixteenth, seventeenth, and eighteenth centuries to handle the administrative and judicial aspects of running the empire. Their spread followed politics and wealth. The earliest *audiencias* were established in Santo Domingo, Mexico, Panama, and Lima and the latest, in the eighteenth century, in Caracas, Buenos Aires (a second time), and Cuzco. Others were established along the way in Guatemala, Bogotá, Charcas, Quito, Manila, and Santiago de Chile. Every important colonial center wanted an *audiencia* and cities lobbied for their creation as a mark of standing. Local government was subject to district royal officials called *alcalde mayores* or *corregidores*, and towns of a certain minimum size where governed by a city council or *cabildo*. A noteworthy colonial

[13] Adame Goddard, "Asimilación y rechazo," 61–65.
[14] Cutter, *The Legal Culture*, 31–43; Dougnac, *Manual de Historia*; Tau Anzoátegui, *La Ley en America.*
[15] Haley, "Foundations of Governance," 190–191.

institution was the General Indian Court of colonial Mexico to hear claims from indigenous peoples in that viceroyalty. Indeed, indigenous legal subjectivity in the colonial era has been studied extensively, indicating that indigenous populations were skillful litigants and consumers of colonial law.[16] At the local level, separate administrative structures were created for some indigenous communities that paralleled communities of Spaniards, and the legal status of indigenous peoples was subject to theological debate and legislative regulation.[17] Indeed, some have interpreted this incorporation of indigenous subjects into the Spanish legal world as an important step in viewing "law as a system of legal rights."[18]

The absence of a constitutional text did not mean that individuals were not protected from government action that was harmful to them. Even before the Bourbon Reforms, the institutions and rules of *derecho indiano* provided various methods through which individuals could establish their claims against actions of the crown.[19] The status of the individual as a person, legally and theologically, was the starting point for any discussion, and by 1500 Queen Isabella had declared the inhabitants of the Americas free vassals of the crown. In the medieval European world, a king should act for the benefit of his vassals, and a vassal had various ways to counter or refute royal action that was to his detriment. These included the tools of petition to the crown, appeal through judicial bodies against acts of agents of the king, supplication before the king, and suspension of the particular action when the action originated with the king.[20] Royal officials were inspected and corrected through *visitas* and *residencias*, official investigations into the administration of an official.[21]

These possibilities were adapted to the Americas and the colonial world. The judicial *amparo* was used in the colonial period of absolutist monarchy until the mid-eighteenth century and fit well within a view of the king and the government primarily as dispensers of justice.[22] The American *audiencias*, with their expanded jurisdiction, in comparison with the same institution on the peninsula, were frequently the fora that heard appeals against government actions. In this capacity – Bravo Lira

---

[16] Haley, "Foundations of Governance," 192–194, 196–197. See, Borah, *Justice by Insurance*; Novoa-Cain, "The Protectors of Indians."
[17] Haley, "Foundations of Governance," 194–196.
[18] Ibid., 196.
[19] Martiré, "Dos lecciones," 11–35.
[20] Bravo Lira, "Protección jurídica," 318, 322–323.
[21] Martiré, "Dos lecciones," 23–26.
[22] Owensby, *Empire of Law*, 49–89.

reminds us – *audiencias* in the Americas served not only civil and criminal functions but also an important function of mediating the affairs of government that increased over time.[23] In addition to judicial resolution of conflicts with royal orders, the suspension of executing royal commands took on a highly scrutinized practice seen as providing flexibility under the response of "I obey, but do not execute."[24] Such supplication or suspension, in which the subject obeyed but did not carry out a particular royal command, was particularly important in implementing royal instructions in the Americas where present conditions might make immediate execution of the royal command ill advised.[25] Despite such checks on government action, royal power in the Americas was unbridled compared to the institutional and customary controls in place on the peninsula. For example, during the colonial period in the Americas, there were no regional assemblies such as the *Cortes* on the peninsula that might raise powerful voices defending customary local rights and interests against royal desires.[26]

In the eighteenth century, with a shift toward enlightened absolutism, the primary role of the king shifted from that of a dispenser of justice to a promoter of public prosperity, morality, and wealth through science, art, and commerce.[27] Royal power and the absolute exercise of royal power became associated with rational plans for implementing specific long-term goals and reforms aimed at improving the economic and social condition. Royal philanthropy was administered through institutions aimed at reducing suffering and increasing prosperity.[28] With these aims in mind, in the same period plans were introduced to increase the economic benefit of the Americas by modernizing commerce and by pulling indigenous populations into the economic sphere of the empire as both producers and consumers.[29]

This new political and economic stance was essential in the Americas' move toward independence and constitutionalism. Reform became an accepted attribute of governance. Government should adopt and change to further a new set of goals for the state that included the well-being and happiness of the people. These reforms might implicate religious

---

23 Bravo Lira, "Protección jurídica," 324, 327, 328, 330, 331.
24 Ibid., 329. For discussions of the aphorism see Mirow, *Latin American Law*, 235 and Phelan, "Authority and Flexibility," 59–60.
25 Martiré, "Dos lecciones," 16–19.
26 Bravo Lira, "Protección jurídica," 324–325.
27 Ibid., 330–331.
28 García Laguardia, *Centroamérica*, 13–15.
29 Owensby, "Between Justice and Economics," 150–155.

conformity, material prosperity, and scientific and cultural growth.[30] These themes provided the idea behind the growth of officially sanctioned societies or economic societies of friends of the country (*sociedades de amigos del país*). Within these organizations, economic and cultural leaders of a country might meet to discuss affairs and ways of improving the country's industry, agriculture, trade, arts, and education. For example, the Economic Society of the Friends of Guatemala was approved in 1795. Havana, Quito, Santiago de Cuba, Bogotá, Puerto Rico, Chiapas, and Lima, for example, all established some sort of society in which the country's nascent ruling class met for lectures, prizes, meetings, and discussions related to improving the country. Although the political composition of such societies was varied, members who espoused French Enlightenment thought or desires for independence most likely could engage others in intellectual debate in a somewhat safe location. These societies probably contributed to a joint sense of regional common purpose and thus to the growth of nationalism within various regions of the Americas. Some of these societies transformed into patriotic societies on independence. In addition to such societies, universities in the Americas provided intellectual outlets for new ideas. Although usually closely regulated and monitored by the church, some universities, such as San Carlos University in Guatemala, provided intellectual spaces for discussion of newer ideas. University documents indicate that views expressed in various prohibited works were addressed.[31]

While Catholic notions of kingship continued to provide justification for monarchy, the ideas of the state and of service to the state came to challenge the central place of the king. Thus, the king came to hold an institutional and beneficent place in the state, and concomitantly monarchy became just one possible form of government.[32] In the midst of these new possibilities, in 1804, Carlos IV attempted to expand royal authority in the Americas even more by appointing his family members as perpetual and hereditary viceroys, something heretofore unheard of, and in 1807 claimed for himself the title of Emperor of the Two Americas.[33]

These shifts aided in viewing the nation as coextensive with the state rather than with the king and monarchy, and these new ideas of administration and service to the state helped a change in perception of the

---

[30] Bravo Lira, "El absolutismo ilustrado," 11–15.
[31] García Laguardia, *Centroamérica*, 43–55, 65–68.
[32] Bravo Lira, "El absolutismo ilustrado," 18–19, 21, 25–27.
[33] Estrada Michel, "Regnícolas," 8–15.

king from the earlier idea of "king-judge" to the newer perception of "king-governor."[34] Representation before the government continued in corporatist lines; municipal corporations, communities, the estates, and corporate entities exercised rights of petition before the crown or its institutions to assert their specific rights, privileges, and liberties. With the newer notions of the public good, these entities might also assert claims based on these broader principles. The basis for such claims were under the *ancien régime* constructions of rights and duties and more specifically the content of *derecho indiano*.[35]

This new agenda and the heightened need for royal funds to put it in motion led to centralization and tighter control of the entire enterprise. The office of the royal regent and new Bourbon structures came into play in the late eighteenth century in the Americas with a continued interest in supervising government and its relationship to a ruled people.[36] A system of intendancies and subdelegations was imposed in the Americas under the government of José de Gálvez during the 1770s and 1780s.[37] Some provinces were characterized as "intendancies" although there was little precision in the use of the terms "province" and "intendancy" in the period.[38] Thus, in addition to the established sources from the Castilian law and the extant compilations of *derecho indiano*, the *Ordenanza de Intendentes* from 1782 and 1783 served as an important source for Spain's ancient constitution. For example, this legislation dictated the creation of various *juntas* depending on the level of importance of each city. In fact, Chiaramonte notes an instance in which the provisions of the *Ordenanza* were used to supply constitutional guidance against the Reglamento of 1811, which made Mendoza politically dependent upon Córdoba in Rio de la Plata.[39]

Although under the viceroys, these new intendants were charged with administration of justice, police, war, and finances, it is little wonder that friction arose with the viceroys and older colonial structures.[40] New financial institutions were put into place to govern and to supervise the finances of cities and important industries such as mining. Freer trade was introduced in 1778 and reached the Americas in the 1790s,

---

34 Bravo Lira, "El absolutismo ilustrado," 31, 32.
35 Lempérière, "La representación política," 57–59.
36 Bravo Lira, "Protección jurídica," 331–332.
37 Benson, *The Provincial*, viii; Hampe Martínez, "De la intendencia al departamento," 340.
38 Benson, *The Provincial*, vii.
39 Chiaramonte, "The 'Ancient Constitution,'" 455, 465, 466.
40 Benson, *The Provincial*, ix; Hampe Martínez, "De la intendencia al departamento," 340–342.

leading to a new economic relationship between the metropole and the Americas.[41] This was also a period of economic interdependence for the Americas. Grafe and Irigoin have recently studied the flows of wealth in the Americas immediately before 1808. They uncovered a system of autonomous colonies that redistributed funds under the direction of the king and his institutions on the peninsula. This economic redistribution provided military defense, a self-sufficient empire, and a satisfied local élite aligned with the empire and its rule.[42]

Thus the system of *derecho indiano* and its peninsular and American institutions functioned quite effectively in running the Spanish Empire in the Americas for close to 250 years before substantial administrative and political changes were introduced. Nonetheless, the system suffered under the weight of an increasingly powerful economic élite, the sale of administrative offices, and a relaxing of administrative oversight. Habsburg control and structures stepped aside after 1700 when Philip V, the first Bourbon king, began his reign. In the context of broader administrative changes in Spain following French models, the Council of the Indies was abolished and a secretary established in its stead. A system of intendants was established by the mid-eighteenth century in the Americas. This reassertion of direct royal and peninsular control was not welcomed by the established hierarchy in the colonies.[43]

In general terms, the characteristics of the Spanish colonies on the eve of Napoleon's invasion of the peninsula are summarized well by John Haley, who wrote, "By the end of the eighteenth century the formal political and legal structures of the Spanish colonial empire reflected the allocations of functions and governmental powers that were to characterize the emerging imperial regimes of the most militarily, economically, and technologically advanced European states."[44] The Bourbon Reforms recognized the well-established division of the Republic of Indians and the Republic of Spaniards in the Americas. All activities were funneled back to the secretaries of state and the Universal Office of the Indies that had taken over much of the work of the Council of the Indies.[45]

Thus with the reforms, new ideas and terminology, such as the public good, the general welfare, the monarchy, and the nation, were employed

---

[41] Lempérière, "La representación política," 63–64.
[42] Grafe and Irigoin, "The Spanish Empire," 260–262. See also Grafe, *Distant Tyranny*, 20–25; Summerhill, "Fiscal Bargains."
[43] Haley, "Foundations of Governance," 199–200.
[44] Ibid., 200.
[45] Pietschmann, "Justicia, discurso político," 24.

at the level of the state. Reformist literature criticized the corporatist system of the *ancien régime* and its privileges, hierarchy, and monopolies.[46] These reforms substantially upset established notions of public offices and public service; the administrative apparatus of the state was professionalized and regulated in service to these new ideas.[47] This "process of administrativization" in the late colonial period was an important step and led to new structures during and after the Cortes and the Constitution of Cádiz.[48] Such developments were projected well into the early republic periods for newly independent states in the Americas.[49]

The administration of justice and judicial offices was also subject to scrutiny and reform.[50] Reforms to the administration of justice might reach into more distant areas of the empire and were, at times, instigated not by central institutions but by local centers of power such as city *cabildos* operating within the same spirit of more national trends.[51] When such activities ran counter to the control of the intendant and empowered local *cabildos*, such as in Tucumán, during the end of the eighteenth century, they provided early experiences of newer forms of government and resistance to imperial representatives.[52] *Cabildos* might assert significant territorial control beyond the city, and the autonomy of *cabildos* in governing expanses of territory became a model for regional government when the king was absent after 1808.[53] With these changes, established practices were transformed through the introduction of institutional novelty and administrative flexibility, perhaps paving the way for even greater changes that would come under the first written constitution governing the area.

Although it is premature to speak of rights in the context of royal absolutism, there were certain expectations subjects in the late colonial period might have in relationship to the king and the royal administration. These were, of course, moderated according to status, particularly in the Americas, and might best be thought of as kinds of liberties. These included expectations of fair trial; of the protection of property;

---

[46] Ibid., 19, 26, 29, 34–43.
[47] Bellingeri, "Introducción," 5.
[48] Garriga, "Orden Jurídico," 48.
[49] Hale, *Mexican Liberalism*, 248–289.
[50] Herzog, "¡Viva el rey!" 90–92; Pietschmann, "Justicia, discurso político," 49–50.
[51] Tío Vallejo, "Los 'vasallos más distantes,'" 217–230.
[52] Ibid., 250–254.
[53] Morelli, "El espacio municipal," 261–285; Ternavasio, "Entre el cabildo colonial," 295–300.

and of liberties of residence, movement, and circulation.[54] Furthermore, despite serious attempts by the crown and Inquisition to limit the spread of "subversive" writings from the French Enlightenment, French revolution, and English works that challenged both royal absolutism and Catholic hegemony, such writings circulated widely on both sides of the Atlantic. These included foundational authors of rationalism and modern constitutionalism – Bacon, Bentham, Condillac, Descartes, Feijóo, Newton, Lavoisier, Leibniz, Locke, Montesquieu, Pradt, Rousseau, and Voltaire. Such works were not always squirreled away among voyagers' belongings; the port of Callao in Peru had one shipment that contained more than 37,000 books. The Inquisition actively investigated reading and circulating books on the Index and increased its supervision during the nineteenth century. This supervision was not limited to religious or political works but might include any work of literature, entertainment, or history that contained any idea that was not approved.[55]

The recognition and drafting of "fundamental laws" reflecting structured approaches to public law in Spain also increased in the eighteenth century. Such explorations of fundamental law and associated doctrinal writings asserted their higher status in the legal hierarchy and also the idea that fundamental laws would endure for a long time in the administration of the state.[56] Francisco Martínez Marina's *Ensayo histórico crítico sobre la antigua legislación de León y Castilla* (1801) enunciated this idea of fundamental laws for Spain and his *Teoría de las Cortes* (1813, published 1814) was a studied justification of the Cortes.[57] The later work was so detailed and contained so much information on the historical constitution of Spain that it was used and quoted in the document written by some deputies to support the absolutist power of the king on his return in 1814, the Manifesto of the Persians (*El Manifesto de los Persas*).[58] There were also comparative works on these topics such as Pedro Rodríguez Campomanes's *Observaciones sobre el sistema general de Europa* published in 1792. In this period, the constitution of Spain was seen as an agglomeration of various customs, practices, and sources, including importantly the *fueros* that served to mediate the power of the monarch. Thus, there was already a constitution in existence composed of

[54] Martiré, "Dos lecciones," 33.
[55] García Laguardia, *Centroamérica*, 18–26, 28–32.
[56] Coronas, "De las *leyes fundamentales*," 18–42.
[57] Abreu y Abreu, "Las ideas constitucionales," 11–13; Escudero, "Martínez Marina," 201–207.
[58] Escudero, "Martínez Marina," 207–208.

ideas about religion, the king, laws and customs, individuals, lawmaking, and adjudication when the French met at Bayona to enact a constitution in 1808 and the Cortes met in Cádiz to draft a constitution in 1810.[59]

From Unwritten to Written Constitutions

The Constitution of Cádiz was drafted in the midst of warfare and political instability during a revolution resulting from a dynastic crisis that befell Spain. Late in 1807, Carlos IV squabbled with his son Fernando VII over succession to the Spanish throne just as Napoleonic forces were bearing down on Spain. Spaniards on the peninsula and Spaniards in the Americas considered Manuel Godoy, chief minister in Spain from 1793 to 1808, an inexperienced upstart who expanded executive power beyond its traditional scope. The popular perception of Godoy created further instability as his detractors supported Fernando VII's bid for the throne and forced Carlos IV to abdicate. The interfamily feud was more or less insignificant in the face of Napoleon's invasion and the presence of French forces in Spain, presumably on their way to Portugal. France took control, and both Spanish kings abdicated.[60] In 1808 in Bayona, Fernando VII passed the crown to Carlos IV, who had already agreed to Napoleon's demands. Napoleon, in turn, designated his elder brother, Joseph, as king of Spain.[61] Spaniards on the peninsula and in the Americas did not recognize the French usurper, and those loyal to Fernando VII were left with a kingdom without a king. On both sides of the Atlantic, this political crisis was also a financial crisis because the well-oiled machine of fiscal interdependence of the empire seized, leading to each region of the Americas to protect its own economic well-being, a certain step toward regional autonomy and eventual independence from the peninsula.[62]

The Constitution of Cádiz brought great change. It substantially modified structures, particularly through its creation of representative bodies, and limited a heretofore absolute executive. It also changed ideas of individual liberties as a system based on assertions of customary entitlements though petition and appeal. Constitutional thought implied some kind of constitutional rights, although probably not individual constitutional rights as we think of them today, and a new judicial mechanism for their

[59] Coronas, "De las *leyes fundamentales,*" 43, 52, 53, 59, 65.
[60] Rodríguez, *Cádiz Experiment,* 31–34; Rodríguez, *Independence,* 49, 5.
[61] Artola, *II La Constitución de Cádiz,* 16–17.
[62] Grafe and Irigoin, "The Spanish Empire," 241, 250–263.

enforcement. The former forms of redressing overreaching by the crown fell to the wayside.[63]

There was also continuity. In noting the continuity between the political world described in the Constitution of Cádiz and the pre-Cádiz unwritten constitution, Lorente focuses on the essential attribute of the corporatist nature of political representation found before and after the Constitution. The oaths required by the Constitution and the role of the church in ensuring complete societal compliance underscored the corporatist, rather than the individualist, nature of society. Thus it is the groups in society that must be given voice, not individuals. Constitutional rights were similarly perceived. Elections functioned not to give a fractional voice to each citizen but to represent the various segments of society.[64] The Constitution of Cádiz and its representative Cortes maintained multiple political subjects more than they replaced these various groups with the new concept of citizen. In fact, citizenship in the Constitution of Cádiz appears to have been derived from the unwritten constitutional understanding of a leading citizen (*vecino*).[65]

Thus, the ideas and structures of Spain's unwritten constitution and *derecho indiano* did much to inform the constitutional drafting process of the period.[66] *Derecho indiano* also served as a basis to legitimize movement toward independence, especially through assertions of the poor administration of justice and of tyrannical exercises of power contrary to established law.[67] The events that led to the Constitution of Cádiz were the same events that led to the first independence constitutions in the Americas. With uncertainty of where allegiance was owed, regions of the Americas could recognize the institutions representing Fernando VII in Spain, create a new direct line of allegiance directly to the absent king, or declare themselves independent. Despite French efforts to attract Americans to Joseph's Napoleonic rule of Spain, this option was rejected quite early by most areas.[68]

It must be kept in mind that for many in Spain's ruling élite on the peninsula, Spain already had a functioning constitution composed of its customs, practices, and law. The force of the regional *fueros* was also still quite significant, with the northern regions of Navarra and the Basque

[63] Bravo Lira, "Protección jurídica," 334.
[64] Lorente, *La nación*, 32–34 citing, for elections, Annino, "Cádiz y la revolución."
[65] Lorente, *La nación*, 33–34.
[66] Botero, "La visión," 785–792; Mirow, "Pre-constitutional law."
[67] García Gallo, "El derecho indiano," 162–167.
[68] García Laguardia, *Centroamérica*, 78–82.

Provinces attempting to opt out of any national constitutional regime. They already had constitutions and did not see the need for another, and other regions had similarly well-developed foral systems of government.[69]

These early independence constitutions arose in an era of "hyperconstitutionalism" running from 1791 to 1830.[70] And, indeed, the Constitution of Cádiz was part of a broader constitutional movement in Europe and the Americas that had a particular impact on the Iberian peninsula.[71] The political shifts of the Americas reflected this trend as some areas of the Americas continued to be loyal to the Spanish crown and thus adopted the Constitution of Cádiz. These included the Caribbean areas of Cuba, Puerto Rico, Florida, and many regions of Central America, Mexico, Peru, and Quito. Other areas such as Río de la Plata and Chile moved toward independence rather early.[72] Such claims of independence from Spain might not include assertions of independence from the absent Spanish king. Santiago de Chile in the midst of political uncertainty swore loyalty to Fernando VII in 1809.[73] The separate Chilean junta created in 1810 was the only American junta to be recognized by the Council of Regency in Spain.[74] During the next ten years or so, Caracas, Buenos Aires, and Mexico similarly recognized Fernando VII as king, but not necessarily the authority of the peninsular institutions claiming to exercise royal power in his absence.[75]

Still other parts of the Americas, such as the areas of Colombia and Venezuela, broke down into province-by-province determinations of their political future. Where areas did not follow the path to the Spanish crown through the Cortes in Cádiz and the Constitution of Cádiz, they established their own constitutional documents.[76] Although decisions of loyalty and independence were usually made within the established political institutions, individuals might steer the process or be shut down by opposition. For example, informed by Enlightenment works and expansive reading, Fray Melchor de Talamantes was an early voice for the independence of Mexico in 1808 and was imprisoned for circulating such views.[77] His writings included a plan for a national congress for

[69] Coronas, "De las *leyes fundamentales*," 71–73.
[70] Botero, "La visión," 793; Corfield, "Constitucionalismo ilustrado," 79.
[71] Mirow, "Age of Constitutions," 229–235; Varela, "El constitucionalismo," 13–51.
[72] Uribe-Urán, "La Constitución de Cádiz," 274–275.
[73] García Gallo, "El derecho indiano," 170–171.
[74] Loveman, *The Constitution*, 314.
[75] García Gallo, "El derecho indiano," 171.
[76] Uribe-Urán, "La Constitución de Cádiz," 274–275.
[77] Pampillo Baliño, "Fray Melchor de Talamantes."

Mexico and a detailed description of the actions it should take toward a constitution.[78] In fact, he was the first to suggest the need of a constitution for an independent Mexico.[79]

Similarly, the promulgation of the Constitution and the required actions under it, such as elections, might provide the battleground upon which long-standing political disagreements were fought. The political infighting in Cuzco provides an example where the constitutional elections for the city council (*cabildo*) were closely contested between constitutionalists and absolute royalists under the Constitution in 1812. When the constitutionalists established power on the council, political battles were not finished as the council vied for power against the governor in some matters and against the *audiencia* in others. In 1813, when the *audiencia* of Cuzco arrested three soldiers accused of a conspiracy and ordered a curfew, civic unrest broke out that led to the deaths of three other individuals. The various local elements used the event to argue against each other. Elections later that year were more peaceful, but in August, 1813, both the constitutionalist position of the city council and the absolutist position represented in the *audiencia* were pushed aside by a local revolution led by José Angulo, who sought a return to traditional freedoms of national sovereignty under his widely circulated fiction that the king had been killed by the French. By early 1815, royalist forces defeated the revolution and put the *audiencia* members back into office.[80] Such political fights were not limited to large and powerful cities. St. Augustine, Florida, also witnessed conflict between the constitutional city council and its governor.[81]

These individual constitutional documents are often properly described as being more liberal or radical in their provisions and as providing greater individual rights than the Constitution of Cádiz.[82] Nonetheless, in many areas, the new constitutions were produced by a "Catholic creole population" that maintained similar racial, social, economic, and political views as their Spaniard counterparts of the *ancien régime*.[83] Thus, significant change on these fronts was exceptional in the new constitutions.

Some of these constitutions seem to have little in common with the provisions of the Constitution of Cádiz and exhibit different institutions

[78] Pampillo Baliño, *El Primer Constitucionalista de México*, 71–78, 105–128.
[79] De la Torre Villar and García Laguardia, *Desarollo histórico*, 12–13.
[80] Peralta Ruíz, "Elecciones, constitucionalismo," 111–112, 115–131.
[81] Mirow, "The Constitution of Cádiz," 284.
[82] Uribe-Urán, "La Constitución," 274–275.
[83] Botero, "La visión," 802.

and structures. Drawing on *derecho indiano*, constitutional documents of the French and U.S. revolutions and ideas from English liberalism and the Spanish Enlightenment, these provincial constitutions reveal a broad range of intellectual and political positions. For example, the Constitution of Antioquia (Colombia) of 1812 established ideas of equality, the prohibition of privileges, and equality in court proceedings, while incorporating the Rights of Man and Citizen into its provisions.[84] These were substantially more progressive positions than those established at Cádiz. Several of these local or provincial constitutions antedate the Constitution of Cádiz.[85]

Early written independence constitutions also must be considered as liminal documents of constitutional thought existing between the unwritten Spanish colonial constitution and the Constitution of Cádiz. Several constitutional documents predate the Constitution of Cádiz in the Spanish colonial world and developed in a symbiotic relationship with the Cortes. These include the Venezuelan Constitution of December 21, 1811; the Quito Constitution of 1812; the Federal Act of the United Provinces of Nueva Granada of November 27, 1811; and the Constitution of Antioquia (Colombia) of May 3, 1812. There were also many drafts of constitutions that never saw the light of day in their own right, but influenced drafters when they were called upon to write constitutions. There were other quasiconstitutional documents that, although not called "constitutions," served constitutional functions. For example, Javier Infante argues that Chile's first constitution dates from August, 1811, under the title *Reglamento para el Arrelgo de la Autoridad Ejecutiva Provisoria de Chile*.[86] Thus, we may view the era not within a limited framework of either constitutional success or failure, but in a more nuanced way with it being a period in which "constitutional laboratories" undertook an unusually high degree of experimentation within new nations and republics.

The language of the Federal Act of the United Provinces of Nueva Granada created a limited federal government over the provinces, which were represented in a congress of elected deputies. Congress took over some of the traditional powers of the king including managing the patronage of the church and foreign relations. Several provinces held off ratifying the constitution until 1814, after Bolívar's success in Cundinamarca.

---

[84] Ibid., 785–792, 803, 806.
[85] Uribe-Urán, "La Constitución," 279.
[86] Infante, *Autonomía*, 90.

Subsequent Spanish reconquest of the area in 1815 meant that the federation it contemplated did not come to fruition.[87]

Venezuela was the first country to declare independence, and it adopted the region's first constitution on December 21, 1811. It created a federal regime, espoused general principles of liberalism, and provided for a republic.[88] It sought to limit presidential power, and indeed earned Bolívar's criticism in this regard.[89] Although it never truly entered into force, the document provided an important landmark in indigenous American constitutionalism. This attempt had little opportunity for implementation before Spain crushed the insurrection.[90]

The Quito Constitution of 1812 created a central government with Roman Catholicism as the official state religion and required Catholicism as a condition of political participation. The Constitution recognized Fernando VII upon his freedom from the French, and despite this religious and royal conservatism, it espoused various aspects of the period's liberalism. Like the Cundinamarca Constitution, it too was a document that lived more in theory than in practice. Spanish authorities gained control over Quito shortly after the constitution was established.[91]

What of the constitutional thought of Latin America's great leaders? Francisco de Miranda, then the failed Venezuelan independence general of the early 1810s, left several texts of plans for government on independence ranging from 1789 to 1808. These works indicate various thought experiments in the possible structure of an independent America. Earlier documents indicate a monarchical structure under a leader with an autochthonous title of "Inca," while other documents are along republican and federal lines. His attempt to weave in indigenous terminology is noteworthy, as most early independence constitutions do not take account of such structures or terminology. Miranda also sought to pick and choose from various constitutional models available, often turning to England and at times the United States for ideas. Other structures are uniquely Spanish, such as his reliance on a system of *cabildos* on the municipal level. These works reveal an ill-defined notion of citizenship, the maintenance of Roman Catholicism as the official state religion with greater toleration for other faiths than usual for the period, and the abolition of the Inquisition. The doctrine of the separation of powers is

---

[87] Loveman, *The Constitution*, 162. See also Safford and Palacios, *Colombia*, 89–90.
[88] Loveman, *The Constitution*, 138–139.
[89] Gargarella, *Latin American Constitutionalism*, 68–69.
[90] Loveman, *The Constitution*, 139.
[91] Ibid., 183.

evident in his works, as is the precocious assertion of judicial review of legislation by ordinary judges to determine constitutionality.[92]

Freedom of the press was an Enlightenment value that came to the fore as Spain battled against the French. When this new right was joined with the abolition of the Inquisition, newspapers stepped in to circulate political events and positions in a new way throughout the Spanish empire. With so many local and regional newspapers, many of them short-lived, broad trends in public opinion regarding the constitutional and independence processes underway were recorded and shaped the debate of deputies and those guiding policy.[93] There was a panoply of various forms of printed communication available to political actors at the time that flowed from the Americas, England, and the peninsula. Among these, Chust notes, "private letters, decrees, newspapers, the *Diario de Sesiones de Cortes* [the official proceedings of the Cortes], pamphlets, single-sheet announcements, commercial correspondence, literature, theatrical works, [and] patriotic songs."[94] Opinions about and news of the Americas were, for example, found in the *Diario Mercantil de Cádiz*, which in 1810 began to run a series called "Americas" and served as an important local source of information.[95]

Various sources were called into play in the construction of new independence constitutions and the Constitution of Cádiz. Chairamonte has noted that Spain's ancient constitution was invoked in various ways on the path to independence. For example, in the Rio de la Plata region, the strictures of such traditional constitutional arrangements might serve the basis for reactionary statements of rejection to chart a new political world.[96] Conversely, early constitutionalists might base their innovations on assertions of continuity with and correction of a preexisting constitutional order. Fray Melchor de Talamantes did this to justify the creation of a junta in 1808.[97] As explored in Chapter 2, continuity with prior constitutional arrangements was, of course, an essential aspect of the reforms of the Constitution of Cádiz.[98]

[92] Constantini, "Les projets," 571–598.
[93] Pérez Guilhou, *La opinión pública*, 17–23, 38–39. See also Safford and Palacios, *Colombia*, 76.
[94] Chust, *América*, 34.
[95] Ramos Santana, "La Constitución," 103–107.
[96] Chiaramonte, "The 'Ancient Constitution,'" 461–463.
[97] Ibid., 463. For a study of Talamantes's constitutional thought see Pampillo Baliño, *El Primer Constitutionalista de México*.
[98] Mirow, "Pre-constitutional law," 313–337.

The chronology and list of possible influences and trends are even less clear than might be imaged. Something must be said of the Napoleonic Constitution of Bayona of 1808. This French constitution for Spain attempted to continue the monarchical line for Spain and the Americas in Joseph, the elder brother of Napoleon Bonaparte. Under this constitution, the prerogatives of the king were not limited, and Joseph would rule with the advice of several corporative institutions created under the constitution for the nobility, clergy, and the third estate. Thus, the organs of state created under the constitution had much more to do with consultation than representation, and the legislative court as constituted under the constitution and that never met, was best viewed as a corporation of corporations.[99] The vast majority of Spaniards were against the French. Some however, known as *los afrancesados*, thought that Spain's future was brighter under French influences.[100] The Constitution of Bayona used American representatives resident in Madrid to lend public legitimacy and imperial credence to the universality of the document. Politics dictated that the American territories be brought within the fold, and the Constitution provided for American deputies and the formal equality of American and peninsular Spaniards under French rule. Under the French constitution, former restrictions on cultivation were removed and trade was opened. These were essential concerns of Americans.[101]

Nonetheless, the speed at which the Constitution of Bayona was drafted and the scant attention it paid to the unique aspects of the Americas caused great concern to those who were familiar with the region and its relationship with the peninsula. For example, by 1808, Benito de la Mata Linares had served on the *audiencias* of Chile and Lima and had been the regent of Buenos Aires. He was an established member of the Council of the Indies when a copy of the Constitution reached him in preparation for the Council's swearing of allegiance and implementation. His notes, carefully analyzed by Victor Tau, indicate that the Constitution of Bayona was woefully deficient in understanding the nature and importance of the Americas and their institutions, including the Council of the Indies itself. Mata Linares sought a greater place for the Americas in the constitutional system, a separate ministry dedicated to the Indies, the continuation of the Council of the Indies (which was not mentioned in the Constitution), the continued efficacy of

[99] Busaall, "Constitution et culture," 79, 82–85, 90.
[100] Artola, *Los Afrancesados*.
[101] Pérez Guilhou, *La opinión pública*, 32–36.

derecho indiano, and the adjustment of constitutional guarantees for the Americas. These observations indicate that the Constitution of Bayona was not drafted with the complexities of the Americas in mind.[102] Other scholars of the Constitution disagree. Eduardo Martiré states that the Constitution was subject to a series of drafts and reviews and that the present state of the peninsula and the Americas was known to Napoleon and the other drafters.[103]

Despite these deficits of information and sensitivity relating to the Americas, the Constitution of Bayona attempted to co-opt American interests. Although official documents calling for the convocation leading to the Constitution did not mention American provinces, six American deputies were appointed to represent American interests, one each from Bogotá, Buenos Aires, Cuba, Guatemala, New Spain, and Peru.[104] Under the Constitution of Bayona, deputies from the colonies were given voice and vote in the Cortes and Americans were equal to Spaniards.[105] French authorities were not deaf to American demands and after a list of requests was submitted by José de Moral of New Spain, the draft was amended to include many of the suggestions. These included the equality of the provinces, no restrictions on cultivation or industry in the provinces, freer trade between provinces, limitations on privileges to export in the provinces, and representation at the Cortes with twenty-two deputies.[106]

The Constitution of Bayona's incorporation of the Americas produced a sea change in Spanish constitutionalism. From this point on, any imperial constitution of Spain would have to take close account of the political place of the Americas in its structure. Eduardo Martiré properly credits the Constitution of Bayona with giving birth to a new *derecho indiano*.[107] Indeed, the Constitution of Bayona was the springboard for the Constitution of Cádiz in the sense that the drafters of the Constitution of Cádiz necessarily had to react to the entire content of the Constitution of Bayona, and the Constitution of Bayona set out many of the areas that the Constitution of Cádiz had to address from broad aspects, such as the structure of government, the representation of the Americas, and what rights citizens were to have, to narrower aspects, such as the codification

[102] Tau, "Las oberservaciones," 243–257.
[103] Martiré, "Algo más," 90–91.
[104] García Laguardia, *Centroamérica*, 87.
[105] Ibid., 87.
[106] Chust, *América*, 20; García Laguardia, *Centroamérica*, 88.
[107] Martiré, "Algo más," 85, 93–94.

of civil law, a topic mentioned in Bayona and again treated in Cádiz.[108] Despite the concessions offered to the Americas in the Constitution of Bayona, the Americas chose different paths.

Conclusion

The tenuous fate of the Spanish monarchy on the peninsula precipitated movement toward independence in the Americans and the necessity to restructure rule throughout the empire. One source for how to proceed was the established unwritten constitution of the empire found in written sources of law, institutions, and in customary practices. For the Americas, *derecho indiano*, Spanish law applied to the Americas, served as an essential source for structuring rule and making arguments about what should follow. More recent forms of imperial administration and ideas about effective political and economic rule informed constitution making in the Americas and on the peninsula.

This period of constitutional limbo arose in an atmosphere of Enlightenment writings that found their way into political thought and debate. These ideas challenged aspects of the empire that had served to maintain peninsular Spanish control such as the rightful authority of monarchs and the place of the church in society. Nascent independent movements and occasional successes led to a number of constitutional texts as models or sources for constitutional drafters on the peninsula and in the Americas. One such text, the French Constitution of Bayona of 1808, intended for the Spanish Empire under Joseph Bonaparte, served to recast the terms of debate and political action. Because it constitutionalized the Americas in written form, any other written constitution for the empire would also have to do the same.

---

[108] Domínguez Nafría, "La codificación"; Fernández Giménez, "El senado"; Martiré, "Algo más," 86.

2

The Constitution of Cádiz

America's Other First Constitution

The Constitution of Cádiz of 1812 stands uncomfortably between two worlds. The Constitution sought to perpetuate monarchy and empire just as monarchical absolutism and imperial structures were revealing pressure factures from Enlightenment political thought and sweeping social changes around the Atlantic. The Constitution contradicted itself by advancing notions of popular representation and national sovereignty in the name of a king. While establishing a perpetual confessional Roman Catholic state, the Constitution espoused liberal ideas and institutions. It established representative electoral bodies at various levels of government, restricted the power of the king, gave rights for the criminally accused, advanced freedom of contract, and affirmed individual property rights. The Constitution abolished seigniorial structures, Indian tribute, forced Indian labor in America, and personal services in Spain.[1] It sought the creation of national codes of law that would be applied equally to all in courts of general jurisdiction without regard to individual status.[2] Thus, the Constitution is an early and important text in the Age of Democratic Revolutions, when absolutism was replaced with constitutionalism and the king's sovereignty was replaced with a people's sovereignty.[3] In fact, in describing the Spanish nation in terms of a population within geographic boundaries, the Constitution of Cádiz has been viewed as an early formulation of the nation-state.[4]

---

[1] Rodríguez, *Independence*, 91.
[2] Domínguez Nafria, "La codificación"; Estrada Michel, *Monarquía y Nación*, 382, 386; and Mirow, "Codification."
[3] Rodríguez, *Independence*, 1.
[4] Artola, *II La Constitución de Cádiz*, 69, 71; Artola, *Constitucionalismo en la historia*, 85–86.

Nonetheless, the Constitution of Cádiz must also be viewed in the context of empire.[5] In the context of U.S. constitutional history, historians have recently "recovered the nexus between empires and constitutions" noting that "empire and constitutional liberties were related and reinforcing."[6] Those working in the field of European and Latin American constitutionalism must take to heart Daniel Hulsebosch's caution that, until recently in the United States, "though some warned against returning to a complacent Whig history that celebrated freedom, the United States' imperial legacy was deemphasized. Constitutional history became a story of the growth of American liberty."[7] Those at the Cortes of Cádiz wanted very much to continue the Spanish Empire as a world player within contemporary interimperial rivalries and power struggles. The empire Spain sought to continue was not a uniform sphere of legal and political influences, but is better seen as a bumpy and fluid legal geography of varying intensities.[8] To continue the sinewy strands of empire, representatives from the Spanish Empire were called from around the world to the Cortes and the Constitution itself carefully defined the territory of "the Spains."[9] Indeed, Lorente's reading of the text as emphasizing competing notions of "nation" to peninsular Spaniards and of "territory" to American Spaniards is compelling in this regard.[10] Thus, in the context of liberalism and in the context of empire, the Constitution of Cádiz and the sessions of the Cortes were transformative.

The Constitution's many transformations of the political world are surprising when one considers that only about a year and a half separated the first meeting of the Cortes of Cádiz in September 24, 1810 from its promulgation of the Constitution of Cádiz on March 19, 1812.[11] This was not much time to draft a new constitution, let alone a new constitution for an extraordinary time. The Treaty of Fontainebleau signed between Napoleon and Carlos IV on October 27, 1807 allowed the presence of French troops in Spain. Through the terms of the treaty, Napoleon sought to control important Portuguese ports in battling the English navy, and for Spain's help, France would recognize Carlos IV as the emperor of

[5] Benton, "Constitutions and Empire"; Garriga, "Cabeza moderna," 100–101; Portillo, "Monarquía," 128–140.
[6] Hulsebosch, *Constituting Empire*, 6, 12.
[7] Ibid., 4.
[8] Benton, *Search for Sovereignty*.
[9] Constitution of Cádiz, Art. 10.
[10] Lorente, *La Nación*, 16.
[11] Morán Orti, *La formación de las Cortes*, 13.

the Americas. Spain's prize in helping France was to be Brazil. Things did not go as expected from Spanish perspectives as France mounted an occupation of Spain.[12]

Before going into exile, Fernando VII charged a junta to govern in his absence and to maintain good relations with the French generals.[13] Most, but not all, Spaniards were against the French. Some, known as *los afrancesados*, thought that Joseph Bonaparte and French ways offered the path to a modern and secular state.[14] Nonetheless, popular sentiment was against the French and against Godoy; regional and local groups of leaders, juntas, called out for maintaining religion, monarchy, and freedom from French rule. There was, however, also nascent sentiment for more revolutionary changes, and some local juntas asserted that sovereignty resided in the people when there was no king to serve as its royal vessel.[15] Spaniards were soon waging guerrilla warfare against the French.[16]

The Cortes of Cádiz were born from this moment of crisis in Spain. More than fifteen regional groups (juntas) on the peninsula and individuals vied for authority in the vacuum created by Fernando VII's departure in 1808.[17] Regional juntas formed in areas on the peninsula that were not occupied by the French and also in the Americas. These juntas rejected the abdication of Fernando VII, decided to govern in his name, and resisted France. Some provinces in Spain summoned their traditional consultative bodies, or Cortes.[18]

Proposals for a united central authority to supplement or to supplant the regional juntas followed. The thirteenth-century collection of laws, the *Siete Partidas*, which carried particular authority in setting out Spain's unwritten constitution, provided for a regency during an incapacity of the king. Thus, some saw the goal of the regional juntas and any central junta as the declaration of a regent or Council of Regency that would govern in the name of Fernando VII. Without universal agreement on how to proceed, the proposals of the Count of Floridablanca head of the junta for Murcia carried the day, and representatives for Asturias, Aragón, Catalonia, Valencia, and northern parts met in Madrid while others met about fifty kilometers to the south in Aranjuez. Representatives

[12] Chust, *América*, 15–17, 19.
[13] Morán Orti, *La formación de las Cortes*, 14.
[14] Artola, *Los afrancesados*; Rodríguez, *Independence*, 59.
[15] Morán Orti, *La formación de las Cortes*, 15–18.
[16] Polk, *Violent Politics*, 20–34.
[17] Chust, *América*, 21.
[18] Rodríguez, *Independence*, 75.

from eight provinces, five cities, and Mallorca participated to create the Junta Central of the Kingdom (*Junta Central, Suprema, Gubernativa del Reino*). Some representatives were excluded on the basis of their locations' historical statuses. Representatives of other localities joined later, but the Junta Central's actions in excluding some representatives and not waiting for others left some hard feelings. The Council of Castile (the Royal Council aligned with France) objected to the creation of both the regional juntas and the Junta Central, but with little effect.[19]

Eventually eclipsing the local juntas, this Junta Central was assembled in September, 1808. It was composed of thirty-nine peninsular Spaniards and nine other Spaniards from America and the Philippines.[20] Leading figures of the Junta Central were José Moñino, Count of Floridablanca, an important conservative thinker; Gaspar Melchor de Jovellanos, considered by most a moderate liberal; and Lorenzo Calvo de Rosas, a more radical liberal.[21] When confronted with questions concerning the legality of the Junta, its supporters invoked the *Siete Partidas* and asserted the proper creation of a regency and the Cortes as a representative body. In the later months of 1808 and the beginning months of 1809, Jovellanos and Calvo proposed convening the Cortes, and Calvo suggested that a new constitution was in order. These proposals led to a Commission on the Cortes and the creation of seven auxiliary juntas by function: Drafting and Regulation, Means and Resources, Legislation, Treasury, Public Instruction, Ecclesiastical Matters, and Protocol.[22]

The scope of activity of the Cortes was already an issue: some asserted that it should narrowly keep to modifying laws and ensuring their observance whereas others, such as Jovellanos in his Instructions to the *Junta de Real Hacienda y Legislación*, sought more sweeping reforms under a new rationalism. These broader reforms included a new constitution, new codes, the abolition of *fueros*, and equality before the law.[23] Charged with examining laws that would need reform, the Legislation junta paved the way for the constitutional reform that was to take place once the Cortes was convinced. The members of this influential body were Rodrigo Riquelme, Manuel de Lardizábal, José Antonio Mon y Valerde, el Conde de Pinar, Juan Pablo Valiente, Alejandro Dolarea, José María

---

[19] Artola, *II La Constitución de Cádiz*, 19–24. For the *Siete Partidas*, see Mirow, *Latin American Law*, 49–53.
[20] García Laguardia, *Las Cortes de Cádiz y la constitutción de 1812*, 6–8.
[21] Flaquer Montequi, "El Ejecutivo en la revolución liberal," 38.
[22] Morán Orti, *La formación de las Cortes*, 19, 21, 23–26.
[23] Ibid., 23–30. For new codes, see Mirow, "Codificación y la Constitución de Cádiz."

Blanco Crespo (later replaced by Antonio Porcel), Agustín Argüelles, and Antonio Ranz Romanillos.[24]

Pushed around by advancing French troops and with grave concern for its security, the Junta Central moved from Aranjuez and passed through Toledo, Talavera, Trujillo, and Badajoz. By the end of 1808, the Junta Central had settled in Seville.[25] It later moved to Puerto de Santa María, on the Bay of Cádiz, as French troops advanced elsewhere in Spain. The Junta Central planned the gathering of the Cortes, which would have the power to pass sovereignty to a Council of Regency.[26] In addition to the function-specific juntas for its legislative activities, the Cortes also created administrative arms through Secretaries of State, War, Grace and Justice, Finance, and Marine.[27]

The revolutionary possibilities of the Junta Central and the Cortes itself, once assembled, were not lost on many of the participants. In light of the Junta Central's regulations that were favorable to religious institutions and property, recent scholars have debated the degree of the Junta's revolutionary activity.[28] Nonetheless, the overall sense for the Junta and the Cortes that Artola conveys for Jovellanos is correct: "[t]he object of Jovellanos was to obtain the revolution without violence, the old Enlightenment notion of using royal power to change society."[29] Indeed, some historians have marked the end of the *ancien régime* in Spain as September 24, 1808, the date of the first meeting of the Junta Central, its declaration of national sovereignty, and subsequent liberal decrees.[30] The story, however, is more complex.

The Junta Central called for the convocation of the Cortes that eventually drafted and promulgated the Constitution of Cádiz. By the middle of 1809, various methods and goals for the convocation of the Cortes were being proposed. Some thought the only permissible action by the Cortes was to establish a Council of Regency. Their view was that the Junta Central existed only to continue the unwritten constitution that existed before the French invasion. In other words, the Junta and the Cortes existed only to perpetuate the current state of affairs, and not to reform legislation and, even less so, to propose a new constitution.

---

[24] Varela Suanzes-Carpegna, *Tres ensayos*, 80–81.
[25] Flaquer Montequi, "El Ejecutivo en la revolución liberal," 38.
[26] Artola, *II La Constitución de Cádiz*, 25.
[27] Flaquer Montequi, "El Ejecutivo en la revolución liberal," 39.
[28] Artola, *II La Constitución de Cádiz*, 22–26.
[29] Ibid., 27.
[30] García Laguardia, *Las Cortes de Cádiz*, 20.

Others sought the Cortes to ratify projects and proposals already well advanced by the Junta Central in the broad areas of defense, government, revenue, and education. Still others saw the convocation of the Cortes as the moment to draft a new constitution establishing national sovereignty and subjecting the power of the king to the popular will. They saw the possibilities not only of improving legislation but also of completely reforming law into new codes that were consistent with new Enlightenment principles. The goals of the Cortes were not clear even before the first deputy arrived.[31]

During the last months of 1809, the Junta Central would move again, this time from Seville to Cádiz, again because of French pressure.[32] On October 28, 1809, a selection process for the Cortes was announced for January 1, 1810, with the first meeting of the Cortes to occur in March, 1810, and letters of convocation for the Cortes were sent from Seville on January 1.[33] The stated goals of convening the Cortes were to preserve the Roman Catholic religion, to free the king, to continue the war against France until the nation was free from Joseph Bonaparte (José I), and to reestablish and improve the fundamental constitution.[34]

At the end of January, 1810, the Junta Central dissolved itself after transferring its authority to a Council of Regency composed of Pedro de Quevedo y Quevedo, Bishop of Orense; Francisco de Saavedra; Lieutenant General of the Marine Antonio de Escaño; Capitan General Francisco Javier Castaños y Aragoni; and Esteban Fernández de Léon, who was quickly replaced with Miguel de Lardizábal.[35] Such changes were not uncommon. The Council of Spain and the Indies published a document requiring all to recognize the sovereignty of the new Council.[36] In October, 1810, the Cortes replaced the Council of Regency with a more manageable Regent (Agar) and substitute Regent (Puig). This change removed the opposition to a new constitution put forth by the Bishop of Orense and Lardizábal.[37] From 1810 to 1814, there were, in fact, four significant Regencies consisting of different members. From the beginning of 1811, the Councils of Regency were governed by Provisional Rules of Executive Power enacted by the Cortes. The Cortes established

[31] Artola, *II La Constitución de Cádiz*, 27–29.
[32] Chasteen, *Americanos*, 53.
[33] Varela Suanzes-Carpegna, *Tres ensayos*, 82.
[34] Meléndez Chaverri, "Las Cortes de Cádiz," 33.
[35] Varela Suanzes-Carpegna, *Tres ensayos*, 83; Flaquer Montequi, "El Ejecutivo," 44.
[36] Artola, *II La Constitución de Cádiz*, 34–35.
[37] Varela Suanzes-Carpegna, *Tres ensayos*, 90.

other rules governing the election of regents and the regency. Despite its control of the regency, the Cortes and the Council of Regency did not always enjoy smooth relations, especially when things did not go well on the battlefield and differing military strategies were proposed. The Council once even offered its resignation to the Cortes that was not accepted. Depending on the composition of the Council and its outlook, some Councils worked well with the desires of the Cortes.[38]

Even before the Cortes was convened and could begin its squabbles with the provisional executive branch, significant issues remained concerning the nature and structure of the Cortes. One frequently debated topic was whether the Cortes would have a unicameral or bicameral structure and how the American and other nonpeninsular provinces would be represented.[39] To rein in the more revolutionary ideas that might be brought by popularly elected representatives to a single house, Jovellanos and others suggested that the Cortes should have two houses, one composed of nobles and ecclesiastics who would serve to check the potentially more radical popular sentiment found in a more representative house. A bicameral structure, however, was inconsistent with the historical unicameral structure of the Cortes in Spain. The issue was debated until the moment the Cortes sat as a unicameral body.[40] The abrupt switch from a bicameral to a unicameral structure appears to have been the product not only of a more liberal view taking hold but also of the practical difficulties associated with assembling a house for the upper estates when nobles and clerics expressed little interest in forming a separate chamber.[41]

A second issue concerned suffrage. The Junta Central decided to include ecclesiastical, military, and popular participation. For the popular segment, the Junta Central selected universal male suffrage, with some notable exceptions when viewed from today's perspective. It refrained from imposing a property requirement, generally found in the early nineteenth century. These decisions led to Spain's first elections law, and the Junta Central used the Census of 1797 to select one deputy for every 50,000 individuals. Two large questions concerning suffrage had been brewing for some time: what to do about deputies for America and what to do about deputies for the occupied areas of Spain. After consultation with the Council for Spain and the Indies, the Junta Central decided to

[38] Flaquer Montequi, "El Ejecutivo," 42–61.
[39] Fernández Giménez, "El senado"; Morán Orti, *La formación*, 31–34.
[40] Artola, *II La Constitución de Cádiz*, 28–33, 38.
[41] Varela Suanzes-Carpegna, *Tres ensayos*, 84.

include American participation but had not announced procedures or the nature of the participation. Nonetheless, after intense negotiations, American participation worked out to about a fifth to a quarter of the deputies at any given time during the sessions of the Cortes. A system of selecting alternate deputies was created for areas that were unable to conduct elections or to send deputies.[42] Both determinations on suffrage were an important marker of maintaining imperial authority: the Spanish Empire by necessity included the Americas, and Spanish imperial jurisdiction continued in territories that were merely subject to the misfortune of being occupied by the French.

It is this division of power among elected representatives, and among judges, courts, and city councils that led Lorente and Garriga to focus on the jurisdictional aspects of the Constitution. They stressed the continuity of the jurisdictional tensions and their constitutional resolution as an essential element in understanding the text and its place in constitutional history. Another important jurisdictional aspect of the Cortes was that a substantial amount of its time was spent hearing and answering petitions rather than legislating in the traditional sense we have come to understand of representative bodies.[43]

On September 24, 1810, the General and Extraordinary Cortes (*Cortes Generales y Extraordinarias*) met in the Regent's Palace in Cádiz. The Cortes was "general" because it represented all the provinces of the monarchy and "extraordinary" because it was not convened by the king and did not include the nobility and clergy as separate estates.[44] From the palace, the deputies went to a nearby church where they swore an oath to uphold the church, the Spanish nation, and King Fernando VII. The deputies began their sessions in a theatre converted for the Cortes's use in the Isla de León, now known as San Fernando, a town on the piece of land that connects the city of Cádiz with the peninsula. By the time the deputies met, there was little doubt that the purpose of its sessions was to draft a constitution for Spain in Europe and America and that the Cortes was in fact a constituent congress.[45] The Cortes declared national sovereignty at its first meeting the same day.[46] It established rules for its internal organization and procedures that underscored its functional independence, keeping executive participation in its activities

---

[42] Artola, *II La Constitución de Cádiz*, 30, 34, 36–37.
[43] Lorente, *La Nación*, 13–14, 38–39.
[44] Rieu-Millan, *Los diputados americanos*, xx.
[45] Artola, *II La Constitución de Cádiz*, 38–39, 283.
[46] Morán Orti, *La formación de las Cortes*, 36.

to a minimum. It importantly required that its proceedings be held in public and even provided space for anyone who wished to attend to listen to the debates.[47] The Cortes continued to meet for about five months in the Isla de León until moving to Cádiz.[48] From February, 1811, to September, 1813, the Cortes held its sessions Cádiz in the Oratory of San Felipe Neri.[49] The main sources for our understanding of what transpired at the Cortes are its official records, a Diary of Sessions and the recorded Acts.[50]

It is important to remember that the activities of the Cortes were not focused exclusively on drafting a new constitution. Running a war in Spain and maintaining control of increasingly fractured American possessions were substantial concerns.[51] There was, after all, an empire to run. In its 1,810 sessions, the Cortes also enacted legislation of immediate applicability in addition to drafting the Constitution.[52] The decrees of the Cortes acting as a regular legislative body foreshadowed many of the reforms the Constitution was to embody.[53]

Attendance at the Cortes varied, and accounts of participation range from as few as 100 deputies at some times to more than 220 deputies at the moment they dissolved the Cortes on September 14, 1813.[54] At the opening of the Cortes, 28 of the 102 deputies represented American interests.[55] About a third of the deputies were from higher levels of the clergy and about sixty were jurists of some kind. The remaining deputies included public officials, university professors, soldiers, estate owners, and men of commerce.[56]

Scholars have divided the deputies into three, sometimes overlapping, groups: royalists, liberals, and Americans.[57] The great majority of liberals were younger, in their late twenties and thirties. They had little political or administrative experience. For example, noted liberals Agustín Argüelles and the Conde de Toreno were thirty-four and twenty-four

---

[47] Marcuello Benedicto, "Las Cortes Generales," 74–81.
[48] Ramos Santana, Cádiz en el siglo xix, vol. 3, 178.
[49] Meléndez Chaverri, *Las Cortes de Cádiz*, 35.
[50] Estrada, "Los Reinos," 211.
[51] Rodríguez, *Independence*, 82.
[52] Meléndez Chaverri, *Las Cortes de Cádiz*, 34.
[53] Varela Suanzes-Carpegna, *Tres ensayos*, 90.
[54] Ibid., 85.
[55] Artola, *II La Constitución de Cádiz*, 38.
[56] Pérez Ledesma, "Las Cortes," 172; for a breakdown of the deputies by profession see Meléndez Chaverri, "Las Cortes de Cádiz," 35.
[57] Varela Suanzes-Carpegna, *Tres ensayos*, 85–87.

years old respectively. An important exception in the liberal camp was Muñoz Torrero, who was forty-nine years old. Conservative royalists were considerably older and experienced in statecraft, with an average age of around sixty years old. The conservative royalists often used their relative age and experience as rhetorical tools to challenge liberal positions in the Cortes.[58] Political positions in the Cortes were often generational. Americans often represented regional interests beyond the peninsular distinctions between royalists and liberals.

A Commission on the Constitution established by the Cortes drafted the Constitution of Cádiz. This Commission was composed of fifteen members: five royalists, five liberals, and five Americans.[59] The Commission based its work on the reports sent to the Junta on Legislation and other suggestions sent directly to the Commission. By August, 1811, the Commission had reported the first four titles of the draft Constitution and their corresponding explanation to the Cortes while the Commission continued to debate the remaining six titles. Along with the draft Constitution, the Commission prepared an explanatory document (*Discurso Preliminar*), an introduction that was highly influential and provides essential intellectual background to the main text. The main drafters of the text of the Constitution were Diego Muñoz Torrero, Evaristo Pérez de Castro, and probably Antonio Ranz Romanillos, who was not a member of the Commission. Agustín Argüelles and José Espiga drafted the Introduction.[60]

This constitutional text was debated by the Cortes, approved by the deputies, and eventually promulgated and published by the Council of Regency on March 19, 1812.[61] March 19 was the feast day of San José, and the Constitution's nickname "La Pepa" comes from the feminine form of Pepe, the nickname for José.[62]

After promulgation of the Constitution, royalists and liberals continued to debate. One issue was the most appropriate location for the

---

[58] García Laguardia, *Las Cortes de Cádiz*, 25–27; García Laguardia, *Centroamérica*, 117.

[59] The five royalists were Francisco Gutiérrez de la Huerta, Juan Pablo Valiente, Francisco Rodríguez de la Bárcena, Alonso Cañedo Vigil, and Pedro María Rich. The five liberals were Diego Muñoz Torrero, Antonio Oliveros, Agustín Argüelles, José Espiga, and Evaristo Pérez de Castro. The Americans were Joaquín Fernández de Leyva (Chile), Andrés Jáuregui (Cuba), Antonio Joaquín Pérez (Mexico), Mariano Mendiola Velarde (Mexico), and Vicente Morales Duárez (Peru). Varela Suanzes-Carpegna, *Tres ensayos*, 91.

[60] Varela Suanzes-Carpegna, *Tres ensayos*, 92–93.

[61] Artola, *II La Constitución de Cádiz*, 39, 77.

[62] Ramos Santana, *Cádiz en el siglo xix*, vol. 3, 182.

convocation of the Ordinary Cortes under the Constitution. Royalists preferred Madrid; liberals preferred the birthplace of the Constitution, Cádiz. The liberals won this debate and the Ordinary Cortes was convened for October 1, 1813, in Cádiz. After electing a Standing Committee, the General and Extraordinary Cortes closed its sessions on September 14, 1813. For reasons of health, the Ordinary Cortes moved its sessions to the Isla de Léon on October 14, 1813, until November 29, 1813, when plans were made to move again to Madrid. On January 15, 1814, the Ordinary Cortes under the Constitution met in Madrid.[63]

Thus, the Constitution stayed in effect until Fernando VII returned to power in Spain and officially renounced the Constitution in Valencia on May 4, 1814. Plaques designating central plazas as Constitution Plazas were removed and liberal members of the Cortes were gathered up and punished. Cádiz, as a hotbed of liberal thought, was subject to particular scrutiny; even liberal cafés, such as the Apolo and the Patriots, were investigated. The most liberal of Cádiz's thinkers, often associated with Masonry, went underground.[64]

The Constitution came back into effect during the "Trienio Liberal," or the liberal three years of 1820–1823 when liberal military forces were successful in their battle with absolutist forces. Fernando VII swore to uphold the Constitution on March 9, 1820. The Constitution governed until, yet again, another French invasion forced Fernando VII to Cádiz in June, 1823. France was to control portions of Spain until 1828.[65]

The Text of the Constitution

The Constitution provides for sovereignty in the nation, rather than in the king. Although maintaining the Roman Catholic faith as the official state religion, the Constitution espouses liberal ideas and institutions including, as stated previously, representative electoral bodies at various levels of government, restrictions on the power of the king, rights for the criminally accused, freedom of contract, and individual property rights. It abolished seigniorial structures, Indian tribute, forced Indian labor in America, and personal services in Spain.[66]

The Constitution is about forty pages in length; its 384 articles are divided into 10 titles. The titles address (1) the Spanish nation; (2) the

[63] Flaquer Montequi, "El Ejecutivo," 62–63.
[64] Ramos Santana, *Cádiz en el siglo xix*, vol. 3, 182–189.
[65] Ibid., 189–198.
[66] Rodríguez, *Independence*, 91.

Spanish territory, its religion and government; (3) the Cortes; (4) the king; (5) tribunals and the administration of justice; (6) the government of provinces and cities; (7) taxation; (8) the armed forces; (9) public education; and (10) the observance and amendment of the constitution.[67]

It is worth noting that the Cortes itself decreed the Constitution under the name of the king, Fernando VII, and the prologue to the Constitution begins "In the name of the name of God Almighty, Father, Son, and Holy Spirit, author and supreme legislator of society."[68] This is quite a traditional frame for what is considered an important document in the history of European and Latin American liberalism. These traditional tropes must be understood in the light of the Constitution's place in straddling the periods of monarchical absolutism and democratic popular sovereignty. From the imperial standpoint, the Trinitarian, Catholic, and monarchical features of the Constitution were probably reassuring phrases of tradition and continuity.

Broadly speaking, the first two titles define the nation and significant aspects such as its territory and religion. Although the chapters of these titles are packed with meanings and political compromises that run the course of this book, a general sense of these provisions is essential to what follows. These provisions define the Spanish nation as including Spaniards "of both hemispheres" and establish that the nation is not the "patrimony of any family or person," that "sovereignty resides essentially in the nation," and that the nation must protect "civil liberty, property, and other legitimate rights of individuals."[69] An article in this chapter also sets out with exactitude who is "a Spaniard," a provision that must be read carefully in conjunction with several articles defining "the Spanish citizen;" they are not the same thing under this Constitution.[70] Thus, near the beginning of the Constitution we find articles defining the territory of the nation in geographic terms, establishing Roman Catholicism as the official state religion, and ordaining a hereditary Monarchy as the form of government.[71] Three following articles tersely declare a separation of powers: the Cortes makes law, the king executes the law, and tribunals apply the law.[72] The bulk of the Constitution follows this structure in the

---

[67] Constitución de Cádiz de 1812, Biblioteca Virtual Miguel de Cervantes, http://www
.cervantesvirtual.com. For an English translation of the text, see Mirow, *Florida's First
Constitution*.
[68] Constitution of Cádiz, Preamble.
[69] Ibid., Arts. 1–4.
[70] Ibid., Arts. 5 and 18–26.
[71] Ibid., Arts. 10, 12, and 14.
[72] Ibid., Arts. 15, 16, and 17.

next 280 or so articles divided into three titles: the Cortes, the king, and the tribunals.

Concerning the Cortes, the Constitution first sets out how deputies were to be elected. Through a system of elections at the parish, region, and provincial levels, one deputy was selected for every 70,000 individuals, with some carefully drafted provisions about who counted for these purposes and how to round off the applicable populations of provinces.[73] Individual citizens of a parish elected parish representatives who, in turn, elected a parish elector or parish electors depending on the population of the parish. The parish was not just a convenient form of dividing the population for administrative purposes. The parish priest, church buildings, the Mass, and *Te Deum* all served in the electoral process.[74] Parish electors met in regional elections to elect regional electors in a similar fashion.[75] In turn, and in similar fashion, regional electors served in provincial juntas to elect deputies, and, in the event elected deputies were unable to serve, to elect substitute deputies to the Cortes.[76] This step into indirect democracy from royal absolutism was a lasting and important transition in the Spanish-speaking world.

The Constitution established procedures for convening the Cortes. These include its place of meeting, what to do about moving the location of the Cortes when necessary, the biennial election of deputies, the oath required of deputies, the king's role in opening the Cortes, the prohibition of deliberation in front of the king, and the immunities of deputies.[77]

Just as Article I, Section 8, of the United States Constitution is a central provision defining the powers of Congress in the United States, Article 131 of the Constitution of Cádiz lists the powers of the Cortes in the Spanish nation. The 26 provisions of Article 131 give the Cortes the power to make laws, to receive the oath of the king to determine various aspects of royal succession, to approve treaties, to create and to remove judicial and public offices, to fix the number and organization of troops, to tax, to borrow, to spend, to invest, to dispose of property, to establish money, to set weights and measures, to promote industry, to plan for public education, to promote the general order though police and health measures, to protect the freedom of the press, to hold public officials accountable, and to ensure the constitutionality of any actions.[78]

---

[73] Ibid., Arts. 27–34.
[74] Ibid., Arts. 35–58.
[75] Ibid., Arts. 59–77.
[76] Ibid., Arts. 78–103.
[77] Ibid., Arts. 104–130.
[78] Ibid., Art. 131.

The process for the Cortes's legislative activity related to the power to make law is described in significant detail. The Constitution established a process of reading, debating, and voting on legislation. A law that passed the Cortes was sent to the king for publication according to a procedure set out in the Constitution. The king could reject the proposed law and return it to the Cortes with his comments. Laws vetoed by the king did not become effective, although if the same proposed law were passed in a subsequent year after two royal vetoes, the law would become effective.[79]

Apart from its regular legislative duties, the Cortes was charged with two other activities under the Constitution. First, at the end of the legislative term, the Cortes was to establish a Standing Committee (*Diputación Permanente*) whose main function was to guard against infractions of the Constitution, convene the Cortes when necessary, and carry out several administrative functions at the beginning of the Cortes. Second, the Cortes might be assembled in extraordinary fashion by the Standing Committee when the crown was vacant, when the king was unable to act, or under any emergency situation.[80] Thus, the Standing Committee served as an important stop gap and check on executive power and stepped in when the king could not act or when the king acted beyond his constitutional bounds.

The authority and function of the king were substantially limited by the Constitution of Cádiz in comparison to the previous unwritten constitution of the Spanish Empire. The Constitution charges the king with executing the laws, conserving public order in the nation, and providing for the exterior security of the state according to the Constitution and laws.[81] Just as Article 131 defines the scope of the Cortes's legislative powers, Article 171 lists the king's powers under the Constitution. These include executing the laws through decrees and regulations, ensuring the administration of justice, declaring war and making peace, naming judges, appointing civil and military officials, appointing archbishops according to the state's control of the church under the *Real Patronato*, bestowing honors, ordering the army and navy, conducting foreign affairs, ensuring money is printed with his likeness and name, allocating funds for public administration, pardoning, proposing legislation, reviewing conciliar decrees and papal bulls, and naming and removing secretaries of state and of the home office.[82]

---

[79] Ibid., Arts. 132–156.
[80] Ibid., Arts. 157–167.
[81] Ibid., Art. 170.
[82] Ibid., Art. 171.

If there is a certain parallelism between Article 131, granting powers to the Cortes, and Article 171, granting powers to the king, the rest of the provisions regarding the king are a clear departure. With no parallel article in the section addressing the Cortes, Article 172 provides for restrictions on the king. The king cannot impede the Cortes or suspend or dissolve it. The king cannot leave the kingdom without the Cortes's consent; if he does, this serves as an automatic abdication. The king cannot transfer either his royal authority or any of the royal prerogatives. The king cannot abdicate without the Cortes's consent. Nor can the king transfer territory of the kingdom. The consent of the Cortes is needed for the king to do any of the following: to form alliances or commercial relations with other countries, to obligate the nation to make payments to other countries, to transfer national property, to tax in any manner, and to marry. The king may not grant monopolies. There are important restrictions on the king's right to take property or deprive individual liberty.[83] The king must also swear to uphold the Constitution, and the text of the oath in the Constitution itself repeats many of the important restrictions found in Article 172.[84] About forty-five articles address the succession of the crown, the creation of a regency during the minority of the king, the rights of the royal family and the Prince of Asturias, and the property provided to the royal family by the nation.[85]

In addition to the king, the executive was divided into seven ministries under the Constitution: State, Government of the Peninsula, Government of Ultramar, Justice, Treasury, War, and Marine. The Constitution also created a Council of State composed of forty individuals, four of whom were ecclesiastics and four were nobles. The remaining members were selected based on their knowledge and ability with the additional requirement that at least twelve would have been born off the peninsula (in Ultramar). The king named the councilors at the suggestion of the Cortes from a list of three candidates for each position. The Council advised and listened to the king concerning legislation, declaring war, making treaties, and appointing ecclesiastics and judges. Unlike similarly named institutions in other countries, the Spanish Council of State was most likely contemplated as an additional check on the king to ensure his actions were constitutional.[86]

---

[83] Ibid., Art. 172.
[84] Ibid., Art. 173.
[85] Ibid., Arts. 174–221.
[86] Ibid., Arts. 231–241; Artola, *Constitucionalismo*, 209.

The extraction of an independent judicial branch from the pre-Cádiz colonial institutions in which various government functions were combined in institutions such as the *audiencia* proved to be a difficult task, and the Constitution of Cádiz dedicates more than sixty articles to courts and the administration of justice.[87] Several articles establish the courts as the exclusive organ of judicial power and make it clear that neither the king nor the Cortes is permitted to exercise a judicial function.[88] The portion of the Constitution addressing the judicial function is divided into three sections: the courts, civil justice, and criminal justice.[89] The courts were granted the exclusive function of applying the law and executing judgments in the sense that other branches of government or institutions must not exercise the judicial function and that the courts must not exercise any function beyond the judicial function.[90] Uniformity in applying law was a theme running though the provisions on the courts. Although maintaining special jurisdictions for the military and church, the Constitution required that procedural law and the substantive civil and criminal law were to be uniform throughout the nation and contemplated modern codes of law.[91] Several provisions addressed the qualifications, removal, and compensation of judges who were also held to be personally liable for failures to observe the law in civil and criminal trials.[92] Responsibility for the overall structure of the judicial branch was granted to the Supreme Court as organized by the Cortes.[93]

Just as Article 131 defines the scope of the Cortes's legislative powers and Article 171 lists the king's executive powers under the Constitution, Article 261 sets out the judicial powers of the Supreme Court. These powers included structuring the judicial branch and the jurisdiction of the *audiencias* (appellate courts), trying government officials, deciding questions of the *Real Patronato* including the use of royal courts in enforcing ecclesiastical judgments (*recursos de fuerza*), reviewing judgments of lower courts including where judges misapplied the law, consulting with other courts and the king, and ensuring the efficient administration of justice.[94]

[87] Constitution of Cádiz, Arts. 242–308.
[88] Ibid., Arts. 242–246.
[89] Ibid., Arts. 242–308.
[90] Ibid., Arts. 242, 243, 245, 247.
[91] Ibid., Arts. 244, 248, 249, 250, 258.
[92] Ibid., Arts. 251–256.
[93] Ibid., Arts. 259–260.
[94] Ibid., Art. 261.

After establishing the nature of the Supreme Court, the Constitution addressed the appellate courts, or *audiencias*. These courts had an appellate jurisdiction over the lower courts in their territory, and were to review *recursos de fuerza*. They were also obligated to assist in the administration of justice in their territories and, in Ultramar, to hear cases concerning the judicial misapplication of the law (*recursos de nulidad*).[95] The Constitution also created lower courts that reported to their respective *audiencias*.[96] It also left open the possibility of distinguishing between judges of fact and judges of law at some point in the future.[97]

Following the structure of the courts, the Constitution established various requirements for the administration of justice by the courts in civil and criminal matters. Almost all provisions dealing with civil justice are related to the availability and usefulness of arbitration and conciliation. Indeed, one article required attempts at conciliation as a requirement for going forward with a case in the courts.[98]

The provisions addressing criminal trials are more extensive than those dealing with civil trials. Spaniards in prison were to be informed of the facts of the crime and were to receive a written judicial order.[99] Before being committed to a prison, the arrested individual was to be presented to a judge within twenty-four hours of detention.[100] Furthermore, within the first twenty-four hours of imprisonment, a prisoner was entitled to know the reason for imprisonment and the name of the accuser.[101] Declarations of the arrested individual were without oath, so that "no one has to take the oath in criminal matters concerning his own actions."[102] Torture was prohibited.[103] Searches of homes were required to be conducted according to law.[104] Criminals *in flagrante* could be arrested and brought before a judge.[105] Property might be seized only in cases in which monetary damages are part of the punishment, and forfeiture of goods as a criminal sanction was prohibited.[106] Guarantors were not subject to imprisonment

---

[95] Ibid., Arts. 262–272.
[96] Ibid., Arts. 273–279.
[97] Ibid., Art. 307.
[98] Ibid., Arts. 280–184.
[99] Ibid., Art. 287.
[100] Ibid., Art. 290.
[101] Ibid., Art. 300.
[102] Ibid., Art. 291.
[103] Ibid., Art. 303.
[104] Ibid., Art. 306.
[105] Ibid., Art. 292.
[106] Ibid., Arts. 294, 304.

when guarantees were permitted.[107] Only the Cortes could dispense with protections concerning arrest in times of extraordinary circumstances.[108] Several provisions address the judicial inspection of prisons.[109]

The remaining substantive provisions of the Constitution address the internal government of the nation, taxes, the military, education, and the observance of the Constitution. *Ayuntamientos* (municipal governments) under the Constitution continued to use the established nomenclature of the Spanish Empire of, for example, *alcaldes*, *regidores*, and *procuradores sindicos* as members of the governing body.[110] Nonetheless, royal control over the appointment and periods of service of these officials were replaced by election by the municipality and periods of service as established by the Constitution.[111] The Constitution also provided for the eligibility requirements for these positions and their duties.[112] The municipalities were charged with the health and comfort of the community; aiding the mayor in ensuring personal safety, the security of property, and the public order; administering the finances and tax schemes of the municipality; overseeing schools, hospitals, roads, bridges, prisons, and other public institutions and structures; drafting municipal ordinances; promoting agriculture, industry, and commerce; and submitting itself for inspection by the provincial government.[113]

Municipal governments were tied to the realm of local representation; the provincial governments were closer to royal executive power. The king appointed the head of the provincial government, the *jefe superior*.[114] The Constitution provided for members of the provincial governments to be elected by the regional representatives who also elected members to the Cortes.[115] The provincial governments were empowered to handle financial matters on a provincial level and supervise similar activities on the level of the municipalities; to ensure that municipal governments were properly constituted; to provide for various public works, to promote education, agriculture, industry, and commerce; to conduct a provincial census and to provide statistics; to oversee pious and beneficent

[107] Ibid., Art. 295.
[108] Ibid., Art. 308.
[109] Ibid., Arts. 297–299.
[110] Ibid., Art. 309.
[111] Ibid., Arts. 312–316.
[112] Ibid., Arts. 317–321.
[113] Ibid., Arts. 321, 323.
[114] Ibid., Art. 324.
[115] Ibid., Arts. 326, 328, 329.

institutions; to inform the Cortes of constitutional infractions; and, in Ultramar, to oversee the economy and conversion of Indians.[116]

After numerous provisions on taxes and the military, both under the jurisdiction of the Cortes, a brief title on public education importantly includes Article 371, which states that "all Spaniards have the liberty to write, to print, and to publish their political ideas without necessity of license, review, or approval prior to the publication, under the restrictions and responsibility established by law."[117] The final provisions of the Constitution concern the Cortes's jurisdiction over infractions of the Constitution and the method of amending the Constitution.[118] Among these provision include the interesting prohibition on changing the text for eight years; Article 375 states, "until eight years after the Constitution being in practice in all of its parts, no alteration, addition, or reform of any of its articles shall be proposed."[119]

With hindsight, one may criticize the overall structure of the Constitution of Cádiz. It lacks the balanced structure of co-equal branches of government that one finds in its contemporary, the United States Constitution, or many modern constitutions. Important provisions for which it is famous are found in unexpected places in its text. For example, the article protecting civil liberty, property, and individual rights is found in the chapter addressing the Spanish nation.[120] The article abolishing *fueros* is found in the chapter dealing with the tribunals.[121] And the article establishing the freedom of the press is located in the chapter dealing with public education.[122] Articles protecting private property from government appropriation and providing for procedural rights for the accused are found in the chapter concerning the authority of the king.[123] Nonetheless, the Constitution took a giant step in the history of constitutionalism.

In some ways, the Constitution of Cádiz is a modern, liberal constitutional document, but not completely. Viewed as a foundational document for the continuation of empire, the structure of the document does not disappoint us from an organizational standpoint. Liberal reforms,

---

[116] Ibid., Art. 335.
[117] Ibid., Art. 371.
[118] Ibid., Arts. 372–384.
[119] Ibid., Art. 375.
[120] Ibid., Art. 4.
[121] Ibid., Art. 248.
[122] Ibid., Art. 371.
[123] Ibid., Art. 171.

although important, are not central. If future drafters of future constitutions chose to focus on these provisions, it was because they could cull the provisions from a text that both bridges and expresses various tensions present at the time. Our present-day biases concerning the expression of particular constitutional ideas within constitutions hinder our ability to understand fully the placement of these ideas within early texts.

Actors, Influences, and Sources

To delve into the remarkable content of this document, a better understanding of the actors who drafted it and their sources will shed light on this Constitution's structure and substance. The division among royalists, liberals, and Americans is a useful way to think about interest groups within the Cortes, although there have been several attempts to characterize the political viewpoints of groups during the drafting of the Constitution and its resultant Cortes.[124] Absolute royalists were drawn to the historical Spanish constitution as a model; Enlightenment royalists considered the English model as best. Liberals, such as Jovellanos, were drawn to the French constitutions and ideas of a rationalist constitution. All of these models were consistent with an imperial notion of Spain after it attained freedom from France. Although it appeared that liberals clearly had the upper hand in the process, they were also savvy enough to realize that more conservative elements would have to be brought along in the process. This meant that direct references to the French sources were limited and that historical justification became an essential element in building broader support for the Constitution within the Cortes.[125]

Numerous contemporary political and philosophical works influenced the drafters of the Constitution of Cádiz. Enlightenment thinkers and their works had been available in Spain for decades preceding the meeting of the Cortes. Montesquieu's writings had the greatest influence and were known and read by liberal and royalist deputies alike.[126] Rallying history and reason against despotism, Montesquieu's *Esprit des Lois* (1748) and the works of Locke, Hume, and Filangieri, among others, commended England's historical constitution as a model that balanced powers in government and provided systems for checks and balances between the branches. These works' focus on the idea of liberty was also an important

---

[124] Fernández Sarasola, *La Constitución española de 1812*, n 47.
[125] Fernández Sarasola, *La Constitución española de 1812*.
[126] Varela Suanzes-Carpegna, *Tres ensayos*, 126–127.

contribution to the drafters of the Constitution.[127] Other deputies were more influenced by the French encyclopedists, or, in the case of the influential cleric Muñoz Torrero, the Spanish Neo-Scholastics.[128] Edmund Burke was known in translation in the Americas and other deputies read Feijóo, Suárez, and Martínez Mariana.[129] Rousseau's writings were similarly influential.[130] Jeremy Bentham's works were hardly known by the deputies with the exception of Agustín Argüelles, who seems to have been influenced by Bentham's thought.[131]

Although not English themselves, a number of these authors stressed English constitutionalism as an appropriate model. It is likely that constitutional anglophilia easily followed from political anglophilia as England battled against the French invaders of Spain. Royalists and liberals alike were influenced by English constitutionalism. England's constitution was, after all, an essential part of the commercial and political imperial success of the country. Spain could aspire to and hope to regain such status even while under the French yoke. The royalists admired the parliamentary structure of England and its representation of nobles and clerics in the House of Lords. Liberals focused on other aspects of England's constitution, such as its freedoms of the press and jury system in trials. Liberals were particularly influenced by the suggestions of the Englishman Lord Holland (Henry Richard Vassell Fox, Third Baron Holland) and the Scotsman Dr. John Allen, both in Cádiz at the time. Lord Holland was an aristocratic Whig who advanced the English constitutional model with a limited monarchy and bicameral legislature as appropriate for Spain. He successfully swayed the thinking of Jovellanos and José María Blanco Crespo. Lord Holland's friend Dr. John Allen was another source of English models. Allen published *Suggestions on the Cortes* which was subsequently published in part in Spanish. Other liberal deputies, such as Agustín Argüelles and the Conde de Toreno, were familiar with English constitutionalism through their first-hand experiences in England. The most lasting influence of the English constitution appears to be in the sphere of the judicial power as set out in the Constitution of Cádiz.[132]

The United States and its Constitution of 1787 were, of course, known to the deputies. Spain under the Cortes very much wanted to maintain

---

[127] Fernández Sarasola, *La Constitución española de 1812*.
[128] Varela Suanzes-Carpegna, *Tres ensayos*, 88.
[129] Torre Villar and García Laguardia, *Desarrollo histórico*, 45–46.
[130] García Laguardia, *Centroamérica*, 132–133; García Laguardia, *Las Cortes de Cádiz*, 48.
[131] Varela Suanzes-Carpegna, *Tres ensayos*, 133, 134.
[132] Ibid., 87–88, 127–131.

control of its provinces in the Americas and very much wanted to keep its king. This greatly differentiated the Spanish nation from the United States, although we must not forget the imperial dimensions of the United States Constitution. The Cortes saw itself as maintaining central power rather than facilitating federalism. Thus, the amount of direct impact and facile citation of the United States Constitution was quite limited. The United States Constitution, however, could not be ignored as the clearest functioning constitutional system with a separation of powers.[133] Indeed, the text and structure of the United States Constitution shouts this idea to all the world with Article I, the legislative branch; Article II, the executive branch; and Article III, the judicial branch. The deputies, however, considered and rejected the federalism that following the United States Constitution would imply. Nonetheless, the anti-aristocratic nature of the United States Constitution, its birth through violent revolution, its patent federalism, and its linguistic distance from Spanish led this document to have relatively minor direct influence on the drafters of the Constitution of Cádiz.[134]

Similarly, the United States Constitution stood in stark contrast with systems espousing "historical constitutions" as some at the Cortes sought. The United States Constitution stood for a structuring of government, its powers, and individual rights that resulted from reason within a constituent convention charged with drafting such a document. From this vantage point, prior politics, history, and societal practices might shape a constitution, but they were not the constitution itself.[135] This radical rationalism was too far a leap for many deputies in Cádiz.

Despite the animosity between France and Spain during the Napoleonic occupation, France had served as a cultural, intellectual, and political model for Spain from the beginning of the modern era. Indeed, military ties between France and Spain existed between 1796 and 1802, and again from 1804 to 1808, as the two countries faced off against England.[136] The Americas were not immune to francophilia.[137] It is not surprising that Spanish monarchical structures would follow French models. For example, the administration of the Spanish state followed French models through the secretariats. And when the Cortes of Castile infrequently met under the Spanish monarchy, it had no legislative power. As just seen,

---

[133] Fernández Sarasola, *La Constitución española de 1812*.
[134] Varela Suanzes-Carpegna, *Tres ensayos*, 89, 123–125.
[135] Fernández Sarasola, *La Constitución española de 1812*.
[136] Ramos Santana, *Cádiz en el siglo xix*, vol. 3, 167.
[137] García Laguardia, *Centroamérica*, 39–40.

French writers led the minds of many of the main actors in the Cortes of Cádiz. The works of Montesquieu, Rousseau, and Sieyès guided their thinking, and the universality of rationalism guiding the French revolution was more easily appropriated than the historical particularity of the English revolution. French distrust of the executive branch was easily transferable to the Spanish situation after its recent experience with Carlos IV and Godoy. The French Constitution of 1791 set out a monarchy controlled by Parliament, exactly what the deputies in Cádiz sought.[138]

Thus, with unwitting irony, the deputies of Cádiz let the French Constitutions of 1791 and, to a lesser extent, of 1793 profoundly influence the structure and substance of the Constitution. Liberal deputies successfully pushed forward an agenda of completely restructuring government, recognizing natural rights of individuals, and establishing sovereignty in the nation, all ideas drawn from the French constitutions and the associated works of the French encyclopedists, Diderot, Voltaire, and Rousseau.[139] Indeed, by way of criticism, Father Rafael de Vélez published an attack on the Constitution in 1818 indicating the parallels between the Constitution of Cádiz and the French Constitution of 1791.[140]

French influences may also have been found in the Constitution of Bayona of 1808, the constitution of the occupying French and José I (Joseph Bonaparte). The Constitution of Bayona was the product of a group of approximately sixty-five notable French sympathizers who drafted the document with suggestions from the Council of Castile and a government junta. It appears an important concession was not submitting Spain to the Napoleonic codes.[141]

Some studies indicate that the Constitution of Bayona served as an unlikely model for the Cortes in Cádiz. There are some broad similarities in the two early written constitutions for Spain. These include their attempt to establish constitutional monarchies under a constitution, their politically necessitated creation of equality between peninsular and American Spaniards, and some of the most general principles of individual liberty, protection of private property and of the home from search, the prohibition of torture, and the support of freedom of the press.[142] As mentioned earlier, Eduardo Martiré properly argues that the Constitution

---

[138] Varela Suanzes-Carpegna, *Tres ensayos*, 136–152.
[139] Fernández Sarasola, *La Constitución española de 1812*.
[140] Ibid., n 57.
[141] Massó Garrote, "Significado y aportes," 6.
[142] Valcárcel, "Bayona," 139–140, 143–144.

of Cádiz owes its very existence to the Constitution of Bayona because it served as the impulse for the Spaniards in Cádiz to do better. There is, according to Martiré, much more. Antonio Ranz Romanillos was active in the drafting process of the Constitution of Bayona. He was a secretary in the council and was responsible for translating the text into Spanish. He later switched sides, went to Seville to support independence from France, and was incorporated into the Commission of the Constitution although he was not a deputy. He was an active member of the Commission, where he prepared drafts during its work. Because of his prior association with Napoleon some doubted his loyalty or value while working on the Constitution of Cádiz.[143]

There are, of course, profound differences in the two documents, particularly in their treatment of and allocation of power to the legislative branch.[144] The Constitution of Bayona's inadequacy in relationship to the Americas has already been mentioned.[145] In fact, when the text was forwarded to the Council of Castile for swearing, promulgation, and publication, the Council stalled in publicizing the document because it feared this would create civic unrest. The Council of the Indies was more compliant, but the actions required for it to comply were less public.[146]

Other lesser known constitutions and constitutional documents were widely available in the drafting process. For example, but only as example, a draft constitution from 1810 with 112 articles provided to Guatemalan deputy Antonio Larrazábal made its way to the drafters and the deputies as a whole. Larrazábal had copies printed and distributed to the deputies on his arrival in Cádiz in 1811 and the topics of many of its provisions are found in the Constitution of Cádiz.[147]

Themes and Contributions

Having surveyed the text and the general influences on the drafters, we should next explore some of the major themes and aspects of the Constitution that have, no doubt, already come to mind when considering its text and sources. The Constitution of Cádiz established written constitutions and constitutionalism in the Spanish-speaking world. Its promulgation marked a watershed in the history of constitutionalism in

---

[143] Martiré, "Algo más," 86, 94–97.
[144] Valcárcel, "Bayona," 144; Fernández Giménez, "El Senado."
[145] Tau, "Las observaciones."
[146] Ibid., 248–252.
[147] García Laguardia, *Centroamérica*, 185–186.

Spain and its possessions. This change is significant enough in its own right.[148] We must not forget this important aspect of the Constitution of Cádiz in the construction of Spanish and Latin American "documentary constitutionalism," a phrase coined by constitutional historian George Athan Billias.[149]

Several themes presented by the Constitution of Cádiz, however, merit closer examination. These themes not only illustrate the constitutional moment of Cádiz but also carry it forward into the world of constitutional thought from this period to the present. They are particularly important for what follows later in this book as it examines the course of Latin American constitutionalism. These general themes are (1) the battle between an "historical constitution" and a "rational constitution;" (2) liberal constitutionalism and constitutional rights; and (3) national sovereignty, popular representation, and empire.

The Battle between an "Historical Constitution" and a "Rational Constitution"

In paving the road to a new constitution, those involved in establishing regional and central juntas, a Council of Regency, and the Cortes repeatedly sought to ground their actions in past practices and legal authorities. This, of course, is not a new trope in revolution or reform.[150] The Constitution of Cádiz and its reforms were, in the eyes of its drafters, justified by established legal texts, past practice, and the historical path of Spain. These sources were used to construct an unwritten constitution for the imperial Spanish monarchy. This constitution delineated accepted compromises in the allocation of political power and agency. In the context of drafting the Constitution of Cádiz, the use of such sources as justifications was often little more than historical fiction, but this process of justification was seen as important. The notion of an unwritten constitution was expanded to include particular rights associated with America through that body of Spanish law directly applicable to the Indies, *derecho indiano*.[151]

Many individual projects and draft proposals for new constitutions made reference to the "historical constitution of the Monarchy" as a

---

[148] García Laguardia, *Centroamérica*, 120–121; García Laguardia, *Las Cortes de Cádiz*, 30–32; Morán Orti, "La Formación," 13.
[149] Billias, *American Constitutionalism*, 8.
[150] Reid, *Constitutional History of the American Revolution*.
[151] Rodríguez, *Independence*, 22, 25, 46–48.

basis for their texts. The invocation of the *Siete Partidas* as a source for justifying the creation of a regency has already been mentioned. Indeed, during the debates on drafting the Constitution, Goméz Fernández, deputy for Seville, proposed that to maintain the historicity of the new document, each article carry with it a citation to the established Spanish law it proposed to modify.[152] Fearing the restraint this would put on the process and substance of the Constitution, the assembly voted the proposition down, but this proposal underscores the importance of the issue of historical justification in the process. Although specific citations to sources setting out the ancient constitution were inconvenient to liberal impulses, general statements concerning the historical continuity of the Cortes, its activities, and the new Constitution were a required part of justifying such radical changes.[153] This did not prevent those charged with drafting law for the nation from rallying their historical sources to support their positions. For example, Antonio Ranz Romanillos, one of the Constitution's drafters, reported to the Junta for Legislation in 1809 on provisions of established Spanish law applicable to the project. The document is divided into three portions: laws regarding the rights of nations, law regarding the rights of the king, and laws regarding the rights of individuals. Applicable laws under these headings are presented following their sources including the *Fuero Juzgo*, the *Siete Partidas*, the *Nueva Recopilación*, the *Fuero Viejo*, the *Fuero Real*, the *Ordenamiento de Alcalá*, the *Ordenamiento Real*, and the *Autos Acordados*.[154]

Once the Cortes had established a text of the Constitution, it appointed two important individuals in the drafting process, Agustín Argüelles and José Espiga, to prepare the Introduction (*Discurso Preliminar*). The main purpose of the Introduction was to provide an historical justification of the text by establishing the conformity of the new text to the established laws of Spain.[155] Using several telling examples, Artola has observed that the drafters were not sensitive to the historical nature or context of their proving texts. He writes, "To legitimate political novelties, the author of the Introduction went to propositions

[152] García Laguardia, *Centroamérica*, 128–129.
[153] Artola, *II La Constitución de Cádiz*, 40–42, 64–65; García Laguardia, *Las Cortes de Cádiz*, 42–43.
[154] *Reunión de las Leyes Fundamentales de la Monarquía Española, clasificadas por el método que prescribe la Instrucción formada por la Comisión de Cortes para arreglar y dirigir los trabajos de la Junta de Legislación en los párrafos 7 y 9, Actas de la Junta de Legislación*, Biblioteca Virtual Miguel Cervantes, www.cervantesvirtual.com. For a description of these sources see Mirow, *Latin American Law*, 15–18.
[155] Artola, *II La Constitución de Cádiz*, 59.

taken from texts from whatever past time, without worrying himself about the changes brought over an interval of centuries. The election of Gothic kings is the argument to justify national sovereignty."[156] How could anything but wildly construed historical precedent in Spain be used to justify things like representative elections with nearly universal male suffrage, natural rights of liberty and property, the call for uniform codes of general application, the abolition of *fueros*, or the suggestion that juries be used in trials?[157] Although not responsible for such wide-ranging changes on a point-by-point basis, Hispanic thought did have a part to play in the development of the constitutional revolution that occurred in Spain after the French invasion.[158] The explanation of Fernández Sarasola that historical justifications were necessary to garner the support of more conservative deputies seems quite correct. Furthermore, the dispersion of sources and their conflicting substance also provided silent support for the need of new structures and features found in the Constitution.[159] History, as Estrada Michel notes, was used "more as a unifying myth than an effective guide," and some deputies were willing to cast away history in favor of practical approaches within a rationalist tradition.[160] Nonetheless, historical justification played an important role in the construction of a new constitutional text that would be acceptable to the Cortes. Then again, the Constitution of Cádiz also signaled a remarkable break from the past.

Liberal Constitutionalism and Constitutional Rights

Liberal constitutionalism and its focus on liberty of the individual led to redefining the place and function of the king, the church, the judiciary, the economy, and the military. Indeed, "liberalism" is more a constellation of ideas than a term with a fixed meaning and this is true particularly in the specific context of the Constitution of Cádiz.[161] The path toward a new liberal constitution was well established by the time of the first meeting of the Cortes in 1810. The documents submitted to the Junta Central and the work of the Junta Central itself demonstrate that a new constitution was in the offing. Some asserted that a new constitution was the natural

---

[156] Ibid., 59–60.
[157] Ibid., 60–63, 67.
[158] Rodríguez, *Independence*, 3.
[159] Fernández Sarasola, *La Constitución española de 1812*, n. 69.
[160] Estrada Michel, *Monarquía y Nación*, 401, 402.
[161] Mirow, review of Carmagnani, *Constitucionalismo y Orden Liberal*, in *Journal of World History* 14 (2003), 421–423.

product of obtaining independence from France. Those fighting to rid the country of the occupying force wanted to know where independence from France would lead. For them, the answer was a constitution reforming laws and institutions.[162] Jovellanos drafted and presented instructions to the Legislative Junta under the Junta Central in 1809. These instructions, in Artola's words, "included the first explicit declaration of a program that contradicted point by point the historical constitution the author invoked: equality of laws, political and legislative unity of the Monarchy, unity of codes, and the abolition of personal and territorial fueros."[163] Also in 1809, others asserted that a new constitution implicated a modern separation of powers among legislative, executive, and judicial functions. Indeed, separation of powers was already reflected in the creation of the Cortes when it assumed legislative power and expressed the idea that executive power was in the king or the Council of Regency.[164]

Much of the Cortes's legislation enacted before the Constitution prefigured the liberalism of the Constitution it was to promulgate. On September 24, 1810, the Cortes's first decree, Decree I, declared that the Cortes was the repository of national sovereignty and by contemplating a constitution, the decree bootstrapped the idea that it was a constituent assembly. Decree I also established the principle of the division of powers and revealed an extreme distrust of executive power. Many of the underlying principles of the Constitution of Cádiz are found in this and other decrees of the Cortes.[165] Decrees by the Cortes established the equality of American and peninsular Spaniards and freedom of the press and abolished a requirement of nobility for military service. Decrees permitted the bearing of arms by members of society who had been denied the privilege and abolished torture and the slave trade. Decrees established freedom of industry, profession, and commerce; they abolished the Inquisition and began reforms in landholding, especially by the church.[166] Much was accomplished to reform Spanish imperial constitutionalism even before the Constitution of Cádiz was promulgated.

The process of drafting the Constitution in earnest was undertaken by the Commission on the Constitution under the Cortes. In 1811, the Commission elected Diego Muñoz Torrero as its president. A central figure in drafting the Constitution, he proposed a plan for the work of the

---

[162] Artola, *II La Constitución de Cádiz*, 45.
[163] Ibid., 47.
[164] Ibid., 48, 50.
[165] Marcuello Benedicto, "Las Cortes Generales," 70–72.
[166] Galván Rodríguez, "El Inquisidor"; Varela Suanzes-Carpegna, *Tres ensayos*, 90.

Commission. This program included the protection of individual rights that were construed in liberal, Lockean terms to include security, liberty, and property. The nation was to have the obligation of protecting these essential rights.[167] Muñoz Torrero viewed liberty as "the power to do everything that is neither prejudicial to society nor offensive to the rights of others."[168] Property included "the fruits of one's talents, work, and industry."[169] Indeed, decrees of the Cortes from 1811 and 1813 concerning agricultural land, and its use and produce, indicate that the Cortes advanced ideas of economic liberalism concerning these assets by leaving the owner to decide the best use and best price for his land and its fruits. At least once, Agustín Argüelles, citing Adam Smith, argued that best way to promote industry was through a free market (*libertad suma*) and the Cortes decreed to decrease greatly the power of guilds to examine members and limit trades.[170] The right to equality meant that the nation would treat all equally both in the distribution of benefits and in the application of the law.[171] These rights were conferred on Spaniards, defined here as "all free men born and resident in the dominions of Spain and their sons."[172]

Jovellanos was an equally influential voice. Although frequently not followed by the Commission on the Constitution or by the Cortes, Jovellanos's suggestions set both the tone and often the agenda. He asserted that sovereignty first resided in the association of all men. Monarchy was consistent with this because a king could serve as the delegated agent of the people's sovereignty. Thus the people had supreme power; the king had sovereign power. The people could constitutionally limit sovereign power. In this sense, Jovellanos was an early proponent of the idea of constitutional monarchy for the Spanish nation.[173]

These ideas were reflected in the final text of the Constitution as well. For example, royal power was prohibited from impeding the convocation of the general Cortes established under the Constitution and the king could not suspend, dissolve, or hinder the Cortes's sessions and deliberations. Because the Constitution was written in hopes of the return of a king, it also realistically contemplated that the king might want to

---

[167] Artola, *II La Constitución de Cádiz*, 52–53; Varela Suanzes-Carpegna, *Tres ensayos*, 112.
[168] Artola, *II La Constitución de Cádiz*, 53.
[169] Ibid.
[170] Pérez Ledesma, "Las Cortes de Cádiz," 198, 202–203.
[171] Artola, *II La Constitución de Cádiz*, 53.
[172] Ibid.
[173] Ibid., 43–44.

suppress it on his return. The Constitution created a mechanism for its enforcement under such circumstances. A Standing Committee of the Cortes would guard its enforcement when the Cortes was not in session and would call an extraordinary session of the Cortes when the king hindered the government. This is just one example of how the Constitution of Cádiz provided a legislative check on the executive, even when the executive was the king.[174] Nonetheless, as Artola has pointed out, the text of the Constitution ignored the possibility of a coup that would sweep away the Constitution with little effort, an eventuality that came about two years after its promulgation.[175]

Many of these quite radical changes moved through decrees and into the Constitutional text with little challenge. There was a comfortable majority of deputies with liberal sentiments so that many novel propositions went through the Cortes with little or no debate.[176] Artola has noted, "The most surprising is that a selection of articles that today we consider most significant for their political consequences were not the object of debate or debate was very brief" when discussing these articles.[177] For example, the provisions for the convocation of the Cortes and the political guarantees of the Constitution were passed by the Cortes with little or no debate.[178]

The provisions establishing courts of general application for all Spaniards, and in effect abolishing most separate tribunals based on individual status through *fueros*, were also passed with little or no debate. Indeed, substituting tribunals established by the king with tribunals whose authority and jurisdiction were defined by a constitution was a significant change in administering justice and in recognizing the separation of powers.[179] Rodríguez summarizes the liberal achievements of the Constitution of Cádiz well:

The Constitution of 1812 abolished seigniorial institutions, Indian tribute, and forced labor such as the *mita* in South America and personal services in Spain; ended the Inquisition, and established firm control over the Church. Freedom of the press, although already a fact, was formally proclaimed... The new charter created a unitary state with equal laws for all parts of the Spanish world. It substantially restricted the king and entrusted the Cortes with decisive power.[180]

[174] Ibid., 56, 72, 74.
[175] Artola, "La Monarquía parlamentaria," 120.
[176] Artola, *II La Constitución de Cádiz*, 64.
[177] Ibid.
[178] Ibid., 67.
[179] Ibid., 68, 72.
[180] Rodríguez, *Independence*, 91.

Liberal sentiments, however, might go too far and be checked by more moderate elements. For example, a proposed Constitutional article that would have given the Cortes the power to adopt "the most convenient form of government" was rejected because of the implicit power to reject monarchy and to adopt a republic.[181] Similarly, although all Spaniards were to be treated equally in tribunals, two articles of the Constitution dealing with the administration of justice continued the *fueros* for the church and the military. Thus, the liberal goal of equality in the administration of justice was tempered by the political realities of the privileged status of these powerful segments of society.[182]

As the church maintained its *fuero*, it also maintained a special constitutional status. Living side by side with liberal constitutionalism were provisions maintaining a privileged status for Roman Catholicism.[183] In fact, the original draft of the provisions providing for Roman Catholicism did not go far enough in the views of the Cortes, requiring further drafting to include the second sentence of the following provision:

Art. 12. The religion of the Spanish Nation is and always will be the Catholic, apostolic, Roman, single true [religion]. The Nation protects it with wise and just laws, and prohibits the exercise of any other [religion].[184]

The document itself opens with "All powerful God, Father, Son, and Holy Spirit," and all levels of society were expected to swear an oath, itself a fundamentally religious act, to uphold it. As Varela Suanzes-Carpegna writes, "In reality, the whole text of the Constitution was saturated with strong religious overtones."[185] This fit squarely with established ideas of the links between civil and spiritual government at the time. Although an empire might include a variety of peoples, territories, and languages, it could not support a variety of confessions. The church and a singular confession served to hold other diverse elements together in the empire.[186] Similarly, Frasquet, noting the parish priest's role in promulgating the constitution by delivering a speech and the religious nature of the oath to uphold the constitution and be faithful to the king, states, "Religion was present as a mental reminder and legitimating element, in the same way as faithfulness to the monarchy was present."[187]

---

[181] Artola, *II La Constitución de Cádiz*, 65.
[182] Ibid., 68, 110.
[183] Ibid., 54, 65.
[184] Ibid., 80.
[185] Varela Suanzes-Carpegna, "El constitucionalismo," 21.
[186] Portillo Valdés, "El problema," 58–59.
[187] Frasquet, "Se obedede [sic]," 219.

Thus, liberal reforms in the Spanish Monarchy were not necessarily linked to anticlericalism or freedom of religious belief. This was to be expected, as was the continuation of the ecclesiastical *fuero*, once we are reminded that "the largest group of deputies at Cádiz consisted of clergymen."[188] The preference for clergy as elected deputies continued in the Cortes under the Constitution.[189] The clerical presence, coupled with the traditional religious beliefs of nineteenth-century Spaniards, ensured that religious intolerance was entrenched in the Constitution. Liberals such as Argüelles were particular disheartened by their inability to usher in an era of religious toleration, but thought that future Cortes might eventually resolve this issue favorably.[190] Nonetheless, the Constitution did begin the process of breaking down a previous condition in which church and state were thoroughly mixed and often overlapped.[191] This combined church–state entity, according to Artola, has not been adequately named and is therefore underappreciated as a particular paradigm of church–state governing authority.[192]

Women may have suffered a setback in status and rights through the Constitution of Cádiz, at least in theory. Under some earlier Spanish practices, when a woman served as the head of a household, she was entitled to cast a vote. The Constitution's clear statement of exclusively male suffrage removed this traditional right. Regular, but not secular, clerics were also deprived a vote.[193] Thus, the liberalism expressed in the Constitution of Cádiz was a form of liberalism unique to Spain at the time, a liberalism that was Roman Catholic, monarchic, imperial, and nationalistic in flavor.[194] It was a highly contextualized and early form of liberalism.

It follows, then, that deputies often preferred to speak of "merit" rather than the term "equality" in the Cortes. Immediately following the French Revolution, the term "equality" raised the specter of Jacobin leveling, anarchy, and blood. On the path to a modern conception of equality, these deputies spoke of "rational equality," "legal equality," and "merit."[195] The idea of merit, in particular, could easily accommodate special places for the church and the military, not to mention a king.

---

[188] Rodriguez, *Cádiz Experiment*, 76.
[189] Ibid., 80.
[190] Varela Suanzes-Carpegna, *Tres ensayos*, 113–115, 146–147.
[191] Artola, "La Monarquía parlamentaria," 121; Benton, *Search for Sovereignty*, 62–63.
[192] Artola, "La Monarquía parlamentaria," 121.
[193] Rodríguez, *Cádiz Experiment*, 98.
[194] Estrada Michel, *Monarquía y Nación*, xxxv.
[195] Pérez Ledesma, "Las Cortes de Cádiz," 175.

Also revealing thought about equality, the Constitution made a distinction between "Spaniards" (*españoles*) and "citizens;" (*ciudadanos*), the latter possessing political rights in addition to civil rights.[196] This distinction was apparently based on the French model of 1789, which separated active citizens, those with political rights, and passive citizens, those with only civil rights.[197] This division would have great significance in relation to Spanish populations in America. On October 15, 1810, the Cortes decreed the equality between Spaniards of the both hemispheres who were born in and whose origin was these territories.[198] Slaves and, more generally, *castas* or blacks were missing from this definition. Arguments to abolish the slave trade or slavery failed against those who raised the economic ruin of masters and the possibility of political upheaval as consequences of dismantling slavery.[199] The independence of Haiti was also a recent event. Although slavery under the Constitution and Cortes is addressed at greater length in the following chapter, it should be noted that slaves were excluded from the term "Spaniards;" freed blacks were included and might, under special circumstances, become "citizens."[200] Citizens had political rights and could elect and be elected to government positions, but under the Constitution, the exercise of citizenship rights could be suspended through judicial decision, incapacity, debt, status as a domestic servant, lack of known employment, accusation of criminal activity, and after 1830, illiteracy.[201] Women and domestic servants were similarly excluded based on a lack of autonomy.[202]

The Constitution placed a positive obligation on the nation to guarantee individual rights in Article 4: "The Nation is obligated to conserve and to protect by wise and just laws civil liberty, property, and the other legitimate rights of all the individuals who make up the Nation."[203] The Declaration of the Rights of Man was of course well known to the deputies and even found its way into instructions sent with a deputy from Guatemala and Jovellanos's suggested a list of now familiar rights in his instructions.[204] Initially, there was no agreement on this structure,

[196] Fernández Sarasola, *La Constitución española de 1812*; Pérez Ledesma, "Las Cortes de Cádiz," 183.

[197] Varela Suanzes-Carpegna, *Tres ensayos*, 105.

[198] Pérez Ledesma, "Las Cortes de Cádiz," 183.

[199] Ibid., 183–184.

[200] Pérez Ledesma, "Las Cortes de Cádiz," 184; Constitution of Cádiz, Arts. 5, 22.

[201] Pérez Ledesma, "Las Cortes de Cádiz," 185; Constitution of Cádiz, Art. 25.

[202] Pérez Ledesma, "Las Cortes de Cádiz," 189.

[203] Artola, *II La Constitución de Cádiz*, 57, 58.

[204] De la Torre Villar and García Laguardia, *Desarrollo histórico*, 51–63.

and in fact, the commission charged with drafting the Constitution first proposed a list of rights of "liberty, security, property, and equality," as defined by the French Constitution of 1793, to be stated at the beginning of the document.[205] Although these ideas were considered by the deputies, the Constitution of Cádiz does not contain a declaration or list or rights.[206] In this regard, it did not follow models of the French or United States Constitutions nor several projects and drafts that included a list of right available at the time of drafting. Instead, the rights found in the Constitution are spread around in different areas of the document.

The Constitution's expression of rights is found in the limitations on the power of the king. In this context, two provisions, both found in Article 172, are particularly important because they address the liberal concerns of property and individual liberty:

> The king cannot take the property of any person or corporation, nor disturb them in possession, use or enjoyment of it, and if in any case it is necessary for the goal of known common utility to take property from an individual, without at the same time being compensated, he shall be given a good sum in the good judgment of good men.[207]
> The king may not deprive anyone of his liberty nor impose by himself any penalty.[208]

The rights expressed in the Constitution are, however, individual rather than collective; thus one does not find a right to assemble or a right expressing freedom of association, as found in the North American and French models.[209]

Scholars have observed that although the drafters of the Constitution were imbued with a natural law theory of rights stemming from the French Enlightenment thinkers, direct attribution or reference to them was obscured for various political and instrumental ends. Liberal drafters may have liked Rousseau's ideas, but a declaration of rights might be seen as just "too French" and just "too revolutionary" for the particular moment.[210] Nonetheless, trolling for rights within the Constitution,

---

[205] Fernández Sarasola, *La Constitución española de 1812*, n. 152 citing Federico Suárez, *Actas de la Comisión de Constitución (1811–1813)*, Instituto de Estudios Políticos, Madrid, 1976, Sesiones de 27 de marzo, 29 de marzo, 2 de abril, 5 de abril y 10 de abril, págs. 76–83.

[206] Varela Suanzes-Carpegna, *Tres ensayos*, 112.

[207] Constitution of Cádiz, Art. 172.10.

[208] Ibid., Art. 172.11.

[209] Fernández Sarasola, *La Constitución española de 1812*.

[210] Ibid.

Fernández Sarasola found a broad range of modern constitution rights including

civil liberty (art. 4), property (arts. 4, 172.10, 294 and 304), personal liberty (art. 172.11), freedom of the press (arts. 131.24 and 371), equality (on the side of not granting privileges, art. 172.9, and in taxation, art. 339), the inviolability of the home (art. 306), the right to remedy constitutional infractions (art. 374) and, finally, procedural rights: preselection of judges (art. 247), the right to public trial (art. 302), the use of arbitration (art. 280), *habeas corpus* (arts. 291 et seq.), and the principle of *nulla poena sine previa lege* (art. 287).[211]

Thus, in many ways, the Constitution demonstrates an articulation of rights but not in the classic form of what we have come to expect. The deputies, particularly with royalist and less liberal members among them, were unwilling to take a full plunge into stating natural rights of equality or liberty outside the particular contexts expressed in the document.[212]

A compelling explanation for the rather limited expression of individual rights found in the Constitution is provided by the work of Marta Lorente, who views the Constitution as continuing established corporatist divisions in society.[213] In her view, the Constitution attempted to continue the empire by recognizing various sectors in society that were represented collectively in the Constitution, and thus the Constitution itself has an overall anti-individualist flavor.[214] Furthermore, some have effectively argued that the Constitution did not recognize the whole area of subjective rights as a basis for a constitutional system; the political and constitutional mindset of those in Cádiz simply had not reached this aspect of modern constitutionalism.[215] These interpretations help to explain why a clear, long list of individual rights was not set out in the text of the Constitution.

Once rights were established on a constitutional level, the effect of such pronouncements within the constitutional system had to be considered. Although the constitutional rights functioned as limitations on the administration of government and the execution of justice, they were not limitations on the Cortes and its legislative power.[216] This followed from the privileged position of the Cortes as the expression of national

---

[211] Ibid.
[212] Ibid.
[213] Lorente, *La Nación*, 11, 13, 14–17.
[214] Ibid., 11.
[215] Lorente, *La Nación*, 125; Portillo, *Revolución*, 382.
[216] Fernández Sarasola, *La Constitución española de 1812*.

sovereignty. Indeed, we must recall that it was the Cortes that was charged with protecting such rights under Article 4.

Artola has observed that once the constitutional process in Spain was underway, the country received an entirely new political vocabulary, not only through reports of what was going on in the Cortes but also though the active circulation of public pamphlets and small publications. These new terms in public discourse included such important words as "national sovereignty, individual rights, liberty, equality, division of powers, constitution, legislative, [and] executive."[217] Such pamphlets were part of a broader intellectual transformation in the Spanish peninsular and American world. In addition to printed materials such as pamphlets and newspapers, cafes, *tertulias* (salons), learned societies, and universities provided new avenues for new Enlightenment thought and discussion.[218] The debates and vocabulary of the Cortes circulated widely. A new constitutional vocabulary reached into the general population, and Spanish society on the peninsula and in the Americas was changed forever. As explored in the next chapter, the liberal constitutionalism of Cádiz was greatly influential in America. For example, Ivana Frasquet has recently and conclusively demonstrated that the Cortes and the Constitution of Cádiz were the point of reference for political thought and structure in Mexico's independence movement and early formation as a nation.[219]

National Sovereignty, Popular Representation, and Empire

In light of the succession battles for the Spanish crown, Napoleon's invasion, and the transfer of the kingdom to Joseph Napoleon (José I), Spaniards on the peninsula and in the Americas asserted notions of national sovereignty that were ultimately reflected in the Constitution of Cádiz itself. As mentioned, the first decree of the Cortes, on September 24, 1810, establishes national sovereignty and the division of powers.[220] The declaration of national sovereignty was essential in justifying the Spanish population's rejection of French rule. Without national sovereignty, Spaniards were bound to the agreements made by Fernando VII and Carlos IV. They would have had to yield to the institutions controlled by the French: the Constitution of Bayona, the Council of Castile, and the

---

[217] Artola, *II La Constitución de Cádiz*, 39.
[218] Rodríguez, *Independence*, 40–45.
[219] Frasquet, *Las caras del águila*. See also, Benson, *Mexico and the Spanish Cortes 1810–1822*.
[220] Fernández Sarasola, *La Constitución española de 1812*.

Supreme Junta of Madrid. National sovereignty was the key to unlocking the nation's freedom, to reject the French, and to continue their allegiance to Fernando VII.[221] Those hoping for constitutional reform and liberal changes also knew that constituent power to draft a new constitution could only come from a recognition of national sovereignty.[222]

Notions of popular sovereignty were well established by this time both on the peninsula and in the Americas. Politicians and thinkers of the period grew up alongside the American and French revolutions, their documents, and the writings of thinkers who inspired these acts.[223] They knew the United States Constitution; the Declaration of the Rights of Man; the French constitutions; and the works of Montesquieu, Rousseau, Bentham, Thomas Paine, and the like.[224] The deputies from the Americas shared in these sources and perspectives.[225]

Spanish sources and history also played a part. The seeds of "popular sovereignty and representative government" can be found not only in Enlightenment thinkers but also in Hispanic thought familiar to the deputies.[226] Deputies drew examples from medieval and early modern legal texts, the Cortes of Burgos (1511), and the practices of the Cortes of Navarra and Aragon.[227]

Assertions of popular sovereignty were everywhere at the time.[228] For example, one Mexican lawyer arguing for autonomy shortly after the creation of the Junta Central wrote, "nowadays no one can ignore the fact that, in the present circumstances, sovereignty resides in the people. That is what an infinite number of publications that arrive from the Peninsula teach us. It is a well-known and recognized truth."[229] Liberal conceptions of sovereignty meant that the constituent congress was empowered to do what it liked, even to the point of establishing a completely different structure of government, such as a republic. The sovereign nation was not limited by historical practices or past relinquishing of popular sovereignty.[230]

---

[221] Varela Suanzes-Carpegna, *Tres ensayos*, 93–94.

[222] Ibid., 100.

[223] De la Torre Villar and García Laguardia, *Desarrollo histórico*, 29–50; Estrada Michel, *Monarquía y Nación*, 65–79.

[224] De la Torre Villar and García Laguardia, *Desarrollo histórico*, 56–63; Estrada Michel, *Monarquía y Nación*, xxxi, 240, 356.

[225] Rodriguez, *Cádiz Experiment*, 47, 51–52.

[226] Rodríguez, *Independence*, 3.

[227] Varela Suanzes-Carpegna, *Tres ensayos*, 94–95.

[228] Fernández Sarasola, *La Constitución española de 1812*.

[229] Rodríguez, *Independence*, 72.

[230] Fernández Sarasola, *La Constitución española de 1812*.

Such ideas were difficult for the Cortes's royalist deputies, who generally followed a Neo-Scholastic view of royal sovereignty set out by Francisco Suárez. In this view, the community had irrevocably transferred sovereignty to the king in a pact that could be altered only through mutual agreement. An absent king might change this situation, but not in its essentials.[231]

The prevailing liberal view of national sovereignty was expressed in Article 3 of the Constitution. Nonetheless, as mentioned earlier, the language did not go so far as to admit that the nation might abandon the monarchy for another form of government.[232] The extent of national sovereignty was still undefined, and national sovereignty in the context of a new constitution was a particularly difficult question. Provisions for amending the constitution provided another area for the scope of national sovereignty. The king was excluded from attempts to modify the constitution, and one provision required that the Constitution not be amended for eight years after its promulgation.[233] The Chilean deputy Leyva argued that this provision prohibiting the Constitution's amendment was, in itself, a violation of national sovereignty because the exercise of sovereignty was always in the nation and could not be alienated or limited. Others disagreed by noting the exceptional quality of a constituent congress and the political need for constitutional stability.[234]

The Junta Central, the Cortes, and the text of the Constitution of Cádiz established representative institutions to exercise this sovereignty. The precise nature of these institutions and the manner in which power would be shared among them was open to substantial discussion. Royalists within the Cortes looked to a British system of "checks and balances," in which distinct organs exercised limited governmental activities, as a model for the construction of the Spanish nation.[235] Influenced more by French Enlightenment thinkers, liberals sought a model based on the strict division of powers among the executive, legislative, and judicial powers: king, Cortes, and judiciary. The same structure could be found in the United States Constitution and the French Constitution of 1791. It was this structure that was to win the day in Cádiz.[236] As incorporated into the Constitution, the idea's French roots were purposefully obscured.

---

[231] Ibid.
[232] Ibid.
[233] Ibid.
[234] Estrada Michel, *Monarquía y Nación*, 232.
[235] Fernández Sarasola, *La Constitución española de 1812*.
[236] Ibid.

Indeed, the deputies of Cádiz followed Espiga's suggestion to replace the French constitutional terminology of "legislative, executive, and judicial" with the more Spanish sounding trio of "Cortes, King, and Tribunals" for the headings in the Constitution. The suggestion was offered particularly to avoid accusations of copying the French Constitution of 1791.[237]

Reflecting this division of power even before the Constitution was drafted, the General and Extraordinary Cortes, not as mere legislative power, but as a "government by assembly" modeled a somewhat impossible separation of powers within itself by providing rules that substantially limited the executive branch, represented by the Council of Regency. For example, proposals for legislation could only come through the Cortes and not from the executive.[238]

The separation of powers and its associated structures were also projected vertically. Varela has elegantly summarized the constitutional structure of the executive and judiciary this way:

The constitutional structure, from an organic point of view, was the following: on one side, the king with his secretaries of Offices and the Council of State, the Councils with their supreme chiefs and the municipalities with their mayors. On the other, the Supreme Tribunal of Justice, the Audiencias, the local judges, and mayors.[239]

First and foremost, of course, was the legislature, or the Cortes. The representative quality of the Cortes was novel and the system employed by the Cortes wrote over the idea of Cortes based on various estates.[240] The Constitution established two new representative structures for provincial and local government, the provincial deputation and the constitutional *ayuntamiento*. The gist of these two institutions was to replace royal officials, councils, and hereditary positions in local and provincial bodies with more representatively selected individuals. The viceroyalties were abolished and their *audiencias*, governing councils with broad powers, were transformed into exclusively judicial tribunals.[241] The provisions for the constitutional *ayuntamiento* greatly increased the number of cities that could have governing bodies incorporated into the system of national representative institutions.[242] All of this was particularly difficult because any meaningful Spanish antecedents to a legislative body

---

[237] Varela Suanzes-Carpegna, *Tres ensayos*, 104.
[238] Marcuello Benedicto, "Las Cortes Generales," 82–86.
[239] Varela Suanzes-Carpegna, *Tres ensayos*, 109.
[240] Artola, "La Monarquía parlamentaria," 116.
[241] Arnold, *Bureaucracy and Bureaucrats*, 56–76.
[242] Rodríguez, *Independence*, 87–89.

with real power in governing or law making were lacking.[243] As might be expected, scholars have entered into a lively debate concerning the exact nature of representation in the Cortes and under the Constitution and the extent to which representation was corporatist, based on the structure of the *ancien régime*, or individual, reflecting newer notions of the individual rights and instrumentality.[244]

Beyond ensuring popular representation in the Cortes based on population, a lasting concern, particularly for Americans, was the issue of the overall structure of the Cortes under the Constitution. Was it to contain one or two legislative bodies? Along with Lord Holland and Dr. John Allen, Jovellanos argued strongly, yet unsuccessfully, for a bicameral system in the Cortes. Liberal concerns related to equality and class, as well as the lack of historical justification for a bicameral legislature, led to a unicameral legislature under the Constitution. The Cortes exercised fiscal power and some powers related to international relations, war, and economic development. Importantly from the standpoint of the Constitution's liberalism, the Cortes was also charged with ensuring individual rights in administrative and judicial actions.[245]

A noteworthy aspect of the Cortes's emphasis on legislative power was that the Cortes was empowered not only to enact law (*ley*) as ordinary legislation in conjunction with the king, but also to issue decrees (*decretos*), official pronouncements of binding rules that bypassed any examination by the king, as executive, whatsoever. This power became especially important during the 1820s, when the Cortes, for example, used decrees to reform fiscal activities and to dispose of national property.[246] The decree power and its uses and abuses have commonly been associated with the executive branch.[247] The use of decrees to shore up the Cortes's power has been linked to its broad understanding of its legislative power within the context of its national sovereignty as a power to control all aspects of legislation through government by assembly.[248]

In this restructuring of powers, the king, as executive, lost to the legislature as a reflection of clearly evident legislative distrust of executive power. Substantial limitations on the executive power were already in effect through the two sets of rules governing the executive power decreed

[243] Artola, "La Monarquía parlamentaria," 115.
[244] Garriga, "Orden Jurídico," 61–77; Portillo, "Monarquía," 174–190.
[245] Artola, *Constitucionalismo*, 196.
[246] Marcuello Benedicto, "Las Cortes Generales," 88–89.
[247] Mirow, *Latin American Law*, 195.
[248] Marcuello Benedicto, "Las Cortes Generales," 89–90.

by the Cortes in 1811 and 1812. A third decree in 1813 also addressed the executive power. The decrees of 1811 and 1812 were aimed at providing strict limitations on the Council of Regency or the king and made clear that the executive was the mere "passive executor" of the laws emanating from the Cortes. The third decree, of 1813, marked a movement toward incorporating the executive into governmental and legislative processes. For example, it contemplated the attendance of the ministers of various executive departments at the Cortes.[249] Although the decree of 1813 indicated a movement toward the Cortes sharing some power and decisions with the executive, it approached nothing close to a parliamentary system where power is shared equally between the two.[250]

Nonetheless, in specific terms that were unusual for constitutions of the time, the Constitution of Cádiz charged the king with enforcing the law, maintaining public order in the nation, and maintaining the security of the state in the international arena.[251] The king continued to have significant functions under the Constitution as the head of the executive including issuing executive orders, appointing public officials, and supervising various executive ministries.[252] These were a far cry from the powers of the king under either an absolutist theory or even the historical constitution of Spain before 1808. The limitations reflected the broader concerns about monarchy the deputies had developed in the years leading up to the arrival of Napoleonic forces.

The judicial branch was, for the most part, left out of the pre-Constitution debates concerning the separation of powers. Decree I of the Cortes of September 24, 1810, maintained the status quo in relation to the courts and the administration of justice. It was only in the Constitution of Cádiz that a new judicial organization and power were recognized.[253] Nonetheless, even before the Constitution, a separate decree establishing the freedom of the press on November 10, 1810, created separate tribunals, *Juntas de Censura*, to be appointed, interestingly because it signals a legislative interference with the judicial function, by the Cortes.[254]

Under the Constitution, an independent judiciary was organized into first-instance courts for civil and criminal matters, tribunals dedicated

---

[249] Ibid., 93–97.
[250] Ibid., 98.
[251] Artola, *Constitucionalismo*, 196.
[252] Fernández Sarasola, *La Constitución española de 1812*.
[253] Marcuello Benedicto, "Las Cortes Generales," 99–100.
[254] Ibid., 102.

to administrative disputes, and appellate-level *audiencias*. A Supreme Court served as the highest court, reviewed lower court decisions and administrative actions, judged government officials including ministers of the executive, and formulated legal questions to be resolved by the king.[255] Oddly, however, when one considers the Constitution's attempt to separate powers, justice was administered in the name of the king, and sentences and provisions issued by the courts were also in the name of the king, as the "First Judge of the Nation" in the terminology of the Constitution's Introduction.[256] The symbol of the king as the fount of justice was, perhaps, too strong to brush aside.

Nonetheless, the distrust of the executive found in the Constitution of Cádiz and its creation of representative bodies to enact laws and, in fact, to govern, remain main features when we consider this document and its influence on constitutionalism in the world. Its methods of representation alone were felt far and wide and "revolutionized America by dramatically expanding political participation."[257] In the context of American political instability, such representative institutions were used by insurgents and others pushing for autonomy in the America. Although never fully establishing active representative participation in national government at the highest level as contemplated by the Constitution, the successes of local participation and the relative successes of provincial participation in thirty-two provinces gave Americans a direct experience of elective representation.[258]

Until 1808 and the arrival of the French in Spain, the country had served as the hub of a highly successful and profitable empire for more than 300 years.[259] The deputies in Cádiz, whether royalist, liberal, or Americans, were the heirs of this imperial tradition and sought to continue both the imperial structures and aspirations of Spain though new institutions. The incorporation of the Americas into the Constitution reveals that American participation in the imperial enterprise was needed. The position of the king, the creation of a Secretary for Ultramar, and the continuation of the imperial control of the church through the *Real Patronato* all led to this conclusion. National sovereignty and liberal reforms bolstered claims of imperial control and an established a path for Spain. They were pieces but not cornerstones of the Constitution of Cádiz.

[255] Fernández Sarasola, *La Constitución española de 1812.*
[256] Varela Suanzes-Carpegna, *Tres ensayos,* 109–110.
[257] Rodríguez, *Independence,* 89.
[258] Rodríguez, *Independence,* 93–94, 97,102–103; Artola, *Constitucionalismo,* 135.
[259] Parry, *The Spanish Seaborne Empire.*

Conclusion

The Constitution of Cádiz contains an unusual mixture of liberal and more traditional ideas that reflect the time and place of its drafting. The Cortes of Cádiz sought a text that would maintain and constitute empire. The crisis on the peninsula necessarily implicated American interests and resources, and the Cortes and Constitution had to take the Americas into account both in Preconstitutional institutions and in the text of the Constitution itself.

The Constitution defined the Spanish nation and its territories, religion, and government. It created a constitutional monarchy in which the king's powers were substantially limited and a Roman Catholic confessional state. With a clear separation of powers, the Constitution established clearly structured legislative, executive, and judicial branches. A number of articles address the rights of the criminally accused and also address detention and torture. The Constitution provided for the freedom to write and to publish political opinions, but does not contain an enumerated list of rights. Education, an essential component of political engagement, was provided for in detail within the text.

The Constitution reflected the debate between historical constitutionalists and those espousing a rational constitution based on newer ideas in vogue. Innovations were often necessarily couched in terms that reflected consistency with historical practices, and this method of legitimizing novelty was employed by Agustín Argüelles in the Introduction (*Discurso Preliminar*) to the Constitution. Cloaking liberal ideas in historical garb was one method of advancing liberal provisions.

The Constitution provided for national sovereignty constructed on a system of popular representation. In this regard, the Constitution's imperial aspirations continued to reach across the Atlantic. Thus, we must next consider "the American question." How did Americans represent their interests in the Cortes and in the Constitution?

3

The Colonies Speak to the Metropole

Transatlantic Constitutionalism

The Constitution of Cádiz is neither wholly European nor wholly American. As scholars unearthed the substantial American contribution to the drafting of the document in Spain, they also revealed that American deputies developed new sensitivities to constitutional thought and governmental structure that were transferred to independence movements and early republics in former colonies.[1] The Constitution had an important influence on American equality within the Spanish Empire, and its traces are observed in the process of independence in Latin America. Recent scholarship has emphasized the global and Atlantic aspects of the Constitution: "one cannot explain Cádiz without America, nor America without Cádiz" writes Frasquet.[2] Chust has aptly described American engagement in Cádiz as addressing the "American question."[3] In his view, American creoles at the Cortes during this period sought autonomy rather than independence.[4] Rodríguez writes, "judging from the Central American experience, the Spanish liberalism that was forged at Cádiz provided key ideological guidelines for a program of modernization and independent existence."[5]

On one hand, the Constitution opened up much that was new on the political, legal and social side. On the other, it has come to mark the final closing of an entire world. The Constitution of Cádiz also had competitors for the recognition of the equality of Americans or American

[1] Rodríguez, *The Cádiz Experiment*, x, xi, 59, 69, 70–74; Rodríguez, *The Independence*, 1.
[2] Frasquet, *Las caras*, 21; see also Frasquet, "Cádiz en América."
[3] Chust, *La cuestión nacional americana*; Chust, *América*, 32.
[4] Chust, *América*, 44.
[5] Rodríguez, *The Cádiz Experiment*, 75.

Spaniards. Equality could be gained by independence, which would shed the American and peninsular dichotomy. Equality was also aptly part of the plan of French occupation of Napoleon, who noted the political expediency of granting the same rights and privileges to the American colonies through the Constitution of Bayona of 1808.[6]

Lorente has noted the split personality in the text of the Constitution: it speaks of both the "Spanish Nation" in the singular and of the "territory of the Spains" in the plural, and many scholars assert that this constitutional period was the cradle of the idea of the Spanish Nation.[7] Influences and communication may be traced from one direction to the other. This chapter looks at what the American territories of the Spains brought to Cádiz, what they sought, accomplished, and lost in the process. The next chapter examines the same exchange from the peninsular perspective. This presents some difficulties because some central issues, such as citizenship, slavery, and trade, ran in both directions.

Americans had been around the city of Cádiz long before the Junta Central and the Cortes. As a center for Atlantic trade and commerce with Spanish colonies, Cádiz always had a stream of Americans flowing through it, and the city grew wealthy as a result of its privileged position. In the decades leading up to the Constitution of Cádiz, the city had experienced interruptions in its trade, and economic hardships resulting from English blockades in 1796 that were lifted in 1802, but then imposed again from 1805 until the middle of 1808.[8] Only Napoleon and the French invasion could lead Spain to accept so readily an alliance with England.

The close connection of Cádiz with the Americas would also continue after the constitutional period. Numerous leaders of American independence had traveled through Cádiz, met with its thinkers, and exchanged ideas with its leading citizens. O'Higgins, San Martín, Bolívar, Nariño, Miranda, and Rivadavia all knew the city and its leaders.[9] Nonetheless, trade with the Americas did not necessarily mean that the Americas were incorporated into the general political mindset of peninsular Spaniards of the day; in some ways the crisis of 1808 forced peninsulars and Americans to examine and to define their relationship in ways that before had not been contemplated. For example, Portillo Valdés notes that the main work on Spanish public law published in 1802, Ramón Lázaro de

---

[6] Massó Garrote, "Significado y aportes," 8.
[7] Lorente, *La Nación*, 27, citing Clavero, *Manual de historia*, 43.
[8] Ramos Santana, "La Constitución," 89.
[9] Ramos Santana, *Cádiz en le siglo xix*, vol. 3, 199–202.

Dou y de Bassols's *Instituciones de derecho público de España*, does not mention the Americas in the context of public law and only makes a brief reference to them in the context of trade and commerce. Dou y de Bassols served as president of the Cortes of Cádiz in 1810. Somewhere between his *Instituciones* in 1802 and his presidency in 1810, he became sorely aware of the place of the Americas in the empire and of the central role they played and would play in the construction of Spain's public, constitutional law. American deputies brought both aspects, trade and economics on one side, and politics and empire, on the other, as they participated in government and constitution drafting in Cádiz.[10]

From 1810 to 1814, there were eighty-six deputies who represented American interests at the Cortes. Their work was spread over different institutions and different segments of time, and one person might have different roles depending on the moment. There were sixty-three American deputies in the General and Extraordinary Cortes from 1810 to 1813, twenty-seven substitutes and thirty-six elected; there were sixty-five American deputies in the Ordinary Cortes from 1813 to 1814, forty-two substitutes and twenty-three elected.[11]

American representation at the Cortes presented many issues. Despite their minority position in assemblies, Americans challenged the composition of the assembly and often set the agenda for the activities of the Cortes. They engaged in broader questions of the nature of a constitutional monarchy: principles of liberty and equality, the decentralization of royal administration, the enforcement of the constitution, and the status of Roman Catholicism as the official state religion.[12] They might also bring forward local or regional concerns that competed with other American interests.[13] New World concerns of the questions of indigenous populations, blacks, and slavery were central to their activities.[14] The commercial success of American traders and ports placed trade restrictions on the agenda and provided the American deputies substantial leverage despite their minority numbers.[15]

To attain their goals, American deputies might always implicitly or explicitly threaten to walk away from the Cortes.[16] When there was a

---

[10] Portillo Valdés, "El problema," 57, 65.
[11] Rieu-Millan, *Los diputados americanos*, 31.
[12] Levaggi, "La constitución," 9–13.
[13] Estrada Michel, "Regnícolas."
[14] Levaggi, "La constitución," 13.
[15] Pérez Guilhou, *La opinión pública*, 66–72.
[16] Volio, *Costa Rica*, 113.

correspondence of interests on the part of American deputies, they might take concerted action, such as the list of eleven demands they made early in the life of the Cortes on December 16, 1810.[17] Other topics, such as the relative power of their various geographical subdivisions or the question of slavery, might divide the American deputies.

For the most part, American deputies were in the liberal camp. They supported national sovereignty, constitutional limitations on the monarchy, and economic liberalism.[18] Mejía Lequerica, a botanist from Quito, was considered one of the leaders of the American deputies whose active liberal members included Miguel Ramos Arizpe (New Spain), Antonio Larrazábal (Guatemala), and José María Gutiérrez de Terán (New Spain). They were often associated with the particularly American issues advanced at the Cortes such as the greater autonomy of the Americas, the rejection of a centralized liberal state without regional autonomy, the nonrepresentative quality of substitutes, the ways that the Constitution fell short in meeting the needs of the Americas, freedom of the press, separation of powers, the abolition of privileges, the abolition of torture, and codification.[19] Despite the best efforts of the Inquisition to limit subversive materials, they were aware of the contemporary Enlightenment and rationalist works from France, England, the United States, and elsewhere. As José Portillo states, "In this entire geography of the Atlantic, the message of the constitutional revolution was received and understood at the height of the crisis of the Spanish monarchy."[20]

Although often aligned with peninsular liberals, American substitute and elected deputies were not monolithic in their perspectives or actions. There are notable examples of conservative deputies such as Francisco de Salazar y Carrillo, a member of the Spanish military who never attacked the actions of Viceroy Abascal of Peru, a target of other American deputies. Francisco de Salazar was well treated after the restoration of absolutism in 1814 and went on to be governor of Huarochirí until 1819, when he joined the side of independence. He was later a deputy, general, and minister of state for Peru. Similarly, José Domingo Rus, deputy for Maracaibo, discussed later, sought military support for his city in the face of Caracas's rebellion and supported the crown, Cortes, and Constitution against the autocratic excesses of Juan Domingo de

---

[17] Salazar, "Puebla," 330, 334.
[18] Rieu-Millan, *Los diputados americanos*, 377–378.
[19] Maldonado Polo, "Científicos americanos," 281–289; Rieu-Millan, *Los diputados americanos*, 378–379, 381, 385.
[20] Portillo, "Monarquía," 153.

Monteverde y Ribas, who led the Spanish military against independence and served as Captain General of Venezuela. Blas Ostolaza, substitute for Peru, supported the person of the king, the Inquisition, and later was one of the sixty-nine total and ten American signatories of the Manifesto of the Persians to Fernando VII urging him to renounce the Cortes and Constitution on his return in 1814. José Cayetano de Foncerrada, elected deputy of Valladolid, Mexico, also signed the Manifesto of the Persians and was rewarded for his loyalty to the crown by being appointed dean of the cathedral of Lérida, Catalonia, in 1814. Several conservative American deputies were informants against liberal American deputies when the king returned to power in May, 1814.[21]

Equality of the Americas: Representation, Indigenous People, Blacks, and Slaves

By far the most pressing and important question was the level of representation Americans would have under the institutions created by the Constitution.[22] The resolution of all other issues affecting the Americas followed from the principal claim of equal representation. With equal representation, Americans would be ready to press for other aspects of the Americas' relationship with the peninsula. These included, among others, free trade among the Spanish provinces and with foreign countries, freedom of cultivation, freedom of profession, the suppression of monopolies, the abolition of Indian tribute, the partition of communally held lands, the compensation of *encomenderos*, the status of *repartimientos*, the mining of mercury (essential for precious metal processing), and restitution for the expulsion of the Jesuits.[23] American deputies used both the equality of the Americas and the distinctiveness of the Americas when advancing their arguments but their plea for identical treatment was a central feature of the deputies' rhetoric.[24] Such assertions led to an

---

[21] Rieu-Millan, *Los diputados americanos*, 368–373, 375–377.

[22] Pérez Guilhou, *La opinión pública*, 96–111.

[23] De Armellada, *La causa indígena*, 40–51; Pérez Guilhou, *La opinión pública*, 112. Until their expulsion from Spain and the Americas in 1767, the Jesuits were an important economic, religious, institutional, and educational force in the empire. As such, and particularly in an age of royal absolutism, they challenged the unbridled authority of the king not only in their daily activities but also in their theological and political writings. It is not surprising that such successes led to their expulsion. García Laguardia, *Centroamérica*, 56–60.

[24] Rieu-Millan, *Los diputados americanos*, 264–267.

entirely new construction of the Spanish monarchy as the American king-doms shouldered their way into the imperial constitutional monarchy.[25]

In determining proper methods of representation of the Americas, numerous fundamental questions were presented to the Junta Central, its Commission on the Cortes, and Council of Regency. These included the status of individuals of Spanish ancestry born in the Americas, the status of indigenous populations for the purpose of popular representation, and the status of people of African descent, particularly slaves who had been forced into labor in America. The resolution of these issues had tremen-dous political consequences for the Cortes, for the representative quality of the assembly, and for its final product, the Constitution of Cádiz.

American Representatives

Considering the question of American representation in Spanish institu-tions of the period, it is important to remember that the issue arose in dis-tinct phases during the period from 1808, when Fernando VII abdicated, to 1814, when Fernando VII abolished the Cortes of Cádiz, its acts, and the Constitution of Cádiz.[26] First, there is the question of American repre-sentation in the Junta Central. Second, there is the question of American representation in the Cortes General and Extraordinary of Cádiz. Third, there is the question of American representation in the General Cortes as convened under the provisions of the Constitution of the Cádiz. To these, we may add a fourth phase when American interests unsuccessfully attempted to renegotiate their representative allotment as the Cortes was established again in Madrid in 1821. Although these issues were similar and related, the results at each stage reflected particular political com-promises and accomplishments of various competing political factions.

Once the Junta Central was established on the peninsula, American representation in the Junta Central was an issue for debate and com-promise. Americans gained a voice, but were disappointed. The Junta Central was aware that French authorities were soliciting American sup-port and could not let American Spaniards drift toward the French.[27] The junta also knew of American financial support of the war effort.[28] For military, economic, and political reasons, the Americas could not be

---

[25] Portillo Valdés, "El problema," 66.
[26] Pérez Guilhou, *La opinión pública*, 54–65; Rodríguez, *The Independence*, 105.
[27] Rodríguez, *The Cádiz Experiment*, 35.
[28] Abreu y Abreu, 30–36; Guerra, *Modernidad*, 178–190; Ramos Santana, "La constitución," 92.

ignored; in fact, they were essential to the survival of the empire.[29] Thus, in the beginning of 1809, the Junta Central requested representatives from the viceroyalties and captaincies general, through an intricate electoral process. In total, ten of approximately thirty-five slots on the Junta Central were allotted to the Americas and Philippines.[30] The American allotment of deputies to the Junta Central was smaller than what Americans would have wanted and some important cities were excluded in the process, but calling for American deputies to the Junta Central was an important step in their recognition and representation.[31] For the Junta Central, there were also international aspects to the representation of the Americas in the junta. By including Americans, the junta weakened the voice of the independent Junta of Caracas on the international scene, particularly as Caracas attempted to garner English support.[32]

The precise nature of this representation is open to interpretation; was it a unitary representation in which each individual was of equal value in selecting the representative or did it continue an older notion of representation based on corporatist institutions such as the city and province?[33] Guerra has explored this topic at length and notes, "When the Royal Order of January, 1809, called Americans to the election of deputies of Junta Central, it is significant that the protests did not primarily concern the corporate and restricted character of the representation – the deputies were selected by the city councils of the principal cities of America – but instead the quantity of deputies that were attributed to America and the number of cities that ought to participate in the selection."[34] In fact, American deputies pragmatically did a bit of both. They represented the provinces that sent them to Cádiz in specific items but also entered into discussions of larger issues that affected both the peninsula and the Americas as a whole.

Lack of knowledge on the part of the Junta Central seems to have led to greater representation than peninsulars had contemplated.[35] Nonetheless, the significance of the moment should not be lost; as Rodríguez writes, "the 1809 elections constituted a profound step forward in the formation of modern representative government for the entire Spanish Nation."[36] The effect was felt in the Americas, where, for example, in Central

---

[29] Ramos Santana, "La constitución," 91.
[30] Rodríguez, *The Cádiz Experiment*, 35.
[31] Rodríguez, *The Independence*, 60–63.
[32] Rieu-Millan, *Los diputados americanos*, 22.
[33] Lorente, "Escenia," 314–346.
[34] Guerra, "El soberano," 6.
[35] Rodríguez, *The Independence*, 77.
[36] Ibid., 61.

America, this process provided a "rewarding electoral experience."[37] This successful rise and spread of elections is discussed later.

Election was not a guaranty of serving on the peninsula. The voyage was difficult and expensive. Manuel Pavón y Muñoz, elected to represent Guatemala in 1809, never left because by the time he was ready to travel, news of the Junta Central's replacement with the regency in January, 1810, had reached him at home. Antonio Larrazábal, the elected deputy for Guatemala in October, 1810, did not arrive to Cádiz until September, 1811, but, as discussed later, stayed on to have an active career in Cádiz.[38] On the Council of Regency, one member out of the five members, Miguel de Lardizábal y Uribe, represented the Americas.[39]

After these elections, the specter of autonomy continued. Indeed, regions that were somewhat neglected in the process of sending deputies to the Junta Central, such as Upper Peru and Quito, responded with bids for greater autonomy. Chuquisaca (today Sucre), La Paz, Quito, Santa Fé (de Bogotá), and several cities in Mexico, notably Valladolid, made varying attempts at splitting from peninsular control, although still in the name of Fernando VII. Similar home rule movements also continued in 1810 in various regions of the Americas, and civil wars began to sprout up in the region.[40]

For the General and Extraordinary Cortes, 30 slots of more than 180 total were allocated to the Americas, with the greatest representation given to the important commercial and financial centers of Mexico and Lima.[41] Elections were held in the provinces, intendancies, and captaincy generals of the Americas. For example, just in Mexico, Benson lists elections conforming to the official call for deputies in Chihuahua, Coahuila, Durango, Guadalajara, Guanajuato, México, Michoacán, Oaxaca, Nuevo León, Nuevo México, Nuevo Santander, Puebla, Querétaro, San Luis Potosí, Sonora and Sinaloa, Tabasco, Texas, Tlaxcala, Veracruz, Yucatán, and Zacatecas.[42]

A desire to get things underway led to the election of twenty-nine substitute deputies from Americans in Cádiz pending the arrival of the elected deputies from the Americas.[43] The Council of Regency ordered

[37] Rodríguez, *The Cádiz Experiment*, 42. See also, Guerra, *Modernidad*, 177–225.
[38] García Laguardia, *Centroamérica*, 103–104, 110, 155–156.
[39] Ramos Santana, "La constitución," 94.
[40] Rodríguez, *The Independence*, 64–73, 77–78.
[41] Levaggi, "La constitución," 9. There were more than 180 signers to the Constitution of Cádiz. Mirow, *Florida's First*, 115–120.
[42] Benson, *The Provincial*, x.
[43] Rieu-Millan, *Los diputados americanos*, 3.

that Americans resident in Spain would select the substitutes from the most distinguished Americans available. Americans were gathered into a General American Congress and selected the substitute deputies on September 19, 1810.[44] Mexico had seven and Peru five substitute deputies. Buenos Aires and Santa Fe (de Bogotá) had three each. Guatemala, Cuba, the Philippines, Chile, and Venezuela had two each, and Santo Domingo and Puerto Rico each had one. The only position not needing a substitute was for Puerto Rico; its elected deputy Ramón Power arrived before the proceedings to select substitutes was finished.[45]

These substitute deputies were challenged by some American interests because they were not elected in the required manner under the applicable acts. Some areas, such as Caracas, which was already well on its way to asserting its independence at the time, expressly revoked the authority of such substitutes with assertions that their appointment ran directly counter to the liberty and independence of the province.[46] Buenos Aires also objected to substitutes and denied their representative quality.[47] Guatemala objected less harshly by expressing its concern that the substitutes had not received instructions and knew little of local conditions.[48] These theoretical concerns perhaps mirrored the financial concerns of the American city councils that were requested to provide the expenses of the substitutes. Funds were in extremely short supply, especially in regions where the choice might be between funding soldiers to suppress rebellion and paying the expenses of a deputy. Some cities, such as Lima, paid one way or another; others, such as Cuzco, refused to pay for a substitute deputy who it claimed had little knowledge of the local situation.[49]

There was also the problem that the substitutes were drawn from a small pool of fewer than 180 American electors in Cádiz, and thus the process was open to concerns that the substitutes elected each other to these positions.[50] As proprietary deputies arrived from the Americas, some substitute deputies shifted to other substitute slots that were still not filled. Shifting substitute deputies to fill other American vacancies was another way to maintain some semblance of American representation.[51]

---

[44] Volio, *Costa Rica*, 39–40.
[45] Rieu-Millan, *Los diputados americanos*, 3–4.
[46] García Laguardia, *Centroamérica*, 145; Molina Martínez, "De cabildos," 146–147.
[47] Molina Martínez, "De cabildos," 147.
[48] García Laguardia, *Centroamérica*, 145–146.
[49] Rieu-Millan, *Los diputados americanos*, 26–27, 48–53.
[50] Chust, *América*, 28; Rieu-Millan, *Los diputados americanos*, 5.
[51] Rieu-Millan, *Los diputados americanos*, 33.

Despite the political instability and insurgencies in some areas of the Americas, most areas were able to elect deputies.[52] Substitute deputies for areas in rebellions, such as Caracas, were seated despite objections on the theory that not to fill the seats would be tantamount to a formal recognition of independence of the particular region. It was only loyal areas of Venezuela, New Granada, and Río de la Plata that elected deputies, so some areas were always covered by substitutes.[53]

Some substitutes took the questionable legitimacy of their representative capacity to heart. For example, El Conde de Puñonrostro, a member of the Lodge of Rational Knights and substitute for New Granada, unsuccessfully tendered his resignation to the Cortes in August, 1811, because he believed that with the independence of his province he no longer represented anyone; he could not, in his mind, debate the text of the Constitution or sign it. Although active many times in debate concerning the Americas and other issues, Mejía Lequerica refused to participate in debates on the Constitution itself because his province, New Granada, had not recognized the Cortes. From the beginning and through its years of functioning, the Cortes had shadows on the legitimacy of its representative character, particularly in relation to the American presence.[54] The case of Caracas provides a good illustration. Despite Caracas's assertions of independence, it was, without its permission, represented by two substitutes who were relatively quiet, royalist members of the Cortes and who went on to serve in the Ordinary Cortes under the Constitution until 1814. Representing Maracaibo, Venezuela, José Domingo Rus came from an established family and was a university-trained lawyer who served as a judge and in various royal positions in the same city. A loyal conservative monarchist who sought to maintain the status quo, he nevertheless advanced several liberal issues on the national level, including the abolition of the Inquisition and free trade.[55]

Because of the nature of transatlantic travel, waves or groups of elected deputies arrived in the city at one time, all on the same ship. From election to arrival in Cádiz, the preparation and journey could reach upwards of one year. Indeed, it was only Cuba, Puerto Rico, and Santo Domingo that sent all of their deputies in a timely fashion.[56] Most elected deputies

[52] Rodríguez, *The Independence*, 78–81.
[53] Rieu-Millan, *Los diputados americanos*, 35, 38.
[54] Rieu-Millan, *Los diputados americanos*, 33–57, 379–380, 385–386, 398–399. The Lodge of Rational Knights was a political organization whose members advanced independence. Infante, *Autonomía*, 162–165.
[55] Langue, "La representación," 2–9, 16.
[56] Rieu-Millan, *Los diputados americanos*, 36, 40, 45.

arrived during the first months of 1811.[57] With one exception, the Central American deputies arrived in July, 1811.[58]

On arrival many deputies lodged with compatriots already established in Cádiz; others lived with merchants who had substantial trading connections with the home of the deputy. For example, Manuel Llanos, substitute for Guatemala, lived with Manuel Micheo, a Guatemalan merchant who had lived in Cádiz for twenty-two years. Joaquín Maniau, an elected deputy for Veracruz, Mexico, lived in the house of Miguel Lobo, a Mexican merchant who had been in Cádiz for thirty-four years. Antonio Larrazábal, deputy for Guatemala, lived with Fermín de Elizalde, a merchant from Navarra, Spain. This was a natural extension of the extensive connections between Cádiz and the Americas.[59]

In Cádiz, American deputies often wound up in various informational and social networks that influenced their actions in the Cortes. For example, information and writings were frequently shared between the Americas, Cádiz, and London where the newspaper *El Español* authored by José María Blanco Crespo provided commentary on the happenings in the Americas and at the Cortes. The Lodge of Rational Knights (*La Logia de los Caballeros Racionales* or *La Logia Lautarina*), a secret society that apparently connected American, even United States, independent liberals, might even offer some kinds of assistance to deputies supporting its ideology and in need of help. For example, the Lodge has been credited with assisting José Domingo Rus's escape from Cádiz to the United States when he was charged with subversion. A number of the electors of substitute deputies were also members of the Lodge. Similarly, American constitutionalists were known to gather together at the house of Manuel Rodrigo, deputy for Buenos Aires, who was thought to form part of a Jacobin club that met with other American deputies in Cádiz and in nearby Chiclana. Liberals were also known to gather at the Apolo café in Cádiz, earning the establishment the nickname of the "little Cortes."[60]

Those selected to represent American interests as substitute deputies were often well suited for the task. For example, the five substitutes for the positions for Peru included a priest and rector of a seminary, two lawyers, and two high-ranking military officials. Although two of the deputies, Dionisio Inca Yupanqui and Antonio Zuaza, had been away from Peru

[57] Chust, *América*, 30.
[58] Volio, *Costa Rica*, 33.
[59] Rieu-Millan, *Los diputados americanos*, 62–64, 66.
[60] Rieu-Millan, *Los diputados americanos*, 366, 374–375, 382–383, 392–393, 400–402. For the Lodge, see Infante, *Autonomía*, 162–165.

for a considerable time, the other three, Vicente Morales Duárez, Ramón Olaguer, and Blas Ostolaza, had recent and long experience in the region. Thus, claims that the substitute deputies were poorly informed representatives of the current situation in the Americas used to undermine their representative legitimacy as substitutes were overstated.[61] Manuel Llanos, who served as a substitute for Guatemala, was quite active in the Cortes and advanced institutional and liberal positions dealing with equality of representation, hospitals, manufacturing arms, and various aspects of military organization and law.[62] On December 14, 1810, he argued for perhaps his most important proposal, to establish a law of habeas corpus for Spain based on the English institution. This was a prescient call for constitutional actions in the Spanish world. He was a signatory to the important American plea for American and peninsular equality of September 29, 1810, which led to a highly negotiated statement on the topic by the Cortes.[63]

The substitutes for Peru just mentioned mirrored the overall education and profession of the American deputies as a whole whether substitute or elected. Of the total eighty-six American deputies, about one-third were clergy and about one-third were lawyers or legal officials. About a quarter of the group was military officials and a slightly smaller group had served in public administration. The primary professions of city council member, large estate owner, merchant, and noble accounted for 5 to 10 percent each. With the exception of a few wealthy and well-financed deputies from Cuba, most deputies had sufficient wealth or funding to cover a servant and a secretary. Where ages are known for the group, more than half were younger than the age of forty, and only three American deputies were known to be older than forty-five years old.[64]

Each deputy was faced with ambiguity about the concept of representation, both generally and in relationship to what the American deputies were expected to do and to represent. This was particularly the case in the General and Extraordinary Cortes. For example, Miguel Ramos Arizpe, representing Coahuila, Mexico, was granted a broad power as deputy, but clearly not powers that contemplated serving in a constitutional convention.[65] Deputies representing American interests might do their best to keep their areas informed of the debates at the Cortes, often supplementing newspaper and other published accounts available in the

[61] Durand Florez, *El Perú*, vol. 1, xv–xvi.
[62] García Laguardia, *Centroamérica*, 147; Volio, *Costa Rica*, 44–45.
[63] García Laguardia, *Centroamérica*, 148–152.
[64] Rieu-Millan, *Los diputados americanos*, 58–62.
[65] Lorente, *La Nacíon*, 109–119.

Americas.[66] Because the substitutes were drawn from creoles in Cádiz and the elected deputies were selected by the city councils of the provincial capitals also composed of creoles, there was little representation in the Cortes of the indigenous population and apparently no representation of blacks.[67] These groups were to play an important role in the debates both for political purposes in promoting the equality of the Americas and as touchstones for the social and political progress that was and might have been made in the direction of Enlightenment values and liberalism. Dionisio Inca Yupanqui, deputy for Peru, was an important voice on these topics at the Cortes, as noted later in this chapter.[68]

Furthermore, whereas some deputies saw their representative duties as geographically tied to the areas they represented, others interpreted their function as serving the nation as a whole.[69] In theory, and according to the Constitution of Cádiz they were to approve, the deputies were not supposed to represent regional interests, but rather the interests of the nation as a whole. Nonetheless, American deputies often advanced items of particular concern to their cities or regions. It was, after all, the city council of the capital of the province that selected the deputy. And the Americas presented unique problems that were not always similar to or even appreciated by peninsular Spaniards.[70] Such concerns could be addressed only on an individual and regional basis.

José Domingo Rus, deputy for Maracaibo, Venezuela, was particularly effective in promoting items of regional importance. The political instability of his region must have made his requests for local support even more persuasive as Spain did not want to lose Venezuela to the independence movement already rejecting the Cortes from Caracas, and Maracaibo had already had its own calls for separation from Spain. Rus was successful in obtaining permission to establish a bishopric with its attendant religious institutions such as a convent and seminary in Maracaibo and in having that status of the city raised to captaincy general. He argued for lower tariffs and for the designation of Maracaibo as a "minor port" within the empire. His loyalty to the crown was rewarded in 1814 when he was made a judge (*oidor*) of Guadalajara, Mexico, a prime position for anyone in the Spanish Empire with legal training.[71] He was later a

[66] Frasquet, "Cádiz en América," 27.
[67] Rieu-Millan, *Los diputados americanos*, 11.
[68] Guerra, "El soberano," 14.
[69] Frasquet, "Cádiz en América," 27.
[70] Rieu-Millan, *Los diputados americanos*, 1–2, 17.
[71] Langue, "La representación," 10–13.

judge of the Mexican Supreme Court.[72] Some deputies, like José Miguel Gordoa, deputy for Zacatecas, left a series of eleven letters written to the council and intendancy of his province. Several were to solicit payment of his expenses but others related his activities at the Cortes, particularly connected to mining, a topic important to his region.[73]

Some American deputies arrived with little more than the credentials required for them to serve in the Cortes. There was even some debate about whether their powers at the Cortes were equal to the powers of the peninsular deputies, and it was agreed that all deputies had full powers.[74] Many others were commonly given extensive instructions concerning the nature of their representation.[75] Guerra found in the provision of instructions to American deputies an extension of the corporatist representation so common of the *ancien régime*.[76] The city councils sought control over and accountability from their agents.

One of the most advised deputies must have been Antonio Larrazábal of Guatemala, who received detailed conferral of power and sixty-five pages of instructions, quite liberal in spirit, from the city council.[77] Supplementary documents included a list of thirty rights, a draft constitution, and what was apparently a more traditional set of instructions of sixty-seven pages from other officials who apparently dissented from the other set of instructions. The Royal Board of Trade (*Real Consulado de Comercio*) provided instructions related to agriculture and trade, and the city council added four other measures related to religion for good measure.[78]

It seems that all this instruction paid off. Larrazábal had a particularly distinguished career at the Cortes. Within two months of arrival, he was elected as one of the thirty-seven presidents the Cortes had during its existence and also received a unanimous vote to serve on the Permanent Deputation of the Cortes. He gave more than twenty-five speeches on the draft of the Constitution and was active in the abolition of the Inquisition, freedom of the press, humane punishment, free trade, the abolition of *mitas*, and the improved treatment of indigenous peoples.[79]

[72] Rieu-Millan, *Los diputados americanos*, 373.
[73] Enciso, "Correspondencia," 186–199.
[74] Rieu-Millan, *Los diputados americanos*, 18.
[75] Marchena, "Revolución," 250.
[76] Guerra, "El soberano," 16–17.
[77] García Laguardia, *Centroamérica*, 156–157, 168; Volio, *Costa Rica*, 48–51.
[78] García Laguardia, *Centroamérica*, 165–185.
[79] Ibid., 158–160.

As another example, Arequipa, Peru, provided its deputy to the Junta Central, Mariano Rivero, with instructions on maintaining the power of local councils, salaries, the creation of a university and college in Arequipa, the recovery of monies paid to convents when their daughters entered these institutions, the shifting of Arequipa from government control from the Audiencia of Lima to the Audiencia of Cuzco, and a request that the compensation and honors due the militia be equivalent to those of the army. Other instructions might include similar lists of local and regional demands related to the creation of universities; the increase of finances to the region; the redistribution of common lands; the assertion of economic, agricultural, and commercial freedoms; the organization of indigenous peoples into reductions; and the rights of the city councils themselves. The content of these instructions might serve as guides to activity before the Cortes, might have been read to the Cortes, or, on rare occasion, published, such as José Domingo Rus's *Maracaibo representado en todos sus ramos*, which appeared in print in 1814.[80]

Whether through their more formal instructions, interventions in debate, or informal conversation, the American deputies spoke to the metropole about the Americas and their situations. There was an admitted and obvious dearth of information about the present state of affairs and sufficient published misinformation about the nature of the Americas and their inhabitants. American deputies spoke, sometimes at length, to introduce and to describe their provinces or captaincy generals. They addressed geography, population, agriculture, trade, mining, educational institutions, the state of the church, and pastoral activities with indigenous peoples – in essence, anything that would increase their effectiveness and legitimacy at the Cortes. Deputies would pass along new information from home to the Cortes as it was received. From 1811 to 1813, there were more than fifteen such informational speeches from American deputies, covering regions of Mexico, Central America, Cuba, Peru, and Santo Domingo, among other areas. At least four American deputies published such materials in Cádiz during the Cortes.[81]

For example, Miguel Ramos Arizpe, deputy for Coahuila, published and presented at length his analysis of the Eastern Internal Provinces, Coahuila, León, Santander, and Texas. He described their geography and population in detail; their various cities, towns, and missions; and their natural resources. He described the provinces' strengths in agriculture

[80] Rieu-Millan, *Los diputados americanos*, 24–25, 28–29.
[81] Ibid., 69–79, 82–98.

and cattle and limited trade and manufacturing. When turning to the provinces' government, Ramos Arizpe becomes more critical. He criticized governors for living in splendor and ruling as arbitrary despots mostly because of the military rather than civilian control of the provinces. Ramos Arizpe saw city councils as a method of improving local government and noted their general lack in the provinces he described to the Cortes. He observed that in the entire province of Coahuila, only the city of Saltillo had a city council. The province of León, with seventeen municipalities, had only three, poorly functioning, city councils. Provisions for the civil administration of justice were equally thin, with military control and huge distances separating individuals from high-level royal courts in, for example, Guadalajara. This dearth of institutions led Ramos Arizpe to solicit the creation of firmer and more powerful governmental structures in the provinces for the prosperity and security of the region. His suggestions included a provincial deputation, a governing superior junta, a regional appellate court, and a purely military authority on the border with the United States. Typical for such regional representation, he also requested free trade, the recognition of more ports, a new university, and honorific titles for cities in the provinces.[82] Such information and requests provided a great deal of necessary information to the Cortes that must have countered extant prejudices and attempts to weaken the political position of Americans in the Cortes.

When American deputies were not heard on their demands, several courses of action were available. Many deputies chose to continue as best as they could in their representative capacity despite an awareness of their diminished abilities to effect change for their American interests. Others, like José Álvarez de Toledo, a Cuban in Cádiz who represented Santo Domingo as a substitute deputy, took more decisive action. The son of an established Cuban Spanish officer and himself trained as a Spanish captain (*Teniente de Navío*), Álvarez lobbied vociferously for American equality at the Cortes.[83] When his petition for representative equality was rejected by sixty-four to forty-six votes in 1811 and his loyalty to Spain was called into question because of ties to England and because he suggested to Santo Domingo that it should declare independence if France conquered Spain, Álvarez was ordered to be imprisoned.[84] He obtained a commission from American representatives to lead an army

---

[82] Ramos Arizpe, *Presencia de Ramos Arizpe*, 9, 10–31, 33–82, 86–100.
[83] Santana, *José Álvarez de Toledo*, 6–12.
[84] Rieu-Millan, *Los diputados americanos*, 374; Santana, *José Álvarez de Toledo*, 12–13.

for the independence of Mexico, Cuba, Puerto Rico, and Santo Domingo, which some have read as a conditional charge if Spain was conquered by France.[85] He then escaped to Philadelphia, where he offered his assistance to James Monroe while supporting independence of the Spanish islands. Álvarez met with advocates of Mexican independence in Philadelphia and sought U.S. assistance in Mexican independence. The first to call for Cuban independence, he later in 1812 continued his work for Mexican and Texan independence from New Orleans. In 1815, when many of these early independence movements had been quieted by Spanish forces, Álvarez sought, and later obtained in 1817, a royal pardon for his treasonous acts. He then became a confidante of royal Spanish officials seeking the pacification of the Americas, eventually serving as the Spanish ambassador to the Kingdom of Naples in the 1830s.[86]

American deputies also pressed for particular quotas of Americans on institutions created under the Constitution. The practice before the Constitution was to provide American representation in a minority on various councils. Five of the fifteen members of the commission who drafted the Constitution were American deputies.[87] For example, the Council of Regency of five members maintained a presence of two Americans, and Americans held positions on the Council of State, as secretaries, and as presidents of the Cortes. The first American deputy elected as president of the Cortes was Antonio Joaquín Pérez Martínez, deputy for Puebla.[88] Fewer assurances were made under the text of the Constitution itself; only Article 232 required a minimum representation of twelve Americans among the forty Councilors of State.[89]

There was also debate about how many ministers would cover the Americas. The final result was just one, a Minister of the Government of the Kingdom for Overseas (*Secretario del Despacho de la Gobernación del Reino para Ultramar*).[90] In the late eighteenth century, there had been several restructurings of the ministries of the executive that affected the Americas and the individual charged with supervising activities in that part of the world. At the Cortes, proposals were made for one minister of the Indies and for two, one southern and one northern, as well as other proposals for divisions based on the subject matter rather than the

[85] Rieu-Millan, *Los diputados americanos*, 386–390.
[86] Santana, *José Álvarez de Toledo*, 13–24.
[87] Chust, *América*, 35.
[88] Salazar, "Puebla," 332.
[89] Rieu-Millan, *Los diputados americanos*, 295; Volio, *Costa Rica*, 142–143.
[90] Rieu-Millan, *Los diputados americanos*, 295–299; Volio, *Costa Rica*, 145–149.

geographic location of the activity. The singular ministry of the Indies under the Cortes was abolished by Fernando VII in 1814 and its duties were assumed by the Universal Ministry of the Indies as it had functioned in 1787.[91]

Indigenous People

Americans in the General and Extraordinary Cortes pushed for greater representation in the body. The inclusion of the Americas also led to the Cortes establishing racial categories that ran contrary to some of its liberal aspirations.[92] In 1810, as a product of declaring that Spaniards "originating from the said European dominions or beyond the seas are equal in rights to those of this peninsula" for the purposes of national representation, the Cortes, by implication, excluded everyone else who otherwise might have been considered to have equal status.[93] These broad declarations of equality served as the basis for American demands of identical procedures for representation, a goal the Americas were unable to attain. While the Cortes voted to ensure equality of representation in the Constitution by a vote of 103 to 4, the application of the same principle to the General and Extraordinary Cortes was rejected by a vote of sixty-one to sixty-nine. Although assurances for identical representation in the Constitution provided a political means of moving forward, the use of two different methods to select deputies to the General and Extraordinary Cortes was a glaring example of a breach of the principle of identical treatment and, in fact, undermined the legitimacy of the Cortes for many.[94] Deputies had sought additional representatives in accordance with peninsular representatives, a formula of one deputy for every 50,000 (later changed to 70,000) inhabitants. Americans claimed inhabitants included both *indios* (Indians or indigenous people) and *castas* (blacks).[95] Racial categories for the purposes of political representation and in society were sometimes undetermined and fluid.[96] Nonetheless, and in theory, "In the Cádiz context, a Casta was anyone with an African trace in his background."[97]

---

[91] Barrios, "Las secretarías," 84, 86–93, 96–97.
[92] Artola, *Estudio preliminar*, 50–51.
[93] Ibid., 303.
[94] Rieu-Millan, *Los diputados americanos*, 12, 14, 276.
[95] Rodríguez, *The Independence*, 83.
[96] Cottrol, *The Long, Lingering Shadow*, 25–52.
[97] Rodríguez, *The Cádiz Experiment*, 54.

Two questions arose in relationship to America's indigenous population: (1) Could Indians serve as electors or deputies? (2) Were Indians counted in the electoral census, if indeed American representation were based on population? American deputies in the Cortes were united in their assertions that Indians should form a part of the political body of the nation and therefore should be counted in the electoral census.[98] Some deputies saw identity as central to selection as a deputy so that Indians should represent Indians by making the parallel argument that someone from Murcia could not represent Catalonia, nor could someone from Valencia represent Galicia, nor someone from Vizcaya represent Andalucía.[99]

As part of a broad list of items in 1810, American deputies argued that indigenous people were included in the population for the purposes of representation and relied on earlier assertions by the regency to the same effect.[100] The question was debated by peninsular and American deputies. In January, 1811, the Cortes decreed that Indians were to be protected and free from prejudice by ecclesiastical, civil, and military authorities.[101] Nonetheless, on considering American proposals to include Indians in the count for representation, some peninsular deputies questioned the natural capacity to vote and thus to be represented. American deputies responded with accounts of pre-Columbian civilizations, the theological and moral works of de las Casas and his school, and specifically the legal argument based on *derecho indiano* that Indians were legally subjects of the Crown of Castile since the early days of the Spanish conquest.[102]

Related to the status of indigenous people was the abolition of Indian tribute. Tribute was originally abolished in Mexico by Viceroy Venegas for political reasons to match the promises that Hidalgo had made to his followers. Similar assurances were made by independent leaders in New Granada, and Manuel del Pombo in 1810 sought to abolish tribute among other beneficial reforms in favor of indigenous people. The Mexican practice of abolishing tribute was extended throughout the Americas in March, 1811. The removal of this tax, coupled with the abolition of forced labor practices such as the *mita*, was an important step in changing the status of indigenous people. This tax was no small matter; the Viceroy of Peru stated that it was the most important source of funds for the viceroyalty and sought to replace it quickly with a "voluntary

[98] Rieu-Millan, *Los diputados americanos*, 19.
[99] De Armellada, *La causa indígena*, 31.
[100] Rieu-Millan, *Los diputados americanos*, 109.
[101] De Armellada, *La causa indígena*, 25–40; Rieu-Millan, *Los diputados americanos*, 110.
[102] Rieu-Millan, *Los diputados americanos*, 112–114.

contribution" at the same rate, a practice that was later condemned. The abolition of tribute also created a financial crisis for clergy ministering to indigenous people when other sources of church income were insufficient. The abolition of tribute and of forced labor such as the *mita* was an important step in normalizing the status of indigenous people and in their political recognition at the Cortes.[103]

Similarly, other proposals sought to improve the status and daily lives of indigenous people as part of incorporating them into the body politic. The Cortes moved to abolish institutions that restricted the liberty of or severely punished indigenous people.[104] Proposals to reintroduce the *repartimiento* were rejected in 1811. The Cortes abolished the *mita*, the *encomienda*, and related payments of money in lieu of the *mita* in 1812, and whipping, a common means of punishing Indians, was abolished in 1813.[105] Interventions by American deputies concerning the institution and its scope informed the actions of the Cortes.[106] Likewise, there were attempts to implement policies that would increase the agricultural productivity of these populations through shifting communally held land to private ownership and by lifting restrictions on what crops might be grown. More specifically, some communally held Spanish land was distributed freely to Indians while some communally held indigenous land was continued as communal holding where necessary. Blacks too were afforded benefits in the distribution of non-indigenous lands. The question of restraining alienation of these distributed lands with the goal of ensuring that large land holders did not sweep in and purchase the newly owned plots was raised and rejected. These plans were approved in 1812 with the provincial deputations serving as the instrument to effect such reforms. To function as citizens in the nation, indigenous people needed, in the eyes of the deputies, religious, academic, and agricultural education. The Cortes considered various proposals along these lines as well.[107] Other related actions by the Cortes sought methods to pacify hostile indigenous groups, to gather dispersed indigenous people for Spanish administrative ease, and to limit the autonomy of missions by placing their activities under the supervision of the provincial deputations or secular bishops.[108]

[103] Rieu-Millan, *Los diputados americanos*, 71, 117, 119–122.
[104] De Armellada, *La causa indígena*, 72–81.
[105] Rieu-Millan, *Los diputados americanos*, 80, 122–127; Volio, *Costa Rica*, 112–122.
[106] Durand Florez, *El Perú*, vol. 1, xxii.
[107] Rieu-Millan, *Los diputados americanos*, 127–137.
[108] De Armellada, *La causa indígena*, 81–83; Rieu-Millan, *Los diputados americanos*, 137–144.

Although the status of indigenous populations did not come up in the selection of representatives in the Junta Central and proved to be of no consequence in arguments for American representation by population in the General and Extraordinary Cortes, it did come up in the context of electing deputies to the General and Extraordinary Cortes. The electoral decree required that deputies be natives of the province. Read literally, this provision would have excluded peninsular Spaniards living in the Americas from consideration! A modification of the decree in 1810 included not only Spaniards born in America, "but also those domiciled and resident in those countries as well as the Indians and the sons of Spaniards and Indians" as eligible for election.[109] As Rodríguez points out, "Indians and mestizos could vote and were eligible to be selected as deputies."[110] In light of this realization, some deputies, Agustín Argüelles among them, raised the unsuccessful concern of whether Indians who did not speak Spanish might serve as electors.[111] Indeed, this formulation was carried through to the Constitution of Cádiz itself, which made Indians and mestizos citizens of the Spanish nation. There are some reports that this characterization produced difficulties in implementation in the Americas where some officials were skeptical of the new status for indigenous people who worked as domestics or who lived in indigenous communities and conditions. It also provided Indians, now citizens, with solid legal authority to attack levies of money and work or social constraints imposed on indigenous individuals.[112] In fact, these provisions were successfully used by indigenous populations in the 1820s to assert that personal contributions of labor were against to the Constitution.[113]

The incorporation of indigenous peoples into the constitutional structures of the empire did not come without cost. All of the aspects of *derecho indiano* that treated indigenous peoples separately disappeared, and although there were many negative aspects in these laws and practices, there were also aspects that maintained and protected community and property rights.[114] The special status some Indian families had as *caciques* earned through their collaboration with the Spaniards during European conquest was diminished, and even the special communal councils recognized in *derecho indiano* as part of the America's Republic

[109] Rodríguez, *The Independence*, 81–82.
[110] Ibid., 82.
[111] Rieu-Millan, *Los diputados americanos*, 19.
[112] Rodríguez, *The Independence*, 92, 93, 101.
[113] Frasquet, *Las caras*, 53–54.
[114] Marino, "Indios," 163–168, 172.

of the Indians were replaced with representative structures under the Constitution. *Caciques* lost their power in relationship to the members of newly elected city councils. In some areas, city councils reflected a majority population of indigenous people that then clashed with a minority Spanish creole population under its jurisdiction. Creoles feared reprisals and in one area boycotted elections to protest their loss of power under the constitutional structures. Sala Vila has suggested that such situations may have been a contributing factor to the rise of creole caudillism where creoles did not want to yield to constitutional institutions populated by indigenous members.[115]

Blacks

The inclusion of blacks in the electoral census for purposes of representation was essentially a question of the extent of American representation at the Cortes. If blacks were included, the population would be greater in the Americas and their allocation of deputies, if based on population in the Americas, would be greater.[116] Indeed, Felipe Anér, deputy for Catalonia, stated that the American deputies sought to include blacks for the sole purpose of increasing American power at the Cortes.[117] This did not mean that the debate was centered exclusively on the question of political representation of the Americas. Questions of equality, representation, and the nature of America's black population were debated heatedly.[118]

American deputies were divided on the questions of inclusion of blacks for representation and the possibility of blacks serving as electors under the representative system. Concerning the inclusion of blacks for representative purposes, some American deputies raised the irrationality of having members of the polity who were excluded from the construction of sovereignty. They argued that just as women and children were represented in this way, all Spaniards, including black Spaniards, were entitled to the same level of representation.[119]

The battle for inclusion of blacks as political actors in the Americas was advanced for reasons of politics and ideology. Blacks were implicitly excluded from political participation under *derecho indiano* and were not included in the electoral provisions of 1810. Nonetheless, Mejía

---

[115] Sala Vila, "La Constitución de Cádiz," 52–54, 63–66, 69.
[116] Guerra, "El soberano," 7.
[117] Rieu-Millan, *Los diputados americanos*, 277.
[118] De Armellada, *La causa indígena*, 69–72.
[119] Rieu-Millan, *Los diputados americanos*, 19, 21, 277.

Lequerica, head of a commission of Americans, raised the issue the opening day of the Cortes on September 24, 1810. His argument was that equality between the Americas and the peninsula meant that all people in the Americas must be counted and that all people in the Americas would be citizens; to exclude blacks would create an inequality inconsistent with the promises of geographic equality. The status of blacks was not abandoned after this initial resolution. Nowhere perhaps was the breach of the principle of identical treatment between the peninsula and the Americas more evident than in the exclusion of blacks from the population for representation of the Americas.[120]

The question was complicated by the presence of black soldiers fighting against Spain in independent uprisings in the Americas and by the desire to have them loyally return to Spain with amnesty and equality. The inclusive policies of Hidalgo in Mexico were well-known.[121] Recent memories of the black rebellion in Santo Domingo and the creation of the Republic of Haiti were used to support arguments on both sides of the question.[122] There were also many loyal Spanish black troops serving throughout the Americas in the royal army and in local militias, especially in Peru. And the number of blacks in some areas was significant; the census of 1792 placed the black population of Lima, for example, at more than 40 percent.[123]

A large majority of American deputies supported citizenship for blacks.[124] In the context of citizenship and the rights of all Spaniards, Manuel Llanos, substitute deputy for Guatemala, argued that blacks in the Americas ought to be considered citizens.[125] José Ignacio Beye de Cisneros, deputy for Mexico stated, "Mexico, sir, desires and honors the reintegration of all races (*castas*) in the rights of citizens."[126] Other Mexican deputies argued that the majority of artisans, miners, and soldiers were black and that those who work for nation should be accorded citizenship.[127] José Miguel Guridi y Alcocer, another Mexican deputy, noted the impossible position blacks were placed in: "After having blacks suffer the injustice of enslaving their ancestors, for this very reason are

[120] Rieu-Millan, *Los diputados americanos*, 147–148, 274, 278–280.
[121] Ibid., 149, 156.
[122] Ibid., 151, 155; see also, Marchena Fernández, "El día que los negros cantaron," 145–181.
[123] Rieu-Millan, *Los diputados americanos*, 155, 163.
[124] Ibid., 154.
[125] García Laguardia, *Centroamérica*, 153.
[126] Rieu-Millan, *Los diputados americanos*, 158.
[127] Ibid., 162.

they to be subjected to the other injustice of denying them the right of citizen? One injustice cannot be the reason or support for another."[128]

Only Peruvian deputies were more divided on the issue.[129] Dionisio Inca Yupanqui, deputy for Peru, noted that Spain had always protected the rights of free blacks and questioned why some sought to limit this in light of the Constitution.[130] Vicente Morales Duárez openly rejected black citizenship in the Cortes in 1811.[131] Debate on the topic was moved to a secret session with the result that Indians, but not *castas*, would be counted. Nonetheless, in this context the result was moot; as mentioned, the proposal for American representation in the General and Extraordinary Cortes based on population was voted down by the assembly.[132]

Just as European Spaniards saw the necessity of developing a system of popular representation that did not lead to an American majority at the Cortes, the Commission of the Constitution was faced with the same problem in drafting the provisions for the permanent Cortes under the Constitution of Cádiz. In their view, the key was to omit "*castas*" from general male suffrage and from population counts for representation established under liberal constitutional principles. In keeping with earlier proposals, the population for the purposes of representation was limited to naturals who had their origins in both branches of their families in the Spanish dominions.[133] Thus, in addition to determining eligibility for voting, the status of the American population surfaced again in the constitutional text describing the method for calculating population for proportional representation. Propositions for proportional representation mentioned those born in and originating from "both hemispheres" and included Spaniards and Indians and their children. The implicit assumption was that blacks were not part of the population to be represented.[134]

The Constitution made a distinction between citizens and natural-born individuals. Article 29 states that for the purposes of proportional representation in the General Cortes contemplated by the Constitution, the base is "the population made up of natural-born individuals who by both branches take their origin from the Spanish dominions."[135] In Europe,

---

128 Volio, *Costa Rica*, 89.
129 Rieu-Millan, *Los diputados americanos*, 154.
130 Guerra, "El soberano," 14.
131 Rieu-Millan, *Los diputados americanos*, 155.
132 Rodríguez, *The Independence*, 83.
133 Artola, *Estudio preliminar*, 55.
134 Rieu-Millan, *Los diputados americanos*, 13.
135 Artola, *Estudio preliminar*, 67.

"naturals" included women and children who were not entitled to vote. In America, did "naturals" include those of Spanish origins with some African lineage (*castas*)? And might this include slaves?[136] One document circulated by the Consulado of Mexico vehemently opposed including Indians and *castas*. It repeated contemporary racist arguments of their inferiority when compared to Europeans. In September, 1811, a report by the Consulado created extreme discord in the Cortes when it broadly attacked the Americas and called into question the ability of Mexican inhabitants to be represented in the empire. It called Indians "stupid," "drunk," "carnal," criminal, and without discernment. Blacks were "drunk, lacking restraint, lazy, without pride, grace or fidelity."[137] The reading of the document prompted American deputies to depart the assembly as a whole, but they were forced to stay by the president and guards of the Cortes.[138] Ramón Feliú of Peru appealed to Rousseau's idea of the social contract and asserted that every individual possessed a natural sovereignty over himself and that every person should be represented as a form of proportional sovereignty in the Cortes. The defense by American deputies was united, swift, and detailed.[139]

The political compromises concerning the status of individuals of African descent were eventually reflected in the Constitution. Article 18, addressing citizenship, states: "Citizens are those Spaniards who by both blood lines trace their origin from the Spanish dominions of both hemispheres and are legal resident in any town of the same dominions."[140]

By a negative inference created in the text of Article 22, slaves and others of African descent were excluded from citizenship: "For Spaniards who by whatever bloodline have or are reputed to have their origins of Africa, the door to the virtue and merit of being citizens is left open..."[141] Peninsular liberals, such as Agüelles, argued that this provided a true opportunity for blacks to become Spanish citizens. American deputies noted that situations in which blacks might employ the provision and meet the high bar were unlikely and that the prohibition would extend for generations. The provision, with the clause leaving open the possibility of citizenship, was passed with 108 votes in favor and 36 against.[142]

---

[136] Artola, *Estudio preliminar*, 67; Estrada, *Monarquía y nación*, 271, 278.
[137] Rieu-Millan, *Los diputados americanos*, 101.
[138] Rodríguez, *The Independence*, 84–86.
[139] Rieu-Millan, *Los diputados americanos*, 15, 102–103.
[140] Artola, *Estudio preliminar*, 80; Mirow, *Florida's First*, 17.
[141] Artola, *Estudio preliminar*, 81; Mirow, *Florida's First*, 18.
[142] Volio, *Costa Rica*, 90, 92–101.

Slaves and *castas*, then, were Spaniards, but not citizens. They were not counted for electoral purposes and could not participate in elections.[143] It was in this context that Chilean deputy Leyva questioned the wisdom of the prohibition on amending the Constitution for eight years.[144] To him, an unjust provisions was made even worse by fixing it into the constitutional structure for eight years. Individuals with African origins were to have the same rights as all others under the Constitution of Cádiz but were excluded from voting and from all positions that required citizenship.[145] The exclusion of blacks provided additional grounds to undermine the legitimacy of the Constitution, particularly as it applied to the Americas. Florencio del Castillo, deputy for Costa Rica, summarized well the position related to blacks:

> And will it not be even more absurd to affirm that some men who may not sit in the national congress or even have passive representation make up a part of this noble and generous nation. Yes sir, in this case they are not called Spaniards, they are not worthy to be an integral part of the nation, tell them rather that they are slaves, or that they are not men, as the Constitution does not count them even for the census that will be made for the future Cortes.[146]

These were lasting scars on the legitimacy of the Constitution.[147]

Slavery and Spanish Liberalism

How did the institution of slavery itself survive the liberal aspirations of the Cortes? Why did not the broader constitutional notions of "liberty" reflected in the thought of the deputies and the text of the Constitution extend to the abolition of slavery? Some regional juntas in the Americas, such as the Junta of Caracas, had voted to abolish the slave trade.[148]

For the Spanish nation, slavery continued. Proposals were made for the immediate or for the gradual abolition of slavery or the slave trade, but American deputies who represented areas highly dependent on slave labor were successful in arguing against them.[149] When in March, 1811, José Miguel Guridi y Alcocer, deputy for Tlaxcala, Mexico, presented a detailed proposal for the progressive abolition of slavery, Andrés Jáuregui, a Cuban deputy, requested that slavery be addressed

---

[143] Chust, *América*, 40.
[144] Estrada, *Monarquía y nación*, 298.
[145] Rieu-Millan, *Los diputados americanos*, 166.
[146] Volio, *Costa Rica*, 137.
[147] Ibid.
[148] Rodríguez, *The Independence*, 112.
[149] Ibid., 87.

only in secret sessions.[150] Approximately one-third of Cuba's population at the time was slaves.[151] The topic was debated at length and with great passion over the course of three weeks of sessions.[152] To maintain union within the Spanish monarchy, even those opposed to slavery on moral grounds voted in favor of slavery to keep the Americas within the nation.[153] Cuban pressure from its deputies and from the Captain General of Cuba, the Marquis of Someruelos, who ominously predicted a slave revolt on the island, were successful in shelving the questions of the abolition of slavery and the abolition of the slave trade.[154] The slave trade was not abolished in Spain until 1817 and Cuban slaves were not freed until 1886.[155] The abolition of slavery in the region was a mid to late nineteenth-century development that was often introduced through laws of free birth before the complete abolition of human property. Chile, Argentina, and Antioquia established laws of free birth in 1811, 1813, and 1814.[156] Gran Colombia established a law of free birth in 1821.[157] Carlos Antonio López, *El Supremo* of Paraguay, introduced a law of free birth in 1842.[158] Slavery was abolished "in New Granada in 1850, in Ecuador in 1852, in Argentina in 1853, and in Venezuela and Peru in 1854."[159] Backsliding on slavery was possible. For example, when William Walker assumed the presidency of Nicaragua in 1856, he legalized slavery, which had been prohibited since 1824.[160]

Furthermore, blacks were excluded from participation in government as well.[161] Perhaps against their own self-interest, in the concomitant battles for independence and autonomous rule in the regions of Latin America, mixed race individuals, free blacks, and slaves, were often decidedly in favor of the monarchy, precisely because of the perceived gains under Spain or promises made by Spain in return for support. Despite the serious flaws of racism and slavery, it must be remembered that in regard

[150] Rieu-Millan, *Los diputados americanos*, 168–169.

[151] Suárez Suárez, "Repercusiones," 335.

[152] Durand Florez, *El Perú*, vol. 1, xxi–xxii; Suárez Suárez, "Repercusiones," 339–366.

[153] Rodríguez, *The Independence*, 87.

[154] Rieu-Millan, *Los diputados americanos*, 169–171.

[155] Suárez Suárez, "Repercusiones," 363; Volio, *Costa Rica*, 114.

[156] Bushnell, *The Making*, 40–41.

[157] Bushnell and Macaulay, *The Emergence*, 213; Bushnell, *The Santander Regime*, 168–174.

[158] Bushnell and Macaulay, *The Emergence*, 138–139.

[159] Safford, "Politics," 387. For Colombia, Bushnell states that remaining slaves were freed by a law of May, 1851. Bushnell, *The Making*, 106–107.

[160] Bushnell and Macaulay, *The Emergence*, 275.

[161] Rodríguez, *The Cádiz Experiment*, 63.

to suffrage, the Constitution of Cádiz, because it did not limit the franchise to only literate or only propertied males, was more progressive than any other constitutional scheme in existence at the time.[162]

The American Agenda

Efforts to increase American representation at the Cortes were instrumental actions to shape the legislation of the Cortes and the content of the Constitution. The general American agenda was to continue the calculated methods of the late eighteenth century to increase prosperity, agriculture, trade, and learning. American deputies sought economic reform that would better the condition of their provinces and the Americas as a whole. They also sought other reforms to change geographic delimitations that would first provide greater benefit to their particular region and second streamline what appeared to be substantially complex and baroque governmental structures.

American efforts often reflected a desire for decentralized governments with local creole authorities to counter what was perceived as central peninsular overreaching. For example, in February, 1811, Ramón Power, deputy for Puerto Rico, asked the regency to withdraw an order granting exceptional powers to the governor. Issued in light of concerns that the Caracas independence movement would spread to Puerto Rico, the governor of the island was conferred, among other powers, the unusual ability to arrest individuals to maintain public peace. American deputies also sought the removal of royal officials when they had exceeded their powers under the Cortes. Several American deputies requested the removal of Viceroy Abascal of Peru in 1811. In 1813, Mariano Rivero, deputy for Arequipa, Peru, complained that, among other overreaching, Viceroy Abascal had improperly abolished freedom of the press in the viceroyalty.[163]

Just as members of the Cortes used arguments based on Spain's ancient or historical constitution to legitimize legislation and the Constitution, American deputies asserted that the Americas had their own historical constitutions. Servando Teresa de Mier asserted that this historical constitution could be drawn from the sources of Spanish administration, the *derecho indiano*, and the customary practices before despotism had taken hold.[164] In Cádiz, he was informed of the arguments being made for a

---

[162] Rodríguez, *The Independence*, 116, 239.
[163] Rieu-Millan, *Los diputados americanos*, 306–308.
[164] Garriga, "Orden Jurídico," 117–120.

Spanish historical constitution, and thought that the peninsular regional arguments for an ancient constitution of the kingdoms of Spain applied in the Americas as well. Americans, too, had their own fount of established unwritten constitutional practices that could be advanced for the protection of customary rights and liberties.[165]

Economic Reform

The American deputies sought to alleviate the economic and social hardships suffered by their regions. Consistent with eighteenth-century liberalism, American deputies advanced proposals for the liberalization of agriculture, manufacturing, and mining; for the abolition of monopolies; and for free trade among the Spanish provinces and with foreign nations.

Underperforming agricultural lands in the Americas drew these deputies' attention. Large landed estates (*latifundios*) often held as entailed estates *(mayorazgos)* were often perceived as being poorly administered and unproductive. American deputies argued that these underutilized estates should be transformed into smaller farms and in some cases new towns. As farms did not produce, American deputies requested and obtained reductions in taxes allocated to these lands.[166]

Restrictions on internal trade and agriculture were another area the American deputies sought to address. State monopolies in the Americas were dismantled from 1810 to 1814, with the tobacco monopoly the last and most difficult to end. In 1811, the Americas were freed from restrictions of manufacturing and industry and guilds were abolished.[167] The questions of inter-province and international trade were much more complex in light of the economic and political interests of the nation in relationship to the Americas. Although free trade had been declared in 1778, such freedoms were repealed in the 1780s because of the difficult economic situation the policy produced.[168] Spanish control of trade through its system of boards of trade (*consulados*) was challenged, especially through attacks on the Board of Trade of Mexico, where animosity already existed between this royal institution and Mexican merchants who blamed the Board for Mexico's poor economic condition. Deputies for provinces or captaincy generals requested a loosening of trade restrictions, particularly so that their ports might trade with adjacent and nearby

[165] Portillo, "Monarquía," 179–180.
[166] Rieu-Millan, *Los diputados americanos*, 175, 176, 178–185.
[167] Ibid., 185–188.
[168] Volio, *Costa Rica*, 124.

ports. For example, the deputy for Chiapas requested permission to trade freely with Guatemala, the Mexican coast, and Peru. Deputies sought the right to hold approved fairs, the reduction of tariffs, and the creation of their own local boards of trade. As an ancillary to improved and freer trade, deputies also sought the improvement of roads and means of transportation.[169]

Like other highly contentious issues of equality of the hemispheres and the status of blacks, international trade was debated in secret.[170] Granting freer trade to the Americas was not only an economic but also a political consideration for the stabilization of the empire. Trade concessions were part of the pacification process and of bringing rebellious provinces back to the fold. English aid in fighting Napoleon was also made contingent on trading privileges. Although peninsular institutions tried to hold on to the economic benefit of restricted trade practices, free trade was established by piecemeal concessions, as in the case of England, or through massive restructuring from May to August, 1811, that permitted Spanish ships to trade with other national ports, including the Philippines, and also to trade directly with foreign countries. There were associated changes in the tariff system. Other economic changes requested by American deputies included the right to coin money at newly created mints, greater local control in the exploitation of mines and over the availability of mercury used for metal extraction, and the creation of local mining tribunals.[171]

New Government Structures and Organization of the Americas

Another method of asserting American power in the Cortes was to engage the question not of representation based on population or status but rather of territory and jurisdiction, particularly as they related to either greater American representation or inter-American political battles and conflicts. Systematic territorial reorganization was contemplated by Article 11 of the Constitution of Cádiz, but this did not stop individual deputies from seeking regional benefits at the Cortes on the municipal and regional level. It has already been noted that under the Constitution, many towns that were formerly unrepresented established elected representatives and gained elected constitutional city councils. For example, Lorente has chronicled the attempts of Tegucigalpa to reassert its jurisdiction through the Cortes in relation to other Honduran interests

[169] Rieu-Millan, *Los diputados americanos*, 188–196.
[170] De Armellada, *La causa indígena*, 21–23.
[171] Rieu-Millan, *Los diputados americanos*, 197–201, 207–216.

during the period.[172] Deputies sought honorific titles for their cities to attest permanently to the noble and loyal quality of the municipality. This was an especially appropriate and cost-neutral way to recognize cities that had fought off or suppressed rebellion against the empire.[173] Cities or provinces might seek economic relief from peninsular trade practices. For example, Florencio del Castillo, deputy for Costa Rica, sought liberalization of the monopolistic restrictions on the cultivation of and trade in tobacco. He also sought the rehabilitation of several important ports and obtained tariff relief for the port of Matina.[174]

Universities were always a way to improve the life of a city, to attract smart people, and to stimulate the economy. Numerous American cities requested permission to found a university, and the University of San Carlos in Guatemala dates from this period and was a result of this process.[175] This university, in turn, served as the model for the University of León, created from a seminary at the request of José Antonio López, deputy for Nicaragua. Mariano Robles, deputy for Chiapas, unsuccessfully sought the creation of a university in Ciudad Real.[176] There were other proposals related to education more generally or the addition of chairs to established universities to increase their power and reach.[177]

Similar attempts to improve cities were found in requests to establish new dioceses centered at the city with a new bishop. This power was assumed by the regency and the Cortes as successors to the Royal Patronage of the church. The church was economically tied to the empire and its evangelization provided an important aspect of legitimizing peninsular power in the Americas.[178] The American deputies seemed to accept the negotiated position of the church in relationship to the state that was a product of more than 300 years of imperial rule; the transfer of the Royal Patronage to the Cortes, and eventually under the Constitution of Cádiz, to the nation was not questioned.[179] In the press, rather than in the Cortes, deputies asserted the necessity of filling episcopal seats with clergy who had received their religious formation and exercised their pastoral duties within the diocese. Although unsuccessful, this was another

---

[172] Lorente, *La Nación*, 49–69.
[173] Rieu-Millan, *Los diputados americanos*, 220–221, 225.
[174] Volio, *Costa Rica*, 181–186.
[175] Rieu-Millan, *Los diputados americanos*, 223.
[176] Volio, *Costa Rica*, 169–170.
[177] Rieu-Millan, *Los diputados americanos*, 224.
[178] Ibid., 258–263.
[179] Adame Goddard, "Asimilación y rechazo," 67–68.

argument to ensure that local creoles were placed in positions of power and leadership in the Americas.[180]

In addition to more powerful churches and new universities, legal institutions also heightened the status and power of cities. The creation of an *audiencia* within the constitutional hierarchy would benefit a city.[181] Citing costs of litigation and delay due to distant courts, deputies requested *audiencias* for their cities. Between 1812 and 1814, deputies requested new *audiencias* for Santo Domingo, the Eastern Internal Provinces of Mexico, the Western Internal Provinces of Mexico, Chihuahua, Valladolid in Mexico, Nicaragua, Maracaibo, and Merida (Mexico). Some new *audiencias*, for the Eastern Internal Provinces of Mexico, Chihuahua, were created through these requests. American deputies also sought reforms to the appointment of judges to the *audiencias* to ensure more legally trained, as opposed to politically connected, magistrates. Except for a provision prohibiting judges from taking on commissions outside the *audiencias*, these criticisms went unanswered.[182]

Some requests for territorial reorganization must have resulted from the labyrinthine nature of political structures and institutions that resulted from hundreds of years of colonial rule. Rieu-Millan notes the particularly complex place that cities such as Tabasco (Mexico), Maracaibo (Venezuela), and the Eastern Internal Provinces of Mexico held in the imperial hierarchy. For each of these cities, political, economic, military, and religious administration might be traced though several different regional authorities that, from standpoints of efficiency or geography, made little sense. To improve the functioning of the contemplated constitutional government, American deputies also sought to strengthen the activities and to lengthen the sessions of the provincial deputations, which, in the Americas, would be charged with many important government functions related to taxation, accounts of the cities, establishing new city councils, public works, promoting education, industry and trade, and ensuring compliance with the Constitution.[183] While requests related to streamlining administrative structures imposed on cities or regions probably had some aspect of municipal or regional benefit for the location concerned, proposals related to the provincial deputations appear to have come from the well-meaning concern of the deputies to

---

[180] Rieu-Millan, *Los diputados americanos*, 267–273.
[181] Estrada Michel, "Regnícolas," 25; Lorente, *La Nación*, 135–183.
[182] Rieu-Millan, *Los diputados americanos*, 254–257.
[183] Ibid., 231–246.

create workable administrative structures rather than from municipal or regional self-interest.

Because provincial deputations were situated in provinces, the very term "province" had to be defined within this context. Surprisingly the meaning of the term had been rather fluid until this time. When attempting to define the territory of the Spains in Article 10 of the Constitution, deputies had debated the content of this long geographical list.[184] The solution for the creation of provincial deputations was to refer to this enumeration of territories in Article 10 of the Constitution, which, because it was drafted to delimit territory rather than establish administrative units, made some important omissions. American deputies jumped in to redefine the term in light of their needs and experience. Between 1812 and 1814, American deputies proposed more than ten new provincial deputations and by implication provinces.[185] For example, in February, 1812, Florencio del Castillo, deputy for Costa Rica, lobbied for the creation of a provincial deputation for Nicaragua and Costa Rica to shed the control the provincial deputation of Guatemala had over his region. It was approved and installed in the city of León later that year. Mariano Robles, deputy for Chiapas, unsuccessfully requested the creation of a provincial deputation in his province.[186] Thus, some suggestions were approved and others rejected. By the middle of 1812, the Americas had twenty provinces. These provinces reported directly to peninsular authorities, and, as a result, the traditional colonial structures of important cities serving as the power centers of viceroyalties and captaincy generals were dissolved.[187] This focus on provinces, coupled with a system of intendants, decreased the importance of the traditional viceregal centers of power in the Americas. This shift also divided American deputies on some issues related to viceroyalties and their kingdoms.[188] Some peninsular deputies were also concerned about the excessive partition of the Americas and the administrative inefficiencies inherent in so many regional centers reporting to Spain.[189]

These regional differences and levels of local power might lead to the diminution of effective collective active on the part of the Americas. Estrada Michel has analyzed the split of American deputies from

[184] Chust, *América*, 39; López Monroy, "El concepto."
[185] Rieu-Millan, *Los diputados americanos*, 246–249.
[186] Volio, *Costa Rica*, 159–161, 169.
[187] Rieu-Millan, *Los diputados americanos*, 248–250.
[188] Estrada, "Los reinos," 221, 225–229.
[189] Rieu-Millan, *Los diputados americanos*, 252–253.

Mexico in relation to their established interests under the extant structures. Deputies from less powerful areas unsuccessfully asserted claims
in the Cortes to challenge the established structures and lines of power.
These less powerful deputies saw promise in constitutional provisions
that sought to reorganize the American territories along more logical
and less historical lines, such as Article 10 of the Constitution. In conjunction with liberal peninsular deputies, American deputies seeking
delay on such changes in territorial delimitation and on the creation
of new *audiencias* that would challenge their historical authority were
successful.[190]

All the deputies recognized the fragility of the constitutional structure
they had just created. Article 375, prohibiting any alteration, addition, or
reform to the Constitution, was a step toward giving the structure a chance
to take hold. American deputies challenged this provision, most likely
with hopes that subsequent Cortes would reflect greater regional power
and thus be able to modify the document to their liking. Again, asserting
the questionable legitimacy of the General and Extraordinary Cortes in
relation to the question of American representation, American deputies
unsuccessfully suggested that the text of the Constitution be submitted to
the first General Cortes under the Constitution for ratification.[191]

The Cortes had other effects in America. Even in areas of the Americas
that established their own juntas and exercised sovereignty apart from
the Junta Central, the proceedings of the Cortes and the text of the
Constitution of Cádiz served as models. The use of the electoral provisions called by the Junta Central as a model for regional American congresses has already been noted. The influence of the Cortes also can be
found in the substantive provisions of new governments in the Americas.
For example, such a regime in Río de la Plata, "expanded education,
restricted the slave trade, abolished tribute, and recognized the political rights of the Indians." A subsequent general assembly in the region
undertook similar reforms. Similar influences are observed in the reforms
in Chile in the same period. Likewise, the autonomous Solemn Pact of
Association of Quito had many similarities to the Constitution of Cádiz.
Mexico's Constitution of Apatzingán, promulgated on October 22, 1814,
also shares much in common with the provisions of the Constitution of
Cádiz.[192]

---

[190] Estrada Michel, "Regnícolas," 19–21, 25–37.
[191] Rieu-Millan, *Los diputados americanos*, 285–286.
[192] Rodríguez, *The Independence*, 129, 141, 149,167.

Implementation

Even before the Constitution of Cádiz was promulgated in Spain, many regions of the Americas swore oaths of loyalty to the Cortes. This occurred in Cartagena, Chiapas, Cuba, Nicaragua, Mexico, Panama, Peru, Puerto Rico, Santo Domingo, Venezuela, and many other parts of the Americas from Florida to Peru. The oaths encompassed all levels of power in the region: civil, military, ecclesiastical. Many areas of the Americas asserted their loyalty through the entire constitutional process and swore loyalty to the Junta Central in 1809 or the regency, and then to the Cortes, and then to the Constitution in 1812.[193] Those in Cádiz knew the stakes, and, for example, in February, 1810, the regency sent high-level special envoys to Quito, New Granada, Mexico, and Lima to announce its installation to the Americas.[194]

The Constitution of Cádiz took American interests into account, and American Spaniards in colonial areas loyal to the Cortes swore to the constitution and did much to implement its provisions. Viceregal administration was dismantled, elections were held, and town councils and provincial deputations were established.[195] Some areas complied closely and apparently quite earnestly in the requirements of swearing to and promulgating the Constitution. For example, Durand Florez reports from the records that many areas of Peru, including small towns, effected the required oaths and ceremonies.[196]

While the Cortes were drafting and debating the text of the Constitution, they also considered the appropriate schedule for the first elections to the Cortes under the Constitution, which had not yet been promulgated. Some deputies thought that this process could be undertaken only after the Constitution was promulgated; other deputies thought that to delay too long might lead to the unraveling of the entire constitutional structure. The date for the convocation of the first General Cortes was shaped by American deputies who knew that American representation would be subject to the vagaries of long distances, difficult travel, and substantial expense. In this light, American deputies sought a later date for the Cortes, and Mejía Lequerica suggested that March 1, 1814, would enable deputies from the Andes region to arrive in time to participate. The General and Extraordinary Cortes could be extended

---

[193] Frasquet, "Cádiz en América," 27–46; García Laguardia, *Centroamérica*, 100, 108.
[194] Rieu-Millan, *Los diputados americanos*, 337.
[195] Massó Garrote, "Significado y aportes," 26.
[196] Durand Florez, *El Perú*, vol. 1, xxiv.

until that date.[197] Despite these objections, the Cortes set the date for October 1, 1813.

Elections were prepared by a Preparatory Council in each province, and again, the question of what was a province in the Americas for the purposes of elections arose. One list was proposed, but it did not include all cities that had provincial deputations, the preferred resolution of the question by American deputies. The Preparatory Council determined the appropriate census, determined the geographic scope of the electoral province, and set the number of deputies for election according to the Constitution. The peninsula was slated to send 149 deputies to the Cortes; and contemporary estimates were that the Americas would send about the same number. Historians attempting to recreate what a full and effective election under this system would have produced under the Constitutional provisions and known census information have come to similar conclusions.[198]

The appropriate elections were held to select representatives to the Cortes and accounts are provided for the expenses of these deputies. Records from Peru indicate the presence of local rivalries and even allegations of electoral fraud.[199] Similar events occurred throughout the Americas. The captain general of Guatemala delayed elections for the Cortes and the creation of the provincial deputation so long that the city council formally accused him of circumventing the Constitution before the Cortes.[200] Viceroy Venegas in Mexico suspended elections on the parochial level because he opposed all the possible electors.[201]

Local government interference with elections was only one problem in applying the voting provisions to the Americas. Lack of funds to send deputies to the Cortes was a significant impediment as well. Thus, of the estimated 143 places for deputies from the Americas, only 65 deputies for the Americas were present in Cortes from October 1, 1813 to May, 1814.[202] American hopes for greater representation at the General Cortes were not fulfilled.

The penetration of the Constitution into the politics and society of daily life varied considerably depending on the region, the composition of the population, the infrastructure, and quality of communication.

---

[197] Rieu-Millan, *Los diputados americanos*, 288–289.
[198] Ibid., 289–293.
[199] Durand Florez, *El Perú*, vol. 1, xxiv.
[200] García Laguardia, *Centroamérica*, 204–212.
[201] Rieu-Millan, *Los diputados americanos*, 54.
[202] Ibid., 31, 294.

Notice of the new status of indigenous peoples under the Constitution must have spread unevenly. Nonetheless, one report from Lima indicates that Indians were aware of their new status as citizens and of their new responsibilities to pay certain taxes. The report not only recognized the new status and obligations but also petitioned the Cortes to abolish whipping and imprisonments as punishments imposed on indigenous people who did not attend the parish. It further requested relief under the Constitution, apparently because it was inconsistent with the abolition of torture and the abolition of the Inquisition. This led to discussion on the topic of whipping as punishment more generally in the Cortes, which took action to abolish the practice.[203]

The freedom of the press guaranteed by the Constitution also met with uneven application in the Americas. For example, Captain General Bustamante of Guatemala, the same person accused of not holding elections, also sought to assert his authority to restrict printing information about the new constitutional regime.[204] Viceroy Abascal of Peru was also accused of suspending this constitutional right in 1813. Ramos Arizpe accused the Viceroy of Mexico of the same unconstitutional conduct in the same year. In the case of Mexico, the Supreme Council of Censorship found that the viceroy's actions were without justification. Similarly, viceroys and other royal officials were accused of sitting on decrees of the Cortes and the Constitution itself by delaying their circulation and publication. Thus, an accepted practice of fluid centralized control that screened and interpreted the actions to take, even in light of clear constitutional provisions, impeded the effectiveness of the new constitutional regime.[205]

A General Cortes under the provisions of the Constitution was called and held in 1813 with deputies (and substitute deputies) representing much of the nation. A second regular session was started on March 1, 1814, after French forces had been beaten.[206]

Repeal of the Constitution

The structure created by the Constitution of Cádiz did not last long. In April, 1814, Fernando VII received word from the army that it would support his abolition of the Constitution. Military support, coupled with

[203] Frasquet, "Cádiz en América," 39.
[204] García Laguardia, *Centroamérica*, 207–208.
[205] Rieu-Millan, *Los diputados americanos*, 308, 310, 312–313.
[206] Rodríguez, *The Independence*, 103–105.

some popular support for his absolute and unconditioned rule without being bound by the Constitution, led Fernando VII to abolish the Cortes and all its acts on May 4, 1814. Some Spaniards voluntarily destroyed or removed public symbols and plaques to the Constitution. With a royal word, the work of the Cortes and the Constitution was swept away and those involved were implicated in treason against the king.[207]

On May 10, 1814, General Eguía ordered the dissolution of the Cortes. Antonio Joaquín Pérez, deputy for Puebla, Mexico, president of the Cortes, did little to protest or to convene the deputies who were not already imprisoned. He received some form of immunity and returned to his position of Bishop of Puebla on his return to Mexico. Other American deputies were less fortunate. The most important deputies, American or peninsular, were ordered to be arrested. Many high-profile American deputies were detained: six Mexicans, two Peruvians, and two from Central America, including Antonio Larrazábal of Guatemala. Larrazábal was sentenced to six years imprisonment under the supervision of the Archbishop of Guatemala. His imprisonment lasted only a year; in 1820 the governor of Guatemala released him on news of the promulgation of the Constitution of Cádiz in Spain that year. In Guatemala, members of the city council who signed his instructions were removed from public office and all copies of the instructions, draft constitutions, and related papers were gathered up and burned.[208]

In the Americas, there was little difficulty dismantling constitutional structures that had been in effect only for less than two years.[209] In addition to the dissolution of constitutional structures on the peninsula and in the Americas and the return of all pre-1808 institutions, the financial obligations owed to the crown under the earlier system were also claimed by Fernando VII.[210] Indian tribute was reinstituted.[211] The Inquisition was reestablished in July, 1814.[212] The Americas lost their constitutional institutions and gained a significant financial obligation to the crown.[213]

Factional civil wars had already begun to divide portions of the Americas. Bolívar decreed a war of independence until death on June 15, 1813. Chile experienced its *Patria Vieja* from 1810 to 1814 with an

---

[207] Rodríguez, *The Independence*, 103–105, 170.
[208] García Laguardia, *Centroamérica*, 162–164, 188–191.
[209] Rodríguez, *The Independence*, 106.
[210] Chust, *América*, 43.
[211] De Armellada, *La causa indígena*, 63–66.
[212] Galván Rodríguez, "El Inquisidor."
[213] Chust, *América*, 43.

autonomous government until, by treaty, it recognized the Council of Regency and the Constitution of Cádiz in May, 1814, the same month the Constitution was abolished. New Granada (today Colombia) experienced its first period of independence from 1810 to 1816, when it was subdued by Spanish forces.[214]

New Spain (today Mexico) had several movements for autonomous rule in their period as well, including the insurgencies led by Miguel Hidalgo and José María Morelos.[215] In 1809 and 1810, attempts to replace viceroys to quell rebellion only led to local action that fed insurrection.[216] These insurrections importantly reached into sectors of the population and rural areas that were mostly detached from the political process until these movements.[217] In 1810, Hidalgo sought to create a representative Junta for Mexico and issued his *Grito de Dolores* in 1811. Although Hidalgo was killed the same year, Morelos continued his rebellion until 1815.[218] Hidalgo was said to have called for the long life of Fernando VII, of the Americas, of religion, and for the death of poor government. Other accounts state that he called for religion, law, country, and purity of customs.[219] In August, 1811, a regional junta, the *Junta Nacional Americana*, was formed in Zitácuro. In November, the Supreme National Congress in Chilpancingo declared independence.[220] These autonomous movements were later effectively crushed by Spain after the restoration of Fernando VII and the abolition of the Cortes and the Constitution of Cádiz. Nonetheless, calls for the restoration of the Constitution formed an important part of independence discourse in the Americas.[221] For example, its spirit and provisions were an important part of Iturbide's Plan of Iguala of 1821 for the independence of Mexico.[222] In some aspects, such as counting *castas* as citizens, the Plan contemplated greater reform than the Constitution.[223] Indeed, in some regions, such as Yucatán, the Constitution played an important part in maintaining the loyalty of the population in the face of pressures for independence.[224]

[214] Rodríguez, *The Independence*, 120, 138, 143,151, 159.

[215] Ibid., 164.

[216] Abreu y Abreu, "Las ideas constitucionales," 46.

[217] Annino, "La ruralización," 348–464.

[218] Abreu y Abreu, "Las ideas constitucionales," 16.

[219] Garriga, "Orden Jurídico," 82, 113.

[220] Abreu y Abreu, "Las ideas constitucionales," 47, 49.

[221] Rodríguez, *The Independence*, 168, 193.

[222] Frasquet, *Las caras*, 84, 86; Rodríguez, *The Independence*, 206.

[223] Frasquet, *Las caras*, 61, 84.

[224] Reid, "The Constitution of Cádiz," 22–38.

The Reinstatement of the Constitution, 1820–1823

By the time when General Riego's insurrection led to the reimposition of the Constitution of Cádiz in 1820, the Americas and their relationship with the peninsula had dramatically changed since the end of the first constitutional period. Although many Latin American countries had established independence, the recognition of this fact by European states was still about five years in the future.[225] Nonetheless, in many areas, as quickly as the Constitution of Cádiz popped out of existence in 1814, it popped back into force in Spain and in royally controlled parts of the Americas on January 1, 1820, when peninsular liberals joined with the Spanish army to insist on its restoration.[226] Several important urban centers quickly followed the call, and Fernando VII created a Provisional Junta to carry out the reconstitutionalization of the monarchy.[227] The procedures of electing deputies to the Cortes under the Constitution were reestablished, and substitute deputies were appointed for the parts of the Americas under royal control, pending the arrival of the elected deputies, who arrived in the first part of 1821. By this time, "Río de la Plata, Chile, and parts of Venezuela and New Granada" were already effectively independent and did not participate.[228] Other areas, such as New Spain (Mexico), Guatemala, Cuba, and Puerto Rico had significant participation in elections under the Constitution. The provisions of the Constitution were imposed on Peru by royal authorities after militarily retaking control in 1820. Similarly, areas of Colombia under royal control were subject to the Constitution of Cádiz in 1820.[229] Despite general compliance with the Constitution of Cádiz, some areas were simultaneously developing their independence and constitutional literature.[230]

As in the Cortes of Cádiz, a main issue of the Cortes of Madrid, held under the Constitution of Cádiz in the early 1820s, was the representation of the Americas. Only thirty substitute deputies were permitted to represent the Americas, and American deputies lobbied for popular representation under the Constitution that provided for a deputy for every 70,000 individuals, a formula that would have given American deputies the majority in the Cortes of Madrid. Frasquet has noted that these issues were heatedly debated not only in Madrid but also in New Spain through

---

[225] Maldonado Polo, "Científicos americanos," 300.
[226] Rodríguez, *The Independence*, 192.
[227] Frasquet, *Las caras*, 29–30.
[228] Rodríguez, *The Independence*, 195,197, 199.
[229] Ibid., 195, 197, 214, 219.
[230] De la Torre and García, 50–63.

the popular press. The issue was a question not just for the Cortes itself but also for the entire population of the Spanish nation. Other issues of similar import, such as the expansion of the number of provincial deputations and the specifics of American administration and government, were also closely followed and discussed in the Americas.[231] Regional interests put forth by American deputies in this period were similar to those they had asserted ten years earlier. For example, Pablo de la Llave, deputy for Veracruz, Mexico, sought the founding of a university in Santa Fe, the capital of New Mexico, and, in keeping with his interest in botany, several agricultural schools. He fought for the principle of equality more generally and for the equal treatment of religious institutions in the Americas and on the peninsula. He addressed questions of mining, the exploitation of natural resources, the tobacco monopoly, trade and tariffs, and the slave trade. By February, 1822, the question of the independence of the Americas was more pressing at the Cortes, and La Llave was a member of a Commission on this topic. When Mexico achieved independence later that year, La Llave returned to Mexico.[232]

Royalist areas of the Americas participating in the Cortes generally hoped for some form of constitutional reconciliation and the construction of independent kingdoms with more autonomy under the king or his appointee, but the various proposals were rejected by the peninsular Spaniards.[233] These proposals would have meant relative autonomy for the areas of Mexico (governed from Mexico City), New Granada–Venezuela (governed from Santa Fé), and Peru–Río Plata–Chile (governed from Lima).[234] Importantly, several proposals presented the specter of federalism to the Cortes. American participation in the Cortes in 1822 faded because the hopes of radically restructuring the relationship between the Americas and the peninsula were not fulfilled by the peninsular-dominated Cortes. The legitimacy of substitute deputies from the Americas and deputies representing areas that had declared independence was called into question, and by the beginning of the ordinary session in 1823, only Cuba, the Philippines, and Puerto Rico continued to have deputies present.[235] Again, there was little hope for a lasting constitutional regime, even on the peninsula. In April 1823, France invaded Spain and supported the absolute rule of Fernando VII who, yet again,

[231] Frasquet, *Las caras*, 31, 33–43, 47–48.
[232] Maldonado Polo, "Científicos americanos," 294–299.
[233] Frasquet, *Las caras*, 69–76; Rodríguez, *The Independence*, 203.
[234] Estrada, *Monarquía*, 618–619.
[235] Frasquet, *Las caras*, 111–112, 114.

abolished the Cortes and the Constitution of Cádiz and pursued the liberals who had supported them.[236]

An interesting result of Cuba's second constitutional period was the creation of chairs in constitutional law at the University of Havana and at the Seminary of San Carlos.[237] Félix Varela held the chair at San Carlos. He was a priest, Cuban liberal, abolitionist, Cuban independence advocate, and deputy to the Cortes for Havana in 1822. After his exile from Cuba in 1823, he became a social reformer in New York.[238] Varela's study of the Constitution based on his lectures was published in 1821 and served as one of the region's first works on public law.[239] He called his chair in constitutional law a "chair of liberty, of human rights, of national guaranties, of the regeneration of illustrious Spain, the fount of civic virtues, and the foundation of the building of our happiness."[240] In 1822, along with other deputies to the Cortes, Tomás Gener and Leonardo Santos Suárez, Varela unsuccessfully proposed greater autonomy for American provinces including Cuba, the recognition of the independent states in the Americas, and the abolition of slavery.[241]

Conclusion

Peninsular Spaniards tried to create a centralized metropolitan nation under new models hidden behind historical practices while American Spaniards increasingly asserted their own form of historically bound sovereignty in light of recent events. This dissonance led to a rupture eventually undermining the aspirational qualities of a broad national monarchy

---

[236] Rodríguez, *The Independence*, 204.

[237] Bahamonde Rodríguez, "Cuba y la Constitución de 1812," 79, 88–89. For Bishop Espada's role in the creation of the chair and his promotion of the Constitution in Havana see Loyda Zaldívar Abad, "El obispo Espada," 124–137. For studies of Félix Varela and his promotion of the Constitution see Fernández Estrada, "Cádiz en Félix Varela," 157–170; Lara Hernández, "Influencia de la Constitución," 138–145; Mondelo García, "Félix Varela," 146–156. For the chair at the University of Havana see Villabella Armengol, "El constitucionalismo español," 212–213.

[238] Bahamonde Rodríguez, "Cuba y la Constitución de 1812," 79, 88–89.

[239] Varela y Morales, *Observaciones sobre la Constitución*; Matilla Correa, "Glosas," 93; Rojas, "De reino," 195–202.

[240] Matilla Correa, "Glosas," 119 citing Torres-Cuevas, Ibarra Cuesta, and García Rodríguez, *Obras. Félix Varela*, 2:4.

[241] Mondelo García, "Félix Varela," 151–153; Portuondo Zúñiga, *Cuba: Constitución y Liberalismo*, 1:136, 141–148. His proposal for American provinces is discussed in relation to other constitutional proposals for Cuba in Prieto Valdés, "La Constitución de Cádiz," 191–207. See also Franco, *Cuba en los orígenes*, 231–279; Valdés Domínguez, *Los antigüos diputados*, 255–270.

under the Constitution. Indeed, the difference of experience led to the same text being read in different ways on each side of the Atlantic and appropriated in national projects in the Americas.[242] In areas loyal to the crown, the Constitution was promulgated and constitutional institutions were created.

The American presence in Cádiz ensured that the Constitution would be a product of American input and effort regarding a host of issues. The level of representation of the Americas in the constitutional process and in institutions was a central question that implicated the construction of legal and political identity for new or less known subjects within the nation such as slaves, blacks, and indigenous peoples. Resolution of their statuses was politicized in the context of representation so that pure liberal or Enlightenment values that were otherwise persuasive in Cádiz did not carry the day. While participating in the construction of a constitutional empire, American deputies were aware of their regional political and economic power in the process. They were also aware of local and regional concerns that might be advanced in Cádiz in concerted efforts or in individual attempts to increase local power against other regions and areas in the Americas. Trade, government, education, and the church were all at issue. The constitutional process and template established in Cádiz were placed over an increasingly uneven political landscape during the first two decades of the nineteenth century. This aspect is examined next.

---

[242] Lorente, *La Nación*, 18–19.

4

The Failures and Successes of Metropole Constitutionalism

> In practice, the Cádiz constitution had little direct impact one way or the other.
>
> John Charles Chasteen, *The Americanos*.[1]

This quote raises the question of the impact of the Constitution of Cádiz. In addressing such a question, one must consider the document both in the context of its contribution to legal and political discourse on the level of ideas and in the context of its implementation as a document creating and structuring real, daily political institutions and legal effects.[2] The implementation of the Constitution of Cádiz on either the intellectual or the practical level must be understood in the light of two facts. First, the Constitution of Cádiz was preceded by numerous decrees and orders of the Cortes that had substantial effects on political structure, activity, and individual status. Second, owing to the mere mechanics of its delivery and promulgation, the Constitution did not click into effect at the same time throughout the Americas.

Previous decrees touched may essential aspects of Spanish rule and the rights of Spaniards. Preconstitutional decrees included the equality of peninsular and American Spaniards, freedom of the press, prohibition of poor treatment of "primitive Indians," removal of tribute payments from Indians and blacks, and abolition of torture and hanging.[3] Thus numerous provisions of constitutional-like status had filtered their way into the American polity before the Constitution, and these must be considered in

[1] Chasteen, *The Americanos*, 91.
[2] Uribe-Urán, "La Constitución de Cádiz," 274.
[3] Ibid., 282.

relation to the package of what the Cortes and the Constitution offered and when they offered them.

The process of dissemination of the Constitution had a great deal to do with geography and the lines of communication of the empire. It was promulgated in Puerto Rico and Cuba in July, 1812, and in Panama in August. In September and October, 1812, it was promulgated in New Granada, Lima, Central America, Mexico, and Florida depending on the region. It was not promulgated in Caracas until December, 1812.[4]

The public ceremonies associated with putting the Constitution into effect were elaborate. They were expected to be conducted in the manner appropriate considering the resources of the city and its circumstances. It appears the decree for promulgation was followed around the Spanish Empire. For example, the small city of St. Augustine, East Florida, of probably about 3,000 individuals, followed the requirements for swearing to and promulgating the Constitution on October 17, 18, and 22, 1812, having been previously selected as the days for promulgation. There was a public ceremony on October 17 and a private gathering of officials on October 22. Sworn statements were forwarded to Cádiz verifying the promulgation. On October 17, Governor Sebastian Kindelán and important officials gathered at the governor's house. Escorted by various military battalions, drummers, and artillery, they processed to various locations throughout the city where three platforms had been constructed for the reading of the Constitution and the decree. The ceremony was followed by a large party at the governor's house, and decorations and lights were set along the main road for the next two days. On Sunday, October 18, the Constitution was read in church by a priest, who then delivered an allegorical homily and celebrated a solemn *Te Deum*. On October 22, all public officials swore to uphold the Constitution in a smaller ceremony.[5] Such activities with minor variations occurred through the constitutional empire.

The ceremonies were a mixture of civic and religious activities. The document itself opens with "All powerful God, Father, Son, and Holy Spirit" and all levels of society were expected to swear an oath, itself a fundamentally religious act, to uphold it. As Varela Suanzes-Carpegna writes, "in reality, the whole text of the Constitution was saturated with strong religious overtones."[6] So too were the ceremonies associated with its promulgation.

---

[4] Ibid., 280–281.
[5] Mirow, "The Constitution of Cádiz in Florida," 280–283.
[6] Varela Suanzes-Carpegna, "El constitucionalismo," 21.

Promulgation did not necessarily mean that the provisions would be put into force. Abelardo Levaggi has noted several regions in Mexico, Peru, and Venezuela, which after promulgating the document, decided to continue with activities, structures, and institutions unchanged.[7] Nonetheless, other areas considered quite peripheral, such as St. Augustine, East Florida, might embrace the practicalities of the Constitution with force; it even built a monument to the Constitution that stands today in the center of the plaza.[8]

The World of Ideas

Positions asserted by American deputies were heard not only in the Cortes but also in public through newspapers and other circulars that enjoyed wide readership under a free press. Newspapers offered not only voice to concerns but also their own popular solutions as to how the Cortes might proceed. The international aspects of these questions as they might affect the relative positions of Spain, France, England, the United States, and Brazil were also expressed and analyzed. The alliance between England and Spain against France was particularly ambiguous in the American context, where England maintained imperial and commercial interests that might directly conflict with those of its ally.[9]

Often referred to as the first liberal constitution, the Constitution of Cádiz failed to incorporate fully the Enlightenment ideas of equality. On one level, the Constitution met American demands for formal equality between Americans and peninsulars. And for the time, it is remarkable that the Constitution and earlier related documents recognizing the political context of such decisions made creole Spaniards and Indians equal in legal status to European Spaniards.[10] On another level, the Constitution racialized representation and citizenship and legally established a form of racial discrimination in the Americas. It sanctioned slavery and only tangentially addressed the question of the Americas' vast indigenous population.[11] Although such racial discrimination was not the product of the Constitution, it concretized the assumption of the legal superiority of white propertied men. Spanish models based on ideas of purity of blood (*limpieza de sangre*) from Jewish and Moorish taint informed the liberal

---

[7] Levaggi, "La Constitución," 17–19.
[8] Mirow, "The Constitution of Cádiz in Florida," 283–302, 309–329.
[9] Pérez Guilhou, *La opinión pública*, 122–144, 192.
[10] Garay, "La idea," 151, 153.
[11] Pérez Guilhou, *La opinión pública*, 173–177.

and Enlightenment notions of citizenship found in the Constitution. Blacks, with African origin and un-free status as slaves, were excluded, and debates about slavery turned mostly on the slave trade rather than on the humanity of the objects of commerce.[12]

Furthermore, the Constitution failed to bridge competing concepts of the nature of representation. Guerra has uncovered a difference in perception between peninsular and American Spaniards in the implementation of the Constitution. Most peninsulars saw the nation as unitary; most Americans saw the nation as a composite of groups of people: kingdoms, provinces, and cities. This distinction produced different ideas of sovereignty and of representation. Nonetheless, to the extent that the Constitution shed notions of corporatist representation, it jettisoned the long-standing idea of the resident (*vecino*) and ushered in a world in which one speaks of the citizen (*ciudadano*). Thus, according to Guerra, the Constitution explicitly recognized a new idea of the individual that produces a modern nation in which the national is distinguished from the foreigner; is entitled to civil rights including property, liberty, and security; and is the holder of political rights as a citizen. Distinctions still appeared in the Constitution of Cádiz: slaves and blacks were almost entirely excluded, and women did not participate politically. Many of the premodern distinctions based on personal status or membership in a collective body with special privileges disappeared. Men and women, Spaniard and indigenous, were citizens.[13]

The Constitution of Cádiz also maintained the privileges of the state in relationship to the church that had been exercised by the crown. The king, under the Constitution, continued to have the power to present bishops and other ecclesiastical officials, to exercise control over the publication and circulation of bulls, and to exercise royal jurisdiction over ecclesiastical matters and everything related to the Royal Patronage. The continuation of the empire as a confessional state and of the status quo concerning the balance between king and pope led to the wide approval of the deputies who were clergy. One notable except was the Bishop of Orense, who placed reservations on his oath to the Constitution and was sanctioned by the Cortes for this action. After the promulgation of the Constitution, the Cortes continued to take actions that indicated it expected to exert power over the church.[14]

---

[12] Garay, "La idea," 130–131, 139, 154.
[13] Guerra, "El soberano," 5–16.
[14] Adame Goddard, "Asimilación y rechazo," 67–68.

The World of Action

For the popular segment, the Junta Central selected universal male suffrage, with some notable exceptions when viewed from today's perspective. It refrained from imposing a property requirement, generally found in the early nineteenth century. These decisions led to Spain's first elections law.[15] Provisions for popular elections at local and regional levels were implemented widely, and large and small cities loyal to the Cortes and the Constitution such as Quito, Lima, Mexico, Cuenca, Cuzco, Guadalajara, Havana, San Juan, and St. Augustine took active practical steps toward effectuating the new constitutional regime.[16]

The introduction of elections to the Americas was an important event in the development of constitutionalism in the region.[17] And the Constitution's reformation of the institution of the city council can be attributed to the successful politicking of Ramos Arizpe.[18] By his careful description of the nature of these elections, Guerra reminds us not to superimpose our modern experiences of elections on these nascent forms of representation. On the lowest level, elections were in the parish and all the implicit underlying social controls of early American nineteenth-century society were in play. These were elections held without candidates, platforms, and electoral campaigns in an atmosphere that greatly lacked meaningful exchanges of public opinion. In this sense, Guerra asserts, such elections were not political but rather symbolic activities that legitimated the exercise of power by the established families and their clients.[19]

The process was much closer to corporatist elections in civil and ecclesiastical governing bodies and chapters of religious organizations than we might at first suspect. Many aspects of the *ancien régime* continued into these representative practices of nascent modernity. Active public debate and opinion, impartial electoral rolls, electoral clubs, and political parties were still things of the future.[20] Nonetheless, these activities were elections. They were new, and it appears there was a much higher level of participation in elections than had been estimated earlier. For example, Rodríguez estimates that "hundreds of thousands, perhaps more than a million, novohispanos participated in electing forty-one deputies to

[15] Artola, "Estudio preliminar," 30, 34.
[16] Uribe-Urán, "La Constitución de Cádiz," 283–284.
[17] Rodríguez, *The Cádiz Experiment*, 42. See also Guerra, *Modernidad*, 177–225.
[18] Rieu-Millan, *Los diputados americanos*, 403–404.
[19] Guerra, "El soberano," 18–23.
[20] Ibid., 24, 26–28.

the Ordinary Cortes in 1813–1814 and five provincial deputations and more than a thousand constitutional *ayuntamientos* in New Spain."[21] Similar participation sprang back on the restoration of the Constitution in 1820.[22]

The effect of these elections on the political development of the region cannot be overestimated. Even the first round of elections in 1809 provided a new model of representative government that had not been witnessed in the Spanish world despite their perpetuation of a relatively closed oligarchical control of local institutions.[23] As Miguel Molina Martínez states, "the experience of the first electoral process was successful in inculcating in the population an irrevocable sense of the necessity of representative participation."[24] It also produced, in the words of Annino, a "territorial revolution" in which local institutions took on essential government functions and provided representatives to the highest level of government.[25]

Following the constitutional requirements, new city councils (*ayuntamientos*) sprung up all over.[26] Guatemala alone had 244 constitutional city councils.[27] Their rise was an essential element in the new representative forms of government contemplated by the Cortes of Cádiz and the drafters of the Constitution. They were governed by the constitutional provisions, a decree of May, 23, 1812, and later a decree setting out specific instructions for the government of the provinces on May 21, 1813.[28] Their history, however, stretched far back to peninsular medieval law and, in the Americas, the *derecho indiano* and the Bourbon Reforms. On both sides of the Atlantic, preconstitutional *cabildos* often fought for local autonomy and municipal freedoms.[29] Depending on the period under examination, *cabildo* membership might be subject to the vote of the *cabildo* itself, and some positions were filled through royal appointment.[30] It was often these city councils that were first faced with questions about where allegiance should lie on hearing news of Fernando VII's abdication. For example, in

---

[21] Rodríguez, "*We Are Now*," 5, 166–186.
[22] Ibid., 241–253.
[23] Molina Martínez, "De cabildos," 142.
[24] Ibid., 144.
[25] Annino, "Cádiz y la revolución"; Molina Martínez, "De cabildos," 151, 153. See also Aguilar Rivera, *Las elecciones*.
[26] Uribe-Urán, "La Constitución de Cádiz," 284.
[27] Molina Martínez, "De cabildos," 154.
[28] Chust Calero, "El poder," 127–128.
[29] Molina Martínez, "De cabildos," 135–136.
[30] Mirow, *Latin American Law*, 26–27.

1808, the city councils of Caracas and Santiago swore their loyalty to the deposed king on hearing such news.[31] Local offices on the city councils, particularly in the Americas, became perpetual and even valuable saleable assets.[32] Some deputies, such as the royalist Peruvian Blas Ostolaza, suggested that restitution for the loss of these offices was appropriate as the positions were converted to elected, nonsaleable positions.[33]

The constitutional city councils did much to standardize territorial administration on the local level. In Spain, the abolition of seigniorial estates (*señoríos*) meant that the special privileges of lords in the products of the land and in jurisdiction over inhabitants were substituted with constitutional structures that were uniform within the peninsula and subjected these lands to freer alienation. These areas were now subject to constitutional city councils. Because these institutions were found only in peninsular Spain, liberals in the Cortes such as Agustín Argüelles argued that their existence was another instance of inequality between peninsular and American Spaniards and sought their abolition. American deputies, such as José Miguel Guridi y Alcocer, deputy for Tlaxcala, New Spain, noted that there were parallel feudal institutions in the Americas that likewise had to be normalized to the newer system of uniform constitutional city councils. Constitutional city councils bolstered expectations and assertions of representative institutions at the local level that exerted a form of sovereignty distinct from the national sovereignty of the Cortes.[34]

New constitutional city councils presented the novel question of areas populated by blacks (*castas*). The Guatemalan deputy Antonio Larrazábal estimated that there were at least thirty such communities in Central America that would require some sort of representation under the new system. Blacks were excluded from citizenship and municipal office under the legislation of the Cortes and under the Constitution. The possibility of their being represented by an Indian or creole Spaniard was rejected because of the established colonial legislation prohibiting communities of Indians and blacks. Such arguments were used unsuccessfully to improve the political status of blacks in the Americas.[35]

As might be expected, entrenched interests also fought to limit the extent and effectiveness of the reforms. As mentioned earlier, while

[31] Molina Martínez, "De cabildos," 137.
[32] Mirow, *Latin American Law*, 26.
[33] Chust Calero, "El poder," 122.
[34] Ibid., 109–113, 116, 119.
[35] Ibid., 123–124.

indigenous peoples gained with the new status of citizen and with the abolition of tribute and forced services, in the new provisions for city councils, they lost the established Indian councils and powers accorded to chiefs (*caciques*) they were permitted under *derecho indiano*. Chiefs were not elected under the new provisions and experienced a significant decline in influence and power.[36] In some areas, local élites misinterpreted voting provisions to exclude indigenous populations from voting or manipulated elections though fraud or force.[37] Such practices of exclusion from municipal representation extended throughout the nineteenth century. This was coupled, for example in Mexico, with a practice of transforming the lands of indigenous *pueblos* into cities with their own, often nonindigenous, city councils under a process that distributed communal property.

And Mexico in the nineteenth century witnessed a series of laws that diminished the existence and legal recognition of communally held lands so that by 1882, Ignacio Vallarta, one of Mexico's outstanding constitutional judges, was able to write of the inexistence of communal lands. The dismantling of communal lands held by indigenous peoples, *ejidos*, was particularly common in the 1890s and resulted in significant resistance from Indians.[38]

Such constitutional city councils also clashed with established royal authorities on the local and regional levels.[39] Nonetheless, numerous new councils were established with the goals of promoting the peace and health of the inhabitants; assisting the local court in ensuring justice; collecting and investing local taxes; maintaining schools and hospitals; constructing and repairing roads, walkways, bridges, and prisons; enacting municipal ordinances; and promoting agriculture, industry, and trade.[40]

Another new institution was the provincial deputation, charged with many important administrative and financial duties for the province. Considered along with the city councils, the provincial deputations have been viewed as an important step in the decentralization of governmental authority and in functioning autonomous control. As such, they were a step toward structures that prefigured federal structures after independence.[41] Although there were attempts to create provincial deputations

[36] Marchena, "Revolución," 253–254.
[37] Uribe-Urán, "La Constitución de Cádiz," 285–286.
[38] Marino, "Indios," 168–198.
[39] Estrada, "Los reinos," 230–231; Quiroga, "Military Liberalism," 452–459.
[40] Marchena, "Revolución," 251–252.
[41] Benson, *The Provincial*, xi–xii; Chust, *América*, 41–42.

by the Cortes before the Constitution of Cádiz, the institution was not created until the Constitution and the specifics of its operation were set out in June, 1813, in an enabling act. Each province was headed by a political chief, an intendant, and a provincial deputation of elected deputies. Importantly, the new structure did not include a viceroy and the political chief took on this role.[42] Thus, with the creation of the provincial deputations, the viceroyalties ceased to exist.[43] This led to a substantial decrease in power even for leaders who had switched from viceroys to political chiefs because their jurisdiction was considered coextensive with the province, as opposed to the former geographical range of the viceroyalty encompassing many provinces.[44]

Thus, the system of election of deputies to the Cortes has been seen as a forerunner of the decentralized control found in the Central American federation. In fact, Costa Rica's second constitution (*Estatuto Político de la Provincia de Costa Rica*) specifically adopted the Constitution of Cádiz's terminology of the "provincial deputation" as a three-person executive branch.[45] Many of these developments point toward greater regional autonomy, but with the American deputies at the Cortes the concerns were limited to either the provincial or viceregal level. The dream of a continental or Pan-American government in the Americas appears to have been an invention of Bolívar and other later independence leaders.[46]

Although the new liberal reforms expressed in the Constitution of Cádiz portended significant institutional change in the Americas, there were many impediments to their effective implementation. One substantial difficulty was the inability of the sixty or so American deputies to change American legal culture. The Constitution of Cádiz arrived on the desks of viceroys and other high-level officials who had established fluid practices of compliance in response to a peninsular government that might be ill suited to legislate specific actions at specific times. This ready ability to interpret and to adapt laws and decrees was imposed on the Constitution and the decrees of the Cortes.[47] It could be used to different ends, and not always in the direction of illiberal despotism. For example, the exclusion of blacks from censuses for the purposes of voting was a factual determination at the taking of the census, and uncertain situations

---

[42] Benson, *The Provincial*, 6–7.
[43] Molina Martínez, "De cabildos," 150.
[44] Benson, *The Provincial*, 8, 10–11.
[45] Volio, *Costa Rica*, 36, 162.
[46] Estrada, "Los Reinos," 226–235.
[47] Mirow, *Latin American Law*, 235–236; Rieu-Millan, *Los diputados americanos*, 313.

might be resolved through discretion to include individuals who might otherwise have been excluded.[48]

Despite these shortcomings, the constitutional experiences garnered by deputies were immediately translated to the constitutional service of new independent states. Miguel Ramos Arizpe contributed significantly to the construction of the Mexican federal state. José Joaquín Olmedo and Vicente Rocafuerte became presidents of Ecuador.[49] Florencio del Castillo, deputy for Costa Rica, became a canon in Oaxaca, Mexico, and served as a substitute deputy at the first Constituent Congress called by Iturbide in 1822. He served on Iturbide's Council of State and in the legislature of the state of Oaxaca.[50] Rieu-Millan lists seven other examples of deputies of the General and Extraordinary Cortes going on to important national service in independent countries of Latin America.[51] Pablo de la Llave, deputy for Veracruz, Mexico, in the Cortes in 1821 and 1822, returned to Mexico and filled a number of executive and legislative positions. Under Iturbide, La Llave was the Minister of Justice and Ecclesiastical Affairs and Minister of Exterior Relations and Finance until 1825. In 1830, he was a senator of the Congress and served as its president.[52] Similarly, the last president of the Cortes, José Miguel Gordoa y Barrios, deputy for Zacatecas, also went on to shape the government of Mexico. In 1820, he was elected as the provincial deputy for Guadalajara at the Provincial Deputation of New Galicia. Two year later, in 1823, he served as a deputy at the first Congress for the state of Jalisco. Putting his experience at the Cortes and in Jalisco to work, he was a deputy to the Mexican Constituent Congress of 1824.[53] Lucas Alamán was a deputy at the Cortes and returned to become one of Mexico's most important conservative jurists who advocated for central authority and a strong executive. He held many high positions in public service and criticized Mexico's institutional structures as being weak in comparison to the constitutional structures created by the United States and France and in Cádiz.[54] There are numerous other examples of deputies returning to assist the drafting of independence and early republic constitutions.[55]

---

[48] Volio, *Costa Rica*, 103–104.
[49] Rieu-Millan, *Los diputados americanos*, 408.
[50] Volio, *Costa Rica*, 65.
[51] Rieu-Millan, *Los diputados americanos*, 408.
[52] Maldonado Polo, "Científicos americanos," 292.
[53] Encisco, "Correspondencia," 177–178.
[54] Gargarella, *Latin American Constitutionalism*, 214. n. 44; Hale, *Mexican Liberalism*, 263–272, 288–289.
[55] Rieu-Millan, *Los diputados americanos*, 410.

The process established by the Junta Central was copied and adapted by regional juntas in Latin America and served as a model of representative elections even in areas that chose not to align themselves with the Junta Central. Autonomous governments in Caracas, Rio de la Plata (Argentina), Chile, New Granada (Colombia), and New Spain (Mexico) found these provisions useful in setting up their own elections.[56] Indeed, the meanings of "autonomy" or "independence" in this context were neither universally accepted nor clear.[57]

The Constitution of Cádiz in Action and in Inaction: The "American Question"

As indicated in Chapter 3, in light of these events, the Americas could not be ignored. Looking from Europe to the Americas, the Cortes and the Constitution had to work with and to consider well American demands. Looking from the Americas to Europe, we find similar influences. Rodríguez has emphasized the centrality of peninsular events in American independence. He writes, "the independence of Spanish America did not constitute an anti-colonial movement, as many assert, but formed part of both the *revolution* within the Spanish world and the *dissolution* of the Spanish Monarchy."[58] This dissolution provided some Americans the opportunity to press for local control and autonomy, often in the name of the Spanish king. Former interpretations that peninsular instability provided an easy excuse for independence in the Americas have been replaced with a more complex narrative of interaction and reciprocal influences.[59]

A viceroy in New Spain, initially appointed by the king, for example, might seek the approval of local institutions, such as a city council (*ayuntamiento*), to continue in power. When local bodies pressed for greater autonomy, they were countered by peninsular representatives and neighboring viceroys who continued to assert the royal authority of an absent king.[60] Some areas were less prone to assert autonomy or independence. For example, scholars have noted a number of factors that isolated Costa Rica from effective revolutionary uprisings. These included a powerful aristocratic creole population that stifled rebellion, a loyal clergy that supported the crown on the popular religious level, few areas of conflict

---

[56] Rodríguez, *The Independence*, 112, 125, 139, 152, 166–167
[57] Rojas, "De reino," 191–220.
[58] Rodríguez, *The Independence*, 1; Rodríguez, "*We Are Now*," 3.
[59] Estrada, *Monarquía*, 184.
[60] Rodríguez, *The Independence*, 53–54.

with peninsular Spaniards, and an apparently low level of social resentment from members on the lower levels of the social hierarchy. Indeed, Costa Rican troops participated in the suppression of the independence movement in New Granada.[61]

There were also some individuals around with truly revolutionary spirits, such as Francisco de Miranda in Venezuela, who twice attempted to establish an independent country with British help in 1806. Although these efforts failed, as the Spanish crown was being placed in French hands, perhaps the moment for independence was ripe. Similarly, the eventual successes of Buenos Aires repelling British forces in 1806 and 1807 added to its regional sense of self-sufficiency and de facto autonomy.[62]

Provisions granting new status and possible rights to the Americas' indigenous and black people under the decrees of the Cortes and the Constitution were effectively deployed on the practical level. For example, indigenous people in Colombia used provisions reducing tribute payments to assert their claims and to negotiate with colonial officials who bargained to maintain indigenous loyalty.[63] Indeed, relief from tribute payments was used as a bargaining chip to garner loyalty either to the crown or to independence movements throughout the region. Similarly, the possibility of release from slavery as another way of mustering troops was used by both royal and independence propagandists. By the time the provision extinguishing tribute from indigenous populations was affirmed in the Constitution of Cádiz, the abolition of this payment and offers of citizenship for indigenous populations and blacks had already been established on the battlefield of independence politics.[64]

One of the implicit goals of the Constitution of Cádiz was to maintain empire. Although the Constitution and the processes leading up to it gave a voice to American interests, it did not and probably could not have given enough to keep American colonies within imperial channels. The representation of Americans was more than token, but less than enough to resolve American concerns in ways acceptable to Americans. Although free trade made it to the agenda and was debated in secret sessions because of the potential international impact such debates might have, a constitutional solution was not found, and by 1812 numerous areas had already split away from the empire and engaged in trade as they liked. Several minor issues related to trade, the choice of profession, and

[61] Volio, *Costa Rica*, 20, 26.
[62] Rodríguez, *The Independence*, 55–58.
[63] Uribe-Urán, "La Constitución de Cádiz," 279 citing Echeverri, "Popular Royalists."
[64] Uribe-Urán, "La Constitución de Cádiz," 282, 286–295, 297–298.

the freedom of cultivation were eventually settled in favor of American demands. Nonetheless, it has been suggested that even when substantive questions were resolved in favor of the Americas, the delay the Cortes exercised in coming to these answers may have been equally fatal to anchor long-term imperial loyalty.[65]

When the Cortes met, republican revolutions had already been successful in the United States and Haiti, and the French Revolution was in recent memory. Several nascent autonomous and independence movements had sprouted up in Spanish America. In 1810, both Caracas and Santa Fé de Bogotá in the north of South America and Buenos Aires in the south declared their allegiance to Fernando VII, but not to the institutions that claimed to represent his government in peninsular Spain.[66] Despite the great distances between these early claims of independence, they may be seen as encompassing a single political event. Buenos Aires, through numerous newspaper reports that were republished throughout the Atlantic region, kept its keen attention on the events in Caracas. Newspaper accounts from the United States and England were translated and circulated in Buenos Aires and helped frame the questions of whether to continue allegiance to Fernando VII, what kind of congress to create, what were the best ways to spread the message of independence to regional areas that may be resistant to such drastic political change, and what sort of constitution might be appropriate. Essential political documents were also published; for example, the Venezuelan Act of Independence was published in Buenos Aires in June, 1812, and the Act of Independence of Cartagena in the same city in November, 1812.[67]

French agents fomented dissent against Spanish institutions loyal to Fernando VII while blaming England for encouraging American territories to rebel. From the Spanish perspective, the vast majority of Spaniards indicated that such territorial assertions of independence or revolution should be met with armed action from peninsular forces.[68]

American deputies were surrounded by and responded to these changes. Independence movements in the Americas not only affected the colonies but also pushed, constricted, and sometimes defined the political moves American deputies were able to make at the Cortes. Some American deputies acted collectively before the Cortes to respond to separatist movements in the Americas. On August 23, 1811, a communication from

---

[65] Pérez Guilhou, *La opinión pública*, 112, 114, 171–173, 176–177.
[66] Ibid., 75–79.
[67] Asdrúbal, "La Revolución, independencia," 55–61.
[68] Pérez Guilhou, *La opinión pública*, 66–72, 80–81, 154–167.

thirty-three American deputies was read in a secret session of the Cortes to address the Americas. With their specific and recent knowledge of the Americas, these deputies sought to explain the reasons for such uprisings as a step toward the better integration of the Americas within the empire and the Cortes. The American deputies stated that the core reason for rebellion was colonial oppression by the peninsula through bad government and poor administration.[69]

The neglect of government and proper assertion of imperial power led to a continuing poor state of the indigenous people, economic crisis due to commercial and trade restrictions, concentrations of power in individuals who might not serve the interests of the empire as a whole, bewildering administrative structures and organizations, and a focus on benefiting the metropole at the expense of the Americas. These were not the only reasons. Americans truly feared the Napoleonic invasion of the peninsula and were perhaps less sanguine about the prospects of Spain shedding what was, until recently, an invincible army. American deputies did not want to see the Americas fall into French hands in the process and by creating juntas in the Americas they did exactly what their peninsular counterparts had done, despite peninsular protests over these actions. Thus, under the circumstances, the creation of a "conditional" or "transitory" junta was probably not unreasonable. Despite the American deputies' continued assertions of loyalty, the recent actions of the Central Junta, the regency, and the Cortes did not signal any new direction in policy addressing the substance of American claims. Their honest assessment of the situation was met with violent displeasure from all but the most liberal peninsular deputies. Furthermore, equivocation about "transitory" or "conditional" independence may not have been, as Rieu-Millan points out, realistic in light of the substantial steps areas in Venezuela and Argentina had taken toward independence and the outbreak of civil war in some areas of the Americas.[70]

The proposed response by American deputies was a general amnesty for members of dissident movements who were willing to swear allegiance to the Cortes and the crown. Mejía Lequerica, deputy for Quito, suggested that assertions of equality of representation at the Cortes should supplement the conferral of amnesty.[71] Amnesties were uncertain remedies and often failed against the political exigencies of the moment.

---

[69] Rieu-Millan, *Los diputados americanos*, 318.
[70] Ibid., 318–335.
[71] Ibid., 335.

The question remained of how the peninsula should deal with the American juntas, whether independent or loyal to the Cortes. On April 10, 1811, a commission to address the provinces set out a three-part division among the juntas. First, there were those that had declared themselves sovereign, such as Caracas, Buenos Aires, and Santa Fe, which would not be offered conciliatory proposals. Second, there were those that had not exercised sovereign power, which the Cortes would recognize and with which the Cortes would communicate. Third, there were those that had recognized the authority of the Cortes but had exercised some aspects of independent sovereignty, such as removing or appointing officials, as in the cases of Quito, Chile, and Cartagena, which the Cortes would recognize both in their existence and actions as long as they returned to an appropriate limited exercise of power. Despite its carefully crafted divisions and courses of action, it is reported that the project had little effect. Attempted communication with the Juntas of Caracas and Chile went without substantive response. The Junta of Cartagena decided not to obey the regency and moved toward outright rebellion and was eventually not recognized by the Cortes. The installation of the General Congress of Venezuela in March, 1811, was a clear indication that another region had decided to go it alone.[72]

The Cortes was not without other ways to deal with the separatist regions. England offered to mediate between provinces that did not recognize the Cortes. England's willingness to step into this situation appears to have been motivated by its desire to maintain good relations with the Spanish Empire as it battled France while simultaneously continuing trading relations with the provinces that had separated from the empire. The offer of mediation was contingent on Spain's permission for England to trade with these areas while negotiations were in process. The ambiguous and conflicted position of England was not lost on the deputies in Cádiz. The Cortes were inclined to approve this arrangement but disagreement about whether Mexico would be included led to difficulties; the Cortes did not consider Mexico to be in such a state of rebellion, but England, with its eyes on Mexican silver, wanted to ensure that these funds would be available for its assistance to Spain. The issue also divided American from peninsular deputies as the Americans on the commission involved with the offer were in favor of including Mexico in the negotiations. The general goals offered by England were to cease hostilities and blockades, amnesty, equal representation at the Cortes, free trade, the imposition

---

[72] Ibid., 340–344.

of creoles as viceroys or governors in the Americas, the loyalty of the provinces to the king, obedience to the Cortes, and American assistance against the French. It appears that England moved forward with attempts to reach out on a diplomatic level with the dissident juntas without much progress.[73]

In the middle of 1811, the Cortes became more insistent on handling rebellious provinces with its military. American deputies did not agree among themselves about the use of force to suppress these areas; they were not uniformly against the idea and it appears at least thirty-three American deputies supported the use of the military. Some Mexican deputies, such as Antonio Joaquín Pérez of Puebla, supported sending royal troops and did not object to and even at times praised Mexican Viceroy Venegas in his victory over the Hildago rebellion, which was marked with greater violence and broader class participation than many other uprisings in the Americas.[74]

The results of reasserting royal control in dissident regions did not necessarily mean that the Cortes, and especially the Constitution and its provisions, would be faithfully followed by the new loyal leadership. When self-appointed Captain General Domingo Monteverde retook Venezuela for the crown in 1812, deputies were shocked to learn of his summary dispatch the following year of eight rebels without trial to the peninsula from whence they were sent to a presidio in Ceuta. This violated the promised amnesty, and deputies objected to his conflation of judicial and executive power that did not comply with the Constitution, the decrees of the Cortes, or even *derecho indiano*. Politics overtook the Constitution in this situation, and the Cortes was unwilling to reprimand Monteverde for his use of arbitrary arrests, summary trials, lack of process, and patent violations of the Constitution.[75]

American interests became important in another possible resolution of the crisis of the monarchy. This proposed solution involved the Infanta Carlota, who was the sister of Fernando VII, wife of the Prince Regent of Portugal, and who had traveled with the Portuguese Court to Brazil in 1807. The idea was to appoint Carlota to the regency as head of the executive. This was also done in light of the possible necessity of moving the Cortes to the Americas if the peninsula fell permanently to the French. Conservative peninsular deputies supported Carlota with the hopes that

[73] Ibid., 345–349.
[74] Ibid., 350–354.
[75] Ibid., 356–359.

she would stem the liberal and constitutional tide at the Cortes. Many Americans too supported her because of her physical presence in the Americas and the regional power that might bring. To make Carlota eligible, the Cortes repealed a Salic Law in December, 1811, but because of her ties to Brazil and the Cortes's broader desires to move forward with a Constitution and an arguably liberal one at that, the plans did not move forward.[76]

The Constitution of Cádiz in Latin American Independence: The Example of Mexico

As Uribe-Urán has observed, the Constitution and the independence constitutions in the Americas served "to erode colonial hegemony on the local, regional, and global level."[77] Once the very idea of a constitution was presented, a new, other, possible world of government was born, and a single model could no longer be presented as a Hobson's choice. As presented in Chapter 3, several areas of the Americas were profoundly influenced by the Constitution, the Cortes, and their political legacy. For example, Central America was closely tied to the activities in Cádiz and Madrid and the implementation of their provisions in the Americas. Guatemala's early independence is impressed with the stamp of Cádiz, and the influence of Cádiz directly, or indirectly through Mexican pressures and, at times, control, has been well documented.[78] Another example is found in the early constitutional documents of Argentina. Abelardo Levaggi has carefully chronicled the influence of the Cádiz Constitution on the Provisory Statutes of 1815 and 1817 and on the work of the official commission whose work was incorporated into the Constitutions of 1819, 1826, and 1853.[79] This section examines the Mexican experience as perhaps the best example of continuity of the ideas of and text of the Constitution of Cádiz into a newly independent country of Latin America.

Mexican independence was closely tied to the Cortes of Cádiz and the Cortes of Madrid held under the Constitution of Cádiz.[80] Mexico under the Cortes of Cádiz in the early years did not experience significant implementation of the Cortes's orders. The Council of Regency

---

[76] Ibid., 360–265.
[77] Uribe-Urán, "La Constitución de Cádiz," 298.
[78] Rodríguez, *The Cádiz Experiment*, 101–211, 229–235.
[79] Levaggi, "La constitución," 26–29.
[80] Frasquet, *Las caras*, 19. See generally, Rodríguez O., "*We Are Now.*"

appointed Francisco Xavier Venegas viceroy of New Spain in 1810. Although Venegas published the decrees of the Cortes, he did little to implement them and governed according to the older notions of a viceroy, rather than being guided by Cortes and the Constitution. Freedom of the press was suspended shortly after the Constitution was promulgated, and Venegas was sanctioned by the Cortes.[81] Estrada characterizes Venegas's compliance with the election provisions of the Constitution as having been "considerably lax," and when creoles were elected instead of peninsulars, Venegas invalidated the election. Venegas's replacement in 1813, Félix María Calleja y del Rey, sought to enforce the Constitution on a broader basis to control the region. New elections produced creoles winners, but claiming lack of funds, Calleja sent only two to Cádiz. He also sought to limit the liberty of the press and was supported by Cádiz in these efforts. He assumed the traditional powers of a viceroy, as the king's representative, and would not be bound by the Constitution. The *audiencia* complained of Calleja's breach of the Constitution, but the question became moot when Fernando VII returned to Spain and revoked the Constitution. This was not a promising start to constitutional monarchy under a new Constitution, and in some circles led to greater independence sentiment.[82]

The Mexican experience leading to the Constitution of 1814, the Constitution of Apatzingán, provides an example of independence constitution making in light of contemporary events and the Constitution of Cádiz. In the wake of the political uncertainty left by Fernando VII's loss of the Spanish throne, important national actors such as Father Hidalgo, Ignacio López Rayón, and José María Morelos called for a constituent congress and a new constitution. Individuals debated privately and publically through correspondence, statements, and publications such as López Rayón's *Elementos constitutionales* and Morelos's *Sentimientos de la Nación*. The positions expressed in these works included how to organize a government, to open up trade, to end Indian tribute and the payment of taxes, to abolish slavery, and whether Fernando VII should be included as the leader of a newly independent state. After taking the title Generalisimo in 1813, Morelos called for a congress to write a provisional and independent constitution that commissioned Quintana Roo, Bustamante, and Herrera to draft the specific language that was later, after debate, adopted in October, 1814.[83]

[81] Estrada, *Monarquía*, 579–581.
[82] Ibid., 582–588, 607.
[83] De la Torre and García, *Desarrollo histórico*, 13–34.

The Constitution of Apatzingán sought to limit autocratic rule and maintain individual guarantees. Its provisions reflect the variety of sources consulted by the drafters and members of the constituent congress: the Constitution of the United States; the Constitution of Massachusetts of 1780; the Constitution of Pennsylvania of 1790; the French Constitutions of 1791, 1793, and 1795; and, of course, the enactments of the Cortes of Cádiz and the Constitution of Cádiz itself. These were typical sources of the period.[84] Although the Constitution of Apatzingán was religiously much more conservative than the Constitution of Cádiz, like the Constitution of Cádiz, it maintained a confessional Roman Catholic state, but it also reserved political rights to Roman Catholics, and apostasy and heresy resulted in the loss of citizenship. Government officials had to swear to uphold the Roman Catholic faith, and the immunity of deputies did not extend to religious nonconformity. Freedom of the press was limited by consistency with Roman Catholic dogma. Thus, this Constitution sought to establish a religious state.[85] The Constitution provided for an executive headed by a troika and gave the government wide authority to maintain internal tranquility.[86]

Nettie Lee Benson has studied the provincial deputations in Mexico in great detail from their creation in 1812 under the Constitution of Cádiz to their role as inchoate state legislatures under Mexican federalism established under the Mexican Constitution of 1824. In their early years, these provincial deputations had a "brief and erratic existence" from 1812 to 1814. They were hardly established and running when the constitutional structures were brought down in 1814, but they did give an important taste of autonomy, particularly on the provincial level.[87]

The return of the Constitution in 1820 provided a moment of substantial popular participation in constitutional government for Mexico and practical experience in running representative institutions within a nation-state.[88] The activities of the Cortes of Cádiz and the Cortes of Madrid, coupled with the text of the Constitution of Cádiz, formed central reference points for Mexican independence under Agustín Iturbide, and Frasquet supports her claim well that "The Constitution of 1812 and

[84] Ibid., 31, 37–44.
[85] Adame Goddard, "Asimilación y rechazo," 70.
[86] Loveman, *The Constitution*, 70.
[87] Benson, *The Provincial*, 9–21.
[88] Frasquet, *Las caras*, 77, 100; Narváez H., "Cádiz."

its laws were the legislative and liberal reference for the Mexican deputies in the construction of their own nation state."[89]

With the Constitution's reimposition in 1820, Mexico promulgated the Constitution throughout the region. Frasquet has noted approximately 500 cities and communities that reported their promulgation of the Constitution in 1820.[90] Mexico also quickly reestablished its provincial deputations, and by the end of the year, the six provincial deputations of Mexico were installed with newly elected members. Over the next three years, there was gradual growth in the number of provincial deputations so that by December, 1823, twenty-three provincial deputations were authorized for Mexico.[91]

In 1821, Agustín Iturbide led a revolt and sought a Mexican empire governed by Fernando VII.[92] Under Iturbide's Plan of Iguala, Mexico would have the three guarantees of "Religion, Independence, and Union," meaning Roman Catholicism and allowing peninsular Spaniards to remain in the country under a constitution promulgated under the Mexican Cortes.[93] Iturbide also recognized the power of the provincial deputations. To battle Iturbide, Political Chief Apodaca engaged in practices that were contrary to the Constitution and transferred his political and military power to Field Marshal Francisco Novella, an action also not permitted under the Constitution. Novella assumed the title of viceroy and also violated the Constitution in his rule. O'Donojú arrived in July, 1821, as the new captain-general and political chief and effectively brokered a deal in which Novella recognized his authority. In August, O'Donojú signed the Treaty of Córdoba that established Mexico as a sovereign and independent nation and a constitutional monarchy, with hopes that it be led by Fernando VII. Until then, the country would be led by a provisional governing junta of thirty-eight persons under Iturbide. A committee went to work on drafting the plans for the first Mexican Congress and new provincial deputations were created under the guiding language of the Constitution of Cádiz.[94]

Thus, by treaty and as subsequently rejected by the Cortes, Iturbide was permitted to rule with the Constitution of Cádiz in effect until a new

---

[89] Frasquet, *Las caras*, 199.
[90] Frasquet, "Se obedede [sic]," 224–245.
[91] Benson, *The Provincial*, 23–60. See also Rodríguez, "*We Are Now*," 166–186.
[92] Benson, *The Provincial*, 40–41.
[93] Aguilar Rivera, *El manto*, 60; Estrada, *Monarquía*, 624; Loveman, *The Constitution*, 72; Rodríguez, "*We Are Now*," 253–263.
[94] Benson, *The Provincial*, 33–36, 40–44, 48–60.

constitution was promulgated.[95] The Plan also contemplated a junta created in Mexico, pending the creation of the Cortes in Mexico that was charged with the same duties as the Cortes under the Constitution of Cádiz. Independent Mexico contemplated following the legislation of the peninsular Cortes, and the Mexican electoral process, although in the end quite different, was guided by the Cádiz experience.[96] Early contentious issues for these newly established Mexican Cortes included the status of regular clerics and the Jesuits, the ecclesiastical *fuero*, and the establishment of courts and appointment of judges in the country.[97] Questions of sovereignty, taxation, the abolition of entails (*mayorazgos*), the election and powers of the Council of State, and the power of the emperor were all debated in light of the Constitution and were often settled by the Constitution and the laws of the Cortes of Cádiz and Madrid.[98]

Deputies even debated what to do when recent Mexican legislation conflicted with a provision in the Constitution of Cádiz, a constitution they had sworn to uphold.[99] This question came to a head with the pending appointment of judges of the Supreme Court of Justice in 1822. The Constitution made it clear that the king, or here Iturbide as emperor, was to appoint the judges. A committee of the Mexican Congress, asserting that it was not necessary to "submit itself slavishly to … the constitution," claimed the power of appointment for itself.[100] Mexicans debated the supremacy of the Constitution of Cádiz in relation to the national sovereignty held by Congress. Many argued that because the Congress was a constituent congress charged with drafting a new constitution, it also had the power to abrogate a provision of the Constitution of Cádiz. The more liberal elements sought this power because it would provide Congress with greater powers to reform government, while, in an odd twist, more moderate deputies maintained that the Constitution of Cádiz was unalterable until a new constitution was promulgated. Politics won the day, and in the end, the Congress voted to make the appointment.[101] Additional areas of conflict were the emperor's exercise of veto power and the creation of military commissions and tribunals to restore peace and order in the country.[102]

[95] Estrada, *Monarquía*, 641–642; Loveman, *The Constitution*, 72.
[96] Frasquet, *Las caras*, 121–126, 129–134.
[97] Estrada, *Monarquía*, 628; Frasquet, *Las caras*, 135–144.
[98] Frasquet, *Las caras*, 151, 162, 167–168, 192, 193–196, 198–200.
[99] Ibid., 200.
[100] Ibid., 205.
[101] Ibid., 205–211; 215–220.
[102] Aguilar Rivera, *El manto*, 62.

Subjecting the Constitution to modification by a congress (although a constituent congress) was bad historical precedent for the supremacy of constitutional law over general legislative acts. It was also, at the time, bad politics. On the heels of this congressional action, Iturbide began a process of dissolving Congress. His actions included the imprisonment of deputies and brought congressional action to a near standstill. Iturbide then acquiesced in Congress's assertion of the power to appoint judges but added a provision that from then on, the Constitution of Cádiz was to control without variation. Iturbide, through his Council of State, created a new military tribunal for conspiracy against the state where the protections of Constitution of Cádiz did not apply. The Congress was then dissolved on October 1, 1822.[103]

When plans for moving forward with a new national government stalled amidst insurrections and tension between two of Iturbide's generals, José Antonio de Echávarri and Antonio López de Santa Anna, the provincial deputations took government on the regional level into their own hands.[104] General Santa Anna sought a republic, and notions of federalism challenged Iturbide and the *Junta Nacional* he created to replace Congress. The Constitution of Cádiz continued to serve as a constitutional reference point both for Santa Anna and for states asserting greater autonomy.[105] General Echávarri proposed the Plan of Casa Mata, which provided that a new congress should be called and that, in the meantime, the Constitution of Cádiz and the decrees of the Cortes would be in effect.[106] Although many provincial deputations signed onto the Plan, Iturbide and his advisors denounced it. When some provincial deputations declared themselves independent of the national government and Iturbide, there was, in effect, no national government left, just the individual provincial governments.[107]

Despite the call for a new congress under the Plan of Casa Mata, Iturbide restored the old congress that gradually reconvened. Many hoped that the old congress would serve as the path new elections, but instead it merely did all it could to stay in power.[108] The Constitution continued to shape the debate about government structure and function in Mexico. A reconvened Congress now set its task as creating a

---

[103] Frasquet, *Las caras*, 229, 243–345.
[104] Benson, *The Provincial*, 60–64.
[105] Frasquet, *Las caras*, 258–259.
[106] Benson, *The Provincial*, 65.
[107] Ibid., 65–73.
[108] Ibid., 76–79.

provisional ruling document (*Reglamento provisional político*).[109] This document was supposed to be a provisional document until the new constitution was drafted. It gave the emperor numerous discretionary powers including control of the military and folded the civil and military powers together for the internal running of the empire. It also reinstated the ecclesiastical and military *fueros*.[110]

Facing the united forces of Santa Anna and Echáverri, Iturbide abdicated in March, 1823, and went into exile in Europe.[111] In 1824, when he briefly returned to Mexico he was executed by firing squad as a traitor.[112] On Iturbide's abdication, the Congress created a triumvirate as the Supreme Executive Power composed of generals Nicolás Bravo, Guadalupe Victoria, and Pedro Celestino Negrete.[113]

With Iturbide's abdication, the treaty that led to his and the country's oath to uphold the Constitution of Cádiz was also gone. Although most deputies in 1822 continued to view the Constitution of Cádiz as Mexico's fundamental law, others began to distinguish the Mexican situation and to characterize the Constitution as "foreign."[114] This criticism of the Constitution of Cádiz continued under the reconvened Congress.[115] As some provinces continued to call for a new congress, others such as Yucatán and Oaxaca declared their complete independence, leading to even greater autonomy in these provinces.[116]

The official recognition of the Constitution of Cádiz as the constitution of Mexico was implicitly revoked in the *Reglamento*, which asserted complete Mexican independence and liberty from other laws, but only, of course, to the extent that actions of the reconvened Congress were accepted by provincial authorities. The Constitution, however, continued in the world of ideas as a reference point; it was now part of Mexico's constitutional legal culture. For example, its provisions and laws from the Cortes informed appropriate procedures in electing a new congress, for creating new tribunals, and for abolishing entails (*mayorazgos*).[117]

In May, 1823, the province of Guadalajara declared its independence as the new state of Jalisco, sought the creation of a new federal nation,

---

[109] Frasquet, *Las caras*, 266.
[110] Loveman, *The Constitution*, 72–73.
[111] Frasquet, *Las caras*, 263; Loveman, *The Constitution*, 74.
[112] Loveman, *The Constitution*, 74.
[113] Aguilar Rivera, *El manto*, 85.
[114] Frasquet, *Las caras*, 234, 237.
[115] Ibid., 271–273.
[116] Benson, *The Provincial*, 82–91.
[117] Frasquet, *Las caras*, 276, 278, 280, 292, 300, 307, 319–328, 366.

and called for new procedures for a new congress. Its plans included a sovereign independent state, Roman Catholicism as the official state religion, a popular representative government, the separation of powers, and the adoption of the Constitution of Cádiz and the decrees of the Cortes as the existing law consistent with the plan. The provincial deputation adopted these plans, and the state elected its first legislature that sat as the Jalisco State Congress on September 18, 1823. The Jalisco Congress dissolved the provincial deputation and assumed its functions. Jalisco broadcasted its actions and founding documents to many other provincial deputations. This new stance was adopted by other provinces.[118]

With only minor variations by mid-October, 1823, Oaxaca, Yucatán, and Zacatecas followed suit by creating state legislatures under the Constitution of Cádiz. This pattern spread, and federalism was the only form of national government available to unite these independent states. A new Constituent Congress of Mexico was installed in November, 1823, where Ramos Arizpe, who had considerable experience at the Cortes of Cádiz, proved to be a driving force as the chair of the drafting committee for the Constitution.[119] It was argued that the Constitution of Cádiz continued to have force in 1823 while the new constitution was being drafted.[120]

The Constitution of Cádiz was one of the primary sources for the drafters of the Constitution of 1824.[121] In addition to Ramos Arizpe, Guridi y Alcocer, another important American deputy in the Spanish Cortes, was instrumental in incorporating provisions from their peninsular drafting into the Mexican Constitution of 1824.[122] Even the federalism of Mexico expressed in its constitution of 1824 found its roots in the petitions of Mexican deputies in Spain.[123] Concerning Ramos Arizpe's contribution and his use of the Constitution of Cádiz in constructing a federal constitution for Mexico, Benson states, "The parallelism between the Spanish Constitution and Ramos Arizpe's *Acta* [*constitucional*] is clear through clause after clause, not only setting forth the same ideas but also employing the same words. In fact entire articles were borrowed, not surprisingly, verbatim from the Spanish Constitution."[124] Thus, as Benson

---

[118] Benson, *The Provincial*, 91–105.
[119] Aguilar Rivera, *El manto*, 90; Benson, *The Provincial*, 98–123.
[120] Frasquet, *Las caras*, 362.
[121] De la Torre and García, *Desarrollo histórico*, 121.
[122] Rodríguez, *The Independence*, 210.
[123] Frasquet, *Las caras*, 23.
[124] Benson, *The Provincial*, 123–124.

demonstrates, the Constitution of Cádiz not only served as a direct model in the process of drafting the Mexican Constitution of 1824 but also was the institutional vehicle for the provincial deputations that led to provincial autonomy, independence, and federal constitutionalism.[125] The Constitution of Cádiz had direct impact.

The Constitution of Cádiz, however, was not the only model text available as Mexico and its states built constitutional structures for independence. Various constitutional possibilities were circulated and propounded in the volatile years of the early 1820s in Mexico. One draft, for example, by Herrera, established a tripartite division of powers among the executive, legislative, and judicial branches. The draft was divided into two parts; the first was broadly on society and the second on individuals in society. The part on society covered rights and duties, the legislative power, the executive power, and the judicial power. The part on individuals in society covered natural, political, and civil rights; taxes; the armed forces; and public education. Rights, such as equality, security, and property, were defined within the Constitution, which also established freedom of thought, expression, and the press and procedural protections for the criminally accused.[126]

José María Luis Mora served as the intellectual leader of Mexican liberalism during the 1820s and 1830s. Like other Mexican liberals of the period, Mora was influenced by the writings of Benjamin Constant, by other French liberal writers, and by the Constitution of Cádiz. His position as the preeminent liberal of Mexico was at odds with his classical academic and religious training. He was a student at the Colegio de San Ildefonso, held a licenciate in sacred theology, and had taken Holy Orders. Mora served as the chair of both the legislation and constitution committees of the influential State of Mexico's constituent congress, which first met in March, 1824. Mora brought his liberal approaches to provisions concerning municipal government, the judiciary, and elections. The Constitution of Cádiz served as his model for the administration of justice in the state constitution, and he turned to a decree of the Spanish Cortes to shape his provisions for the State of Mexico's law on *ayuntamientos*. The influence of Constant can be seen in Mora's advocacy for jury trials. Mora put similar liberal constructions forward on a national scale after 1830.[127]

---

[125] Ibid., 129.
[126] De la Torre and García, *Desarrollo histórico*, 82–112.
[127] Hale, *Mexican Liberalism*, 55–61, 69–87, 91, 95, 96, 103.

The approved text of the Federal Constitution of the United States of Mexico of 1824 reflected the widespread participation of the middle and élite classes in its drafting. The Constitution provided for a tripartite division of powers, with the legislative power in Congress split between a Senate and House of Deputies. In addition to general legislative powers, Congress was charged with thirty-one exclusive powers, including to tax, to declare war, to approve treaties of peace and friendship, to establish public works, to regulate commerce, to establish the territorial organization of the country, and to maintain the political freedom of the press. The chief executive officers were the president and vice president, who were charged with the publication and execution of the law; proposing legislation; designating secretaries of executive departments; selecting civil, military, and judicial officers; deploying armed forces; declaring war; reaching concordats with the Holy See (the Constitution maintained the status of Roman Catholicism); and ensuring the administration of justice, among other activities. The judicial power was assigned to the Supreme Court, circuit courts, and district courts, whose jurisdiction included diversity jurisdiction arising from federalism.[128]

Ramos Arizpe argued forcefully for the inclusion of emergency powers in the Constitution, but liberal arguments against such powers won the day when the Congress considered the final text and they were not included. Emergency powers to maintain public tranquility, however, were debated outside the Constitution the same year in an attempt to create such powers extraconstitutionally. And although the proposal gained traction and even was approved in general, debate on the details of the provisions led to the proposal's downfall.[129] Aguilar Rivera argues that the lack of emergency powers helped foster constitutional instability. He writes, "If the Constitution of 1824 had included ordinary provisions to meet extraordinary situations, perhaps the Constitution would not have been violated repeatedly during emergencies... Unconstitutional extraordinary powers and *ad hoc* military law brought *more* abuses than what possibly could have occurred with constitutional emergency powers."[130] In fact and surprisingly in light of the Congress's earlier rejection of emergency powers, in the last day of its session the constituent congress granted extraordinary powers to the president to deal with perceived threats to the independence of the country. The benefits of the law were

---

[128] De la Torre and García, *Desarrollo histórico*, 117.
[129] Aguilar Rivera, *El manto*, 93–97, 104–115.
[130] Ibid., 118.

often debated and it was repealed in May, 1826. This and similar laws in the 1820s revealed inherent defects in the Constitution.[131]

As one might expect from the brief description here, some contemporaries criticized the Constitution of 1824 for the strong parallels one finds to the United States Constitution. Nonetheless, as Benson has demonstrated, there is much of the Constitution of Cádiz in its provisions as well, and where would skilled drafters look to find a constitution that provided a good template for a working federal government other than the Constitution of the United States?[132] Some elements were clearly not found in the United States Constitution. The nation's duty to protect the Roman Catholic church, for example, was a distinguishing feature adopted from the Constitution of Cádiz.[133]

Federalism appeared to be the only way of maintaining some sort of political union for Mexico in the face of the political reality that many areas had already expressed their own separatist tendencies and actions. Central America, Chiapas, Yucatán, Texas, Coahuila, Nuevo Léon, Tamaulipas, and Jalisco had already moved substantially in an independent direction. Other areas, namely Oaxaca, Puebla, Zacatecas, Michoacán, and Guanajuato, had also declared a federal form. Ramos Arizpe's federalism moved toward unifying Mexico through a federal constitution, and apart from the United States, there were other models of federalism in the region and in political tracts and writings.[134] Reflecting federal or centralist sentiments during the 1820s, political actors gravitated toward one of two Masonic lodges, one following the Scottish Rite and the other the York Rite.[135] York Rite Masons included important federalists, such as President Guadalupe Victoria, and Scottish Rite Masons were often aligned with centralists.[136]

The federal structure served other regions as well. For example, Central America was annexed to Mexico in 1822, but soon reacted with a Constitution in 1824 that provided for a republican, representative, and federal system incorporating the electoral system found in the Constitution of Cádiz. More than a mere experiment, the structure lasted until 1835.[137]

---

[131] Ibid., 127–142.
[132] Benson, *The Provincial*, 123–124; De la Torre and García, *Desarrollo histórico*, 112–117, 121–122.
[133] Adame Goddard, "Asimilación y rechazo," 71.
[134] De la Torre and García, *Desarrollo histórico*, 124–138.
[135] Aguilar Rivera, *El manto*, 123–124.
[136] Bushnell and Macaulay, *The Emergence*, 66–68.
[137] Ibid., 73–74; De la Torre and García, *Desarrollo histórico*, 138–144.

Conclusion

Considering the projection of the Constitution and Cortes of Cádiz across the Atlantic and into the Spanish world in the Americas, the document and its institutions had a direct impact. They shaped ideas of government, constitutionalism, representation, and sovereignty. Electoral institutions and practices served as models for Latin American practices in the early nineteenth century when the region's political future was in flux. Ideas and practices of independence incorporated and adopted the Constitution and acts of the Cortes. Regions and provinces moved along a continuum from complete loyalty toward the absent Spanish king and his Cortes to sovereign independence. These movements occurred in the minds of the Americans and through military battle. The Constitution had similar effects elsewhere in the world, but as the example of Mexico illustrates, it shaped early Latin American constitutionalism in profound and lasting ways.[138]

The following chapters will examine how the ideas, institutions, and practices developed in the Americas from the Constitution of Cádiz and Cortes took shape during the independence period, the nineteenth century, and over the last century. Central issues debated in Cádiz and mediated through the Constitution of Cádiz were repeated over the next 200 years. Sovereignty, representation, the political and social status of indigenous and black peoples, the power and role of the church, institutional structure, the allocation of powers among the branches of government, and especially the scope and breadth of the executive were all challenges faced, but not settled by, the Constitution of Cádiz.

[138] Ferrando Badía, "Proyección exterior de la Constitución de 1812."

5

Latin American Constitutionalism
after Independence

The political and military independence of many parts of Latin America was obtained during the first half of the 1820s. The final battles included Ayacucho, Peru, in December, 1824, and an attempted Spanish invasion of Veracruz, Mexico, from Cuba in 1829. Although some countries, such as Mexico, had a very uneven and ill-defined journey into independence as seen in the previous chapter, others did not. All countries had to wrestle to create new governments and constitutions. All faced questions of whether to create a republic, by far the most popular option, of whether they should adopt centralist and federal structures, of how to balance legislative and executive powers, and of where important institutions such as the military and the church fit in their new constitutional orders. For the most part, new nations did this in an atmosphere of political and economic instability that impeded the effective creation of stable constitutional regimes, regardless of their particular content and resolution of these basic questions. The colonial legacy and wars of independence did little for the countries' economic conditions, administrative structures, or sense of national unity; it was, indeed, the perfect moment for strong men to step in as caudillos to run autocratically their slice of the country or a major city with promises of establishing order and seeding prosperity.[1]

It is then somewhat odd that nations latched onto constitutions as means of resolving crises that were essentially political and social. A new constitution seemed to offer a way to resolve the crisis even if its provisions were never fully implemented. It was a common response; Latin America produced more than 100 constitutional texts in the nineteenth

---

[1] Loveman, *The Constitution*, 53, 54–55, 59–61, 368–369.

century.[2] Furthermore, since at least the Constitution of Cádiz, liberalism was advanced and established in constitutional form and was widely implemented in the mid- to late nineteenth century.[3] As Aguilar Rivera writes, "The center of the liberal project was constitutionalism."[4] And elsewhere he correctly observes, "Spanish America constitutes the great post-revolutionary liberal constitutional experiment."[5] Nonetheless, liberalism did not offer a panacea for nineteenth-century political organization. Indeed, some scholars argue that flaws inherent in liberalism, in addition to social and economic factors, hindered effective constitutional development in this period.[6] Others have argued that liberalism contained an internal tension between goals of limiting government and of centralizing power.[7] In crafting political responses to various challenges and in light of advancing political stances in different countries, drafters of constitutions turned to similar sources.

Sources of Independence Constitutionalism

With the traditional analysis focused on the great European political tracts of Montesquieu, Locke, and others as background, Chiaramonte has recently argued for a shift of focus toward the broader intellectual structures, the "social consensus" that shaped the underlying ideas of independence constitutionalism. This would seem appropriate considering the common nature of constitutional responses to political uncertainty. A restructured analysis of the ideas of this period leads the scholar to canon and Roman law, the survival of the *ius commune* tradition, and above all, deeply embedded understandings of natural law.[8] Chiaramonte makes a compelling argument that an ancient constitution based on these sources was "far more than mere rhetoric."[9] These sources were often explicitly saved in early constitutional documents that upheld their

[2] Ibid., 62, 368.
[3] Safford, "Politics," 353–354. For compilations of primary sources on liberalism see Aguilar Rivera, *La espada y la pluma*; Aguilar Rivera, *Liberty in Mexico*; Botana and Gallo, *Liberal Thought in Argentina.*
[4] Aguilar Rivera, *La geometría*, 12.
[5] Aguilar Rivera, "Introduction," xiv.
[6] Aguilar Rivera, *El manto*, 1–4, 269–273.
[7] Negretto, "Repasando," 217.
[8] Chiaramonte, "The 'Ancient Constitution,'" 458, 461, 476, 487. Bentham apparently had a greater impact in Mexico than in other countries of Latin America. See Hale, *Mexican Liberalism*, 148–187. For disputes concerning the use of Bentham in Colombian classrooms see Bushnell, *The Santander Regime*, 192–193; Safford and Palacios, *Colombia*, 115, 142.
[9] Chiaramonte, "The 'Ancient Constitution,'" 470.

applicability absent an inconsistency with the new policies of freedom and independence found in the document.[10]

A better appreciation of natural law and the way it informed the social consensus leads to a comprehensible coherence in understanding independence constitutionalism, regimes of constitutional exceptionalism, caudillism, and dictatorship. The characterization of caudillos and nineteenth-century dictators as simplistic power mongers ruling with tyranny belies their often impressive intellectual background in law, theology, and natural law more generally. The influence of these studies, Chiaramonte suggests, provides important clues to the relatively unexplored intellectual underpinnings of these forms of government in Latin America.[11] Such models continued well into the twentieth century and today. Leaders such as General and President Juan Vicente Gómez of Venezuela successfully transferred the idea of the caudillo as a rural leader, benefactor, and protector into the highest levels of government while advancing liberal and economic reforms. He ruled the country for twenty-eight years, from 1908 to 1935.[12]

Spanish colonial law was far from being jettisoned on independence or on constructing new republican states. The sources of *derecho indiano*, colonial customary practices, and institutions discussed in Chapter I continued as fundamental aspects of law and government within legally trained minds after independence. The late colonial *Ordinanza de intendentes* served as a constitutional touchstone even into the early republic period.[13] Just as a great deal of private law survived shifts to independence in Latin America, many aspects of governing and liberties associated with longstanding Spanish legal traditions might also shape the minds and products of those drafting constitutions.

Experience with monarchy led to a heavy reliance on the executive branch. While recent works of political theory discussed the nature of the legislative branch and of establishing balances of power, legislatures and congresses were relatively new. Thus, one important aspect of early independence constitutions was their attempt to create a government under a congress. Although substantial European antecedents existed, congresses in this constitutional sense were relatively new political entities. The Cortes of Cádiz served as recent examples, and many of the approximately eighty Latin American constitutions from the period 1810 to 1850

---

[10] Ibid., 471; Mirow, *Latin American Law*, 125.
[11] Chiaramonte, "The 'Ancient Constitution,'" 469, 470, 473–487.
[12] Velasco Ibarra, *Expresión política*, 55–56.
[13] Chiaramonte, "The 'Ancient Constitution,'" 469.

sought to establish the place of congress in relation to an established tradition of a strong executive that predated the independence period and was present in the Bourbon Reforms of the late colonial empire.[14]

The use of foreign sources in constitutional drafting is an important aspect in this period. The influence of the United States Constitution as a model has been noted by scholars and even negatively correlated with the endurance of constitutions in Latin America. Early emulation of the United States Constitution led to the frequent adoption of presidentialist systems.[15] Although the influence of U.S. language was felt throughout the region at various times, Argentina is particularly noteworthy for its willingness to adopt not only constitutional language, but also the sources and case law of U.S. constitutionalism during the period. Mexico, too, was greatly influenced by U.S. language and practice.[16] This was the case at least until the United States ceased to be a model and became an aggressive invader in 1847.[17] A practical guide to drafting constitutions could be found in works such as Benjamin Constant's *Curso de política constitucional* (1814) that stressed the place of individual liberty in stopping assertions of arbitrary authority. Constant's work and thought were frequently employed in writing and arguing about constitutions.[18]

The Politicization of Constitutions

Since the first written constitutions to incorporate the Americas into the Spanish Empire, such as the Constitution of Bayona and the Constitution of Cádiz, constitutions were viewed as political documents rather than foundational texts that transcended political demands, position, or exigency. Bolívar's influence on early political and constitutional structures serves as an illustration of the continued politicization of constitutions during the independence era and into the post-independence period. Bolívar's dream of Pan-Americanism quickly succumbed to regional and national interests, battling ideologies, and civil wars.[19] Frank Safford writes that the "Napoleonic state as advocated by Simón Bolívar" was one of two constitutional formulas from

---

[14] Bravo Lira, *El estado constitucional*, 16, 22–23.
[15] Cheibub, Elkins, and Ginsburg, "Latin American Presidentialism," 1707–1716.
[16] Hale, *Mexican Liberalism*, 188–214; Miller, "The Authority," 1483–1572.
[17] Hale, *Mexican Liberalism*, 188–189, 302–303.
[18] Aguilar Rivera, *La geometría*, 1, 25–27; Aguilar Rivera, *El Manto*, 21,
[19] Loveman, *The Constitution*, 137.

the period of independence to the mid-nineteenth century, with the Constitution of Cádiz serving as the other.[20]

Bolívar's nature as a constitutionalist remains a vexing question for scholars today, and Safford notes that "constitutions based on the Napoleonic-Bolivarian model were short-lived."[21] There is no easy answer to the degree of Bolívar's liberalism, and his views changed from the early years of independence to the mid-1820s and his drafting of the Constitution of Bolivia.[22] This grand leader of independence eschewed the ideologies of the French Revolution and the Haitian Revolution and claimed that Americans could learn little from them in constructing their own independence. Wary of foreign influences in drafting constitutions, he nevertheless turned to foreign models he considered appropriate. For example, in the *Jamaica Letter* of 1815, he questioned the applicability of representative institutions at the moment, and yet advanced a proposal for two chambers, one representing the people and the other composed of élite independence fighters and their descendants modeled after English practice.[23] His views in this period indicate he did not think that complete liberty was appropriate for newly independent peoples of the Americas. If democratic republics were a goal in Latin America, they were not, according to Bolívar, suited to the present situation, customs, and character of the people. An intermediate phase of paternal government was necessary.[24]

While leading the charge for independence, Bolívar was given military and civil powers over Venezuela with combined military, executive, and legislative powers.[25] By 1819, in his Angostura Discourse, he continued to argue for a hereditary upper house and a strong executive.[26] Attempts to put the federalist Constitution of 1811 back into effect were thwarted, and an assembly under Bolívar adopted the Constitution of Angostura of 1819, a liberal, centralist text granting Bolívar considerable military and civil authority and wide emergency powers for the president of the Republic of Colombia.[27] Following the ideas of Benjamin Constant, the Constitution also contained a fourth power, the Moral Power, to supervise

---

[20] Safford, "Politics," 361.

[21] Ibid., 366.

[22] Adelman, "What's in a Revolution?" 190.

[23] Gargarella, *Latin American Constitutionalism*, 66–68, 224, n. 4.

[24] Castagno, "El pensamiento," 737–739.

[25] Loveman, *The Constitution*, 140.

[26] Gargarella, *Latin American Constitutionalism*, 67.

[27] Loveman, *The Constitution*, 140–141.

education, virtue, and morality.[28] Under this constitution, the senate was composed of members who served for life. Nonetheless, Bolívar expressed the opinion that because of its complexity, the Constitution of 1819 was ultimately unworkable.[29]

Under the Constitution of Cúcuta of 1821, Bolívar led Colombia under various titles until 1830 while trying to gather the areas of Colombia, Venezuela, Ecuador, Bolivia, and Peru into one large country. This constitution provided for centralized control by a strong executive and included provisions for extraordinary powers in times of crisis.[30] The presidential term, like that under the Constitution of 1819, was set at four years.[31] Regional and local officials were appointed by the president and there were no state legislatures. The electorate was limited to and filtered through indirect elections.[32] Tension with the church was avoided, but the Congress of Cúcuta abolished the Inquisition and began to chip at the secure foundation of ecclesiastical property by dissolving smaller monasteries and convents.[33]

The region was still in the process of establishing military independence, and quotidian executive duties fell to the vice president Francisco de Paula Santander. Administration was hampered by colonial practices of referring decisions up the chain of command, by excessive attention paid to questions of etiquette in official communications, and a shortage of competent individuals to fill official positions leading to multiple offices being held by the same individual. Nonetheless, Bushnell concludes that Santander's achievements in administration and the maintenance of constitutional legality were notable. Tensions between Santander and Bolívar were to grow over the next decade as they developed and applied differing notions of constitutional rule. Santander's consultation with Congress concerning the executive authority of Bolívar while absent from Colombia irreparably changed their relationship.[34]

As Bolívar's military success increased, he became more influenced by Napoleon and French thought concerning law and constitutionalism.

[28] Barrón, "La tradición republicana," 271–274.
[29] Castagno, "El pensamiento," 740–741.
[30] Loveman, *The Constitution*, 141–143, 162–163. For extraordinary powers see Bushnell, *The Santander Regime*, 31–34. For the legislative enactments of the Congress of Cúcuta see Bushnell, *The Making*, 52–54.
[31] Castagno, "El pensamiento," 743.
[32] Safford and Palacios, *Colombia*, 108.
[33] Ibid., 113. Bolívar subsequently revoked the law related to closing the monasteries. See Safford and Palacios, *Colombia*, 141.
[34] Bushnell, *The Santander Regime*, 14–22, 34–44, 69–75.

Bolívar considered himself not only a great general but also a great lawgiver.[35] Thus, French models of constitutionalism gained greater appeal for him by the mid-1820s. Nonetheless, his hopes for regional unity continued throughout the various permutations of his rule.[36] The ideas of a lifetime executive and constitutional consul became prominent in his thinking.[37] In this period, considering the political instability around him and convinced that recently independent states were not ready for democracy, Bolívar argued for the idea of a presidency that carried a life term. He drew these ideas from the Napoleonic models and from what he considered the success of Pétion as president for life in Haiti. There were no other early independence constitutions using life presidencies that may have served as models. In 1826, the Constitution of Bolivia established life tenure for the president and four powers.[38] Following the constitutional thought of Benjamin Constant, the fourth power, contained in the censors, mediated between the other powers and sought to guarantee individual liberties.[39]

A year after the Congress of Gran Colombia withdrew Bolívar's extensive powers in 1827, when Bolívar sensed that most people wanted to reform the Constitution of 1821 despite the Constitution's own prohibition of reform for ten years and despite Santander's objections, Bolívar sought constitutional change in 1828.[40] "For Bolívar," writes Velasco Ibarra, "the life of the Republic and the will of the people were more valuable than the text of a quickly written law."[41] After an uprising in April, 1828, the constitutional limitations were dispensed with and by August, 1828, Bolívar assumed sweeping dictatorial powers under an emergency decree. One of his several nationalist opponents, Santander, who strongly supported Colombian nationalism and federalism in the face of Bolívar's more expansive desires and who championed the rule of law and constitutional limitations, was sentenced to death, a sentence that was later commuted to exile.[42]

---

[35] Castagno, "El pensamiento," 745–746; Mirow, "The Power of Codification," 83–116.
[36] Loveman, *The Constitution*, 140.
[37] Gargarella, *Latin American Constitutionalism*, 67.
[38] Castagno, "El pensamiento," 742–744, 748–750; Loveman, *The Constitution*, 143.
[39] Barrón, "La tradición republicana," 275–278; Safford and Palacios, *Colombia*, 119.
[40] Safford and Palacios, *Colombia*, 120.
[41] Velasco Ibarra, *Expresión política*, 67.
[42] Loveman, *The Constitution*, 142, 144, 161. See also Bushnell, *The Santander Regime*, 348–359. Constitutional reform through the Convention of Ocaña from March to June, 1828, did not unfold as Bolívar had hoped. The Colombian Constitution of 1830 drafted by the "Admirable Congress" was too late to avoid the collapse of the republic it sought to preserve. See Safford and Palacios, *Colombia*, 123–125, 129. See also Bushnell, *The Making*, 71–72.

Pan-Americanism was a central aspect of Bolívar's constitutionalism. He often spoke and wrote about the brotherhood of Spanish America and the union of the people of the Americas. While he realized that political differences would maintain separate countries in the region he worked for and envisioned cooperation and confederation between the independent states of Latin America. In 1824, he invited Chile, Colombia, Guatemala, Mexico, and Río de la Plata to the Congress of Panama. Meeting in 1826, the Congress did not fulfill his expectations for confederation and common action.[43] Nonetheless, Bolívar's aspirations in this area continued to be a powerful call or at least a convenient trope for regional reform.

Bolívar's actions also led to constitutional change as a reaction to his overreaching. Because of Bolívar's sweeping assumptions of dictatorial power, Colombia's early constitutions unusually did not provide for emergency extraordinary powers in the executive or regimes of exception.[44] Colombia's first national constitution was adopted in 1832. It attempted to strike a balance between central and federal perspectives, but its substantial grant of authority to the provinces was not sufficient to prevent a civil war, the War of the Supremes, between religiously conservative elements and the government between 1839 and 1842.[45]

After the war, the government took the opportunity to limit provincial power through a more centralist constitution in 1843. Under this constitution, the provinces were pulled under central control and the president appointed provincial governors.[46] The Constitution of 1843, drafted by Mariano Ospina Rodríguez and José Eusebio Caro, was a conservative reaction to the War of the Supremes and attempted to follow more radical French positions in the recent past.[47] The constitution limited popular participation and government powers.[48] Presidents and often their subsequent constitutions were the products of liberal and conservative oscillation. Nonetheless, transition from president to president was relatively peaceful, reflected the electoral process, and occurred at the end of presidents serving their full terms.[49]

Following the constitutional history of Colombia forward from these early documents illustrates many of the various positions and policies

---

[43] Castagno, "El pensamiento," 751–752.
[44] Loveman, *The Constitution*, 145, 161.
[45] Gargerella, *Latin American Constitutionalism*, 71; Loveman, *The Constitution*, 163–165; Safford and Palacios, *Colombia*, 146–151.
[46] Loveman, *The Constitution*, 165.
[47] Gargarella, *Latin American Constitutionalism*, 71.
[48] Bushnell, *The Making*, 97.
[49] Loveman, *The Constitution*, 166.

presented during the nineteenth century. From 1849 to 1886, Colombia was guided by liberalism and the examples of the European revolutions of 1848. The Jesuits were, once again, expelled and ecclesiastical property was secularized. Federalism led to the creation of the Confederation of Granada from 1851 to 1861, and then the United States of Colombia.[50] Constitutional reforms of 1853 moved the country toward greater federalism; established universal male suffrage; and provided for direct election of provincial governors, the attorney-general, and Supreme Court justices. One province, Vélez, under this reform provided for women's suffrage in 1853 but the Supreme Court annulled the provision. The reforms of 1853 made no specific provisions for the church and opened the door to religious toleration.[51]

A civil war from 1859 to 1862 and a resulting liberal victory led to a convention at Rionegro to draft a new constitution.[52] The federalist Constitution of 1863 greatly diminished the power of the president and, among other liberal reforms, guaranteed the right to bear arms, leading to insecurity and attacks against the government.[53] The constitution also contained several anticlerical aspects. Concerning the constitution's liberal provisions, Bushnell and Macaulay write that "in almost every respect the Colombian Constitution of 1863 represents the most advanced form of liberalism that any Latin American nation achieved (or was afflicted with) in the past century."[54] It appears that Mexican developments under Benito Juárez served as models for Colombian liberalism in this period. The Rionegro Constitution, or Constitution of 1863, would serve as Colombia's constitutional text until 1886.[55]

Elected to his third term in 1866, President Mosquera dissolved Congress and assumed extraordinary powers. He was subsequently removed by a coup led by moderates who wanted to avoid war. It is noteworthy that the Colombian Constitutions of 1853 and 1863 were the only Latin American constitutions of the nineteenth century that did not include extraordinary powers for the executive in times of emergency

---

[50] Velasco Ibarra, *Expresión política*, 68–70. See also Safford and Palacios, *Colombia*, 188–221. The Jesuits returned in 1857 under President Mariano Ospina Rodríguez. See Bushnell, *The Making*, 114. They were expelled again in 1861 under General Tomás Cipriano Mosquera. See Bushnell, *The Making*, 120.

[51] Bushnell, *The Making*, 108–109.

[52] Safford and Palacios, *Colombia*, 221–227.

[53] Loveman, *The Constitution*, 171.

[54] Bushnell and Macaulay, *The Emergence*, 217.

[55] Bushnell, *The Making*, 121–124.

or regimes of exception.[56] Marginalizing or excluding the conservative voice in debates and drafting, liberals, radicals, and the armed forces constituted the main powers in their construction.[57]

Liberal and conservative governments came in and out of power in Colombia until 1886, when conservatives constitutionalized their victory in the war of 1885.[58] When almost all other nations in the region were making a decidedly liberal turn, Colombia entered a markedly conservative period known as the Regeneration from approximately 1878 to 1900 with the Constitution of 1886 as a central feature.[59] Responding to civil unrest and economic problems, Rafael Nuñez sought to "restore" the country based on moderate liberal and conservative principles, including former, more conservative constitutions. In 1886, a constitutional commission of élite jurists, including the conservative Miguel Antonio Caro and the liberal José María Samper, drafted a conservative constitution to restore order and reinstitute Roman Catholicism as a central moral guide for the country. Just as they had excluded conservatives in the past decades, liberals and radicals from the prior period were now excluded in the process.[60]

The Constitution of 1886 centralized authority, established a clear and favorable relationship with the church, and greatly strengthened the executive power.[61] It created a strong executive that had recourse to extraordinary powers during regimes of exception. Conservatives who also controlled access to administrative positions in the government effectively controlled elections.[62] The states of earlier constitutions were now departments with the president appointing governors of departments and governors appointing mayors. The president appointed lifetime members of the Supreme Court and appointed other judicial officers. The presidential term was lengthened to six years. A transitional article permitted censorship of the press, and in keeping with the new place of the church under the constitution, a Concordat of 1887 as amended in 1892 placed the church in control of civil registries, cemeteries, and education.[63] The

[56] Loveman, *The Constitution*, 161, 172.

[57] Gargarella, *Latin American Constitutionalism*, 40.

[58] Bushnell and Macaulay, *The Emergence*, 219–220; Loveman, *The Constitution*, 172–174; Safford and Palacios, *Colombia*, 239–246.

[59] Gargarella, *Latin American Constitutionalism*, 30; Loveman, *The Constitution*, 161; Palacios, *Between Legitimacy*, 1, 27–30. See also Bushnell, *The Making*, 140–148.

[60] Gargarella, *Latin American Constitutionalism*, 40–41, 79; Safford and Palacios, *Colombia*, 246. For Caro, see Herrera Andrade, *Miguel Antonio Caro*.

[61] Velasco Ibarra, *Expresión política*, 71.

[62] Loveman, *The Constitution*, 174–175, 177.

[63] Palacios, *Between Legitimacy*, 29.

turn of the nineteenth century, from 1899 to 1902, saw Colombia in civil war, known as the War of a Thousand Days, resulting in a conservative victory and the loss of Panama from Colombia.[64] The following thirty years were a period of political conservatism and economic liberalism.[65] And these developments are discussed in the next chapter.

Venezuela

Venezuela's first stance regarding events on the peninsula in 1808 was loyalty to Fernando VII. Attempting to maintain the status quo, the city council and captain general sought to create a regional junta in 1808, and signatures were gathered to advance the creation of this new institution when faced with a representative of the Junta of Seville requesting that it be recognized as the legitimate representative of royal authority. The proposal for a regional junta was rejected and the Junta Central in peninsular Spain was recognized by Caracas in 1809. The election in 1809 was unsuccessful because the representative was rejected for being a non-native of the region. The following year, in 1810, the election was successful for a representative to the Junta Central, but Caracas soon received word that the Junta Central had been replaced by the Council of Regency. This transfer from one institution to the other was not readily accepted by Caracas, which, fearing that the regency usurped royal sovereignty, opted to establish its own *Junta Suprema Conservadora de los Derechos del Señor Don Fernando VII* in April, 1810. The Cortes of Cádiz that convened shortly afterwards was met with skepticism in Caracas, which refused to recognize its authority. The Caracas Junta sent troops against the city of Coro, loyal to the regency, and at the beginning of 1811, Captain Feliciano Montenegro, who was loyal to the regency and Cortes, arrived in Caracas with documents addressed to the city council of Caracas, but not to the Junta of Caracas. This was taken as a great affront by the Junta. The denial of representative capacity of the substitute deputies by the Junta has already been mentioned. Caracas established its own electoral laws to create a government for Venezuela.[66] A constitution was soon to follow.

A subsequently gathered congress declared independence from Spain on July 5, 1811 and promulgated the federal Constitution of Venezuela in December, 1811. In April, 1812, Congress dissolved itself and granted

[64] Bushnell, *The Making*, 148–154; Palacios, *Between Legitimacy*, 37–39; Loveman, *The Constitution*, 178; Velasco Ibarra, *Expresión política*, 71.

[65] Palacios, *Between Legitimacy*, 48.

[66] Quintero, "La iniciativa," 187–207.

extraordinary dictatorial powers to Francisco de Miranda to conduct war against Spain. Domingo de Monteverde conquered the territory for Spain and ruled Venezuela as captain general and governor with little regard for the Constitution of Cádiz for which he was supposed to have fought. His unwillingness to pardon those associated with independence, his control over the promulgation of the Constitution, and his summary imprisonment of individuals were criticized in Venezuela and on the peninsula, but were apparently outweighed by his suppression of the independence movement in the region. After a brief occupation by Simón Bolívar for part of 1813 and 1814, Venezuela was once again under the control of Monteverde. Thus, during the first constitutional period, Venezuela did not experience a full implementation of the Constitution of Cádiz. It did, however, participate in elections in the second constitutional period after 1820, but this ended in June, 1821, when the independent movement won in Carabobo and moved forward with its own government.[67]

José Antonio Páez, who had led an effort to sever Venezuela from Colombia in 1826 and obtained significant concessions from Bolívar in 1827, served as president of Venezuela from 1830 to 1835 and from 1839 to 1843. He ruled autocratically and implemented various liberal reforms although Venezuelan historians sometimes refer to the Páez years as the "Conservative Oligarchy."[68] The following period from approximately 1848 to 1858 is known as the "Liberal Oligarchy" during which military rulers shared the presidency under the eye of the Liberal Party. After a protracted power struggle known as the Federal War from 1858 to 1863, victorious liberals promulgated a Constitution of 1864 that included a federal structure, assertions of equal rights for citizens, and universal male suffrage. In 1870, Antonio Guzmán Blanco assumed power and pressed for modernization. He reduced the power of the church, established civil marriages, and advanced economic liberalism. He left the presidency for the last time in 1887.[69]

Argentina

Argentina similarly offers important perspectives on the issues steering constitutionalism in the nineteenth century. Concerning the first half of the nineteenth century in Argentina, Negretto states, "From the Revolution of 1810 until 1852, Argentine political history can be summarized into

---

[67] Ibid., 208–215.

[68] Bushnell and Macaulay, *The Emergence*, 102–107; Safford and Palacios, *Colombia*, 117–118, 121.

[69] Bushnell and Macaulay, *The Emergence*, 238–242.

the extensive fight between Buenos Aires, opposed to a federal form of government, and the rest of the provinces, which found in such a system the best protection for their political and economic interests."[70] The revolution of May, 1810, led to liberal reforms such as the abolition of titles of nobility and entailed estates (*mayorazgos*), the freedom of the press, and the emancipation of slaves.[71] From 1810 to 1829, the region was subject to a variety of individual or collective governing bodies including supreme directorates, juntas, triumvirates, and congresses, some declaring loyalty to Spain and others pressing for greater independence.[72] These bodies sometime issued constitutional documents. A draft Constitution of 1812 mirrored many of the provisions of the Constitution of Cádiz, while substituting a directorate for the king and making other liberal modifications such as introducing a jury in trials.[73] A bit later the Provisional Statute of 1815 included a declaration of the Rights of Man and expressed additional liberal values.[74] The country fell into battles between centralists and federalists and regional conflicts.[75] A Congress held in Tucumán declared independence in 1816.[76] The Constitution of 1819 provided for corporate representation to outweigh the strong political pressure held by caudillos in areas outside of Buenos Aires. It provided for a centralized state and Roman Catholicism as the official state religion without prohibiting the public exercise of other religions. This permissive approach to other religions appears to have been a concession to English traders and others who had close economic ties to Buenos Aires and its commercial activities. The Constitution of 1819 did not receive support from the provinces, which set out on their own courses while demanding a federal structure and a high degree of political and economic autonomy. In light of the failure of the 1819 Constitution, a Junta for Buenos Aires conferred full governmental powers on its governor as some provinces declared themselves independent republics under caudillos. Both the provinces and Buenos Aires experienced political chaos throughout the 1820s. It is estimated that in the single year of 1820, Buenos Aires had more than twenty governments.[77] After the Constitution of 1819, Bernardino Rivadavia attempted to centralize national power through

---

[70] Negretto, "Repasando," 224.
[71] Velasco Ibarra, *Expresión política*, 76–82.
[72] Loveman, *The Constitution*, 266.
[73] Botana, "El primer republicanismo," 164.
[74] Loveman, *The Constitution*, 270–271.
[75] Botana, "El primer republicanismo," 164–165; Loveman, *The Constitution*, 265–266.
[76] Botana, "El primer republicanismo," 160.
[77] Loveman, *The Constitution*, 272–276.

the Constitution of 1826.[78] It too provided for a central structure with protections of civil rights that were, in effect, suspended for reasons of security of the country.[79]

Buenos Aires province was to have its own caudillo, Juan Manuel de Rosas, who ruled in one fashion or another from 1829 to 1852.[80] Rosas brought the rural areas into the picture while maintaining his control over Buenos Aires.[81] Appointed "provisional governor" of Buenos Aires after various military factions were subdued, Rosas championed federalism, Roman Catholicism, and personally vested extraordinary powers to obtain internal security in the country. Legislative bodies granted him these powers, and in 1835 a plebiscite confirmed his status as a constitutional dictator with full control over all aspects of government. His use of terror to promote his ends has been documented. Such tight-fisted control led to his overthrow by Justo José de Urquiza, the caudillo of Entre Ríos province in 1852, who assumed the title of "provisional director" with extensive executive powers.[82]

By 1853, plans were under way in Santa Fé for a new constitution.[83] The Constitution of 1853 established Argentina as a federal republic that borrowed a great deal of structure and ideology from U.S. sources.[84] As Billias has noted of this Constitution, "This document relied more heavily on the U.S. Constitution than did any other Latin American charter of the nineteenth century."[85] The Constitution adopted a liberal democratic political model, with rights and liberties for citizens and a program to foster the country's educational and economic condition. Under the Constitution, provincial government was left to each province, which retained all powers not specifically allocated to the national government. The Constitution did, however, provide for the granting of extraordinary powers to the executive when a state of siege had been validly declared under its provisions.[86] It also provided for a strong central government and executive power, and the Chilean Constitution of 1833 served as a model in this respect.[87] In this way, the Constitution

---

[78] Velasco Ibarra, *Expresión política*, 79.

[79] Loveman, *The Constitution*, 277.

[80] Loveman, *The Constitution*, 274; Bushnell and Macaulay, *The Emergence*, 125–131.

[81] Velasco Ibarra, *Expresión política*, 80.

[82] Loveman, *The Constitution*, 278–282.

[83] Velasco Ibarra, *Expresión política*, 81–82.

[84] Loveman, *The Constitution*, 283.

[85] Billias, *American Constitutionalism*, 133.

[86] Loveman, *The Constitution*, 283–285.

[87] Negretto, "Repasando," 211, 229.

contained a mix of liberal and conservative views by drafters of differing viewpoints in the same constitutional document.[88]

The mastermind behind this lasting document of Argentine constitutionalism was Juan Bautista Alberdi, who had produced a study of contemporary comparative constitutionalism in the context of the country's constitutional history, *Bases and Points of Departure for the Political Organization of the Argentine Republic*.[89] Born in Tucumán; raised in Buenos Aires; and with degrees in law or legal qualifications from Córdoba, Montevideo, and Valparaíso, where he wrote his famous study, Alberdi was well prepared to assess the constitutional condition of Argentina and the region.[90] Following the path of Esteban Echeverría's intellectual tradition, Alberdi attempted to construct a useful history for constitutional development in 1847 in his *La República Argentina 37 años después de su Revolución de Mayo* that would later be echoed in the *Bases*.[91]

In 1853 he entered into a public and polemical debate with President Domingo Faustino Sarmiento through a series of letters. Cast as an academic, Alberdi stressed the rich past and constitutional tradition of Argentina, while Sarmiento, the pragmatist, argued for following successful models from abroad, especially those of the United States. Unsurprisingly influenced by von Savigny, Alberdi stressed local customs, habits, traditions, and history in a study of the Argentine Constitution of 1853. He noted that Chilean experience, rather than that of the United States, served as a better model. Foreign models were, in his view, too far removed from the realities of Argentina's social and political world. Alberdi also noted that Sarmiento, in the previously published work *Facundo* (*Civilización y Barbarie: Vida de Juan Facundo Quiroga*), had asserted the important role the system of caudillos had in creating political institutions and structures.[92] As might be expected, Alberdi ensured

---

[88] Gargarella, *Latin American Constitutionalism*, 30.

[89] Botana, *La tradición republicana*, 309–311; Loveman, *The Constitution*, 283. See also Alberdi, *Bases*. See generally Adelman, "Between Order and Liberty;" Negretto, "Repensando."

[90] Alberdi, *Bases*, 7–8.

[91] Adelman, *Republic of Capital*, 172–181. "Echeverría was a romantic poet and political writer who assimilated the ideas that originated in France and Italy (not yet considered a nation) in the 1830s and were presented, with the force of a creed, mainly through four authors: Giuseppe Mazzini, Alexis de Tocqueville, Félicité de Lamennais, and François Guizot." See Botana and Gallo, "Introduction," xi. He is considered a leader of the "Generation of '37." See Botana and Gallo, *Liberal Thought*, 428.

[92] Gargarella, *Latin American Constitutionalism*, 63–66, 78, 226, n. 22. See also Botana, *La tradición republicana*, 340–408; Botana and Gallo, "Introduction," xii.

that his works and opinions were widely circulated among policymakers. On receiving a copy of *Bases*, General Urquiza noted the timeliness and importance of the work.[93]

Alberdi focused on commercial and economic growth and found fault both in the Spanish *derecho indiano* and the Latin American constitutions of the first half of the nineteenth century because they did not adequately promote these interests.[94] In Alberdi's view, the constitutions of the regions were oriented too much toward independence and philosophical notions of liberty and not enough toward material progress, stimulating population growth through immigration, navigation, industry, and economic interests. This is the broad theme he used to critique the contemporary constitutions of Argentina, Chile, Peru, Mexico, Uruguay, and Paraguay. The Chilean Constitution's religious restrictions impeded foreign capital and investment. The Peruvian Constitution of 1830 was overly restrictive of property and other rights for non-Peruvians. According to Alberdi, the constitutions of countries issuing from Gran Colombia were tainted with Bolívar's fears of foreign powers and foreigners. Mexico's constitution too was overly restrictive of foreign ownership of property and religious practice. Uruguay did not foment economic progress, and Paraguay was excessively presidentialist and hostile to foreigners.[95]

Thus, none of these constitutions merited imitation, and Alberdi argued for originality in meeting the needs of the Argentine state on both the constitutional and legislative levels. The region, he proposed, required constitutions that encouraged economic growth, immigration and population, transportation, and industry. These were the pressing issues of the day and took precedence over ideas of the former needs for liberty and independence. Where, then, should Argentina look for suitable constitutional models? California was his answer. California was a model of economic growth, tolerance, and progress where religious beliefs were absent from politics and where mixed marriages were protected by the constitution to stimulate an increase in population through

---

[93] Gargarella, *Latin American Constitutionalism*, 218, n. 23. As an interesting aside, it seems that President Lincoln's suspension of habeas corpus informed President Domingo Faustino Sarmiento of Argentina when he considered the need for emergency powers of the executive. See Botana, *La tradición republicana*, 376–377.

[94] Alberdi, *Bases*, 12–13. Alberdi was only one of several important Latin American constitutionalists to address this question. The Mexican Mariano Otero saw the distribution of property as an impediment to functional constitutionalism and the Colombian Murillo Toro also linked constitutional improvement to economic reform. See Gargarella, *Latin American Constitutionalism*, 49, 52.

[95] Alberdi, *Bases*, 17–19, 21–41.

immigration.[96] He carried this admiration of Anglo-America even into his vision of public education: "[t]he English language, as the language of liberty, industry, and order, ought to be even more required than Latin" and reading and writing English should be a requirement for all university degrees.[97] Thus, he argued for policies of immigration; religious tolerance; transportation, particularly railroads supported through state privilege and foreign capital; and free trade within the country, all recognized in the constitutions, substantive codes, and piecemeal legislation. Furthermore, Alberdi noted the possibilities international law offered for locking in economic and individual rights for immigrants and foreigners. Treaties, he argued, could serve as an additional state guarantee of these rights for non-citizens.[98] Alberdi wrote, "Every treaty will be an anchor of stability holding the constitution."[99]

Alberdi addressed at length a question that haunted Argentina from the beginning of its split from Spain – whether a centralized or federal state was the appropriate structure for the country. Noting both the unitary and federal antecedents and the impossibility of a purely unitary or a purely federal government, Alberdi argued for a hybrid or mixed structure of both structures with the United States, Switzerland, and Germany as the primary successful examples of such a system but cautioned against blind imitation of such structures. Nonetheless, Alberdi was not hesitant to quote Joseph Story's *Commentaries* or *The Federalist* in defending his constitutional plans. Representation would be provided through two houses, one representing the entire republic based on population and another representing the provinces with an equal number of representatives from each province. Similarly, Alberdi contemplated a divided judiciary with courts on both the provincial and federal levels. The federal level of government would be able to promote projects related to the infrastructure and economy of the country that were too large to be handled by individual provinces. It would also provide national identity for political and economic purposes, especially as these activities interacted with the international sphere through diplomatic relationships and treaty obligations.[100] Indeed, Alberdi's recognition of Argentina as a state with exterior obligations and benefits was a noteworthy step in constitutionalism of the period.

[96] Ibid., 17, 25, 41–43, 44–47, 56, 177–184.
[97] Ibid., 53.
[98] Ibid., 62–81, 88–96, 189–191.
[99] Ibid., 189.
[100] Alberdi, *Bases*, 81–88, 99–115, 117, 119–120, 122–129, 131, 158–159. See also Botana and Gallo, "Introduction," xvii–xviii.

Concerned about the long-standing regional battles between Buenos Aires and the provinces, Alberdi asserted that Buenos Aires should never serve as the capital of his newly created united federation. This assertion was made in light of the conflict between Rosas and Urquiza, the president as Alberdi wrote, and Alberdi's assessment that Buenos Aires stood in the way of creating a united constitution for the country while capitalizing on its position as de facto leader of the region.[101]

Although provinces were limited in their powers under Alberdi's proposal, they, like the states of the United States of America, retained all powers not specifically granted to the federal government.[102] With the Chilean experience in mind, Alberdi seemed resigned to the necessity of a strong executive in the Argentine constitution and in constitutions of the region. He saw the burst of liberty expressed in early post-independence constitutions as a stage of constitutional development to be substituted by a responsible, that is constitutional, construction of a strong executive, but always under a constitution.[103] He wrote, "This development of executive power is the main need of constitutional law in our days in South America."[104]

Alberdi contemplated a constitutional order that was consistent between text and political reality; he decried constitutions in the region that were not reflected in the political reality of their countries.[105] Echoing this desire for political and legal consistency, he wrote, "It is not the laws that we have to change, it is people and things."[106] Alberdi sought to create a lasting and effective constitutional order and viewed constitutional interpretation, commentary, and case law as essential pieces in establishing and maintaining this goal.[107] Changes in the presidency should not lead to new constitutions. For him, the constitution might be thought of as a ship that may change captains but would continue on its established course.[108] Alberdi's constitution would incorporate his economic policies of progress under the general structure by first setting out general rights and guarantees followed by a set of institutions to administer or to ensure these principles, rights, and guarantees.[109]

---

[101] Alberdi, *Bases*, 140–154, 201–211.
[102] Ibid., 132–133, 240 (Art. 99 of Alberdi's draft constitution).
[103] Ibid., 133–140.
[104] Ibid.,
[105] Ibid., 175, 184–187 (noting the lack of implementation of guarantees in the Bolivian Constitution).
[106] Ibid., 175.
[107] Ibid., 194.
[108] Ibid., 198.
[109] Ibid., 194, 198, 212–242.

Debate on the constitution was conducted for only ten days, as Urquiza wanted a document to maintain the Confederation as quickly as possible.[110] The place of the church in Argentina's political structure was the primary area of debate. Conservatives sought to privilege the church and Roman Catholics in public life, and to ensure Catholic education and the proper patronage of the church by the state.[111] The Constitution established a federal system in which the federal power might step into provincial matters to maintain "republican principles."[112] It established three branches of government, a powerful executive, a bicameral legislature, and judiciary with a set of basic rights for citizens including property, travel, work, worship, and publication without censure.[113]

The response of Buenos Aires initially was not to adopt the constitution but rather to promulgate its own Constitution of 1854 and to select Mitre as governor who squabbled with Urquiza's confederation until 1859, when Urquiza gained the military upper hand. The Constitution of 1853 was accepted as a national constitution in 1860 and Mitre became president in 1862.[114] President Mitre instituted numerous liberal reforms under a team led by noted jurist and codifier Dalmacio Vélez Sársfield. Several liberal-leaning administrations under Domingo Sarmiento, Nicolás Avellaneda, and Julio Argentino Roca provided stability and economic growth.[115] Battles between Buenos Aires and provincial caudillos continued into the 1880s, with states of siege used as means to suppress uprisings. Congress had the authority to void a declaration of a state of siege, but never exercised it. In 1865, the Supreme Court of Argentina also assumed the power to void presidential decrees as unconstitutional. Through the end of the nineteenth century, political conditions led to presidents availing themselves of extraordinary power under the Constitution and the state of siege. Significant economic expansion in the final decades of the century led to the consolidation of economic power and, in turn, the ability to control political power. In 1898, General Roca's second presidency called for order and progress, the positivist's call for social and economic improvement. Political life in Argentina in the final years of the century became imbued with the rise of labor movements, anarchy,

---

[110] Adelman, *Republic of Capital*, 201.
[111] Gargarella, *Latin American Constitutionalism*, 35.
[112] Adelman, *Republic of Capital*, 207.
[113] Ibid.
[114] Loveman, *The Constitution*, 286–287. See also Botana and Gallo, "Introduction," xx.
[115] Gargarella, *Latin American Constitutionalism*, 36.

and socialism, which were met with even more calls for dramatic action under states of siege.[116]

Uruguay

Neighboring Argentina, Uruguay in the early nineteenth century experienced civil wars and from 1817 to 1825 was controlled first by Portugal and then Brazil. From 1825 to 1828 it was the object of war between Brazil and Argentina. A treaty between these countries left Uruguay subject to their control until 1835, when it was declared independent but continued under the effective powers of Uruguayan caudillos until the mid-nineteenth century. Nonetheless, under English pressure and in the midst of Argentine and Brazilian squabbling, Uruguay adopted its Constitution of 1830, a document that recognized the Argentine and Brazilian intervention in the country. The Constitution of 1830 created a conservative centralized government in which even the heads of each regional department were selected by the president. Elections were under the sway of the president and would remain so for most of the nineteenth century. The Constitution provided for extraordinary powers in the executive when the country was threatened.[117]

Fructuoso Rivera, the first president, opposed Argentine caudillo Juan Manuel de Rosas's ambitions in the region and was associated with the Colorado Party. Manuel Oribe, the second president, was associated with Rosas and the other main political party, the Blanco Party. These two parties would shape Uruguayan politics for the remainder of the nineteenth and well into the twentieth centuries. From 1836 to 1851, Montevideo favored the Colorados while the areas outside the capital favored the Blancos. During the late 1840s, Rosas attacked Montevideo while England and France bolstered the Colorados by keeping shipping open to the city and attempted to blockade Buenos Aires. On the defeat of Rosas, Brazil moved troops into the country and militarily controlled the country until the 1850s. Brazil and Argentina continued to influence affairs in the 1850s and 1860s through the parties and their leaders. From 1865 to 1870, Uruguay was brought into the triple alliance with Argentina and Brazil against Paraguay. This war led to the modernization and professionalization of the Uruguayan army and, as a result, its greater role in the political life of the country. The country was run by a series of military leaders from the late 1870s through the 1880s who treated opposition

---

[116] Loveman, *The Constitution*, 287–289.
[117] Ibid., 291, 294–296.

harshly and stressed authoritarian and centralized control that included the civilian jurisdiction of military courts in specified situations and the military's responsibility for internal public order.[118]

Paraguay

Paraguay successfully repelled Argentine assertions of control after 1810 and would be ruled by a succession of individual dictatorships until the aftermath of the Paraguayan War in 1870 when Brazil imposed a constitution on the country. In 1813, a congress in Paraguay made José Gaspar Rodríguez de Francia, who asserted independence from Spain and Argentina, the supreme dictator and in 1816, the Congress appointed him perpetual dictator. Francia controlled the country in all aspects until his death in 1840 and there was little need for a constitution. Indeed, he realized he had little need of other collective governing bodies such as the Asunción City Council, which he dissolved in 1825. The main source of private law was the *Recopilación de las Leyes de las Indias*, mentioned earlier, and he personally reviewed judicial decisions. Francia was followed by a junta of three army officers to maintain order, who were, in turn, replaced by another three individuals. A subsequent congress appointed Carlos Antonio López and Mariano Roque Alonso as co-consuls for three years without a constitution. The first constitution-like document was issued in 1844 under López, who had received a ten-year term under a law establishing public administration. Congress was to meet every five years, which it did, sanctioning all actions by López and in 1854, electing him for another ten-year term. On López's death in 1862, his son, Francisco Solano López, who had been the commander of the army, succeeded him. Solano López called a Congress that appointed him president for a ten-year term. He died in battle in 1870 during the Paraguayan War. Brazil occupied the country until 1876 and gave Paraguay its first constitution, the Constitution of 1870.[119]

The Paraguayan Constitution of 1870 was a liberal document with an extensive list of civil rights. It established freedom of religion, the abolition of slavery, and the abolition of military and ecclesiastical *fueros*. It also abolished grants of extraordinary executive power from Congress and prohibited dictatorships, but it left the door open for states of siege in response to internal commotion, among other triggering factors. The Constitution of 1870 was to last through the remainder of the nineteenth

---

[118] Ibid., 298–301.
[119] Bushnell and Macaulay, *The Emergence*, 136–140; Loveman, *The Constitution*, 305–309.

century and into the twentieth century. Presidents typically found internal unrest to justify extraordinary executive powers to maintain their presidencies and the influence of the Colorado Party.[120]

Ecuador

Ecuador's experience in the nineteenth century varied from the countries already discussed. Presidential succession in the period was usually decided by force. Ecuador split away from Bolívar's Gran Colombia, of which it was part until 1830, having been under control of General Antonio José de Sucre. The country obtained a new constitution on this date under the control of Venezuelan General Juan José Flores, who was to rule the country autocratically for the next fifteen years despite his liberally worded constitution and internal resistance from supporters of Ecuador's return to the Colombian federation. During a second period as president from 1839 to 1843, Flores promulgated a new constitution in 1843 that was called the "Charter of Slavery" by those not aligned with Flores. The Constitution provided for increased executive powers, a new institution called the "Permanent Commission," a committee of five people that had legislative power when Congress was not in session, and the continuation of the military *fuero*. Military rule continued in the country, despite attempts in the Constitution of 1845 to limit the president's control of the military without congressional assent, but internal unrest and another new Constitution of 1852 ensured that the pattern of the use of extraordinary powers continued. General Urbina ran Ecuador from 1845 to 1860 and Dr. García Moreno from 1860 to 1875. With low voter participation, regionalism, and the lack of political parties, Ecuador was ruled, often ruthlessly, by these individuals. García Moreno's political conservatism was reflected in the Constitution of 1861 that strengthened ties to and the power of the church. His self-assured sense of godly mission led to frightening oppression of those who disagreed with him. The Constitution of 1869 stated that only Roman Catholics could be citizens, limited public assembly to activities that respected the church, and gave the Holy See ultimate authority over the dissolution of religious organizations in the country.[121]

García Moreno faced substantial criticism from thinkers such as the radical Juan Montalvo, who advanced the importance of associations in political life to stand up to despotism and anarchy, ideologies that in his

[120] Loveman, *The Constitution*, 309–311.
[121] Ibid., 180–194.

view often relied on separating and isolating citizens.[122] García Moreno was replaced by a conciliatory liberal in 1875 after being assassinated by liberals and opposing members of the military. The presidential exercise of extraordinary powers under Garciá Moreno's constitution did not lessen with a shift in political perspective. Subsequent presidents declared prior constitutions revoked or reinstated depending on their political leanings. The liberal Constitution of 1878 stated that the military was not to carry out orders that were unconstitutional. The final decades of the nineteenth century in Ecuador were marked by a distinctly conservative period of civilian presidents under a close group of powerful families that exercised oligarchical rule until 1895, when another liberal regime came to power. The Constitution of 1897 reduced the power of the church and its institutions in the political arena, and in 1900, births, deaths, and marriages in Ecuador became the province of civil registers.[123]

Peru

In Peru, creole élites sought to maintain allegiance to Spain; the idea of independence was linked to the republicanism and disorder that would challenge this small ruling class's control. Racial control over the indigenous population was a central concern since the Tupac Amaru revolt of the 1780s. Similar concerns were apparent in Upper Peru (Bolivia), which after 1776 was politically tied to the viceroyalty of Rio de la Plata. Bolivia's separate course was set by Pedro Olañeta, who opposed the restoration of the Constitution of Cádiz in the early 1820s and declared himself ruler of Rio de la Plata in absolutist monarchical loyalty to Fernando VII. General Sucre quickly wrested power from him and declared the region independent in 1825 as the republic of Bolivia. Peru was ruled by General San Martín, who promulgated a central authoritarian constitutional text in 1822. A constituent congress in Peru appointed José de la Riva Agüero in 1823, but the country was soon placed under the control of Bolívar.[124] Nonetheless, the Peruvian Constitution of 1823 reflected radical and liberal principles that led to hopes for a unicameral legislative body representing the popular will. Special procedures provided for the legislative branch electing the executive, controlling executive activities, and limiting presidential functions.[125] Peru and Bolivia were ruled directly by Bolívar on independence until 1826 and then continued in political

[122] Gargarella, *Latin American Constitutionalism*, 60.
[123] Loveman, *The Constitution*, 196–201.
[124] Ibid., 204–207, 209–210.
[125] Castagno, "El pensamiento," 749–750; Jamanca Vega, "El Liberalismo Peruano," 13–30.

and constitutional disorder for several decades. Bolívar's Constitution of Bolivia of 1826 famously created a centralized government, presidency for life, and ample powers in the executive. His hopes of incorporating these countries into a Pan-American federation were checked by local caudillos and nationalism at the regional level.[126]

General Andrés Santa Cruz governed over a confederation of Peru and Bolivia in the second half of the 1830s, creating military conflicts with neighboring Argentina and Chile. Military officers would guide the region into the 1860s, and Peru's five constitutions between 1823 and 1839 did little to remove the central place of the military in the country's political life. Indeed, the Peruvian Constitution of 1839 focused on maintaining peace and order through a strong executive branch with the possibility of delegating extraordinary powers to provincial officials in times of crisis to save the country.[127] Dissent from the executive and military stranglehold could be noted in the works of important Peruvian constitutional thinkers such as Francisco de Paula González Vigil, who produced numerous political tracts during the period. He asserted the importance of associations to combat relatively successful attempts to keep individuals distanced from political life.[128]

The presidencies of Ramón Castilla from 1845 to 1851 and from 1855 to 1862 were notable for his desire to place legislative and fiscal activity within constitutional bounds under a prosperous economic period resulting from fertilizer mining and sales. Each term produced a constitution, with the second constitution, of 1856, reducing the power of the executive in favor of the legislature and limiting the power and influence of the church and military.[129] Congress took full advantage of its new powers and at one point turned itself into a constituent congress to draft a new constitution and to exact compromises from Castilla. This resulted in the Peruvian Constitution of 1860 that was to serve, with a few short interruptions, until 1920. The Constitution, with the justification of the country having too many laws, provided for a relatively weak Congress that met in sessions every two years. With assertions that the country was not ready for universal suffrage, the Constitution also substantially cut back on the extent of the franchise.[130] This constitution continued the

---

[126] Loveman, *The Constitution*, 207, 214–216. See also Bushnell, *The Santander Regime*, 331, 336–337.
[127] Loveman, *The Constitution*, 207–208, 218–221.
[128] Gargarella, *Latin American Constitutionalism*, 60–61.
[129] Loveman, *The Constitution*, 223–224.
[130] Gargarella, *Latin American Constitutionalism*, 217, n. 16.

military's function of maintaining internal order while providing for significant control over the executive by the legislature. It maintained Roman Catholicism as the official state religion with the control of ecclesiastical appointments in the presidency. Peru did not have a civilian president until the 1870s. This was a period of economic and industrial expansion, but by the late 1870s, Peru was at war with Chile, with a Chilean occupation of Lima in 1881. When Chile left, with significant loss of Peruvian territory, Peru turned to its military, which secured a greater role in the political life of the country into the twentieth century.[131]

Bolivia

Bolivia's first constitutional experience was under Bolívar's Constitution of 1826. With Bolívar's departure from the region in 1826, the constitution was never completely in effect or for very long. General Sucre controlled the country until 1828. Similarly, Bolivia's ten constitutions from 1826 to 1880 permitted a continued use of extraordinary powers and dictatorial rule in a period of coups, civil wars, and violence under broader debates over conservative and liberal principles. When General Santa Cruz came to power in 1829, he assumed autocratic power and later instilled the Constitution of 1831 that gave him broad executive and extraordinary powers to control the entire government and military, to dissolve the congress, and to rule through decrees when the council of state agreed.[132] From 1829 to 1850, General José Miguel Velasco was president five times, and from 1825 to 1899, as Loveman writes, "every Bolivian president faced uprisings and coup attempts; several were assassinated in office, others after leaving office, and almost all failed to complete their terms. Nowhere else in Spanish America did so many presidents and former presidents participate personally in assassinations, executions, direct command of barracks revolts, and large-scale insurrections."[133] An anecdote reported by Loveman about President Malgarejo sums up the approach. After enacting the Constitution of 1868, the president is reported to have said that as he put the Constitution of 1861 in his left pocket and the Constitution of 1868 in his right pocket "and that no one but me rules Bolivia."[134] This was probably true until his personal and political excesses led him to be overthrown in 1870 by General Agustín Morales, who sought to overturn many of Malgarejo's unpopular and

[131] Loveman, *The Constitution*, 210, 227–229.
[132] Ibid., 208, 234, 237–239.
[133] Ibid., 235.
[134] Ibid., 252.

ruinous policies. Morales promulgated a new constitution in 1872 that provided for the innovation of public exercise of non–Roman Catholic religions in immigrant settlements to encourage foreign investment and immigration. Morales was not above using the military for political purposes. At one point he closed Congress by having soldiers occupy the chamber when it attempted to limit his budget. He labeled the legislators "corrupt traitors" among other strongly worded criticisms. Morales's renunciation of Malgarejo's decrees concerning international agreements with Chile paved the way to the War of the Pacific from 1879 to 1883. These agreements served as a central political question during the late nineteenth century, with coups and the installation of new presidents leading to rejection or recognition of the agreements made with Chile. Another constitution in 1878 served to legitimate the presidency of Hilarión Daza, who entered war with Chile, and this constitution was to provide Bolivia with a constitutional text until 1938. Seeking peace with Chile, General Nicolás Campero followed Daza and was named president under the Constitution of 1878. In Bolivia, the end of the nineteenth century witnessed liberal and conservative changes in control, with liberals coming into power during the first decades of the twentieth century.[135]

Bolivia's disperse population, large landed estates, and many indigenous communities created particular challenges for instilling functioning constitutional regimes. Although often not formally excluded from political participation under constitutions of this period, Indians and blacks were excluded socially from political life and activities. In fact, Indian tribute was the largest source of national income when General Sucre abolished it in the second half of the 1820s. With a high proportion of indigenous peoples, Bolivia excluded many from participation with literacy and property requirements. It is estimated that in a country of more than one million people, only approximately 20,000 voted in national elections in the 1870s. Thus, it was not until the 1870s that proposals for some sort of federal structure surfaced in Bolivia.[136]

Chile

After its initial independence from 1810 to 1814, Chile was again subject to Spanish control from 1814 to 1817. San Martín's independence army crossed the Andes Mountains and established Bernardo O'Higgins as the first president of the country in 1818. The first independence period never

[135] Ibid., 254–261.
[136] Ibid., 211, 233, 234, 238.

clearly broke with the empire and a set of provisional constitutional rules from 1812 (*El Reglamento Constitutional Provisorio de 1812*) provided for three branches of government with expectations that Fernando VII would accept the Constitution in the same way he was expected to accept the Constitution of Cádiz on his return to the active throne of the empire. As Spain battled to retake the region, several short-lived directorates, dictatorships, and factions under Francisco de la Lastra, José Miguel Carrera, and Bernardo O'Higgins took shape. Lastra operated the government for less than half a year under a new set of rules for a provisional government in 1814 that gave the executive full powers with no provisions for civil liberties or extraordinary powers in the executive because it already had a full grant of powers under the main articles of the document. By the time the royalist General Mariano Osorio was sent to ensure Chilean compliance with the Constitution of Cádiz, Carrera was able to let the general know that the Constitution was no longer in effect. Osorio was victorious in routing the first push for Chilean separatism, and Chile remained under Spanish control until 1817.[137]

After San Martín and O'Higgins entered Santiago, its city council offered O'Higgins the supreme directorship of the province. He proclaimed independence in February, 1818, and prosecuted the war into the 1820s. O'Higgins promulgated constitutions in 1818 and in 1822. The first constitution made O'Higgins the supreme director for six years and provided for a senate of five people to amend the constitution. This document provided for a centralized government for the particular moment of crisis in which the country found itself. Despite O'Higgins's strong liberal leanings; independence spirit; and association with the *Logia Lautarina*, a secret organization that advanced American independence, his Constitution of 1818 provided for Roman Catholicism as the official state religion. It also provided for extensive powers in the supreme director to command the military; to develop all forms of commerce, industry, and agriculture; and to supervise all branches of the state. The Constitution ensured other liberal rights in property, liberty, civil equality, honor, and security, all of which might be set aside in times of danger to the country. O'Higgins was also the impetus behind the Constitution of 1822 that resulted from a conflict he had with the senate, which did not want to relinquish as much power as he requested. A preparatory

---

[137] Ibid., 314–318. For a discussion of the *Reglamento de 1812* see Infante, *Autonomía*, 102–107. For a discussion of historiography of this period see Infante, "La historiografía constitucional."

convention promulgated the Constitution of 1822 that divided powers between the supreme director as the executive; a senate in which various corporate groups were represented such as the church, the military, and the universities; a Chamber of Deputies selected though departmental elections; and a Cortes to undertake legislative activities when Congress was not in session. Notwithstanding this division of power, the powers of the executive still could be quite extensive; the executive held all powers necessary to maintain public order in addition to the control of the administration of the church, state, and military. Political overreaching and unrest led to O'Higgins leaving office in 1823.[138]

In 1823, a national junta replaced O'Higgins and selected his opponent, Ramón Freire, as the new supreme chief of Chile. Freire set about a new constitution. The Constitution of 1823 was a complex conservative document drafted under the influence of the important thinker Juan Egaña.[139] The constitution included a Cámara Nacional that was to function as a censure whose function, among others, was to mediate between the executive and legislative powers.[140] Interestingly, the constitution charged the legislature with drafting a moral code for citizens at each step of their lives to increase civic and moral virtue in the country. The constitution was never put into effect because Freire resigned shortly after its completion and, in turn, the senate granted him extensive executive powers and declared the constitution void. This led to Freire's rule eventually being recognized only in Santiago. Other provinces embarked on their independent rule. Freire eventually called another congress and resigned again in 1826. The next two years were even more politically unstable, with an attempted coup and the senate appointing Freire president again followed, again, by his resignation. Francisco Antonio Pinto became president on Freire's resignation and led efforts toward the Constitution of 1828.[141]

---

[138] Loveman, *The Constitution*, 318–323. See also Collier and Sater, *A History of Chile*, 42–48. For the *Logia Lautarina* see Infante, *Autonomía*, 162–165. For the Constitution of 1818 see Infante, *Autonomía*, 185–196, 203–206. For the Constitution of 1822 see Infante, *Autonomía*, 213–219.

[139] Loveman, *The Constitution*, 324. For the complexity and importance of Juan Egaña's constitutional work and his draft constitution from 1811 see Infante, *Autonomía*, 110–134. For the relationship between Egaña's draft of 1811 and the text of the Constitution of 1823 see Infante, *Autonomía*, 230–249.

[140] Infante, *Autonomía*, 233–234. A similar institution was found in Egaña's draft constitution of 1811. Ibid., 233.

[141] Loveman, *The Constitution*, 322–326. See also Infante, *Autonomía*, 253–256.

The Chilean Constitution of 1828 was a liberal document that sought to maintain order while recognizing the liberal rights of liberty, property, and equality. It maintained Roman Catholicism as the official state religion, but abolished the entailed estates (*mayorazgos*) of the large landholders. It attempted to strengthen the legislative branch and rein in the executive branch and the military to a workable balance. Congress was ceded control of important aspects of the budget, the military, and appointments in the administration including the justices of the Supreme Court.[142] Nonetheless, the liberal Constitution of 1828 was not to govern for very long; in 1830 a civil war ended with a definitive conservative victory and established a conservative government through the mid-1850s.[143]

General José Joaquín Prieto and Diego Portales formally and informally governed the country on the death of President Ovalle in 1831 and for most of the 1830s. Portales's goal of restoring order served as justification for his use of fear and intimidation in political life. The Constitution of 1833 was greatly influenced by the thought of Mariano Egaña, who stressed a centralized authoritarian structure and eschewed popular participation and liberal ideas. Under this constitution, the president had a veto power over legislation. The president also had an effective supervision of elections to promote his ends, and members of the senate were almost always seated through presidential approval. Presidential terms were five years with the possibility of a second five-year term. For nearly the next forty years, as might be expected, all presidents served for both terms. The Constitution contained a number of provisions for extraordinary executive powers.[144] The president had ample power to appoint and remove national and local officials either in consultation with the senate, for example, in the case of judges, or by himself as in the case of the Council of State. These powers reflected the centralist structure of government under the Constitution that created a clear chain of authority from the central machinery of government to local official.[145] As might be expected, the Constitution of 1833 maintained Roman Catholicism as the official religion and prohibited public worship by religions other than Catholicism.[146] Andrés Bello, who participated in the reforms, wrote in

---

[142] Loveman, *The Constitution*, 328. See also Collier and Sater, *A History of Chile*, 49–50.
[143] Collier, *The Making*, 3. See also Infante, *Autonomía*, 278–291.
[144] Loveman, *The Constitution*, 327–333. For electoral control see Collier, *The Making*, 31–37. See also Collier and Sater, *A History of Chile*, 54–60.
[145] Collier, *The Making*, 22–26.
[146] Ibid., 118.

favor of the amendments in 1833 and expressed the opinion that the provisions would govern for a substantial time and be amended according to the Constitution's text.[147]

Despite the Constitution's provisions for executive powers, Portales stated that when the country was threatened it was necessary to violate the Constitution. Portales was assassinated in 1837 after being taken prisoner by rebel Colonel José Antonio Vidaurre. President Prieto held on to extraordinary powers during the war against Peru and Bolivia but in 1839 declared that the powers were no longer in effect. Nonetheless, the range and exercise of martial law was significantly expanded with the General Ordinance of the Army in 1839. The Ordinance defined the military *fuero*, merged military and civilian authority on the provincial level, and expanded the jurisdiction of military tribunals over civilians in particular circumstances. Furthermore, states of siege were declared intermittently over the next few decades when needed by the executive.[148] "Order and progress" was a catchphrase for the political goals of the day and the Constitution of 1833 was credited with advancing these goals.[149]

Prieto's nephew and successor, General Bulnes, served as president from 1841 to 1851, with a brief leave for illness in 1844. Although the period remained firmly within the conservative ambit of the Constitution, liberal political and social organization began to take shape in the latter days of Bulnes's second term. A central aspect of the liberal opposition was to reform the Constitution of 1833, and liberal and conservative positions were expressed in numerous political treatises of the day.[150] Bulnes accepted congressional controls over the budget, took a moderate and conciliatory position in the country, and supported the growth and exercise of the judicial and legislative bodies under the constitution. Although he opened up the participation in government to other branches, he simultaneously crafted a system of oligarchical rule by several important landed, military, and political families. In the late 1840s and 1850s, liberal voices, such as José Victorino Lastarria, and radical voices such as Francisco Bilbao criticized such conservative concentrations of power. Lastarria was a particularly forceful advocate of the possibilities of associations in political life to counter the bad influences of self-interest and

[147] Guzmán Brito, *Vida y Obra*, 107–109; Jaksić, *Selected Writings*, 255–260; Jaksić, *Andres Bello*, 102–103.
[148] Loveman, *The Constitution*, 329, 333–338.
[149] Collier, *The Making*, 124, 127.
[150] Ibid., 62–95, 132–144.

individualism that had in his view captured the country.[151] Slightly later, this important figure entered into an extended debate with Andrés Bello concerning the place of tradition and history in Chilean constitutionalism and political structure. Lastarria criticized colonial structures and institutions and argued for sweeping political reform and the preservation of individual rights. In his view, the colonial legacy had to be routed out.[152] Andrés Bello, on the other hand, took a deeply historical approach and sought to use such studies to inform the country's constitutional and political future.[153]

Bulnes's selected successor, Manuel Montt, who had served as Bulnes's interior minister, was somewhat more conservative than Bulnes and faced growing and significant liberal opposition.[154] Montt served as president from 1851, during which time he faced a civil war from revolutionaries in Concepción in his first year. This necessitated his assumption of extraordinary powers but also consolidated his support so that he was reelected in 1856 and served until 1861.[155] During the end of his first term, tensions between the state and the church were heightened when religious members of the Santiago cathedral appealed the dismissal of a sacristan from the cathedral to the Supreme Court. It became a national incident concerning the place of the church in Chilean society.[156] Montt's presidency provided a certain amount of stability, an opportune moment for legal reform, such as Andrés Bello's famous *Civil Code* (1855), and conditions favorable for foreign investment.[157] Chile's stability as a successful republic in the region prompted calls for it to lead efforts for regional integration and Pan-American union.[158] Nonetheless, liberal opposition sought constitutional reform in second half of the 1850s when, for example, radicals supported the ideal of a new constituent congress.[159] Montt dealt with a second civil war from 1858 to 1859. Calls for constitutional reform continued.[160]

---

[151] Gargarella, *Latin American Constitutionalism*, 8, 15, 61, 339–340. See also Collier, *The Making*, 80–92.

[152] Gargarella, *Latin American Constitutionalism*, 73–74; Jaksić, *Andrés Bello*, 131–139.

[153] Gargarella, *Latin American Constitutionalism*, 75; Jaksić, *Andrés Bello*, 131–139.

[154] Collier, *The Making*, 69, 91–98.

[155] Loveman, *The Constitution*, 340–343. See also Collier, *The Making*, 98–102.

[156] Collier, *The Making*, 199–205; Collier and Sater, *A History of Chile*, 110–111.

[157] Guzmán Brito, *Andrés Bello*; Jaksić, *Andrés Bello*, 156–176; Mirow, "Borrowing Private Law in Latin America," 299–301.

[158] Collier, *The Making*, 147, 172–175. Ideas of international union are also found in Alberdi's thought. See Botana, *La tradición republicana*, 396–397.

[159] Collier, *The Making*, 218–222.

[160] Collier and Sater, *A History of Chile*, 112.

Montt's selected his successor as José Joaquín Pérez, who also served two terms until 1871 without ever invoking extraordinary executive powers, even during a war with Spain in 1866. In 1870, the Constitution was successfully modified to establish a six-year presidency of one term that could not be immediately renewed and, in 1875, the ecclesiastical and military *fueros* were substantially limited.[161] During the War of the Pacific from 1879 to 1884, the executive did not resort to extraordinary powers or states of siege. Nonetheless, President José Manuel Balmaceda had to contend with Congress's attempt to exert its constitutional powers in light of the economic prosperity brought by commercial expansion and nitrate sales. When the senate decided to delay essential budgetary legislation pending the president's appointment of cabinet officials, the president countered that he would simply adopt the previous year's budget. Opposition members in Congress established a revolutionary junta under navy captain Jorge Montt. This action led Balmaceda to assert complete control over the government in light of the navy's challenge to the Constitution, despite the absence of any provision empowering him to do so. Civil war broke out, with Balmaceda losing in August, 1891, and committing suicide later that year. Congress had established its supremacy and the Constitution of 1833 would continue through the end of the century and into the next. Jorge Montt continued as president from 1891 to 1896. He reformed electoral procedures to lessen the influence of the executive branch and to increase the autonomy of local authorities. A new threat in the form of organized workers, labor movements, and unions would come to challenge political stability in Chile in the final decade of the nineteenth century.[162]

Central America

In Central America, despite overall similarities, each country's constitutional history in the nineteenth century is extremely complex and riddled with the promises of new constitutions, the nonconstitutional transfer of power from one government to the next, executive despotism under the guise of a constitution and its provisions for emergency powers, and little constitutional entrenchment in the period. Here, it is possible only to highlight some of the distinctive features from the countries of the region. From 1823 to 1838, Central America established a federal structure under the Federal Constitution of Central America of 1824. Individual members

---

[161] Loveman, *The Constitution*, 344–346. See also Collier, *The Making*, 238–252; Collier and Sater, *A History of Chile*, 121–122.
[162] Loveman, *The Constitution*, 347–350.

of the Central American Federation promulgated their own constitutions. Notably, the Costa Rican Constitution of 1825 created a conservatory authority similar to the supreme conservatory power later found in the Mexican Constitution of 1836.[163] The Costa Rican Constitution of 1824 also gave the president power "to act as he deems most convenient to save" the state when it was threatened with a risk, a broad power for executive discretion, and invitation for presidential autocracy.[164]

Liberal and conservative rivalries in the 1830s led to the dissolution of the Federation. Guatemala, for example, entered a period of liberal reforms in this decade that included many of the central cores of liberalism and an attempted borrowing of the codes drafted by Livingston in Louisiana. When jails were needed under new criminal law, Governor Manuel Gálvez turned to forced Indian labor. He ruled through the military and through regimes of exception available under the constitution. The Guatemalan Constitution of 1851 marked a conservative victory and was amended in 1855 to give Rafael Carrera the presidency for life, a constitutional structure that continued after his death until a switch to liberalism under the Constitution of 1879. In contrast, Honduras had eighty-five presidents or interim presidents between 1821 and 1876 and six different constitutions during the nineteenth century. It was the location of particularly brutal civil wars during the period.[165] William Walker's North American intervention in Nicaragua in 1856 and 1857, and his association with liberalism, "ensured Conservative control of every Central American republic for at least a decade and a half after 1856" in response to his intervention.[166]

Within the independent states of Central America, similar back and forth movements between conservative and liberal powers in Central America led to constitutions reflecting these choices during the second half of the nineteenth century. El Salvador had a series of constitutions after 1845 that reflected the ongoing civil wars between conservative and liberals. New constitutions appeared in 1864, 1871, 1872, 1880, 1883, 1885, and 1886.[167] As an example of liberalism in El Salvador,

---

[163] Ibid., 91–136. Manuel Vidaurre in Peru also advanced the ideas of a Supreme Conservative power in the late 1820s and early 1830s. See Gargarella, *Latin American Constitutionalism*, 214, n. 41.

[164] Loveman, *The Constitution*, 98.

[165] Bushnell and Macaulay, *The Emergence*, 281; Loveman, *The Constitution*, 102–106, 116.

[166] Bushnell and Macaulay, *The Emergence*, 275.

[167] Loveman, *The Constitution*, 112–113.

amendments to its Constitution of 1886 established freedom of religion, the separation of church and state, the secularization of cemeteries, and civil marriage, divorce, and property registers. Honduras witnessed similar liberal successes in the 1870s through the 1890s, and Nicaragua in the 1890s.[168] Nonetheless, these successes in constitutional text were often shrouded in daily governmental practices that withheld democratic processes and constitutional guarantees. Writing of the period after 1858 about Nicaragua, Loveman summarizes the state of affairs this way: "Presidential dominance, suspension of selected *garantías* in times of internal tumult, presidential authority to arrest, incarcerate, or exile suspects when internal order was subverted, and the de facto dominance of military authorities would reign in Nicaragua for the remainder of the nineteenth century."[169]

From the 1840s to the 1860s, Costa Rica had more than five different constitutions or similar texts, until the Constitution of 1879 that managed to govern the country for over fifty years. These short-lived texts were often the result of violent political changes and the governments du jour.[170] The Costa Rican Constitutions of the 1840s contained some unusual social provisions related to the loss of rights. For example, the Constitution of 1848 removes rights for "ingratitude to parents," "abandoning one's woman or children," and "failing to meet family obligations."[171] Panama too had a rapid succession of constitutions as it moved in and out of the Colombian federation in the 1850s to the 1880s, with constitutions in 1853, 1855, 1859, 1863, 1865, 1868, 1870, 1873, 1875, and 1886. Its permanent "independent" status was constitutionalized in the Constitution of 1904, itself copied from the Constitution of 1886 and the product of significant diplomatic and political pressure from the United States in the process of establishing the canal.[172]

Mexico

Considering the importance of the Mexican Constitution of 1917 in the development of Latin American constitutionalism, a fuller description of Mexican developments in the nineteenth century is warranted. Mexico and Central America too reflected general shifts in the region during the nineteenth century from initial liberalism to a conservative

---

[168] De la Torre and García, *Desarrollo histórico*, 191–198.
[169] Loveman, *The Constitution*, 125.
[170] De la Torre and García, *Desarrollo histórico*, 204–209.
[171] Loveman, *The Constitution*, 129.
[172] De la Torre and García, *Desarrollo histórico*, 210–214.

reaction, followed by a firmer liberal entrenchment that set the stage for the social and political transformation of social constitutionalism at the first part of the twentieth century. After early independence constitutions embraced the economic liberalism and social change implicit in French doctrine and the Constitution of Cádiz, Mexico experienced a conservative reaction in its constitutions during the first part of the nineteenth century. This was followed by a period of firmly established liberalism in the later part of the century.[173] Mexico's turbulent constitutional history leading to the Constitution of 1824 was discussed in the previous chapter. The Constitution of 1824 provided a federal structure for the states of Mexico that had moved toward independence. Its provisions were generally liberal, such as providing for free speech and limited powers in the president, who was elected indirectly by the states. Nonetheless, the Constitution maintained a privileged position for the church and the military and gave the president control over the military.[174]

After Mexico's liberal and federal Constitution of 1824, which governed until 1835, the country experienced instability and a quick succession of republics each guided by one or more constitutional documents. A Spanish expedition in Veracruz in 1829 led to a call for and granting of extraordinary powers to deal with the foreign threat, but this was one of many exceptional circumstances. And perhaps expectedly, President Guerrero used extraordinary powers far beyond their expected reach. His decrees were used to confiscate property, pay the military, grant pardons, control the press, and abolish slavery, among many other actions. Such overreaching was not without a reaction, and Vice President Bustamante, Santa Anna, and Melchor Múzquiz ousted President Guerrero at the end of 1829, and the new government with Bustamante as chief executive executed Guerrero in 1831. Bustamante's rule has been described as not having any concern whatsoever for the constitution and as not seeing the need for any sort of constitutional justifications for its actions. His actions were defended by Lucas Alamán in his *Examen imparcial de la administración del General Bustamante.*[175]

Often discussed in contrast to Alamán, during the 1830s, José María Luis Mora continued as an important voice of Mexican liberalism. He took aim at corporatist powers of the church as reflected in clerical privileges and the ecclesiastical *fuero*, although he did not align himself

[173] Ibid., 145–223.
[174] Loveman, *The Constitution*, 75–76.
[175] Aguilar Rivera, *El manto*, 126, 149–153, 160–161.

with the official toleration of all religions. Charles Hale sees the seeds of nineteenth-century anticlericalism in an essay written by Mora in 1831 on church property in which he advocated state control over entailed property, a key asset of the church. Expressing concern about the military *fuero*, Mora, however, thought that such unstable times required its continuation. Even after his departure to France in 1834 and after a substantial hiatus from an ability to shape Mexican political change, Mora was called on by liberal governments from 1847 to 1849 as an adviser on reform and source of intellectual guidance. He died in Paris in 1850.[176]

As Brian Loveman tallies, "Between the years 1833 to 1855, the presidency of Mexico changed hands thirty-six times, with Santa Anna its occupant on eleven different occasions."[177] Similarly, between 1824 and 1857, Aguilar Rivera counts sixteen presidents and thirty-three provisional presidents and a total of forty-nine different governments.[178] Such instability and change do not permit detailed discussion of all constitutional shifts and political developments within the period. The country was a centralized republic from 1835 to 1846, returned to a federal republic from 1846 to 1853, and again centralized without a governing constitution from 1853 to 1855. In a country and period lacking infrastructure, communications, and transportation, it was not surprising that regional rule expressed through federalism would be an attractive option. These changes were not the result of peaceful democratic processes.

For example, acting against the Constitution of 1824, Antonio López de Santa Anna dissolved Congress and convened another to his liking to promulgate the centralist *Siete Leyes*, or the Constitution of 1836.[179] This document provided for a declaration of rights, a bicameral legislature, a personal executive with an eight-year term and reelection, and new provisions regarding the judiciary and its functioning.[180] It did not contain emergency powers, a lack felt strongly when Mexico attempted to repel French forces in 1838.[181] It maintained Roman Catholicism as the official state religion.

The constitution also provided for an unusual institution, the supreme conservatory power, a body of five people that could void legislation as unconstitutional, overrule executive and Supreme Court decisions,

---

[176] Hale, *Mexican Liberalism*, 105–149, 178–179, 290–292.
[177] Loveman, *The Constitution*, 75.
[178] Aguilar Rivera, *El manto*, 167.
[179] De la Torre and García, *Desarrollo histórico*, 149–151, 154.
[180] Gargarella, *Latin American Constitutionalism*, 214, n. 43.
[181] Aguilar Rivera, *El manto*, 173–174.

suspend Congress for a limited time, review constitutional reforms, and enforce compliance with its orders.[182] This institution was introduced by Lucas Alamán and Manuel Sánchez de Tagle.[183] Its genesis was the work of contemporary constitutional theorists such as Benjamin Constant, who developed the idea of a power to moderate the other three. As it took practical effect in Mexico, this "moderating power" was transformed into another source of executive power under Santa Anna.[184] This somewhat odd fourth power was dropped in 1843, when another constitutional document, the *Bases Orgánicas* under Santa Anna, returned to a three-part traditional structure of legislative, executive, and judicial branches.[185] Political changes occurred in 1841 and again in 1845, when General Mariano Paredes Arrillaga rose against the sitting president and called for a constituent congress in 1846.[186] Mexico and the United States entered into war in 1846 and in the following years the Caste Wars, indigenous uprisings in the Yucatán and Huasteca regions, challenged the country.[187] Returning from Cuban exile in 1846, Santa Anna led the country against the United States and successfully called for a return to the Constitution of 1824.[188] From 1846 to 1848, Mexico was at war with the United States with concomitant calls for emergency powers to prosecute the war.[189]

The military defeat led to the rise of a conservative party under Lucas Alamán, whose intellectual and political positions influenced Mexico until his death in 1853. He embraced Spanish heritage, institutions, and the church and rejected liberalism and foreign influences.[190] Aguilar Rivera has noted the development of Alamán's thought from more liberal positions in the 1820s and 1830s to his characterization as the "father of Mexican conservatism" in subsequent decades.[191] He even sought

---

[182] Loveman, *The Constitution*, 78.

[183] Barrón, "La tradición republicana," 278–280.

[184] Aguilar Rivera, *La geometría*, 36; Augilar Rivera, *El manto*, 125–126, 170–172; Gargarella, *Latin American Constitutionalism*, 17–19.

[185] Aguilar Rivera, *El manto*, 184–191; Loveman, *The Constitution*, 79–80.

[186] De la Torre and García, *Desarrollo histórico*, 155, 157. For an analysis and description of the composition of the congress and its complicated mix of deputies from agriculture, commerce, mining, manufacutring, the army, and the clergy, among other groups, see Aguilar Rivera, "El verdicto," 161–162.

[187] Hale, *Mexican Liberalism*, 11.

[188] Aguilar Rivera, *El manto*, 169, 191; Loveman, *The Constitution*, 81.

[189] Aguilar Rivera, *El manto*, 188–194.

[190] Hale, *Mexican Liberalism*, 15–22.

[191] Aguilar Rivera, *La geometría*, 28, 31–35.

to rekindle Bolivarian dreams of a united Hispanic-American effort to counterbalance North American aggressions.[192]

The Constitutive Act or Constitution of 1851 laid the groundwork for war and the liberal reforms that were to follow. The Act was centralist and conservative, recognizing the validity of large landed estates, of taxes paid to the church, and of the consolidation of powers in the president as supreme chief. In 1854, the archbishop declared that the position of president was perpetual with the right to appoint a successor. On his death, the president was followed by loyal military leaders.[193] These ideological conflicts led to civil war from 1854 to 1867.[194] In the words of Aguilar Rivera, three important events punctuated this period: "the dictatorship of Santa Anna, supported by the conservative party, the anticlerical reform and the Constitution of 1857, and the French intervention that brought an Austrian prince to the Mexican throne."[195]

Santa Anna returned to the presidency in 1853, but in 1854, the *Plan de Ayutla* rejected his leadership and aimed at establishing a popular representative republic.[196] Santa Anna left the presidency in 1855 and new liberal leaders such as Ignacio Comonfort, Melchor Ocampo, Miguel Lerdo de Tejada, and Benito Juárez rose in political stature.[197] While Ignacio Comonfort served as president, radicals in Congress pressed for liberal and radical reforms. Acts passed limited the special legal status of the church and the role of military in civil matters, confiscated property from civil and religious corporations, settled parochial taxes, and suspended forced contributions to the poor.[198]

President Comonfort, who served until 1857, called for a constitutional convention that was composed of mostly moderate liberals and promulgated an *Estatuto Orgánico Provisional* to serve while the new constitution was being drafted.[199] Some conservatives called for the return of the Constitution of 1824, but this proposal lost by a close vote. The convention chose another direction and presented its draft in 1856.[200] Conservatives were excluded from the constituent congress and the commission to draft the constitution was composed of radical liberals

[192] Hale, *Mexican Liberalism*, 31.
[193] De la Torre and García, *Desarrollo histórico*, 160–161.
[194] Hale, *Mexican Liberalism*, 38.
[195] Aguilar Rivera, *La geometría*, 49.
[196] Aguilar Rivera, *El manto*, 196; De la Torre and García, *Desarrollo histórico*, 178.
[197] Aguilar Rivera, *El manto*, 196; Loveman, *The Constitution*, 81–82.
[198] De la Torre and García, *Desarrollo histórico*, 178, 179.
[199] Aguilar Rivera, *El manto*, 197.
[200] Gargarella, *Latin American Constitutionalism*, 42.

and moderates who still argued over issues such as presidential and emergency powers, the nature of the legislature, the place of the church, and the death penalty.[201]

The liberalism of the Constitution of 1857 was accompanied by important piecemeal legislation advancing liberal positions. In the late 1850s and early 1860s, Benito Juárez put forth a series of reform laws that nationalized ecclesiastical property, established civil marriage, created a civil register, secularized cemeteries, suspended religious holidays, provided for freedom of religious belief, secularized hospitals and other charities, and extinguished religious communities.[202] Many of the liberal reforms of the mid-1850s, the *Ley Juárez* concerning ecclesiastical and military *fueros*, and the *Ley Lerdo* effecting the forced transfer of church property, were solidified and restated in Mexico's Constitution of 1857. The introduction of the jury trial was debated but was narrowly defeated by its opponents, who included the famous jurist and Mexican expert on Anglo-American law, Ignacio Luis Vallarta. Vallarta also served to check more radical proposals for the reorganization of property and agrarian reform by arguing for economic liberalism and the nonintervention of the state in such matters. Questions of poverty and the poor condition of agricultural labors were also raised, but eventually not practically addressed in the final text.[203] As may be expected, Roman Catholicism was not established as the official state religion and the pope denounced the constitution. Adherents to the constitution were expelled from the church.[204]

The Constitution of 1857 contained a bill of rights and increased the power of the federal government in relationship to the states. It also established a broadly worded article that gave the president, with forms of congressional consultation, the ability to declare a regime of exception.[205] The Constitution of 1857 was also the first Mexican constitution to include broad emergency powers and these were evoked during the Reform War from 1858 to 1861 and frequently during its subsequent application.[206] Despite its assertions of popular sovereignty, the constitution gave the vote only to the approximately 15 percent of the population who were literate, and élite control of the electoral process in

---

[201] Aguilar Rivera, *El manto*, 204–230.
[202] De la Torre and García, *Desarrollo histórico*, 182.
[203] Gargarella, *Latin American Constitutionalism*, 42, 43, 45.
[204] Safford, "Politics," 400–401.
[205] Loveman, *The Constitution*, 82–83.
[206] Aguilar Rivera, *El manto*, 201, 203, 231–250, 260–267.

the following decades has led some to conclude that elections were little more than a show of democratic ritual.[207] Many were discontent with the final document because it had gone too far; fewer thought it did not go far enough. Detractors included President Comonfort himself, who led a military coup against it and closed Congress. These actions led to his stepping down shortly after the coup.[208]

This Constitution was in effect during Benito Juárez's presidency in the 1860s. When Juárez did not honor foreign debt in the midst of economic difficulties, the path was paved toward European intervention in 1861.[209] Furthermore, Juárez had lost the support of more conservative elements in Mexican society and such a broad sweep in one direction prompted the conservative and imperial response that placed Maximilian as emperor of Mexico.[210] The intervention was short lived partly because of Maximilian's unwillingness to yield his somewhat more liberal positions to Mexican conservatives, and he was executed by firing squad in 1867.[211] Benito Juárez returned to the presidency, and the Constitution of 1857 continued in effect during the presidency of Sebastián Lerdo de Tejada in 1872 after the death of Juárez.[212] The following ten years were a period of liberal rule.[213]

Lerdo de Tejada was ousted by Porfirio Díaz in 1876.[214] Despite early concerns about Díaz's seizing power, the positivists supported the shift and his new policies.[215] Díaz was in direct or indirect control of Mexico from 1876 to 1911, a period known as the Porfiriato. It was a time of technological and economic expansion and of Mexico's openness to foreign ideas, including those from the United States, and to foreign investment. Nonetheless, increases in wealth and prosperity did not reach far enough into Mexican society and the result was the political and constitutional revolution in Mexico discussed in the next chapter.[216]

Liberalism continued as the predominant political philosophy in the wake of Juárez's victory, and during the late nineteenth century, Mexico was shaped by various manifestations of liberalism and positivism,

---

[207] Ponce Alcocer, "Las elecciones," 303–307.
[208] Gargarella, *Latin American Constitutionalism*, 43.
[209] Aguilar Rivera, *El manto*, 232; Loveman, *The Constitution*, 84–85.
[210] De la Torre and García, *Desarrollo histórico*, 183.
[211] Aguilar Rivera, *El manto*, 233.
[212] Ibid., 202; Loveman, *The Constitution*, 85–87.
[213] Aguilar Rivera, *El manto*, 233–234, 250–260.
[214] Ibid., 233; Loveman, *The Constitution*, 87.
[215] Hale, *The Transformation*, 55–63.
[216] Mirow, "*Marbury* in Mexico," 66.

serving as underlying political approaches of Porfirio Díaz. Liberalism, as transformed though its political interaction with positivism, was linked to constitutionalism, the secular state, and private property.[217] Hale notes the important speech in 1867 of Gabino Barreda, charged by Juárez to reform education, as emphasizing a new scientific approach to government and calling for the positivist principles of law, order, and progress.[218]

Positivism and the notion of "scientific politics" took off in the last quarter of the nineteenth century and shaped political viewpoints espoused by *"científicos,"* in 1890s who by then sought constitutional constraints on executive power and an independent judiciary. Informed by the political and social writings of Auguste Comte and Herbert Spenser, adherents of this approach called for constitutional revision to bring the Constitution of 1857 into line with the society and goals of the day. Indeed, along with attacking liberalism and generally advancing strong governmental authority, scientific politics sought constitutional reform, and positivists set out these claims through *La Libertad*, a newspaper published from 1878 to 1884 and led by Justo Sierra, Francisco G. Cosmes, and Telesforo García. This publication served as a mouthpiece for positivist proposals for constitutional reform. In their view, the Constitution of 1857 overly reacted to the Santa Anna dictatorship and created absolute protections and rights that were inconsistent with the needs of society. Themes included constitutional enforceability, stronger executive powers, the strengthening of administrative powers and functions in government, and limiting the franchise through literacy and professional requirements. There were also proposed reforms related to the judiciary. These were disentangling the office of vice president from the position of chief justice of the Supreme Court and the creation of life tenure for judges. Public education and its constitutional status were important parts of this scientific approach, one that echoed the relationship of constitutional provisions for public education with political engagement going back to the Constitution of Cádiz.[219]

The relationship between positivist positions and constitutional reform continued throughout the period, with the late 1870s and early 1890s as particularly active years for constitutional debate and speculation. As part of these debates and modifications in political structure, a

---

[217] Hale, *The Transformation*, ix, 3–4. The Mexican historiography of this period has expectedly been charged with various contemporary political positions and the associated creation of national history and myths to live by. See Ibid., 14–20.

[218] Ibid., 5–6, 245.

[219] Ibid., 11, 20–22, 25–63, 123–204.

new senate was convened in 1875.[220] A central issue in the early 1890s was the independence of the judiciary and the irremovability of judges.[221] As Hale has demonstrated, positivists and the *científicos* embraced constitutional change and were not blind supporters of Porfirian authority.[222] Concerning their suggested reforms in 1878, Hale writes, "A lengthened presidential term, a suspensive veto, restricted suffrage, the retention of a senate, a separate vice presidency, and life tenure for judges – these changes would make the constitution conform to social reality and would avoid the need to suspend it at moments of crisis."[223] In a few decades, Mexico would introduce the most profound constitutional changes in Spanish America since independence and the Constitution of Cádiz.

New Trends in Constitutionalism

This survey of some of the major constitutional developments in a few of the region's countries illustrates that constitutions were employed to political ends during the nineteenth century. Constitutions were used to legitimate new regimes regardless of the constitutionality of the regimes' rise to power and control. Constitutions were subject to strong rulers who either exercised the broad powers given them through their constitutions or sometimes ran things as they pleased without constitutional backing. Constitutions, however, were important. Presidents appealed to them and signaled new political arrangements through their promulgation. Differing camps of political ideology also formed more clearly in this century, and the terms such as "liberal" and "conservative" took on more clearly defined sets of viewpoints. Following ideological cohesion, political parties also grew in importance and definition. Constitutions also continued to grapple with the construction of the constitutional states, the role of the executive, the place of the military and church, and the recognition of rights.

Despite appeals to history, a number of dominant political theories competed for priority in the political construction of post-independence states of Latin America. Gargarella has argued for a tripartite division of political loyalties that played against each other to shape nineteenth-century constitutionalism in the region. These are radicalism, conservatism, and liberalism. Central features of radicalism included the

---

[220] Ibid., 83, 64–101.
[221] Ibid., 108–121.
[222] Ibid., 246.
[223] Ibid., 246.

political equality of individuals, land reform, strict separation of powers, unicameralism in the legislature, and a limited judiciary.[224] Although ideologically influential, its presence here serves particularly as a foil to conservatism and liberalism, "The history of radical constitutionalism in America is the history of failure."[225]

Radicalism, or Republicanism, placed a high value on self-government and majoritarian political control encompassed a broad franchise. Majoritarian rule was a higher goal than the maintenance of individual autonomy. This political theory of the general will and moral populism was consistent with new republics' turn from colonial rule with monarchical structures, closely held power in a ruling élite, and a powerful church. Relying on politically active citizens with shared values, this view supported universal suffrage and egalitarianism, including at times the redistribution of land toward these ends. Egalitarianism in political voice and in the enjoyment of property were even, but rarely, extended by constitutional theorists of the nineteenth century to include indigenous populations. There were, however, exceptions, and Gargarella notes that this was the case of the Peruvian radical José Carlos Mariátegui.[226]

Conservatism highlighted elitism, as might be reflected in a strong senate; moral perfection, especially through a privileged position of the church; a strong executive and military that might benefit from states of siege or exception; and private property. Conservatives sought to build constitutions around a unified, often Roman Catholic, notion of the good as expressed by an élite with an active political voice. Although not a requirement of conservative constitutions, some constitutions, as suggested in the writings of Bolívar, sought the creation of a "moral power" as a fourth power as a source of civil virtue, education, and national improvement.[227] And some early independence constitutions were grounded in the thought of the Catholic Enlightenment and its hopes of remodeling society and encouraging civil virtue. The Constitution of the United Provinces of 1819, the *Constitución Moralista* of Chile of 1823, and the Peruvian Constitution of 1823 have been read in this light. Such hopes were often short lived and often led to dictatorial regimes.[228]

Conservatism, however, was second to liberalism in having the greatest influence in constitutionalism. Liberalism sought to carve a middle

[224] Gargarella, *The Legal Foundations*, 9–89.
[225] Ibid., 49.
[226] Gargarella, *Latin American Constitutionalism*, 6, 7–11, 54.
[227] Ibid., 6, 11–14, 90–152.
[228] Corfield, "Constitucionalismo ilustrado," 79–83.

way between the extremes of conservatism and radicalism, of anarchy and tyranny, and yet it provided dramatic changes from the constitutional perspective of the pre-independence sources. Liberalism's chief attributes were the autonomy of each person that led to the abolition of privileges for certain groups in society such as the military and the church. Similarly, communal landholding by indigenous peoples and slavery were to be abolished with this justification. Liberalism also sought to have legislatures do as little as possible and therefore sought to limit the strength of popular organs and set suffrage requirements of property or social standing, producing, in Gargarella's terms, a *sovereignty of reason* rather than of people.[229]

Liberalism was equally skeptical of the executive and sought to curb the executive's claims to extraordinary powers. In relationship to a system of governmental checks and balances, liberals supported notions of judicial review despite its countermajoritarian attributes. Rights, and particularly the absolute right to property, were central to the idea of liberalism, and the right to property coupled with a preference for minimal legislative activity led to the nonintervention of the state in economic activities.[230] The Constitution of Cádiz was probably the most influential text in the development of liberalism in Latin America.[231]

Property ownership was seen as a defining factor for suffrage within each of these political ideologies. Gargarella has cited the example of the Mexican liberal José María Mora, who equated citizenship with property ownership because the poor and disadvantaged were subject to the economic, and thus political, influence of the wealthy; poor people lacked the necessary political independence to engage actively the state. Similarly, Gargarella has noted Lucas Alamán's connection of property with effective democracy. Liberal and conservatism's paternalism of the poor led to the following solutions: indirect elections, property qualifications for voting, and literacy and other property requirements for political participation. This meant that those who were elected were the "best" and "noted people" who had already been screened through an electorate limited by restrictions of age, property, gender, capacity, education, income, and the like.[232]

---

[229] Gargarella, *The Legal Foundations*, 153–214, 170 (for sovereignty of reason); Gargarella, *Latin American Constitutionalism*, 6. See also Aguilar Rivera, *La geometría*, 19–23.

[230] Gargarella, *The Legal Foundations*, 153–214; Gargarella, *Latin American Constitutionalism*, 14–17.

[231] Gargarella, *Latin American Constitutionalism*, 17.

[232] Ibid., 47–49, 227, n. 26.

General divisions between liberals or conservatives developed into political parties in the national context. The rise of political parties as a central actor in political direction has been noted by scholars. For example, concerning the presidency in Chile in the nineteenth century, Velasco Ibarra writes, "until 1860, it governed over the parties. From 1860 to 1890, it governed with the parties. From 1890 to 1920, the authority of the president disappeared and the parties governed by themselves."[233] Collier and Sater's extensive and complicated charts of Chilean political parties illustrate this well.[234]

Thus, the radical, liberal, and conservative perspectives existing in the independence period quickly formed into political parties on the national level.[235] At times, these parties took on these very names. If the period from 1810 to 1850 was one of developing the centrality of congress in the constitutional state, then, according to Bravo Lira, the period from 1850 to 1920 witnessed the development of political parties during which about sixty constitutions were promulgated. Nonetheless, much of the workings of political parties within constitutional systems were extraconstitutional, meaning that the constitutions themselves did little to address the new aggregation of power exercised by political parties as they controlled congresses in countries of the region. Parties did not guarantee broad political representation but were often used to consolidate oligarchical power through the party.[236]

For the same period, from approximately 1850 to 1900, Gargarella has noted an important confluence of interests between liberals and conservatives that effectively marginalized the radical voice. Because both liberals and conservatives based political control within the élite, agreements leading to shared power or at least alternating power were possible in the face of the more drastic demands and programs of radicalism. Liberals and conservatives could agree that the franchise should not be opened up and that land and other property should not be redistributed. These agreements might take priority over disputes concerning the extent of individual rights, a central aspect of liberalism and not a core principle of conservatism, and even the place of the church in society. Points of agreement are noteworthy. These different perspectives could agree on a right to property and the resultant exclusion of nascent ideas of social and economic rights within the constitutional sphere and a limited scope

---

[233] Velasco Ibarra, *Expresión política*, 51.
[234] Collier and Sater, *A History of Chile*, 121, 193, 257.
[235] Velasco Ibarra, *Expresión política*, 147.
[236] Bravo Lira, *El estado constitucional*, 24–25.

of political rights. Gargarella noted that thinkers as polarized as the conservative Andrés Bello and the liberal Juan Bautista Alberdi agreed that political power in the popular majority was a bad idea. Constitutions resulting from this "fusion," as Gargarella calls it in this period, provided for greater religious toleration but often maintained a privileged position for Roman Catholicism; checks and balances but with a thumb on the scale for the executive; a centralist system with some nods to federal or local power; little representation of the disadvantaged; few methods for mass political participation; and little recognition of social or economic rights. Gargarella finds many examples throughout the second half of the nineteenth century: Argentina's Constitution of 1853, Mexico's of 1857, Peru's of 1860, and Paraguay's of 1870.[237]

Constitutions and the Constitutional State

Constitutions served various functions during this period. First and foremost, constitutions served as guiding documents for political structures, representative governments, and the protection of various civil rights. Constitutions were often used to legitimize autocratic and dictatorial regimes that wanted to cloak themselves in the legitimacy of having or of promulgating a constitution. Constitutions also permitted countries to extend their economic and political activities on the international stage because they needed the formal documentation to delineate their domestic constitutional laws of foreign relations. This was particularly important in the context of establishing treaties and binding countries on the international level.[238]

Although constitutions often played an important function in legitimizing political change, they could also be used as springboards for political reform. For example, Gargarella has noted the way the Venezuelan Constitution of 1811 was used by Bolívar as a scapegoat for political difficulties in the post-independence period. Gargarella also gives the examples of the conservative Mexican Lucas Alamán's criticisms of the liberal Mexican Constitution of 1824 and of the liberal José Victorino Lastarria's objections to the conservative Chilean Constitution of 1833.[239] Thus, constitutions played roles at both ends of political change, as the legitimizing force for a new regime and as the object of criticism that could be blamed for problems necessitating change.

[237] Gargarella, *Latin American Constitutionalism*, 20–34.
[238] Loveman, *The Constitution*, 253.
[239] Gargarella, *Latin American Constitutionalism*, 69–70.

Constitutions have then responded to and been subject to the political power of the moment. An additional question is the ability of constitutions to create new constitutional states. Bravo Lira sought to study the question of when Latin American constitutions effected a functioning constitutional state. His research indicates that the approximately 200 democratic constitutions promulgated over the last 200 years in the countries of the region rarely accomplished their stated goal of establishing constitutional states.[240]

Bravo Lira, as others studying Latin American constitutionalism, first noted that most of the constitutions were short lived. In his estimation, there were only a dozen or so that governed for any significant length of time. Of these, nine came from the second half of the nineteenth century and only one from the twentieth century. Uruguay's Constitution of 1830 was in effect until 1917. Chile's Constitution of 1833 was in effect until 1924. The Mexican Constitution of 1857 was in effect until 1917; and the Peruvian Constitution of 1860 was in effect until 1920. Bolivia, Colombia, Guatemala, El Salvador, and Paraguay also had constitutions that lasted more than fifty years. The Argentine Constitution of 1853 and the Mexican Constitution of 1917 still govern in their revised forms.[241]

Nonetheless, Bravo Lira pointed out that there is a big difference between having a constitution that is nominally the governing instrument of the nation's political structure and having one that is truly functioning as intended. His test then became the existence of a functioning congress under the constitution; and here the most important factor was not the duration of the document nominally serving as constitution but its penetration into the political life of the country as measured by congressional participation and consistency.[242]

By the measure of congressional activity, Bravo Lira concluded that the Chilean Constitution of 1833 served as a basis for an effective constitutional regime because the Chilean Congress meet consistently for ninety-one years under it, until 1924. Similarly, the Argentine Constitution of 1853–1860 had eighty-six regular annual sessions of Congress under its rule. These were exceptional instances in the history of Latin American constitutionalism. Uruguay, under its Constitution of 1830, by 1903 had

[240] Bravo Lira, *El estado constitucional*, 6–12.
[241] Ibid., 12–14. The amendment to the Argentine constitution in 1994 is often referred to as the Argentine Constitution of 1994. Oquendo, *Latin American Law*, 151–157.
[242] Bravo Lira, *El estado constitucional*, 13–17.

twenty-five different governments, mostly disconnected from the text of the Constitution, with two presidential assassinations, nine successful coups d'état, and ten unsuccessful ones. The experiences of Bolivia, El Salvador, Paraguay, and Guatemala with their long-lasting constitutions were similar. The experience of Colombia was somewhere in between, with five significant interruptions by 1991 in congressional activity under the Constitution of 1886.[243] Although not a perfect proxy for effective constitutional rule, the idea of a functioning congress under a constitution brings the study of Latin American constitutionalism one step closer to the facts of constitutionalism and one needed step away from merely an examination of constitutional texts.

Related to the functioning of constitutional states are the questions of regimes of exception and the place of the military in politics and government. These were other important attributes of nineteenth-century Latin American constitutionalism. Whereas many have viewed the invocation of a regime of exception as an unbridled bid for tyrannical autocratic rule, Chiaramonte has successfully placed these commonplace occurrences of Latin American constitutionalism into a more coherent intellectual framework. When viewed from the perspective of the social consensus of the *ius commune* tradition and internalized ideas of natural law, such suspensions of constitutional rights, normal governmental functions, and divisions of governmental exercises of power gravitate toward theoretical consistency. Using Roman history and Roman law as a basis of the argument, early republic constitutionalists successfully asserted that individual security and nascent constitutional rights were to be suspended in times of great threats to the security of the state. As in ancient Rome, dictatorship was a necessity, despite its costs, and the social consensus might even give consent to such an arrangement.[244] This tradition was folded into the Spanish law through the *derecho indiano*.

Although the Constitution of Cádiz contains a suspension of provisions on search and seizure when required by order and state security, it is the Cortes, rather than the king, that was empowered to take exceptional action.[245] Under Napoleon's Constitution of Bayona, the senate had the power to suspend the protection of individual liberties.[246] This does not

---

[243] Ibid., 17–20.

[244] Chiaramonte, "The 'Ancient Constitution,'" 481–485; see also Rosenkrantz, "Constitutional emergencies."

[245] Constitution of Cádiz, Art. 356; Loveman, *The Constitution*, 20, 43; Mirow, *Florida's First Constitution*, 58.

[246] Martiré, "Algo más," 93.

mean that the military could not take action to maintain order, and in fact, the Constitution of Cádiz charges the military not only with the external defense of the empire but also with the conservation of internal order. This second prong, maintaining internal order, became a central and self-initiated function of the military in the century after the Constitution of Cádiz. Furthermore, in the battles between constitutional and absolutist royal regimes in the period from 1812 to 1823, the Spanish military, and by extension the military serving in the Americas and militias, took on greater political affinities and aspirations.[247]

Brian Loveman has extensively studied the origin and impact of regimes of exception in Latin American constitutionalism and asserts that such regimes constitute the "juridical foundations for constitutional dictatorship."[248] Just as Bravo Lira has noted that effective constitutional regimes when congresses functioned regularly were infrequent, Loveman takes a close look at the other side of the coin. Regimes of exception and the exercise of extraordinary power became "a habit" in the nineteenth century and have become frequently a part of today's constitutional structures in the region. Loveman identifies five kinds of actions that may be implicated in a constitutional regime of exception: (1) the suspension of civil liberties, for example, the freedom of assembly for a limited time or permanently during the state of exception in all or part of the country; (2) a declaration of the particular state or situation required by the constitution or other constitutional law; (3) suspension of the constitution with dictatorial powers exercised by one branch of the government, usually the executive or military; (4) the granting of extraordinary powers for a stated time or indefinitely during the state; and (5) the imposition of military law. From the north to the south, such regimes of exception were a common element in mid-nineteenth century Spanish American constitutions.[249]

Aguilar Rivera offers another perspective on provisions for regimes of exceptions within nineteenth-century constitutions. Liberalism, as reflected in constitutions of the period, "was deficient because it did not provide governments with legitimate means to face emergencies."[250] The rejection of emergency powers in constitutions of the period followed the work of various European liberal writers, particularly Benjamin Constant. This led to governments necessarily abandoning constitutions and acting

---

[247] Loveman, *The Constitution*, 43, 46, 50–51.
[248] Ibid., 56.
[249] Ibid., 6, 18, 64.
[250] Aguilar Rivera, *El manto*, 7.

extraconstitutionally because liberal constitutions did not include emergency powers or actions that would permit a constitutional government to battle through difficult challenges. The later inclusion of emergency powers, for example, in the liberal Mexican Constitution of 1857, marked an important change to bolster, not to undermine, constitutional rule. Lack of emergency powers in constitutions, in Aguilar Rivera's view, eroded the prestige of constitutions.[251] He writes, "Extraconstitutional measures are less adequate than constitutional powers of emergency."[252]

When considering the role of the military within the context of nineteenth-century constitutionalism, the positions of Spanish colonial society and the importance of the military *fuero* cannot be overestimated. In the late eighteenth century, the military *fuero* was extended to colonial militia in the Americas, and the maintenance of these special rights, like those of the church, was a hotly contested topic in the battle between liberals and conservatives.[253] As described previously, these debates continued throughout the nineteenth century.

In light of the role military governments have played in the constitutional and extraconstitutional histories of Latin American countries during the nineteenth century, it is important to examine the relationship between militarism and constitutionalism in the region during this period. Militarism is part of a panoply of institutions and devices that coalesce into a usually unwritten form of autocratic rule. Other aspects include the state of siege, presidentialism, and decree laws. Writing in 1992, Bravo Lira observed that "there is hardly a year in which a civil government does not replace a military one or vice versa in one of the twenty Iberoamerican countries."[254] This observation led Bravo Lira to conclude that constitutionalism and militarism are two sides of the same coin, inseparable and somehow maintaining an informal law of the conservation of militarism in the region. Rooted in military officials serving in civilian leadership roles in the late colonial era and the important part military officials played in national independence, militarism, in which the armed forces become an institutional form of government rather than a momentary solution to crisis, is a newer phenomenon. The reason or excuse for military intervention in government has typically been the poor or inefficient performance of civil government and the resulting anarchy that will befall the country without military action. Once

[251] Ibid., 10–21, 41–57.
[252] Ibid., 117.
[253] Loveman, *The Constitution*, 27–28.
[254] Bravo Lira, *El estado constitucional*, 167.

institutionalized, military governments form competitors for governing power against civil governments.[255]

Rights and Their Protection

Following natural law and Enlightenment ideas, constitutions after 1824 almost always contained a list or bill of rights. These often included the classically liberal rights of property, equality, security, and liberty and constitutions in the period often adopted lists of enumerated civil liberties.[256] Similarly, the drive for penal reform in the era often led to quite specific statements in constitutions assuring procedural due process for the criminally accused with set time periods and the transparent actions of judicial and prison officials.

Conservatives and many liberals did not argue for the redistribution of land held by large landholders, the church, or underproductive owners. Radicals and some liberals, however, sought such changes as a necessary element for implementing meaningful constitutional and political reform. Although the call for such action was not loud and only somewhat successful in the twentieth century, there were, of course, nineteenth-century and even colonial antecedents to these desires. Reformist liberals such as the Mexican Mariano Otero advanced ideas of redistribution, as did the Colombian liberal Manuel Murillo Toro. These thinkers were quick to perceive the relationship between landholding and political power, a dynamic that could be disrupted only through redistribution.[257]

Constitutions had to determine the status of the nations' indigenous populations, although many did so with little success. The Constitution of Cádiz racialized citizenship in the Spanish world by recognizing indigenous peoples and by excluding for the most part slaves and blacks from political participation.[258] Although indigenous peoples might be extended formal equality through constitutions, the social and actual political positions of such individuals were greatly compromised.[259] In 1828, Simón Bolívar reintroduced Indian tribute as the most efficient means of collecting national taxes from indigenous peoples.[260] As late as 1918, legislation prohibiting imprisonment for debt impacted most importantly the indigenous community, which was still noted to lack adequate educational

---

[255] Ibid., 167–183.
[256] Loveman, *The Constitution*, 369, 371.
[257] Gargarella, *Latin American Constitutionalism*, 80–81.
[258] Garay, "La idea," 146–156.
[259] Velasco Ibarra, *Expresión política*, 97–98.
[260] De Armellada, *La causa indígena*, 66.

and health services.[261] Many of the same issues related to the Americas' indigenous population that arose in the context of the Cortes were revisited by newly independent states. For example, one scholar notes that from Venezuela's Constitution of 1811 until the middle of the twentieth century, Venezuela had to construct specific laws for its indigenous community. These laws addressed the equality of indigenous people, the relationship between indigenous people and religious missions, specific mistreatment of Indians, the abolition of *mitas*, Indian tribute, personal services, the distribution of indigenous communal property, forms of punishment, and education.[262]

The mere expression of rights under a constitution was not enough. Judicial mechanisms were needed to enforce such rights. The efforts of Manuel Llanos, substitute deputy for Guatemala, to study English habeas corpus and its possible application at the Cortes are an early example. On December 17, 1810, a commission of Llanos, Pedro Rich, Domingo Dueñas, Vicente Traver, and Joaquín Leiva was appointed to draft a law that would ensure the individual liberty of citizens. In April, 1811, the Commission of Justice presented a draft of a law of habeas corpus that was discussed by the Cortes and became Article 287 of the Constitution Cádiz.[263] This article states: "No Spaniard may be imprisoned without a preceding summary information of the deed, for him who deserves to be punished with corporal punishment according to law, and also an order of the judge in writing, which notifies him and the prison in the same order."[264] This, of course, was not new as there were several earlier models from the United States and France, and the Constitution of Bayona had a similar provision.[265] The Cortes of Cádiz debated many of these protections and the final text of the Constitution of Cádiz included a significant specified list of safeguards for the accused.[266]

Although there were colonial antecedents in *derecho indiano*, the modern *amparo* was born in Mexico. As part of substantial reforms to the Mexican Constitution of 1824 enacted in 1847, the first general aspects of this judicial relief for actions inconsistent with the constitution were set out.[267] The *amparo* was part of a consistent liberal reformist plan

---

[261] Velasco Ibarra, *Expresión política*, 97–98.
[262] De Armellada, *La causa indígena*, 78–89.
[263] Volio, *Costa Rica*, 109–110.
[264] Mirow, *Florida's First Constitution*, 50.
[265] Martiré, "Algo más," 93.
[266] Mirow, "The Legality Principle," 189–205; Mirow, *Florida's First Constitution*, 50–51 (Arts. 286–308).
[267] De la Torre and García, *Desarrollo histórico*, 176–177.

laid out by Mariano Otero in the 1840s. In addition to a popular action for the protection of constitutional rights, Otero advocated for a federal secular government, greater judicial independence (essential for effective *amparos*), and jury trials. Otero's liberalism reached toward the examination of property holding in Mexico, and he sought systems of redistribution of land held by the church and large landholders as well as lands that were unproductive. With such a perspective, Otero contemplated an *amparo* that would protect even poor citizens.[268] By 1900, some sort of constitutional action of habeas corpus or *amparo* were present in all the countries studied here.[269] Such actions are discussed more fully in Chapter 7.

Related to the protection of constitutional rights though judicial procedures is the question of the judicial review of legislation to determine its constitutionality. On the path to complete powers of judicial review, the first Latin American constitution to give a supreme court the power to declare forms of legislation, in this case municipal ordinances, unconstitutional was the Colombian Constitution of 1853.[270] A number of countries explored notions of judicial review in the nineteenth century, but this was mostly a late twentieth century development, and is also discussed more fully in Chapter 7.[271]

The Church

Although the Constitution of Cádiz contemplated different territories, races, nations, and even languages, the idea of a Spanish Empire with different religions was most likely unthinkable to the Cortes.[272] A singular confession bound the empire together and had even provided the grounds for territorial expansion into the Americas throughout the colonial era. This idea was reflected in the text of the Constitution of Cádiz and in various nineteenth-century independence constitutions of the new republics. At the beginning of the nineteenth century, the Chilean Juan Egaña noted his belief that commercial relations were possible across faiths, but citizenship in a country across faiths was not.[273] This belief reflected the common conservative view that perceived moral

[268] Gargarella, *Latin American Constitutionalism*, 80–81.
[269] Loveman, *The Constitution*, 369–370.
[270] Ibid., 169.
[271] See, for example, Mirow, "*Marbury* in Mexico."
[272] Portillo Valdés, "El problema," 58–59; Portillo, "Monarquía," 171–172; Van Young, "El momento," 247–248.
[273] Alberdi, *Bases*, 29.

disintegration following independence could be checked by Roman Catholicism and a centralization of authority.[274] Nonetheless, by the mid-nineteenth century, some exceptions began to arise in the region. Another example, The Honduran Constitution of 1839, while maintaining Roman Catholicism as the official state religion, provided for freedom of conscience and of religion.[275]

Situating the church in new republics was a challenge for constitutions in the period. Providing the church with privileges or crushing its economic stature followed the political outlook of those in power and drafting constitutions. Although the Constitution of Cádiz maintained the privileged position of the church, radical and liberal thought was already present in public discourse. Early republics went further to suppress the wealth of the church and its role in the public sphere. Such moves against the economic, political, and social influence of the church were often aligned with liberalism and liberal parties of the period.[276] For example, Colombia under Santander in the early 1820s experienced several anticlerical reforms related to education, property holding, and the exercise of the *Real Patronato*.[277]

In Argentina, Rivadavia, and in Chile, Pinto suppressed religious orders and confiscated ecclesiastical property.[278] Mexico's independence was recognized by Spain and the Vatican in the same year, 1836.[279] In Mexico, the church's close ties with Santa Anna in the early 1850s were later put asunder by the Mexican Reform of 1854 and the economic and social secularization under Juárez.[280] The Constitution of 1857 provided that federal power was exercised over religion as determined by law.[281] After a period of toleration of the church under Porfirio Díaz, the church in Mexico in the second decade of the 1900s was placed under national control and there were even calls for the creation of a national Mexican church.[282] The Constitution of 1917 denied legal personality to the church and in doing so removed any collective constitutional rights for it.[283] Nonetheless, most Latin American countries maintained the

---

[274] Gargarella, *Latin American Constitutionalism*, 3.
[275] Loveman, *The Constitution*, 117.
[276] Ibid., 372.
[277] Bushnell, *The Santander Regime*, 183–248.
[278] Velasco Ibarra, *Expresión política*, 87.
[279] De la Torre and García, *Desarrollo histórico*, 150.
[280] Velasco Ibarra, *Expresión política*, 87–89.
[281] Adame Goddard, "Asimilación y rechazo," 71.
[282] Velasco Ibarra, *Expresión Política*, 89–90.
[283] Adame Goddard, "Asimilación y rechazo," 71.

privileges of the Roman Catholic church and only six countries did not follow suit by the end of the nineteenth century.[284]

Freedom of religion might be advanced not through ideology but for practical economic reasons. For Alberdi, "beneficial" immigrants who brought trade and capital were often non-Catholics, and he criticized constitutional provisions that placed religious restrictions on the activities of these people so needed to populate the region.[285] Freedom of religion or at least no prohibition on public worship was a concession or cost in the battle to attract foreigners and their wealth. An early example of this concession may be found in the Argentine Constitution of 1819, which maintained Roman Catholicism as the official state religion but did not prohibit the public exercise of other religions, most likely with the international trading community of Buenos Aires in mind. Following this reasoning, some of the early provisions providing for the free exercise of religion were targeted toward commercial and foreign communities in efforts to increase foreign trade, foreign investment, and foreign investment, as in the Bolivian Constitution of 1872.[286] During the nineteenth century, more than fifteen countries of the region had constitutions that permitted freedom in public worship, but such changes might be swept away by another, more conservative, constitution that recognized greater rights for and exclusivity of the Roman Catholic church.[287] Furthermore, facially conservative constitutions, such as the Chilean Constitution of 1833 as interpreted in 1865, were read to provide some toleration of other religions, particularly in private.[288] Accommodation of other religions, particularly other Christian religions, might be accomplished through means other than constitutional amendment or reform.

Conclusion

The nineteenth century was truly a period of constitutional fractionation, as each new republic tried to mediate political battles and compromises through its constitutions. As learned from earlier periods, governments in power saw constitutions as key tools in political legitimacy and stabilization. Indeed, constitutions were frequently enacted to legitimize and to legalize governments that came to power through unconstitutional

[284] Loveman, *The Constitution*, 371.
[285] Alberdi, *Bases*, 28
[286] Loveman, *The Constitution*, 256, 273.
[287] Ibid., 372–373.
[288] Gargarella, *Latin American Constitutionalism*, 39.

or extraconstitutional means.[289] For example, summarizing the several Venezuelan constitutions of the second half of the nineteenth century dating from 1874, 1881, 1891, and 1893, Loveman writes, "In every case, the main incentive for calling constituent assemblies was to regularize presidential succession for interim presidents or dictators, increase or decrease the length of presidential term, or allow the incumbent to remain in office despite prohibitions on reelection. In Venezuela, as clearly as anywhere in Spanish America, constitutional reform after 1864 became the key to resolving crises of presidential succession."[290]

Constitutions reveal political solutions and aspirations for conservatism and liberalism, for federalism and centralism, for unicameral and bicameral representative bodies, for the separation of powers and the place of the executive, for the expression and protection of constitutional rights, for redistribution of land, and for the capture of the political process by powerful parties. Constitutions met the challenges of economic expansion, nationalism, the judicial protection of rights (*amparo*), and the weak penetration of legal structures.

Although some of these themes were to continue into the twentieth century, others were not. Foundational questions of government structure and the nature and composition of legislative bodies were eclipsed by ideas of social rights and expanding representation while those holding the executive and military reins often held fast. Politics and political power, just as in the Constitution and Cortes of Cádiz, would continue to shape Latin American constitutionalism.

---

[289] Loveman, *The Constitution*, 151.
[290] Ibid., 156.

6

The Legacy of the Constitution of Cádiz

Twentieth-Century Latin American Constitutionalism

Constitutionalism has not had a very happy existence in Latin America.[1]
Bernardino Bravo Lira, 1991

The Constitution of Cádiz was a liberal constitution establishing constitutional rights, a representative government, and a constitutional monarchy. It influenced ideas of American equality within the Spanish Empire, and its traces are observed in the process of Latin American independence. To these accepted views, one must add that the Constitution was a lost moment in Latin American constitutional development. By the immediate politicization of constitutionalism after 1812, the document marks the beginning of constitutional difficulties in the region. The ways the Constitution of Cádiz was viewed in historical and constitutional thought help explain the path, the successes, and the challenges of Latin American constitutionalism. Before discussing this perspective more fully, some important twentieth-century developments in constitutionalism must be addressed.

Late nineteenth- and twentieth-century Latin American constitutionalism responded to new economic and social realities of the period. England grew as an important economic power in the region and, in Gargarella's view, liberals seeking progress and conservatives seeking order joined hands in an alliance for positivism that was to exclude the radical aspects of extreme or utopian reform. Autocratic governments advanced agendas of order and progress of positivist thinkers such as Auguste Comte. Positivist theories of science, technology, and bureaucracy in government

[1] Bravo Lira, "Protección jurídica," 335.

were summoned to establish social quietude and economic gains. The pushback from this powerful alliance took shape in revolutionary, socialist, indigenist, and agrarian movements that were effectively excluded but also that surfaced to overcome this established structure of compromise. Student voices as a political force also developed in this period. Beginning in Córdoba, Argentina, in 1918, reform-minded students exerted political power to push for radical or populist changes.[2] Thus, a shift from the liberal to the social may be observed. As Botana and Gallo write, "The 1922 ruling by the Argentine Supreme Court of Justice that a law approved by the national Congress authorizing the regulation of urban leases was constitutional marked the beginning of the end of liberal ideas in Argentina."[3]

Nascent socialist parties began in Argentina in the 1890s and in Chile in the 1910s. The first calls for women's political representation were made. For example, in Argentina, feminist, doctor, and socialist Alicia Moreau de Justo, wife of Socialist Party founder Juan B. Justo, unsuccessfully advocated for women's suffrage; the proposal was struck down by conservatives in the senate. Indigenous and black people were recognized as exploited laborers in the writings of Peruvian José Carlos Mariátegui, founder of the Peruvian Socialist Party. Central institutions of government such as the judiciary were subject to criticism based on class. For example, Peruvian anarchist Manuel González Prada criticized judges for blindly serving the interests of wealth and power.[4] Following French scholars, radicals and reformist liberals sought to redefine property itself placing social limitations on it through the social function theory of property.[5] Some constitutions picked up this idea that provided the intellectual underpinnings for agrarian reform.[6] Other constitutions sought to give voice to various groups in society through corporatist representation. For example, in the 1920s and 1940s, Ecuador's constitutions included representatives for leaders of industry and peasants, journalists and the army, merchants, workers and academics, and indigenous leaders. These were substantially reduced by the Constitutions of 1946 and 1967.[7]

The effective inclusion of social thought into constitutions of this period stemmed from these usually submerged and secondary ideologies.

---

[2] Gargarella, *Latin American Constitutionalism*, 84–86, 92–93.
[3] Botana and Gallo, "Introduction," xxix.
[4] Gargarella, *Latin American Constitutionalism*, 93, 94, 230 n. 15, 230 n. 21, 231 nn. 23 and 26. For Juan B. Justo, see Botana and Gallo, "Introduction," xxvi–xxvii.
[5] Gargarella, *Latin American Constitutionalism*, 94–95; Mirow, "Origins of the Social Function," 1183–1217.
[6] Mirow, *Latin American Law*, 219–227.
[7] Gargarella, *Latin American Constitutionalism*, 235 n. 35.

Radicalism made its way into the political thought of the time, but less frequently into successful reforms that transformed the political landscape. Nonetheless, new ideas of property, work, and social rights were concretely expressed in constitutions. Gargarella astutely notes that these developments occurred in the shadow of the Bolshevik Revolution in 1917 and of the increasing U.S. presence in the region, which fomented resistance and protest. The right to strike, however, was not automatically listed in such constitutional provisions of rights.[8]

A discussion of twentieth-century Latin American constitutionalism must begin with Mexico because of the importance of the Mexican Constitution of 1917. After surveying some other countries of the region during the nineteenth century, this chapter will turn to a broader analysis of main themes and issues presented. This is a lot of ground to cover. There were 103 constitutions in force in the region from 1900 to 2008 with an average life span of about 23 years per constitution, and from the 1970s forward, there was a significant increase in adopting new constitutions in Latin American countries.[9]

Mexico

From 1876 to 1911, Porfirio Díaz autocratically governed Mexico under a liberal regime that sought foreign investment, infrastructure improvement, and industrial expansion.[10] Although the Porfiriato in Mexico is often viewed as a period of economic expansion and social stability, Porfirio Díaz's harsh regime suppressed a number of political and social factors that would eventually lead to the Mexican Revolution. Racial and agrarian instabilities, rampant criminal unlawfulness, and areas under regional control of strongmen all challenged this seemingly quiet period.[11] Politicians and political thinkers such as Justo Sierra and Emilio Rabasa provided positivists positions that bolstered Díaz's agenda of progress and stability guided by science. Although both proposed reforms, they also provided legitimation for Díaz's rule. Rabasa, who was influential during the later years of Díaz, was able to transfer his ideas into to revolutionary period.[12] A critic of the Constitution of 1857, Rabasa argued that Benito Juárez and Porfirio Díaz were forced to become dictators

---

[8] Ibid., 91, 120, 236 n. 29.
[9] Negretto, *Making Constitutions*, 20–21.
[10] De la Torre and García, *Desarrollo histórico*, 237–238.
[11] Knight, *The Mexican Revolution*, Vol. 1, 15–77; Loveman, *The Constitution*, 87.
[12] Gargarella, *Latin American Constitutionalism*, 86–88. See Hale, *Emilio Rabasa*.

because of the impossible limitations placed on them by the Constitution. These ideas found expression in Rabasa's book, *La constitución y la dictadura* (1912).[13]

New movements for anarchy, socialism, labor, and land rights coalesced to raise their demands to the national arena.[14] Political opposition grew in the first decade of the 1900s and gained articulation. For example, the *Plan de Partido Liberal* drafted in 1906 from the safe distance of St. Louis, Missouri, contained both theoretical constructs and concrete steps that would flourish in the impending revolution. The *Plan* was characterized by workers and peasants' rights, anticlericalism, freedom of the press, education, equality, and protection of indigenous peoples. It sought to bar the reelection of Díaz, abolish the death penalty, hold public officials accountable for misfeasance, create public schools that provided a lay education, prohibit Chinese immigration, fix the work day to eight hours, prohibit child labor, improve working conditions, establish employer liability for work accidents, limit worker debts and fines, and improve the *amparo*, among other goals.[15]

Francisco Madero, Díaz's main opposition, spoke throughout Mexico to support the cause of "anti-reelection" through a political party of the same name in 1909. After elections were conducted under oppressive constraints in July, 1910, the *Plan de San Luis* in October declared the elections null, refused to recognize Díaz, declared Madero the provisional president, sought the freedom of political prisoners, pushed for agrarian reform, and called for armed battle the following month.[16] By the beginning of the 1910s, critics of the Porfiriato gained power, and revolutionary movements led by Emiliano Zapata in Morelos and Pancho Villa (Doroteo Arango) in the north challenged Díaz.[17] There were several other armed insurrections in the period that added to the political instability of the country. Madero established Ciudad Juárez as a provisional capital and appointed a cabinet. Díaz fled from Veracruz and in June, 1911, entered Mexico City. The Anti-reelectionist Party became the Progressive Constitutional Party.[18] Madero effectively obtained the cooperation of protestant leaders in Mexico and promised them freedom of

[13] Aguilar Rivera, *La geometría*, 55, 57.
[14] Loveman, *The Constitution*, 87.
[15] Carpizo, *La Constitución*, 18–20.
[16] Ibid., 25–26; Knight, *The Mexican Revolution*, Vol. 1, 55–77.
[17] Gargarella, *Latin American Constitutionalism*, 98; Knight, *The Mexican Revolution*, Vol. 1, 123, 309–319; Knight, *The Mexican Revolution*, Vol. II, 34–36.
[18] Carpizo, *La Constitución*, 26–28. For the Madero regime, see generally Knight, *The Mexican Revolution*, Vol. 1, 171–490.

belief and a role in public education.[19] Despite this political sea change, some recent scholars have noticed continuity with the positivist and *científico* approaches found during the Porfiriato.[20]

Nonetheless, Madero was not without his critics. Claiming that Madero had tricked the people and failed to implement the *Plan de San Luis*, Zapata, in November, 1911, announced the *Plan de Ayala*.[21] Through the Plan, Zapata's followers sought the political and economic empowerment of agrarian peasants through land redistribution.[22] Henry Lane Wilson, U.S. ambassador to Mexico, did not support Madero, and threatening intervention by the United States in the midst of more than 2,000 deaths, reached an agreement by which Madero stepped down from the presidency in February, 1913, to be replaced by his general Victoriano Huerta. Despite assurances of safe passage by Huerta, Madero and his vice president, José María Pino Suárez, were murdered a few days later.[23]

In turn, Huerta was rejected by Venustiano Carranza, governor of Coahuila, who called for a "constitutionalist" movement while Zapata in the south and Villa in the north also fought under a call for the constitution.[24] Carranza's *Plan de Guadalupe* refused to recognize Huerta and established Carranza as head of the constitutional army while federal power devolved to state governments.[25] Carranza's executive power was to be temporary until elections could be held. In September, 1913, Carranza appointed his first cabinet in Hermosillo, where he spoke eloquently about the social struggle of peasants and the need for education and clean water. In this context, he spoke of the need for a new constitution. During the same months and into 1914, Huerta lost the support of the United States, which invaded Veracruz and negotiated his removal as president. Carranza, Villa, and Zapata filled any vacuum Huerta's departure created.[26] Carranza was much less ideologically focused and his *Plan de Guadalupe* as first announced lacked any content on land and workers. His goal was constitutional restoration, but later political

---

[19] Bastian, "Los propagandistas," 326.

[20] Hale, *The Transformation*, 257.

[21] Carpizo, *La Constitución*, 29.

[22] Gargarella, *Latin American Constitutionalism*, 99.

[23] Carpizo, *La Constitución*, 30–32. For Henry Lane Wilson's involvement see Knight, *The Mexican Revolution*, Vol. 1, 485–489. For the Huerta regime generally see Knight, *The Mexican Revolution*, Vol. 2, 1–171.

[24] De la Torre and García, *Desarrollo histórico*, 238; Knight, *The Mexican Revolution*, Vol. 1, 478–480; Knight, *The Mexican Revolution*, Vol. II, 11–33.

[25] Knight, *The Mexican Revolution*, Vol. II, 104–106.

[26] Carpizo, *La Constitución*, 36–37, 39–41.

developments led him to add ideological content to garner popular and military support.[27] Indeed, some scholars assert that Carranza was influenced by earlier notions of scientific politics and positivism, and such an administrative approach to governing would have been consistent with avoiding the great social questions of the time.[28]

The Aguascalientes Convention in 1914 was a meeting of Carranza and Villa's representatives, who were later joined by Zapatistas. The needs of the country raised at this convention included agrarian reform and the recognition of Mexico's racial and indigenous composition.[29] Thus, the *Plan de Ayala* served as common ground for the basis of discussion.[30] Although successful in creating some unity among the opposition movements in their desire to legislate for the Mexican people as a whole, it did not produce a text.[31] It was, in the terminology of Carranza, an attempt to create a "preconstitutional" government while social reforms might wait for a later date.[32]

In November 1914, the United States left Veracruz and a few weeks later, Villa and Zapata entered Mexico City, creating a great deal of unrest. Carranza expanded his *Plan de Guadalupe* with economic, social, and political reforms that included the equality of all Mexicans; agrarian reform; the partition of large estates and the restitution of improperly taken lands; improvements for peasants, miners, and workers; a new judicial system; the revision of civil, commercial, and criminal codes; and new laws related to natural resources and their exploitation. Governors of the states of Mexico began to legislate along these lines, and in May, 1914, Villa published his own agrarian law.[33] Carranza's injection of social rights in the Plan was necessitated by political pressure from the successes of Villa and Zapata as well as from Alvaro Obregón, Carranza's chief military officer whose political views were much more reformist than Carranza's views. Obregón favored agrarian reform, redistribution of property, and the nationalization of natural resources, and these views no doubt helped him sway Villa at important moments of the revolution, although their working in concert was temporary.[34]

[27] Hernández Campos, "El constitucionalismo," 144–149, 151.
[28] Hale, *The Transformation*, 257.
[29] Gargarella, *Latin American Constitutionalism*, 99–100, 103; Knight, *The Mexican Revolution*, Vol. II, 254–263.
[30] Carpizo, *La Constitución*, 42.
[31] Gargarella, *Latin American Constitutionalism*, 99–100.
[32] Hernández Campos, "El constitucionalismo," 149–150.
[33] Carpizo, *La Constitución*, 42–44. For developments in agrarian reform see Knight, *The Mexican Revolution*, Vol. II, 185–196.
[34] Hernández Campos, "El constitucionalismo," 150–151, 157–163.

In October, 1915, Zapata issued his program of reforms in response to Carranza's additions to the *Plan de Guadalupe*.[35] As the "constitutionalist" movement under Carranza took shape, he found support among the protestant communities in Mexico and those in the United States who exerted political influence to argue for nonintervention by the United States. There was, of course, a natural confluence of perspectives between the anticlericalism of the revolution and the anti-Catholicism of missionary protestant communities.[36]

After Carranza had effectively defeated Villa's forces, the United States gave de facto recognition to Carranza's government. Carranza's call for a constitutional convention was announced at Querétaro in 1916 with the aim of reforming the Constitution of 1857. Following the call for a constituent assembly and the arrival of the deputies, the preparatory meetings dedicated a substantial amount of time and effort to weeding out deputies who were politically suspect for being too conservative or for having ties to the Díaz government. The detailed political scrutiny of deputies produced speeches and long defenses. Deputies had to establish their revolutionary merit and allegiance to Carranza.[37] Nonetheless, the overall composition of the assembly took on a much more reformist and radical hue; this greatly shaped the final text that would become the Constitution of 1917.[38]

Under the presidency of Luis Manuel Rojas, the assembly reviewed the draft submitted by Carranza, whose initial proposals were far less reformist than the final product.[39] The authors of the draft were Luis Manuel Rojas and José Natividad Macías with assistance from Félix Palavicini and Alfonso Craviota. Considering the care the assembly took in selecting and certifying its delegates, it is not surprising that it also took substantial time to create committees for the internal workings of the assembly and to debate the membership of these committees. Indeed, the composition of the important Constitution Committee was finally decided by vote of the assembly rather than through more informal means. As a whole, the congress was a diverse group of constitution makers including workers, farmers, miners, and railroad employees in addition to the expected assortment of lawyers, doctors, engineers, professors, and professionals who had usually comprised constituent and

---

[35] Ibid., 152.
[36] Bastian, "Los propagandistas," 332, 342–347.
[37] Carpizo, *La Constitución*, 45, 50–62.
[38] Hernández Campos, "El constitucionalismo," 165.
[39] Carpizo, *La Constitución*, 62; Gargarella, *Latin American Constitutionalism*, 100.

legislative bodies in the region.[40] The theme of the needs of the Mexican people was reiterated by Carranza at the Querétaro Convention as he attempted to build consensus among conservative and radical interests.[41] Knight describes the constituent congress as being "middle-class," with half of the delegates coming from the professions with a quarter of the total having university education. Nearly one-third of the delegates held some military rank.[42] Examining the composition of the congress, Knight suggests, "The myth of 200 sage legislators sedately deliberating their country's needs requires correction; but so, too, does the standard image of moderates and jacobins clashing in fierce ideological debate, the jacobins' triumph determining Mexico's future radical course."[43] Nonetheless, Gargarella noted the importance of the people's voice at the Querétaro Convention where regular folks, "women, men, and children" sought to inform the delegates present on social and economic needs.[44] From Gargarella's point of view, this provided a new dynamic in Latin American constitutionalism. Knight viewed popular participation as being more limited. He writes, "The new Constitution only imperfectly represented popular, revolutionary hopes: it was conceived without direct popular participation; it was drawn up in haste and chaos, rather than calm deliberation; and its limpid provisions contrasted with the murky reality which existed outside the Querétaro Palace of Fine Arts."[45]

Nonetheless, Carranza's draft was an entirely new text in Latin American constitutionalism. Important or new aspects included individual guaranties, the secularization of education, limitations on employment contracts, freedom of the press, procedural rights for the criminally accused, freedom of religious belief, provisions for expropriation, citizenship by birth, electoral reform, a reduction of the presidential term to four years, provisions for the Supreme Court and the *amparo*, the supremacy of the state over the church, and the secularization of marriage and personal status.[46]

The main issues for debate on the draft and areas that were often pushed toward greater reform by the assembly were provisions addressing the church, education, work, and land. The place of the church in

[40] Carpizo, *La Constitución*, 63–64, 72.
[41] Gargarella, *Latin American Constitutionalism*, 100.
[42] Knight, *The Mexican Revolution*, Vol. II, 473–474.
[43] Ibid., 475.
[44] Gargarella, *Latin American Constitutionalism*, 103–104. See also Carpizo, *La Constitución*, 50.
[45] Knight, *The Mexican Revolution*, Vol. II, 470.
[46] Carpizo, *La Constitución*, 64–71.

society and political structure had been an issue since colonial times; the incorporation of Roman Catholicism as the official state religion was an extremely important attribute of the Constitution of Cádiz. The Mexican Constitution of 1857 had done much to separate church and state, but the Constitution of 1917 went even further by imposing the supremacy of the state over the church. The debates that led to the texts of Article 24 and Article 130 of the constitution indicated that the assembly sought to move beyond even the supremacy of the state over the church. Article 130 gave federal authorities an exclusive jurisdiction in religious affairs, prohibited Congress from establishing or prohibiting any religion, placed determinations of civil status within civil authorities, removed the legal personality of churches, gave local legislatures the power to determine the number of priests and ministers in each state, required that members of religious orders be Mexicans by birth, prohibited religious officials from criticizing fundamental laws and public authorities, prohibited religious officials from voting, removed official recognition from seminary studies, prohibited religious publications from commenting on political affairs, prohibited political meetings in religious buildings, and prohibited religious officials from inheriting unless the bequest came from a family member within the fourth degree, among other restrictions and prohibitions. These provisions passed without record of the number of votes.[47]

Article 24 prohibited religious ceremonies or activities in public, outside of religious buildings. Debates about these articles revealed that some deputies wanted to discuss the possibility of prohibiting auricular confession, which was seen as a means of not only moral and religious control but also political control. The marriage of priests younger than fifty years of age was also debated. These more radical perspectives did not win favor, and the article passed by of vote of ninety-three to sixty-three.[48]

Addressing the topic of education and in keeping with its general views on the church, the Congress sought to laicize education and particularly remove the strong influence the church and its personnel had on primary education. Considering the foundational role education had in society and politics, the Congress sought lay and rational bases for the educational system which was, in effect, charged with constructing the future of the country. It was recognized that mere freedom of education or letting parents decide the education of their children would permit the church to play a strong role in education, and prohibitions were seen as

---

[47] Ibid., 71, 97–98.
[48] Ibid., 93–96.

necessary to shape the future.[49] The resulting article of the Constitution of 1917 passed by ninety votes to fifty-eight and provided that education should be free and that it should be lay at all levels. As might be expected, primary education received special attention. Religious corporations and ministers of any religion were prohibited from running primary schools, which were also subject to official control and would provide free tuition.[50]

Reforms came from commissions at the convention to study the "social question," issues related to land, work, and poverty. The commissions, headed by deputy Pastor Rouaix, Minister of Industry, produced the famous social articles that were incorporated into the Mexican Constitution of 1917, especially Article 27 dealing with land and property and Article 123 dealing with work.[51] Article 27, drafted by Molina Enríquez, established fundamental ownership of property in the state and a view of property that is moderated by its function in and use by society. Large landholders (*latifundios*) were to be divided and distributed to develop smaller agricultural plots, and the property of religious and civil corporations was limited.[52] In seeking an equitable distribution of land and wealth, the country would establish small land holdings and agricultural centers to ensure that all centers of population had needed land and water.[53] Article 27 also established principles for regulatory regimes governing coal, oil, hydrocarbons, and minerals. Direct ownership of land and water was limited to Mexicans; churches and religious associations were prohibited from ownership of lands. Lands that were improperly taken from groups, including indigenous peoples, would be returned according to law and held communally.[54] The debates within the commission produced an article related to property that was both sweeping in its scope and specific in its detail. The debate within the Congress on Article 27 were confused, rushed, and conducted in one afternoon and evening under candlelight because the electricity had failed.[55] Article 27 was passed unanimously.[56]

---

[49] Carpizo, *La Constitución*, 72–80.
[50] Mexican Constitution of 1917, Article 3; Carpizo, *La Constitución*, 80.
[51] Gargarella, *Latin American Constitutionalism*, 101; Hernández Campos, "El constitucionalismo," 168–169.
[52] De la Torre and García, *Desarrollo histórico*, 242; Knight, *The Mexican Revolution*, Vol. II, 475.
[53] Gargarella, *Latin American Constitutionalism*, 101.
[54] Carpizo, *La Constitución*, 98–109.
[55] Knight, *The Mexican Revolution*, Vol. II, 475.
[56] Carpizo, *La Constitución*, 103.

Workers had begun organizing and creating mutual aid societies, cooperatives, and nascent unions during the latter half of the nineteenth century and into the first two decades of the twentieth century. The liberal reforms of Juárez in the 1850s and 1860s served as precursors to the significant societal and political changes of the beginning of the twentieth century. When the revolution was in place, the text of the Constitution of 1857 no long expressed the desires of the winners. The radical positions of the revolutionaries now were central in the drafting process. The times produced a very new constitutional text for Mexico, Latin America, and the world.[57] This was particularly true regarding new labor and working conditions and rights drafted in response to deplorable working conditions and oppressive exploitation.[58] Solutions to these concerns had been shaped by the courts for some time in Mexico.[59] Now the Constitution would speak. Article 123 sets out various rights for labor and provided the constitutional grounds for the extensive labor legislation that followed in Mexico.[60] It recognized trade unions and spelled out in detail conditions and rights related to work including provisions addressing hours, minors, women, wages, vacation, safety, accidents, strike, arbitration, dismissal, and social security.[61] The maximum hours of labor each day and the maximum length for a contract for labor were debated at length. The provision was novel for its content not only in redefining the status of the worker in Mexico but also in its specificity. Article 123 is specific and regulatory. The article, along with Article 5 addressing other and related aspects of workers' rights, passed by unanimity and was seen as a great advance for human and workers' dignity.[62] There was surprisingly little debate on this article.[63] With Article 27 on property, Article 123 of the Constitution of 1917 serves as an intellectual monument to the goals and spirit of the Mexican Revolution. Indeed, Article 123 was the most advanced statement of protection of workers' rights at the time.[64] In addition to its new approaches to labor and property, the Constitution of 1917 also further defined the scope of the *amparo*.[65]

---

[57] De la Torre and García, *Desarrollo histórico*, 236–237, 239.
[58] Carpizo, *La Constitución*, 81.
[59] James, *Mexico's Supreme Court*; Suarez-Potts, *The Making of Law*.
[60] De la Torre and García, *Desarrollo histórico*, 240–241.
[61] Gargarella, *Latin American Constitutionalism*, 101–102.
[62] Carpizo, *La Constitución*, 81–93.
[63] Knight, *The Mexican Revolution, Volume II*, 475.
[64] Hernández Campos, "El constitucionalismo," 168.
[65] De la Torre and García, *Desarrollo histórico*, 242.

Many of the most important reforms of the Constitution of 1917 were not part of Carranza's original draft, and after his election as president in March, 1917, he did little to advance the social and redistributist agenda enshrined in the Constitution. He removed local authority to act in such matters, created fiscal barriers to redistribution, and worked slowly in these matters. The principles of Article 123 were not shaped into laws and regulations, and Carranza disavowed the right to strike. Disagreeing with anticlerical aspects of the revolution and the Constitution, he sought the return of some church property and to reform Article 3 of the Constitution dealing with education. He no longer carried sufficient political power to effect these goals, and there was little social or military support for his views. Alvaro Obregón was elected president in 1920 and implemented these policies further than Carranza.[66]

Regional Influence

The Mexican Constitution of 1917 radically changed constitutionalism in the Spanish-speaking world. From this moment forward there was an entirely new set of political and civil rights that may be thought of as constitutional rights.[67] This earliest, clearest, and most influential statement of social constitutions in Latin America may be viewed in the context of a global shift toward "the social."[68] The Constitution of 1917 and its provisions on property, for example, served to cement antiliberal policies in Mexico and to inspire other constitutional drafters away from liberalism in Latin America.[69] Nonetheless, Aguilar Rivera has observed, "The continuity of liberalism is one of the founding myths of the Mexican nation."[70]

Numerous constitutions in the region after 1917 followed the new economic, social, and political aspirations set out in the Mexican Constitution and other important sources. These argued for the expansion of educational and social services to the population, for the development of an interventionist state that would increase the economic and social capacity of the country, and for the creation of specialized bureaucracies to advance these agendas. Central to these transformations was the redistribution of property and particularly the redistribution of rural

[66] Hernández Campos, "El constitucionalismo," 172–173, 176–177.
[67] Bravo Lira, "Protección judícial," 339.
[68] Kennedy, "Two Globalizations."
[69] Aguilar Rivera, *La geometría*, 67–69.
[70] Ibid., 74. See also Aguilar Rivera, *El fin*, 15–19, 23–24.

lands through systems of agricultural reform that would dissolve the landholdings of the privileged few and redeploy these assets into the hand of farmers closer to the land.[71] Frequently antagonistic to the church and its interests, governments and constitutions sometimes reached truces with the church that had developed its own theology of property in the face of industrialization and Marxism. Laicism was a cornerstone of the project, but the overwhelming Roman Catholic presence in personal faith and political action could not be discounted. Panama and El Salvador reached such understandings in the 1940s.[72] The clergy might continue to have a powerful influence. For example, despite constitutional prohibitions on political engagement, Mexico's clergy had an unofficial but powerful voice in political life and change from the 1930s to today.[73]

The Constitution of 1917 provided for a number of new social rights. When Venustiano Carranza took office as president, Congress agreed with his request for extraordinary powers. Using presidential decrees in keeping with the spirit of the new constitution, Carranza restructured the Mexican government with broad institutional and substantive reforms. These reforms addressed many core areas of government and society: property, public health, labor, the economy, the church, and criminal law.[74] In the words of Loveman, "Extraordinary powers were the ordinary instruments of government" as they would be for more than twenty years.[75]

The Constitution, however, did not usher in a new period of agrarian revolution. As much as the provisions of the constitution contemplated a regenerative redistribution of resources, landholders and invested members of Mexican society, including Carranza himself, effectively blocked many of the social and political promises of the document. Despite its anti-imperialist claims, the Constitution of 1917 permitted imperial structures to endure.[76] Indeed, in the 1920s, Mexico experienced a number of military uprisings in part as a result of the various military officers and local caudillos who had participated in a successful revolution. In 1928 the precursor to the *Partido Revolucionario Institucional* (PRI) was formed under General Plutarco Elías Calle, whose call to political action brought soldiers, workers, and farmers together. This led to the presidency

---

[71] De la Torre and García, *Desarrollo histórico*, 225–226, 229. See also Alviar García, "The Unending Quest," 1895–1914.
[72] De la Torre and García, *Desarrollo histórico*, 230.
[73] Reich, *Mexico's Hidden Revolution*.
[74] Loveman, *The Constitution*, 89.
[75] Ibid.
[76] Carpizo, *La Constitución*, 113–115.

of the socialist Lázaro Cárdenas, who served from 1934 to 1940 while advancing land reform and nationalizing Mexico's oil companies. Since then, the one-party system in Mexico has effectively controlled – with the exception of one opposition candidate's success in 2000 – the country through executive legislation.[77] State-sanctioned organizations were created to represent various interests within the working population, and programs of social security and agrarian reform have ebbed and flowed according to the political moment.[78]

The Constitution of 1917 successfully effected a stable form of constitutionalism that provided for the regular functioning of Congress under its language.[79] These provisions proved to be greatly influential in the region. Central American countries that required highly intensive manual labor, such as Guatemala with its coffee, bananas, and railroad expansion, turned to the labor provisions as their worker and popular movements gained political power. El Salvador, Honduras, and Nicaragua took similar steps in the first half of the twentieth century even when, in some instances, such reforms were advanced by dictatorial or oligarchical leaders.[80] The Cuban Constitution of 1940, influenced by the Spanish Constitution of 1931 and the Weimar Constitution, contained similar social provisions and sought to institutionalize principles of the Cuban Revolution of 1933 that expelled General Machado from power. It sought to replace the idea of separation of powers with the idea of a socialist unity of power.[81] The Constitution of 1940 was suspend when Fulgencio Batista seized power in 1952 and issued his own Constitutional Law in 1952.[82] The Cuban Constitution of 1959, the Constitution of 1940 as reinstated in 1959, carried these ideas further by empowering the executive to carry out a program of change from above and to act consistently with a "dictatorship of the proletariat."[83] The Council of Ministers served a legislative function and supported a strong central executive in the hands of Fidel Castro, who accomplished dramatic institutional restructuring of the army, the state bureaucracy, popular organizations, the media, and the economy in the first few years of his control.[84]

[77] Gargarella, *Latin American Constitutionalism*, 102; Loveman, *The Constitution*, 89–90.
[78] Gargarella, *Latin American Constitutionalism*, 108–109.
[79] Bravo Lira, *El estado constitucional*, 19.
[80] De la Torre and García, *Desarrollo histórico*, 244–247, 250–267.
[81] Gargarella, *Latin American Constitutionalism*, 125–126.
[82] De la Torre and García, *Desarrollo histórico*, 270–271.
[83] Gargarella, *Latin American Constitutionalism*, 126.
[84] Ibid.

Although Fidel Castro's legislation advanced such social programs immediately on his seizure of power, notably with agrarian reform legislation, Cuba's movement toward a new socialist constitution was not officially begun until the 1970s.[85] With the Soviet Constitution of 1936 in mind, the Cuban Constitution of 1976 increased the role of the Communist Party and solidified state control of the economy, social and health services, and education. It also created two new conciliar bodies and the National Assembly, all supporting the general will of the executive.[86] The First Congress of the Cuban Communist Party approved the Constitution in 1975, as did a plebiscite in 1976. The Constitution describes Cuba as a "socialist state of workers and peasants and other manual and intellectual workers."[87] In such an environment, law as a subject of academic study declined dramatically; in 1965, the law school of the University of Havana had no graduates.[88]

Thus, numerous countries in the region were drawn to social principles. The Cuban Constitution of 1940 created a Council of Ministers reporting to the Congress and incorporated many of the social aspects common in the region at the time. Similar developments can be noted in the Constitutions of Uruguay in 1934 and Bolivia in 1938. The Costa Rican Constitution of 1949 enacted many of the provisions common in the region. It also sought to rein in presidential power and took the unusual step of abolishing the military, which removed this central player in Latin American political and constitutional life from influence in the country.[89]

Twentieth-Century Constitutional States

While the Mexican Constitution of 1917 ushered in a new era of social rights and interventionist economic theory, the same period signaled the collapse of efforts to erect functioning liberal representative states. Two general categories of Latin American constitutional governments are set out by Bravo Lira in his work on constitutional states: noncompetitive (and often extraconstitutional) constitutional governments and competitive forms of constitutional government. Military rule and Argentina's

---

[85] De la Torre and García, *Desarrollo histórico*, 273–275.
[86] Gargarella, *Latin American Constitutionalism*, 126.
[87] Bravo Lira, *El estado constitucional*, 96.
[88] Gargarella, *Latin American Constitutionalism*, 238 n. 47. Legal study rebounded in subsequent decades. See Mirow, *Latin American Law*, 233.
[89] Gargarella, *Latin American Constitutionalism*, 112–114.

alternating between civil and military rule are set aside for separate analysis in his study. As examples of noncompetitive forms, Bravo Lira provides, among others, Mexico's dominant party system, Colombia's biparty system, and Cuba's unitary party system. Competitive forms during the twentieth century include Chile's experience from 1933 to 1973 with competing oligarchies, Uruguay's experience since 1930 with autocracy and military rule, Costa Rica's experience with presidentialism and party rule since 1952, Venezuela's party rule, and the presidentialism of the Dominican Republic since 1965.[90]

These examples warrant some discussion. For example, in Mexico since 1930 the PRI established itself as the only sanctioned party to carry the mantle of the revolution and exercised complete extraconstitutional control over the government and its goals and processes. The country's experience with long periods of autocratic rule under presidents who refused to leave office such as Juárez and Díaz in the second half of the nineteenth century established a strong presidentialist structure that was easily carried into the post-revolutionary period. The president of the PRI was, for all intents and purposes and in actuality, the president of Mexico.[91] The *Partido Acción Nacional* (PAN) was founded in 1939 by Manuel Gómez Morin and Efraín González Luna. It reflected some aspects of prerevolutionary Mexican liberalism such as the rejection of state intervention in many aspects of life but its assumption of Roman Catholic social doctrine was inconsistent with established liberalism.[92] Nonetheless, Congress was structured to ensure a PRI majority, and in any case, its sessions were limited to four months out of the year. Thus, some opposition was permitted after 1940, but Congress's main function was to "provide a constitutional façade. Without congress, the Mexican president would appear in the eyes of foreigners as a dictator."[93] This arrangement, according to Bravo Lira, is a "completely original" form of Latin American extraconstitutional government.[94]

As will be remembered from the previous chapter, Colombia, under the Constitution of 1886, is another example of extraconstitutional arrangements that block competition in the political arena.[95] From the late nineteenth century and during the first half of the twentieth century,

[90] Bravo Lira, *El estado constitucional*, 35–97, 99–200.
[91] Ibid., 37–39, 45.
[92] Aguilar Rivera, *La geometría*, 90–97.
[93] Bravo Lira, *El estado constitucional*, 41.
[94] Ibid., 47.
[95] Ibid., 49.

liberals and conservatives traded positions of power back and forth. The War of a Thousand Days, from 1899 to 1902, led to conservative continuation of power until 1930.[96] The Constitution underwent important amendments in 1910 that reduced the term of the president to four years, provided for the direct election of the president, and removed the presidential power of appointment of Supreme Court justices who were now subject to a five-year term. The Supreme Court's power of judicial review was expanded and the death penalty was abolished. Congress was required to meet annually instead of the former practice of every two years.[97] From 1914 to 1930, a period of "conservative hegemony" meant that the church was particularly influential in political matters and some priests went so far as to equate liberalism with sin and atheism.[98]

From 1930 to 1946, liberals were in control. Labor movements and local violence led to the use of exceptional powers, and until the late 1960s, Colombia would live most of its time under states of siege under the constitution.[99] The entire period of the mid-1940s until the mid-1960s was known as *La Violencia* because of political fighting that often turned to murder and massacre. It is estimated that 300,000 Colombians lost their lives from acts of vengeance, feud, and atrocity.[100]

From 1934 to 1938, President Alfonso López Pumarejo advanced labor reform and partisan reforms under a program entitled "Revolution on the March."[101] In addition to establishing agrarian reform, he supported constitutional amendments in 1936 that redefined property in light of social rights, removed requirements that public education should be consistent with Roman Catholicism, and eliminated a literacy test for voting.[102] He had a second term from 1942 to 1945 during which he gained support for constitutional reform to have senators elected directly.[103] Liberal leader Jorge Eliécer Gaitán's assassination in 1948 in Bogotá led to violent rioting in the city and elsewhere on April 9, dubbed the "Bogotazo," which was suppressed by the government.[104] Seeking a "revolution of order," President Laureano Gómez became president in 1950 while the country was under a state of siege. In fact, every change

[96] Palacios, *Between Legitimacy*, 36–48.
[97] Ibid., 63. See also Bushnell, *The Making*, 161–162.
[98] Palacios, *Between Legitimacy*, 72–74.
[99] Loveman, *The Constitution*, 178–179; Safford and Palacios, *Colombia*, 288–292.
[100] Palacios, *Between Legitimacy*, 135–137.
[101] Bushnell, *The Making*, 185–192.
[102] Ibid., 189.
[103] Palacios, *Between Legitimacy*, 100–113, 116, 121.
[104] Bushnell, *The Making*, 194–204; Palacios, *Between Legitimacy*, 139–143.

in government between 1945 and 1958 happened during a state of emergency or outside the constitutional requirements under dictatorial rule.[105]

The Liberal and Conservative Parties lost control when General Gustavo Rojas Pinilla came to power in 1953, and his populist military government that also embraced the country's industrialists ended in 1957.[106] It was during Rojas Pinilla's rule that women attained the vote.[107] Working together to oust Rojas Pinilla, the parties agreed through a National Front to an extraconstitutional coalition that would, despite their fundamental political differences, ensure that they had at least some of the power and that the country would have some modicum of stability and peace.[108] The conservatives were led by Laureano Gómez and the liberals by Alberto Lleras Camargo. Negotiations were held in Benedorm and later Sitges, Spain.[109] All important government positions were allocated fifty–fifty, with the president maintaining the balance when appointing officials. Anyone who was not a Liberal or Conservative was, of course, excluded from service in politics. The solution for the presidency was simple: take turns. Under these conditions, elections became the means to justify and to legitimate the political agreement.[110] This unique form of power-sharing is described well by David Bushnell:

> These rules, devised by the top leaders of the two traditional parties and then approved by popular plebiscite, laid the basis for the peculiar bipartisan coalition regime, known as the National Front, that remained in control of the country until the 1970s. It ... followed a set of mathematical guidelines written into the constitution itself, so that everyone might know the exact rules of the game and would also know that these rules could not be casually changed from one day to the next.[111]

An amendment in 1968 provided for its phase-out.[112]

When Rojas Pinilla stepped down, a plebiscite in 1957 confirmed the solution of the National Front. Lleras Camargo was the first president elected under the system.[113] This agreement, coupled with expanded

---

[105] Palacios, *Between Legitimacy*, 93–94, 146–148.
[106] Palacios, *Between Legitimacy*, 132–133; Safford and Palacios, *Colombia*, 321–324.
[107] Bushnell, *The Making*, 216–217.
[108] Bravo Lira, *El estado constitucional*, 49–51.
[109] Gargarella, *Latin American Constitutionalism*, 123. See also Palacios, *Between Legitimacy*, 153–157.
[110] Bravo Lira, *El estado constitucional*, 53–56.
[111] Bushnell, *The Making*, 223–224.
[112] Ibid., 225.
[113] Gargarella, *Latin American Constitutionalism*, 123–124. See generally Safford and Palacios, *Colombia*, 324–335.

executive powers under a state of siege, led to a redefinition of the role of Congress, which was now relegated to public criticism of the government, commentary on current events, and an escape valve for hot issues.[114] The predictability of the system, and the exclusion of the Left, led to apathy and disinterest on the part of many Colombians.[115] The National Front encompassed four successive presidents elected by popular vote with alternate party affiliations, and the system was not dismantled completely until 1986.[116] Carlos Lleras Restrepo, president from 1966 to 1970 under the National Front, led a set of constitutional reforms in 1968 that improved proportional representation and abandoned a two-thirds requirement for most legislation in the Congress. Planning for the economic health of the country was concentrated in the executive branch and the possibility of an "economic emergency" was given constitutional form.[117] The following decades were overshadowed by the rise of powerful leftist guerrilla movements and the drug trade.[118] In 1985, M-19 guerrillas seized the Palace of Justice. More than 100 individuals died in the battle to retake the building and subsequent fire. Eleven of the twelve justices died.[119] In 1989, presidential candidate Luis Carlos Galán was assassinated at a political rally through orders of a drug cartel.[120]

In 1990, President Gaviria called a constituent assembly that included Liberals, Conservatives, and the Democratic Alliance (the political party formed from former M-19 guerrillas). The resulting Constitution of 1991 demonstrated a continued faith in constitutions as a means for political progress in the country.[121] Indeed, the Constitution has been viewed as an attempt to refound a state in the midst of crisis.[122] The Constitution of 1991 advanced many human rights, now identified as third- and fourth-generation rights. It recognized indigenous territorial units and enabled a law of Afro-Colombian communities. It created a new Constitutional Court and strengthened other institutions of the judicial branch. Nonetheless, it maintained a strong presidency.[123] And, as Loveman points out, it maintained

---

[114] Bravo Lira, *El estado constitucional*, 58–59.
[115] Gargarella, *Latin American Constitutionalism*, 124.
[116] Bravo Lira, *El estado constitucional*, 56, 61; Palacios, *Between Legitimacy*, 170–171.
[117] Palacios, *Between Legitimacy*, 187–188. See also Bushnell, *The Making*, 231.
[118] Bushnell, *The Making*, 252–268; Palacios, *Between Legitimacy*, 190–206; Safford and Palacios, *Colombia*, 339–342, 354–370.
[119] Palacios, *Between Legitimacy*, 207; Safford and Palacios, *Colombia*, 360.
[120] Palacios, *Between Legitimacy*, 212.
[121] Bravo Lira, *El estado constitucional*, 61.
[122] Safford and Palacios, *Colombia*, 336.
[123] Palacios, *Between Legitimacy*, 246–253.

the traditional constitutional escape clause of the region, a provision for states of exception and of internal commotion, which now includes provisions for social and environmental causes for its implementation.[124] A controversial provision was its prohibition of extradition of Colombians, a prohibition that was reversed in 1997.[125]

Cuba's noncompetitive system stems from Fidel Castro's reinstating the Constitution of 1940. Executive power was held by the president and prime minister; a Council of Ministers legislated. Elections or Congress was not necessary. In 1965, his United Party of the Revolution became the Communist Party of which Castro became the First Secretary.[126] The Cuban Constitution of 1976 provides for a National Assembly of the Popular Power that meets in two sessions a year. When not in session, the Council of State under the presidency of the chief of state and government tend to affairs.[127]

Other Latin American countries developed systems of political competition. Bravo Lira identified Chile from 1830 to 1924 as a stable political system with a congress that met regularly during the period. The presidency and Congress vied for power during this time. At first, the system was heavily presidentialist, but after 1860, political parties – conservative, liberal, national, and radical – rose in power and parties' control of congress meant that the president had to govern with the aid of his party or at times became substantially less powerful if there was a conflict with the party controlling Congress. This competitive system was challenged by the revolution in 1891 but continued more or less intact until the 1920s, when new conflicting political forces arose through two competing caudillos and the army. Arturo Alessandri was a populist who shed the party-based structure of control; Carlos Ibáñez was a caudillo born from the higher ranks of the military.[128]

This shift was the result of the political elements in play during the last decade of the nineteenth century and the first two decades of the twentieth century in Chile to address the new political landscape of unions, labor movements, socialism, and communism. Although extraordinary executive powers were unusual from 1894 to 1919, they would come to be relied on more after this period and under the new Constitution of 1925.[129]

[124] Loveman, *The Constitution*, 179–180, 391.
[125] Safford and Palacios, *Colombia*, 340.
[126] Bravo Lira, *El estado constitucional*, 95–96.
[127] Ibid., 96.
[128] Ibid., 102–109.
[129] Loveman, *The Constitution*, 350–351.

The Constitution of 1925 can be viewed as a sea change in the movement toward "the social" in legal and political thought.[130] The decades leading to the Constitution were guided by three major changes. First, electoral reforms created a parliamentary system that produced deadlocks and ministerial instability.[131] Second, a new class mentality arose from organized workers.[132] Third, the military intervened in politics as Alessandri was removed and reinstated though military force in quick succession.[133] A liberal nominating convention composed of the Liberal, Radical, and Democrat Parties put Alessandri's name forward, and he was elected in 1920. He sought a stronger executive, social reform consistent with the age, legislation that would be responsive to the country's needs, and, of course, a new constitution.[134] These goals were, at first, effectively blocked by conservatives, but on his reelection in 1924, his subsequent removal and reinstallation by differing factions of the military, and assumption of the presidency in 1925, Alessandri was able to move forward with these projects.[135] For the first time in Chilean history, the armed forces seized control of the government in 1924 and replaced the president and Congress with a council of government that selected Alessandri as president.[136] Under Alessandri a new, presidentialist constitution was drafted that, when promulgated in 1925, removed the country from direct military rule.[137]

The social question was addressed directly in his new constitution. These reforms included redefining property under the constitution as a social function, rather than as an individual right.[138] Although the Mexican Constitution of 1917 approached property with its social role in mind, the Chilean Constitution of 1925 was the first to adopt this definition, after extensive debate and direct presidential intervention, based on the writings of French constitutionalists Henri Hayem and León Duguit.[139] Such shifts in the concept of property were essential elements

[130] Kennedy, "Two Globalizations," 648–674; Mirow, "Origins," 1186.
[131] Mirow, "Origins," 1187; Rector, *History*, 130.
[132] Collier and Sater, *A History*, 199–200; Mirow, "Origins," 1187.
[133] Collier and Sater, *A History*, 209–211; Mirow, "Origins," 1187–1188; Rector, *History*, 132.
[134] Collier and Sater, *A History*, 201–205; Mirow, "Origins," 1188.
[135] Collier and Sater, *A History*, 210–214; Mirow, "Origins," 1188; Rector, *History*, 131–132.
[136] Bravo Lira, *El estado constitucional*, 107.
[137] Ibid., 109–110.
[138] Mirow, "Origins," 1188.
[139] Ibid., 1189–1209; Mirow, "The Social Obligation Norm," 191–226.

in creating systems of agrarian reform and land and urban redistribution in Latin America during the twentieth century.

The Constitution also contemplated constitutional review without providing for a Constitutional Court to ensure the constitutionality of legislation or enforce the newly established constitutional right. A legislative review panel, the Senate Committee on the Constitution, Legislation, and Justice, examined the constitutionality of legislation and undertook the task with seriousness and prestige. Respected senators who had often been judges before entering the legislature were members of the Committee.[140]

Supported by the political parties, Ibáñez governed from 1927 to 1931, and from the early 1930s until 1973, the Chilean government was shaped by competition between the political parties and the presidency. An increase in presidential power in the 1950s was challenged by the arrival of ideological and international parties – socialists, communists, and Christian Democrats – and a rise in terrorism in the 1960s.[141] In 1964, substantial changes were implemented under President Eduardo Frei including land reforms, programs aimed at poverty, and the nationalization of copper.[142] Salvador Allende's presidency was the last in the line of this competitive structure when it was brusquely terminated by General Augusto Pinochet and a military council of government.[143] The period of Allende's presidency was marked by competitive voices in the public arena. The opposition forced Allende to sign a Statute of Constitutional Guarantees that ensured he would protect basic rights and liberties.[144] The Statute protected rights of expression, assembly, education, and ensured compensation for the expropriation of property. After the economically significant moves of nationalizing the copper industry and other companies and of instituting land reform, Allende obtained a constitutional reform in 1971 that supported claims of nationalization and the state's ownership of natural resources. Eduardo Novoa Monreal was a key figure in setting out the law in relation to Allende's reforms and indeed attacked the Supreme Court for its unwillingness to bend in the

---

[140] Couso, "Models of Democracy," 1525.
[141] Bravo Lira, *El estado constitucional*, 111–116. See also Collier and Sater, *A History of Chile*, 237–263.
[142] Gargarella, *Latin American Constitutionalism*, 234 n. 18. See also Collier and Sater, *A History of Chile*, 305–325.
[143] Bravo Lira, *El estado constitucional*, 116–118.
[144] Gargarella, *Latin American Constitutionalism*, 127. See also Collier and Sater, *A History of Chile*, 328.

winds of change.[145] Novoa Monreal's use of extant legislation that had been dormant for decades, "forgotten precepts," as justification for many of these desired changes in the legal topography was a controversial yet creative and effective means to enact new measures.[146] Despite the severity of the transformations sought by Allende, he employed constitutional provisions and arguments to support his actions.[147]

Faced with opposition from the Supreme Court in these matters, Allende asserted the executive's power over the judicial power when fundamental questions of social transformation were at issue. Congress also viewed executive actions as exceeding appropriate authority and countered with legislation limiting expropriations. In August, 1973, the Chamber of Deputies went so far as to publish a statement expressing concern over the lack of constitutional actions and legality by the state, and on September 11, 1973, General Augusto Pinochet's coup removed Allende, who committed suicide during the attack.[148]

The Constitution of 1980 drafted under Pinochet's rule established the basis for dictatorship under constitutional language and the exercise of military jurisdiction over civilians.[149] The Ortúzar Commission produced a constitution that privileged the military and created a number of areas that ensured Pinochet's authoritarian control. These included senators for life, designated senators, electoral practices that blocked opposition voices, and a National Security Council.[150] Nonetheless, others have seen the Constitution as contemplating a return to rule by civilian authorities and political parties, excluding the Communist Party.[151] In any event, the broad executive powers in the Constitution of 1980 were built upon a long foundation of states of siege and extraordinary powers that were already very familiar in Chilean constitutionalism.[152] Subsequent constitutional amendments reduced the presidential term to four years and eased the requirements for amending the Constitution.[153] In 1990, Patricio Aylwin assumed the presidency and restored Congress.[154] Although the

---

[145] Gargarella, *Latin American Constitutionalism*, 127, 237 n. 43; Villalonga, *Revolución y Ley*.
[146] Gardner, *Legal Imperialism*, 166–169; See generally Villalonga, *Revolución y Ley*.
[147] Collier and Sater, *A History of Chile*, 347–356.
[148] Gargarella, *Latin American Constitutionalism*, 128. See also Collier and Sater, *A History of Chile*, 356–358.
[149] Loveman, *The Constitution*, 353.
[150] Gargarella, *Latin American Constitutionalism*, 149.
[151] Bravo Lira, *El estado constitucional*, 117–118; Collier and Sater, *A History of Chile*, 364.
[152] Loveman, *The Constitution*, 390.
[153] Collier and Sater, *A History of Chile*, 381.
[154] Bravo Lira, *El estado constitucional*, 121.

Constitution of 1980 remained in force after Pinochet, the reforms of President Ricardo Lagos and others over the next three decades moved the document and its institutions toward a more inclusive democracy.[155]

Other countries were caught in cycles between military and civil governments. To illustrate this structure, Bravo Lira selected Argentina in the twentieth century as an example because it was nominally governed by the Constitution of 1853. Bravo Lira saw the rise of military government in Argentina as a reaction to the lack of or failure of civil government, particularly in response to the world-wide depression of 1929. What began as temporary solutions to a present crisis transformed into a method of government unto itself as it created institutions and government structures that became permanent.[156] States of siege with suspension of civil rights became common in the first half of the twentieth century in Argentina.[157]

General Juan Domingo Perón, with his wife Eva, embodied hopes for social and political transformation. Perón came to power through a military coup in 1943 and then was elected president in 1946.[158] The Peronist Party was founded in 1947 to shape Argentina toward social justice, economic liberty, and political sovereignty. Perón replaced the Constitution of 1853 with the Constitution of 1949 that echoed the core ideas of transforming society and work in the country.[159] The Constitution sought to restrict the electorate and expand presidential powers. Negretto correctly views this constitutional episode as a prime example of constitutional change to consolidate power in which a new powerful political party effects a new constitution reflecting the party's political and policy positions. This included the heavy-handed impeachment of the Supreme Court in 1947 to create a judiciary that was amenable to finding various legal reforms consistent with the Constitution then in effect.[160]

The intellectual force behind the Constitution of 1949 was Arturo Sampay, who argued for the state's intervention in the economy and society. Gargarella noted a number of defining attributes of this important document, including the rejection of liberalism and an acceptance of the role of the state to serve the common good of citizens, the acceptance of principles of Roman Catholic social justice, the doctrine of the

---

[155] Gargarella, *Latin American Constitutionalism*, 149.
[156] Bravo Lira, *El estado constitucional*, 146–147.
[157] Loveman, *The Constitution*, 289–290.
[158] Gargarella, *Latin American Constitutionalism*, 119.
[159] Bravo Lira, *El estado constitucional*, 147–148.
[160] Negretto, *Making Constitutions*, 11, 113–137.

social function of property, a state as a supporter of Christian morality, and, of course, a powerful executive centering on Perón's personality.[161] Solidifying executive gains, the Constitution also permitted immediate presidential reelection and the power to push uncooperative local governments aside to further federal goals.[162] In retrospect, Sampay concluded that the Constitution, in fact, did not go far enough in the sense that it did not fundamentally change the institutions under the Constitution and the way power was organized under it to bring about the contemplated changes.[163] The Constitution of 1853 was placed back into service after Aramburu's coup against Perón in 1955 and was Argentina's constitution until 1994.[164]

In contrast to the Chilean experience, Congress in Argentina since 1930 has had an on-again, off-again existence. Indeed, Loveman estimated that from 1930 until 1970, Argentina was under a state of siege for approximately 45 percent of the time.[165] Congress functioned from 1932 to 1943 and then from 1946 to 1953. Under Perón, Congress was a place of discourse but not action. Another period of activity from 1958 to 1966 was without the influence of Perón, but then again under Peronism from 1973 until 1975. Congress was closed after the military coup of 1976, but after the military government was discredited in the Falklands/Malvinas War, it opened again in 1983 under President Raúl Alfonsín and functions today.[166]

For much of this period, Congress was not needed to enact laws. Extraconstitutional action by the executive through decree-laws supplemented or surpassed congressional legislative action. In 1955, the president was, by decree, given the legislative capacity held by the Congress under the Constitution. In 1966, decree-laws stopped being named as such and took on the more regular title of simply "law." Again, extraordinary temporary solutions became the norm. Similarly, the military council that took control after Perón's death removed the president, dissolved Congress, and abolished political parties.[167] Many of the atrocities of the dirty war were cloaked with the constitutional authority of the state of siege.[168] After the death of Perón, the military junta violently suppressed

[161] Gargarella, *Latin American Constitutionalism*, 119–121.
[162] Negretto, *Making Constitutions*, 123, 133.
[163] Gargarella, *Latin American Constitutionalism*, 186–187.
[164] Bravo Lira, *El estado constitucional*, 155.
[165] Loveman, *The Constitution*, 290.
[166] Bravo Lira, *El estado constitucional*, 149–150, 159.
[167] Ibid., 150–151, 159.
[168] Loveman, *The Constitution*, 290.

opposition. More than 10,000 guerrilla troops, sympathizers, suspects, and innocents were "disappeared."[169]

Thus, Bravo Lira observed that since 1930, Argentina has alternated between constitutional and extraconstitutional governments. He importantly noted that extraconstitutional governments were not without constitutions, but were recent examples of unwritten constitutions that expressed common elements and methods. The indications of such a situation were the powerlessness of Congress, the irrelevance of political parties, and the expansion of presidential powers.[170] Under these circumstances, military governments swept in with their own unwritten way of proceeding which formed a plastic constitution not subject to the checks of a written document held as the supreme law.

Peru provides another important example of the fluctuation between civil and military governments in the twentieth century. From 1919 to 1930, President Augusto Leguía sought to challenge congressional inaction and congressional parties.[171] Coming into power after various civilian governments through a coup, Leguía sought to stem the tide of communism. The Peruvian Constitution of 1920 promulgated under his presidency was a liberal document with protections for civil rights, but Leguía exercised extraordinary powers that included suspending guarantees that were constitutionally not able to be suspended. Leguía was ousted by a military coup in 1930 that was followed by the Constitution of 1933 that recognized the military as a force to maintain public order.[172]

In response to the rise of Peronism in Argentina and incorporating the ideology of the Mexican Revolution, Víctor Raúl Haya de la Torre founded APRA (*Alianza Popular Revolucionaria Americana*) while in exile in Mexico.[173] APRA had regional aspirations to counter U.S. imperialism and to unify Latin America. It sought to nationalize lands and industries and to create solidarity between all oppressed classes and people.[174] It was an important political actor since its founding but did not have an official APRA victory until Alan García won Peru's presidential election until 1985.[175]

---

[169] Feitlowitz, *A Lexicon*; *Nunca Más*; Rock, *Argentina*, 367–368.
[170] Bravo Lira, *El estado constitucional*, 160–161.
[171] Ibid., 162.
[172] Loveman, *The Constitution*, 230–231.
[173] Bravo Lira, *El estado constitucional*, 162.
[174] Velasco Ibarra, *Expresión política*, 149–150.
[175] Bravo Lira, *El estado constitucional*, 163.

The Peruvian Constitution of 1933, nominally in effect until 1980, served as the palimpsest on which a series of extraconstitutional civil and military governments were sketched.[176] The text of the Constitution provided for numerous social rights and limitations on the executive branch, which was under the control of the Council of Ministers and could be censured by Congress.[177] Congress met infrequently under the constitution.[178] In 1948, General Odría removed President Bustamante y Rivero and was himself selected president in 1950. The next president, Manuel Prado, was also removed by the army in 1962. There was then a three-way split for succession between Haya de la Torre of APRA, former President Odría, and the leader of a new party, Fernando Belaúnde, who was selected by the armed forces and elected to the presidency. He was removed by the army in 1968 on complaints of government inefficiency and replaced with General Juan Velasco Alvarado, who governed from 1968 to 1975. He was removed by the army and replaced with General Francisco Morales Bermúdez, who, in 1980, began the process of leading the country back to civilian rule. Belaúnde was elected in 1980 and Congress was opened. He was succeeded by the Aprista Alan García in 1985.[179]

Two constitutions were produced by the military governments of this period, one in 1968 and another in 1979. The provisions on the state of siege in the Constitution of 1979 served as the basis for extraordinary powers in the 1980s as these governments battled the *Sendero Luminoso*.[180] The Constitution of 1979 was a compromise between APRA and the Popular Christian Party. It attempted to install various institutional checks between the executive, the Council of Ministers, and the Chamber of Deputies.[181] On the heels of discontent over García's handling of domestic terrorism, Alberto Fujimori came to power in 1990 and ruled with expansive autocratic power.[182] Fujimori suspended the Constitution of 1979 in 1992 and ruled through presidential decrees. Through these decrees he waged war against Peru's rebel groups and transformed Peru's economy by instituting neoliberal policies including the privatization of many state-held assets, all without the need of Congress.[183]

---

[176] Ibid.,
[177] Gargarella, *Latin American Constitutionalism*, 234 n 14.
[178] Bravo Lira, *El estado constitucional*, 163.
[179] Ibid., 163–165.
[180] Loveman, *The Constitution*, 232.
[181] Gargarella, *Latin American Constitutionalism*, 234 n. 13.
[182] Bravo Lira, *El estado constitucional*, 165.
[183] Loveman, *The Constitution*, 232–233. See also Boza, *Doing Business*.

Bolivia continued with states of siege and extraordinary powers under the constitution in the twentieth century. Extraordinary powers were exercised during the social revolution of 1952 and incorporated into the Constitution of 1967.[184] Picking up some of the social rights expressed in prior constitutions, the Constitution of 1967 expanded the franchise, agrarian reform, and education while nationalizing mines.[185] Under Víctor Paz Estenssoro's second presidency, he invoked a state of siege in 1985 to suppress striking miners who were protesting his neoliberal reforms.[186]

Uruguay shed military rule during the first decades of the twentieth century. President José Batlle y Ordóñez, a member of the Colorado Party, sought significant economic and social reforms, including the reduction of presidential power and an increase in minority party representation on the executive council.[187] He sought to advance the working classes, to counter foreign influences, and to establish a plural executive in which members took turns addressing the political needs of the country.[188] These reforms were partially instilled in the Constitution of 1918.[189] For example, the Constitution creates an executive that shared power between the president and a National Administrative Council. Uruguay experimented with methods of diluting presidential power and in 1952 instituted a system in which a National Council of Government composed of four members was coordinated by the president. The country returned to a single executive under the Constitution of 1967.[190] Nonetheless, emergency provisions in the Constitution were still present, and during the twentieth century, Uruguay's executive was faced with sufficient justification to declare states of internal war and the suspension of liberties under the Constitution, particularly when confronted by social unrest and guerrilla movements in the second half of the century. Proposals for a new constitution in 1980 were not successful.[191]

In Paraguay, the first decade of the twentieth century brought a liberal military coup with Argentine help against an entrenched Colorado Party president. Nonetheless, the same pattern of rapid presidential succession

---

[184] Loveman, *The Constitution*, 261–262.
[185] Gargarella, *Latin American Constitutionalism*, 237 n. 39.
[186] Loveman, *The Constitution*, 262.
[187] Ibid., 302.
[188] Gargarella, *Latin American Constitutionalism*, 97.
[189] Loveman, *The Constitution*, 302–303.
[190] Gargarella, *Latin American Constitutionalism*, 97–98.
[191] Loveman, *The Constitution*, 304–305.

continued into the 1920s with presidents leaving office every year or two.[192] The aftermath of the Chaco War with Bolivia from 1932 to 1935 led to a new constitution, the Paraguayan Constitution of 1940, that continued the possibilities of the state of siege and of limiting civil liberties under dire circumstances. This Constitution was an early example of outlawing Marxism; Article 35 prohibits "preaching of hatred or class conflict."[193]

The situation in Central America in the twentieth century reflects many of these themes. Guatemala experienced presidential and military control from the late nineteenth to the mid-twentieth centuries. Its twentieth-century constitutional trajectory was punctuated by an unsuccessful social revolution from 1944 to 1954.[194] The Constitution of 1945 provided for a number of social and workers' rights, legalized unions, and sought to reduce presidential powers through a Council of Ministers supervised by the Congress of this "republic of workers."[195] Intervention by the United States in 1954 continued the tradition of military control after Guatemala's social revolution until the 1980s, but the country did not shake military influence and regimes of exception.[196]

States of siege, military control, decree-laws, and constitutional dictatorship were equally a part of El Salvador's experience, even after the civil wars of the 1970s and 1980s.[197] These facets of government similarly remained ensconced in Honduras after its transition to civil government and a new constitution in 1982.[198] Such instruments of power were not limited to conservative regimes or to the right. Article 185 of the Nicaragua Constitution of 1986 of the Sandinistas states, "The President of the Republic may suspend, in all or part of the national territory, the rights and guaranties consecrated in this constitution in the case of war or when national security, economic conditions or a national catastrophe demand it."[199]

Similarly, Venezuela was governed by Juan Vicente Gómez from 1908 to 1935 after he ousted an already absent president. He used the emergency powers under Venezuela's Constitution of 1904 and various

---

[192] Ibid., 311.
[193] Ibid., 312.
[194] Ibid., 108–109.
[195] Gargarella, *Latin American Constitutionalism*, 112.
[196] Loveman, *The Constitution*, 109.
[197] Ibid., 115.
[198] Ibid., 121.
[199] Ibid., 126.

reforms to cloak his activities with constitutional justification.[200] The Venezuelan political writer Laureano Vallenilla Lanz in his *Cesarismo democrático* provided a theoretical justification for the caudillo-style rule of Gómez, a tradition Vallenilla traced to Bolívar himself. Such dictatorial control, in Vallenilla's view, was necessary to protect the country from war and despotism.[201] Many of Gómez's same tools were employed by Marcos Pérez Jiménez, who led the country from 1948 to 1958.[202] To avoid continued military regimes, representatives of the three main political parties and exiles met in New York City and signed a pact to make political changes. Shortly afterwards in 1958, the same leaders, excluding the Communist Party, which had also sought to act against Pérez Jiménez, signed the Pact of Punto Fijo. They sought a common program, respect for the electoral process, and a coalition government.[203] The same year, Rómulo Betancourt was elected, and under his presidency the country promulgated the Constitution of 1961. The Constitution strengthened social provisions and established a presidential system without reelection. It is known for its provision giving the president extraordinary powers to handle economic crises and to issue legislative decrees. The Constitution is also known for advancing social rights and in other areas actually limiting the executive power, such as a ten-year waiting period before presidential reelection of the same person. Two of the three original Punto Fijo parties maintained control of the government until the 1990s, when the government responded to social protests in Caracas with violence, the "Caracazo," and it was challenged by two unsuccessful military coups. Hugo Chávez was elected president in 1999.[204]

Presidentialism, Legislative Decrees, and the Military

Another common characteristic of Latin American constitutionalism, presidentialism, continued in this period. The idea that presidentialism is the national extension of the caudillo system has been asserted by several scholars.[205] Constitutions that stressed centralized power in a strong executive or president often mandated infrequent congressional sessions. During the nineteenth century, congresses rarely sat for more than ninety

---

[200] Ibid., 158–159.
[201] Gargarella, *Latin American Constitutionalism*, 88–89.
[202] Loveman, *The Constitution*, 159.
[203] Gargarella, *Latin American Constitutionalism*, 121–122.
[204] Ibid., 121–123, 234 n. 13.
[205] Velasco Ibarra, *Expresión política*, 116–121.

days in a year. Some constitutions only mandated a congress every two years.[206] As described above, there might be long periods during which no congress, or no meaningful congress, had sessions.

With few instances of true constitutional states functioning with congresses doing most of the legislating, alternate methods of making law sprang up to enable some sort of effective government. Decree-laws, legislative decrees, or decrees with the force of law were and are the result of executive or military law making in the absence of or inability of functioning constitutional legislative bodies.[207] Thus, the rise of the decree-law was the reverse side of the weakening of congress as an effective legislative body. Further methods of limiting congressional action included the political subordination of the Congress to political parties, such as the case of Mexico, and reductions in the duration of congressional sessions ensuring that congress simply did not have enough time to act or to address particular problems.[208] The scope of political parties themselves was restricted during the mid-twentieth century as Latin American countries responded or were made to respond to the Cold War. The Communist Party became illegal in Chile, Colombia, Costa Rica, and Peru in 1948, and in Venezuela in 1950.[209]

Some political parties might result from not only internal needs but also perceived external threats or transnational ideologies. In the 1920s and 1930s, parties representing international socialism appeared in Argentina, Chile, Cuba, Mexico, and Peru.[210] Peru's APRA Party sought to counter U.S. imperialism, unify Latin America, nationalize lands and industries, internationalize the Panama Canal, and create solidarity between all oppressed classes and people.[211] Other parties reflected national positions, such as Chile's National Falangist party founded in 1935 and Mexico's PRI, founded in 1929.[212]

It was also possible to replace Congress by order or decree with a new, usually smaller body beholden to the executive or the military. For example, in Chile from 1972 to 1990, legislative power resided in the council of government composed of the chief military officers. Where Congresses

---

[206] Loveman, *The Constitution*, 389.
[207] Bravo Lira, *El estado constitucional*, 29; Loveman, *The Constitution*, 382–384.
[208] Bravo Lira, *El estado constitucional*, 203, 206–207.
[209] Gargarella, *Latin American Constitutionalism*, 110.
[210] Bravo Lira, *El estado constitucional*, 32.
[211] Velasco Ibarra, *Expresión política*, 149–150.
[212] Bravo Lira, *El estado constitucional*, 32.

remained, their functioning might take on a ritualistic, formalistic, or legitimizing function.[213]

Decree-laws were common in the region. From 1930 to 1980, Argentina enacted approximately 6,000 legislative acts and 9,000 extra-constitutional decrees. From 1949 to 1959, Colombia enacted 165 legislative acts and approximately 3,000 decree-laws. Even though Chile had a functioning congress from 1933 until 1973, from the period 1924 to 1989, it enacted nearly 14,000 legislative acts and approximately 5,500 decree-laws.[214] Some constitutions placed the power in Congress to activate these powers; others in smaller government councils, and others at the discretion of the executive branch itself.[215]

Regimes of exception and states of siege under constitutions that provided for extraordinary powers in the executive branch during times of danger to the country were another essential aspect of constitutionalism in this period. Such powers might easily be exercised politically to the disfavor of opponents and to suppress dissent. While well recognized in the twentieth century, these devices of autocratic control have a long history in the region and date well back to the founding constitutional documents of the region. Indeed, only two constitutions from the nineteenth century did not have some sort of regimes of exception, the liberal Colombian Constitutions of 1853 and 1863.[216]

Powers under states of siege were not always limitless or without definition. Declarations of a state of siege might require congress being out of session, approval by another body of the government, subsequent legislative ratification or review, or other elements expressed in the constitution. The extent of the suspension of constitutional guarantees also varied from time to time and from constitution to constitution. Some constitutional states of siege suspended all civil rights; other constitutions allowed only a partial suspension based on geography, time, or the nature of the right. Furthermore, such devices were not the exclusive tool of the right or the left; they have been used by conservative military dictators and far-left autocratic ideologues, with the opposition usually declaring their objections to such centralized, unchecked, and at times cruelly brutal power in the executive. Neither communism nor authoritarian anti-communist dictators invented these regimes of exception. Both effectively exercised such regimes not only for the stability of the state but also for

---

[213] Ibid., 208–211.
[214] Ibid., 30, 205.
[215] Loveman, *The Constitution*, 380–382.
[216] Ibid., 375–377.

political and ideological repression. Enemies, even citizen enemies, could be characterized outside the law, outside the constitution and its constitutional protection of civil rights.[217]

Such exercises of power were effectively without review. Presidents were never prosecuted for going beyond the scope of their grant of power nor subject to impeachment. Judicial procedures for protecting the constitutional rights of individuals such as habeas corpus and *amparo* were not used to challenge executive extraordinary powers in the nineteenth century. This reflected the relative weakness of the judiciary and its reliance on the executive. Furthermore, the idea of judicial review of other branches of government was not well developed. For example, when it seemed the Supreme Court of Argentina was about to challenge actions by the executive branch its members were dismissed, in 1946, 1955, 1966, 1973, and 1976.[218]

Considering the broad role of the military in the political and institutional life of Latin American countries, some have suggested the military should be properly considered as a fourth branch of government. Charged with much more than external national defense in many constitutions, the military was often required to maintain internal peace and order. Even without a constitutional requirement, the military often assumed this duty.[219] In this light, one study has recorded more than 170 military coups in Latin America during the twentieth century.[220] The military might assume the role of constitutional protector in light of perceived illegal or unconstitutional actions by other branches of the government. This means that the idea of military *intervention* in politics is a misnomer because the military was an incorporated constitutional entity *within* the ambit of the constitution. The problem of subjecting civilians to military jurisdiction, where injustices are thought to be more likely, is linked to this position of the military within the constitutional order. The reduction of the constitutional place of the military and the limitation of military jurisdiction over civilians are steps toward civic government in the region. Constitutions have also attempted to check military power or influence in civil government by making military officers ineligible for the presidency and other public offices.[221]

---

[217] Ibid., 385–392, 395, 404.
[218] Ibid., 392–393.
[219] Ibid., 399–400.
[220] Gargarella, *Latin American Constitutionalism*, 109.
[221] Loveman, *The Constitution*, 401–402, 405.

The Cádiz Effect: Politicization of Constitutional
Texts and Processes

These challenges are not new to the region, but rather are the product of each nation's constitutional and legal development. Although regional generalizations are subject to dangerous inaccuracies, some broader trends can be noted. Tracing the historiography of Latin American constitutionalism is a daunting task, and indeed scholars have observed that no full study has been undertaken.[222]

Bravo Lira suggests that the region's constitutional history may be divided into three stages: (1) a parliamentary stage from approximately 1810 to 1850 during which countries attempted to establish representative legislatures under characteristically strong presidents; (2) a political party stage from approximately 1850 to 1920 during which congresses are subject to the control of party politics; and (3) a congressional crisis and monocratic stage beginning in 1920 during which congresses and congressional parties fall into decadence and the executive governs through decree. This is, of course, only one scholar's approach and it has its conceptual difficulties, among them how to overlay military governments, which was addressed more or less separately by Bravo Lira at the end of his work on this topic.[223]

The success of independence movements was the result of military might, and strong generals led to the rise of military leaders. Thus, according to Rodríguez, in northern South America, "men of arms dominated men of law."[224] As mentioned earlier, the strong executive and lifetime presidency created under Bolívar's Constitution of Bolivia in 1826, for example, share little in common with the legislatively strong provisions of the Constitution of Cádiz.[225] In populations accustomed to the ordinary politics of constitutions through the Cádiz experience, the path toward caudillism, presidentialism, autocracy, and indeed military rule was already being cleared. Many of these autocratic exercises of control were effected through regimes of exception that continue today as an important element of Latin American political and constitutional life. The necessity of maintaining order and checking unconstitutional exercises of power by elected presidents has often been the justification for ouster by the military. The ouster of President Allende in 1973 by the

---

[222] Bravo Lira, *El estado constitucional*, 7.
[223] Ibid., 22–34, 167–229.
[224] Rodríguez, *The Independence*, 240, 243.
[225] Ibid., 234–235.

forces of General Pinochet was justified by a declaration that Allende had violated fundamental rights and was leading the country into anarchy and economic ruin. The military claimed that it took upon itself the moral duty to depose the government. Thus, the constitutional and political place of the military in society was a central characteristic of Latin American constitutionalism.[226]

Seeing regimes of exception as central to the constitutional challenges in the region today, Brian Loveman found grave error in their creation in nineteenth-century constitutions and writes, "The constitutional foundations for repression, exile, trial of civilians in military courts, newspaper closures, dissolutions of Congress, and internal war – albeit updated somewhat with new laws for the protecting of the internal security of state – were the legacy of the liberals and conservatives of the nineteenth century."[227] Thus, he sees the reform of these provisions as a necessary step toward meaningful constitutional government in the region.[228] Conversely, such provisions can be viewed as important escape valves in times of crisis to maintain constitutional continuity.[229]

Concern about the region's constitutional order and the promotion of democracy is not new.[230] In 1943, Velasco Ibarra wrote confidently of a regional ideal of South American constitutionalism and of "hispano-american constitutional law."[231] Despite noting variation by country in the region, Velasco Ibarra recognized that institutional and social impediments hindered a functioning constitutionalism in the region. These included the need for constitutionalism to match the political and social realities of the country, to address the place of religion in the political sphere, to recognize peasants and particularly indigenous populations, and to educate the citizenry in the political process.[232] He also noted common attributes such as presidentialism, the strength of the executive power in relation to the other powers, and the role of political parties.[233]

By 1952, Jesús de Galíndez traced constitutional instability in the region from the independence period to the date of his study. Noting a brief respite from new constitutions in Chile, Argentina, Uruguay, and Mexico during the second half of the nineteenth century as exceptions

---

[226] Loveman, *The Constitution*, 14–15, 374.
[227] Ibid., 8.
[228] Ibid., 9.
[229] Aguilar Rivera, *El manto*, 10–21, 41–57, 117.
[230] González Marco, "Comparative Law."
[231] Velasco Ibarra, *Expresión política*, 13, 105–168.
[232] Ibid., 38–43, 83–93, 95–104, 123, 131, 157, 159–168.
[233] Ibid., 110–12, 143–157.

to a continuous state of flux, de Galíndez found that most countries in the region during the twentieth century began again repeatedly to enact new constitutions.[234] Constitutional instability was coupled with many forms of political instability, autocratic or military rule, and rapid turnover of governments.[235] By one estimate, Bolivia experienced 200 coups in 155 years as a republic by the year 1980 with concomitant constitutional flux.[236] Venezuela has had more than twenty-five constitutional texts since 1811.[237] Some countries had long periods of the same constitution in place, but most constitutions were short lived, and even where constitutions had long lives, this fact alone reveals nothing of healthy functioning constitutional governments.[238]

As observed in this chapter, writing in the early 1990s, Bravo Lira assessed Latin American constitutionalism since 1920 as caught in an apparently endless cycle of constitutionalism, anarchy, and militarism in which constitutional and military governments shift back and forth.[239] Looking out his window in the 1990s, Bravo Lira observed, "The fact is that for more than a century and a half, there is hardly a year in which a civil government is not replaced by a military one or vice versa in one of the twenty Iberoamerican countries."[240] Bravo Lira finds several causes for this "constant oscillation."[241] These include, in his view, the attempt to instill foreign institutions through constitutions that were not consistent with the region's historical development, the lack of an historical response to an oppressive metropole in the colonial context that failed to lead to a desire for self-government, and the rise of a new militarism seeking functioning governments in the face of civil governments' perceived failures. The results are extraparliamentary laws, the subordination of the legislative to the executive, the shortening of legislative sessions, the suspension of legislatures, and a decline in the value of elections. Although he asserts the descriptive accuracy of this cycle and these factors, Bravo Lira believes it is possible to break the cycle.[242]

Can we really blame the Constitution of Cádiz for all this? Other students of the region's constitutional history see countries' attempts

[234] De Galíndez, "La inestabilidad constitucional," 5.
[235] Bravo Lira, *El estado constitucional*, 7.
[236] Rivera, "La evolución político-institucional en Bolivia," 102, 104.
[237] Ayala and Casal, "La evolución político-institucional de Venezuela," 553.
[238] Bravo Lira, *El estado constitucional*, 12–19.
[239] Ibid., 3, 196.
[240] Ibid., 167.
[241] Ibid., 169.
[242] Ibid., 172–177, 189, 197–200, 204–210.

to establish more meaningful constitutional regimes as challenged by their constitutional past.[243] For example, concerning the back-and-forth swings between civil and military rule in the region, Bravo Lira writes, "The point of departure for the coming and going in Iberoamerica, and also in the Iberian peninsula, of civil government to military government, is the political vacuum created by the collapse of the enlightened monarchy at the beginning of the nineteenth century."[244] The resulting constitutionalism was, in Bravo Lira's view, "foreign [and] difficult to adapt to these countries."[245] Thus, "historically, militarism is born in Iberoamerica in conjunction with constitutionalism as a result of its failures."[246] The Constitution of Cádiz, for all its movement toward liberal constitutionalism, representative institutions, and separation of powers, failed to take root and failed to raise constitutions and constitutional law above the politics of the day.

Conclusion

The twentieth century continued a process of the politicization of constitutionalism. Constitutional practices shifted dramatically toward the social, and the Mexican Constitution of 1917 serves as a bridge to the modern era. The unique structure and content of this Constitution marked a strong break from past constitutional practices and past models, making it a watershed document in Latin American constitutional development. The text of the Constitution and the debates surrounding it reveal important national and regional shifts in ideas of social rights, nationalization of natural resources, agrarian reform, and the place of the church in public and political life. The Constitution of 1917 asserted a number of economic and social rights related to housing, education, health, and work. It foreshadowed aspects of environmental and cultural rights. Although some of these issues arose before 1910 and the Mexican Revolution, the Mexican Constitution of 1917 must be a focal point of study in Latin American constitutionalism of the twentieth century, as the Constitution of Cádiz is for the nineteenth century. The provisions of the Mexican Constitution of 1917 served as a model throughout the region as countries considered constitutional changes to reflect various

---

[243] Rivera, "La evolución político-institucional en Bolivia," 143.
[244] Bravo Lira, *El estado constitucional*, 195.
[245] Ibid.,
[246] Ibid., 221.

social or political revolutions. Furthermore, the twentieth century witnessed a recrafting of political liberalism into economic liberalism. As Aguilar Rivera states, "if during the nineteenth century the constitutional aspect of liberalism was hegemonic, what happened in the twentieth century was that political liberalism was eclipsed by different authoritarianisms. Although individual liberties and democracy are from the beginning incompatible with dictatorships, the free market was not. Thus, in the countries of the Southern Cone, liberalism was reduced to one of its components, the economic."[247]

Latin American constitutionalism continued into the twentieth century with characteristic attributes of presidentialism, states of exception, decree-laws, militarism, and authoritarianism. Following the practices of the earliest constitutions in the region and the Constitution of Cádiz, the politicization of constitutions and constitutional law continued to be an attribute of Latin American constitutionalism in the twentieth century.

[247] Aguilar Rivera, *La geometría*, 141.

7

Constitutional Promise

Latin American Constitutionalism Today

The later twentieth and early twenty-first centuries remain a mixed bag when one considers constitutions and constitutional effectiveness in the region. Since the 1970s, countries have sought to shed autocratic and dictatorial rule, and in this process, a new era of Latin Constitutionalism has responded to awakened desires to create effective democratic and participatory constitutional governments. It has not been a smooth process. Many of the challenges of the past 200 years continue to hinder this goal. Political instability, social insecurity, violence, organized crime, wealth discrepancy, and corruption have been at times insurmountable obstacles over the past forty years.

Constitutions continue to be subject to replacement or frequently amendment on a political level.[1] The relatively rapid turnover of constitutions has produced varied and sometimes unexpected outcomes and effects. Oquendo has properly attributed instability in political and social environments as causes of constitutional turnover and has characterized this relatively rapid promulgation of new constitutions as a form of national catharsis that seeks to leave a less desirable past behind.[2] In writing about their findings obtained through their path-breaking Comparative Constitutions Project, Elkins, Ginsburg, and Melton have charted the difficulties that arise from a rapid turnover of constitutions. Constitutions need time to create habits of obedience, political stability, effective institutions, a united polity, and economic welfare.[3] Similarly,

[1] Ortiz Gutiérrez, "La evolución político-constitucional de la República de Colombia," 266–272.
[2] Oquendo, *Latin American Law*, 124.
[3] Elkins, Ginsburg, and Melton, *The Endurance*, 5–6, 17–22.

Schor has written of "constitutional entrenchment" in the Latin American context.[4] Criticism and concern for many constitutions in a short period of time in Latin America is not entirely new. Writing more than sixty years ago, de Galíndez expressed his frustration this way:

The maximum difficulty that confronts any student who tries to analyze constitutional law in Latin America is the instability that even now predominates in many of its countries. It is almost impossible to be current; and of course every comparative study winds up antiquated a few years after coming off the press.[5]

De Galíndez attributed the rapid succession of constitutions in the region to their texts focusing too much on political agendas rather than on lasting institutional structures.[6]

There has also been little consistency in constitutional design; the region is experiencing many independent and autonomous developments within each state that do not represent regional and uniform solutions.[7] As Negretto observes, "Although it is true that institutions tend to outlive the conditions of their creation and the original intentions of their designers, the relationship between institutional change and institutional effects is more dynamic than is often assumed, particularly in unstable political environments."[8] Difference in design and structure in modern constitutions of the region is not necessarily a bad thing; countries have increasingly sought their own solutions to their own challenges, and in light of this, one might expect varying structures and designs.

The region still claims a litany of challenges in the realm of constitutions, constitutional law, and the protection of constitutional rights. In addition to a recent history of short-lived constitutions and rapid turnover of constitutional texts, Latin America continues to experience periods of autocratic authoritarianism in the executive and armed intervention in the political and constitutional process.[9] Political instability, corruption, abuse of power, and a perceived disregard for the rule of law challenge effective constitutionalism.[10] Political parties are often viewed as prime actors in these activities.[11] Indeed, since 1978, constitutions in

---

[4] Schor, "Constitutionalism," 27–34.
[5] De Galíndez, "La inestabilidad constitucional," 3.
[6] Ibid., 20–22.
[7] Negretto, *Making Constitutions*, 224, 227, 237, 241–242; Negretto, "Shifting Constitutional Designs," 1805.
[8] Negretto, *Making Constitutions*, 241.
[9] Nogueira Alcalá, "Preámbulo," 12.
[10] Carpizo, "Presentación," 17–18.
[11] Reinaldo Vanossi, "La desconstitucionalización," 81–99; Rivera, "La evolución político-institucional en Bolivia entre 1975 a 2005," 116, 118.

the region usually reflect the input and policy choices of two or more national parties.[12]

A recent survey of the constitutional condition of South America from 1975 to 2005 reveals that, despite notable progress, difficulties remain.[13] The situation is well known, and few examples are sufficient. The successful and failed unconstitutional seizures of power by the military through coups d'état were common in the period.[14] Legislatures were closed by authoritarian or military order.[15] Constitutional programs for agrarian reform have been slow to move forward, creating perhaps even more social unrest than if such promises had not been made in the first place.[16] Promises of diluting central power through federalism in countries with this system have not resulted in regional control and self-determination. Indeed, Levaggi cautions that as federalism has played out in Latin America, it has taken on very different attributes than those contained in the U.S. system. He writes of "the progressive decline of federalism and its *de facto* transformation into a unitary regime" and of Argentina today having a "relatively opulent national treasury" with "mere nominal federalism."[17]

Presidents have sought constitutional reform, when sufficient electoral backing was present, to ensure their ability to be immediately reelected, and the region has witnessed a general trend toward more permissive presidential election since the mid-1980s.[18] The Argentine Constitution of 1994 is one example.[19] President Menem sought a constitution that would permit his immediate reelection and entered into an accord with former President Alfonsín.[20] With the backdrop of President Alfonsín's use of extraconstitutional decrees to address economic crisis in the

---

[12] Negretto, *Making Constitutions*, 226, 239.
[13] Nogueira Alcalá, *La evolución político-constitucional de América del Sur 1976–2005*.
[14] Ayala Corao and Casal, "La evolución político-institucional de Venezuela 1975–2005," 552; Carrasco Delgado, "La evolución político-constitucional de Chile," 306; García Belaunde and Eguiguren Praeli, "La evolución político-constitucional del Perú 1976–2005," 464, 480, 485–386; Ortiz Gutiérrez, "La evolución político-constitucional de la República de Colombia 1976–2005," 214; Rivera, "La evolución político-institucional en Bolivia entre 1975 a 2005," 106; Sagüés, "Evolución institucional argentina," 24; Salgado Pesantes, "Treinta años de democracia," 399, 413–414.
[15] Bravo Lira, *El estado constitucional*, 117, 149, 150, 163.
[16] Alviar García, "The Unending Quest," 1895–1914; Mirow, *Latin American Law*, 221–224. See generally Azuela, "Property in the Post-post-revolution," 1915–1942.
[17] Levaggi, "Three Matters," 8283.
[18] Negretto, "Shifting Constitutional Designs," 1785–1788.
[19] Negretto, *Making Constitutions*, 11.
[20] Oquendo, *Latin American Law*, 152–153.

1980s, President Menem, elected in 1989, adopted and expanded the practice significantly and attempted to address the crisis through trade liberalization, national austerity, and privatization. Cleared in 1990 by an amenable Supreme Court constructed through court-packing, these decrees became even more frequent.[21] A frequent trope, economic crisis empowered and concentrated the executive. The resulting Constitution of 1994 did much more than effect the possibility of consecutive presidential terms and transfer some presidential powers to a coordinating minister, the latter being one of Alfonsín's requirements.[22] It permitted consecutive presidential election, a president with no local powers, the appointment of federal judges through a system using a National Judicial Council, the presidential appointment of Supreme Court justices with Senate approval, and the legality of the kind of decrees employed in previous years.[23] In bids for constitutional provisions permitting consecutive reelection, sitting presidents are sometimes forced to make structural and institutional concessions that create new constitutional landscapes.

Military governments or strong presidents used decree powers to enact laws often under the constitutional cover of emergency powers.[24] Decrees might even serve to enact constitutional texts. Authoritarian regimes operated with impunity and sometimes with subsequent full or partial immunity.[25] The judiciary and particularly members of the highest courts were subjected to summary removal, replacement, and public distrust.[26] Social protest is sometimes the only viable manner for the public to express its disenchantment with the current state of affairs. Yet popular participation can easily become co-opted or suppressed by the executive or its party, for example, in the naming of judges in Ecuador under President Correa in 2011.[27]

The continuation of modern states of siege and states of exception is another substantial roadblock to more meaningful constitutional activity.

---

[21] Negretto, *Making Constitutions*, 140–143, 147–148.

[22] Oquendo, *Latin American Law*, 153.

[23] Negretto, *Making Constitutions*, 162–163.

[24] Bravo Lira, *El estado constitucional*, 204–206; Ortiz Gutiérrez, "La evolución político-constitucional de la República de Colombia," 211, 218; Sagüés, "Evolución institucional Argentina," 25, 29, 33.

[25] Nogueira Alcalá, "La evolución político-constitucional de Chile," 338–339, 343; Sagüés, "Evolución institucional Argentina," 28–29, 50.

[26] Miller, "Evaluating the Argentine"; Sagüés, "Evolución institucional Argentina," 37, 42, 45.

[27] Gargarella, *Latin American Constitutionalism*, 174, 190–192, 245 nn. 6–8.

Attempts to rein in the scope and exercise of such powers are merited, but also difficult to effect on the ground.[28] Because executive dominance may make internal governmental checks unworkable, strengthening these branches in respect to the executive, president, and military seems to offer one of the only possibilities for reform within such a system. Indeed, some have viewed this aspect of modern Latin American constitutionalism as a critical and lasting flaw in constitutional design.[29] Others suggest that there are institutional design mechanisms that may recognize, incorporate, and limit governance under such situations. For example, Rosenkrantz suggests that the best solution for regulation of emergency powers is a legislative ex post examination of executive conduct based on Roman law principles rather than greater judicial engagement.[30] Still others suggest such power enables constitutional structures to stay in force during moments of crisis.[31]

Militarism in Latin American changed after the 1960s when the United States perceived the threat of Cuban and Soviet communism at its doorstep. Military regimes that espoused anticommunist ideologies became favored in the region, and from the perspective of the United States there was no hurry for transformation to civil, constitutional rule that could produce undesired results in the midst of the Cold War. More recently, concerns about national security, particularly from domestic terrorism, have done much to create a professionalized and institutionalized form of military government.[32]

Scholars and politicians have also viewed movement toward constitutional states as a transition to democratic rule. Bravo Lira is wary of a discourse of "transition" from military rule to a constitutional state. Given the challenges of the region, some conclude that military governments can be good or bad. Bravo Lira sees both constitutional states and military governments caught in the same oscillating cycle. Indeed, in his view, constitutionally elected presidents who may be fraught with ineffective leadership, corruption, and rent seeking might even be complicit in their own overthrow by military authorities – just one more way to escape public scrutiny and to garner international sympathy.[33] Furthermore, Bravo Lira is concerned about the rhetorical deployment

---

[28] Loveman, *The Constitution*, 395; Valadés, *La dictadura constitucional*, 155–158.
[29] Loveman, *The Constitution*, 396–398.
[30] Rosenkrantz, "Constitutional Emergencies," 1579–1586.
[31] Aguilar Rivera, *El manto*, 10–21, 41–57, 117.
[32] Bravo Lira, *El estado constitucional*, 186–189, 212–213.
[33] Ibid., 193–195, 197.

of "transition to democracy" in which any reform sought by any government can be clothed in the garments of democracy to achieve particular political ends.[34]

Bravo Lira offers important and deeply researched analysis of the relationship between constitutionalism and militarism. Indeed, writing in 1992 about Venezuela and the failed military coup of February 4, 1992, led by then military officer Hugo Chávez, Bravo Lira stated, "Everything seems to indicate that we are facing the appearance of a new form of militarism in Venezuela, tied to the preservation of the supreme and permanent interests of the country, similar to those that arose in Iberoamerica in the 1960s."[35] Nonetheless, militarism and dictatorship in the region still rely on constitutions to lend legitimacy to their practices. Constitutions are essential in autocratic rule in the region.[36]

Some scholars have suggested that the military is properly considered a fourth branch of government, and these arguments are compelling.[37] Because the military in many Latin American countries was constitutionally linked to the maintenance of internal order and became, in effect, an institution that intervened readily in moments of political crisis, it seems appropriate that its interplay between the civil branches be accorded this kind of status.

The use of states of emergency and the associated assumption of legislative and decree power by the president are characteristic traits of Latin American presidentialism.[38] The use of these tools does not seem to be declining. In the past decade, constitutional reforms in Ecuador have strengthened presidentialism. The president of Ecuador has the power to name important state officials as well as to grant pardons for common crimes. Where legislative powers were formerly shared between the legislative and executive branches, more and more of these powers have been shifted to the executive exclusively. The president now establishes implementing regulations and proposes legislation and constitutional reforms. When the matter is of "urgent" economic importance, an executive decree-law establishes the new legal requirements. New institutions reflecting state functions, such as the electoral function and the popular participation function, serve to modify and to complicate the traditional balance of powers within the branches of government. In practice, even

---

[34] Ibid., 214–219.
[35] Ibid., 222.
[36] Loveman, *The Constitution*, 63.
[37] Ibid., 6–7, 115.
[38] Cheibub, Elkins, and Ginsburg, "Latin American Presidentialism," 1720–1727.

these new functions and powers have been subjected to powerful executive and presidential control.[39]

The situation is similar in Venezuela with the appearance of new institutions to further political participation, such as the "citizens' power" that, in effect, served to channel the power of the executive, President Chávez, who promised constitutional reform as part of his election.[40] Indeed, the Venezuelan Constitution of 1999 contains five powers: executive, legislative, judicial, civic, and electoral.[41] The Venezuelan Constitution of 1999 expanded the legislative functions of the president, increased the term to six years, and provided for reelection. Congress was empowered to and has turned over legislative authority to the executive, an area that was limited to economics under the Constitution of 1961.[42] Deflecting both a coup d'état and general strike in 2002, Chávez was reelected in 2006 under the Constitution of 1999. He did not always obtain the constitutional amendments he sought. In 2007, for example, Venezuelans rejected numerous constitutional amendments proposed by the president including some that would have expanded his extraordinary power.[43] Nonetheless, exceptional powers are now possible under a range of extraordinary circumstances that quickly become ordinary, including the state of exception, state of alarm, state of internal commotion, and state of economic emergency.[44] Gargarella has noted the Venezuelan Supreme Court's rejection of the notion of "checks and balances" in favor of a new principle of "unity of power."[45] Popular political participation has been welcomed and encouraged, but only when the outcome supports the ruling executive; inconsistent results, such as in local decisions, are suppressed. Responding to criticism by the Organization of American States (OAS), Venezuela has sought to limit the scope of the OAS and has denounced the American Convention on Human Rights.[46]

Indeed, some scholars now write of "deconstitutionalization" in the region, meaning that unconstitutional laws are not challenged or laws needed for the implementation or enforcement of constructional norms simply do not exist.[47] Others have even used the term "failed states" or the

---

[39] Gargarella, *Latin American Constitutionalism*, 173–174.
[40] Ibid., 175; Oquendo, *Latin American Law*, 171.
[41] Oquendo, *Latin American Law*, 189.
[42] Gargarella, *Latin American Constitutionalism*, 175.
[43] Oquendo, *Latin American Law*, 194–195.
[44] Gargarella, *Latin American Constitutionalism*, 175–176.
[45] Ibid., 176.
[46] Ibid., 176–177.
[47] Reinaldo Vanossi, "La desconstitucionalización," 64–74; Sagüés, "Evolución institucional Argentina," 59.

idea that constitutions may have lost their significance at certain points in recent history.[48] Gargarella asserts that the meaningful protection of social and civil rights can come only when constitutions are drafted so that their institutional apparatus is consistent with their goals of protecting rights. The process of grafting social rights onto constitutional structures that are ill equipped to effect such political and social change leads to certain contradictions that impede the sought-after goals.[49] A strong centralized executive is not the only problem in establishing equality.[50] He writes, "The whole representative system shows a preoccupying difficulty in meeting its most basic promises of inclusion and representation. The worst of it is that the system is not in a position to fulfill those promises, even by getting condoned for its worst sins."[51] Other proposed solutions to these difficulties include the strengthening of legislatures, courts, political parties, and other civilian institutions.[52] Loveman warns, "Without such radical changes, transitions to elected civilian governments guarantee neither democracy nor constitutional rule."[53]

Negretto writes that the Colombian Constitution of 1991 serves as a good example of a constitution created to respond to state failure. Issuing from a period of unsuccessful governments, multiple and fractionated political parties, failing public security, and economic difficulties, the Constitution was seen as a way to address violence and social discord. The new Constitution was drafted with the goals of reducing corruption, strengthening the courts, decentralizing power, enforcing human rights, and limiting states of exception. The new Constitution revised the electoral process by prohibiting presidential reelections, downsizing Congress and increasing its participation in policy decision, and creating special districts for indigenous communities. Other changes increased the efficiency and effectiveness of Congress and brought in new institutions such as the Constitutional Court, Attorney General, and Prosecutor General.[54]

In the Ecuadorian Constitution of 1998, Negretto similarly finds an example of a constitution responding to a situation in which the

[48] Ortiz Gutiérrez, "La evolución político-constitucional de la República de Colombia," 215; Salgado Pesantes, "Treinta años de democracia," 418–419.
[49] Gargarella, *Latin American Constitutionalism*, 165–168; Gargarella, "Grafting Social Rights," 1537–1555.
[50] Gargarella, *Latin American Constitutionalism*, 207.
[51] Ibid.
[52] Loveman, *The Constitution*, 404.
[53] Ibid.
[54] Negretto, *Making Constitutions*, 166–176, 181,189–192, 195.

institutions of government are no longer operating properly. The previous Constitution of 1978 created a structure in which the Congress and president could stop the other's actions that led to a freezing of governing functions. Presidents under the Constitution sought solutions that would empower them to break such standstills, but legislators refused; instability and corruption continued. By the mid-1990s, there appeared to be broad support for a new constitution and this solution was part of the platform of Pachakutik, a newly formed indigenous party. In 1997, a referendum succeeded that called for a constituent assembly while also affirming the appointment of interim president Alarcón. Among many realignments of institutional power, the president's powers were expanded and the office's agenda-setting authority was increased, creating a stronger executive.[55]

Recent constitutional changes in some countries have attempted to address the various challenges to functioning states and effective democracy. In the past forty years or so, on one hand, there has continued to be a host of impediments to fuller constitutionalism in the region. On the other hand, there are some promising developments.

Some Promising Signs

The path of Latin American constitutionalism has had more than its fair share of difficulties. Many recent events demonstrate promise for the development of meaningful democratic constitutionalism. The region has seen more peaceful transitions of democratically elected presidents. Gargarella states that since the 1980s the region has entered "a new period of democratic stability that exists today."[56] In 2011, noting the recent expansion of democratic participation and constitutional rights, Uprimny opined, "To some extent, Latin America is now enjoying its first true wave of constitutionalism."[57] In many ways, just as the early republic period can be characterized as a period of rapid constitutional experimentation, recent decades have witnessed Latin America entering a second phase of creative development and experimentation.

A persuasive argument may be made for a new era of Latin American constitutionalism. Negretto, studying constitutionalism in the region, embraces the notion of experimentation and notes that since 1978, countries in the region have either replaced or substantially amended their

---

[55] Ibid., 199–204, 215–217, 220–221.
[56] Gargarella, *Latin American Constitutionalism*, 111.
[57] Uprimny, "The Recent Transformation," 1599, 1601.

constitutions. These new constitutions have improved the representative quality of elections, the legislative oversight of executive cabinets, judicial independence, and political decentralization. Other improvements include broader ideas of political participation; recognition and privileging indigenous rights, claims, and property; sharing in the benefits of property; intergenerational environmental and sustainability rights linked to an early tradition of social rights; and rights to concepts that are just emerging, such as rights to cultural property, technology, or the city. These developments led to the conclusion that despite the challenges for the region, there is much reason to be hopeful in Latin America's new dawn of constitutionalism. Many of these changes in constitutional text are the result of multiparty coalitions responding to a perceived need for institutional change in the face of political, economic, or security crises.[58]

Structural Changes

Recent constitutions have significantly changed the political and constitutional landscape in Latin America. Latin America had fifteen new constitutions created between 1978 and 2008. Most of these incorporated the modern terminology and standards from European and world practices flourishing after World War II. In the Latin American context, many have perpetuated the privileges and powers of the executive in relation to the other branches. New constitutions have sought to change the allocation of power between the branches of government in many ways. There have been notable changes in the limits and functions of the executive branch in the region in the past forty years.[59] Presidential powers have been modified by constitutions; some changes have limited their powers while others have increased their ability to effect legislation.[60] Thus, Gargarella has noted the paradox of "more presidentialism and more rights" in Latin America in the present period. Some, however, have asserted that strong centralized executive authority is necessary in the region to secure the effective implementation of a new rights policy.[61] At the same time that electoral reform has increased the possibilities for participation and representation, other reforms in some countries have led to greater possibilities for presidential reelection and agenda-setting powers while somewhat unexpectedly reducing other presidential powers in the

---

[58] Negretto, *Making Constitutions*, 2, 8, 11.
[59] Ibid., 17.
[60] Negretto, "Shifting Constitutional Designs," 1788–1792.
[61] Gargarella, *Latin American Constitutionalism*, 155–165.

executive and legislative spheres.[62] Furthermore, the work of Negretto has demonstrated that the role of institutional inertia in subsequent constitutions is probably much less than what we generally might have assumed.[63]

New public controlling bodies, such as those established under the "citizens' power" of the Venezuelan Constitution and the Colombian Procurator General, Defender of the People, and Controller General, are institutions that attempt to create greater public oversight of the actions of government. Furthermore, new constitutions, such as those in Argentina, Colombia, and Peru, have created some sort of ombudsman to monitor and to improve human rights in the country.[64] Another recent development since the late 1980s has been the creation of judicial councils. These institutions and the participation of senior judges in them vary from country from country. They tend to administer the resources of the judiciary, participate in the appointment of judges, and manage judicial careers and discipline, especially in light of concerns about judicial favoritism and corruption.[65]

Institutions have also been created or adapted to respond to new rights and the effective enforcement of all constitutional rights. Provisions establishing constitutionally protected rights have gained recognition by courts, individuals, and society in general. Nonetheless, the incorporation of new mechanisms or sets of grafted social rights into constitutions that are institutionally ill suited for the introduction of such things have also challenged the effectiveness of the new elements. Thus, the successful grafts or transplants of these new elements are a function of their matching an institutional structure under the constitution that is ready to receive them.[66] There have also been changing popular conceptions of human and constitutional rights with an increased involvement of regional international institutions and legal provisions.[67]

Even modifications to existing constitutions can accomplish significant change. For example, over the past thirty years the Chilean Constitution of 1980 promulgated under President Pinochet's power has been opened to encompass many favorable democratic practices and institutions. From

---

[62] Negretto, *Making Constitutions*, 30–42; Negretto, "Shifting Constitutional Design," 1778.
[63] Negretto, *Making Constitutions*, 103.
[64] Uprimny, "The Recent Transformation," 1594, 1596–1597.
[65] Pozas-Loyo and Ríos-Figueroa, "The Politics of Amendment," 1807–1833.
[66] Gargarella, *Latin American Constitutionalism*, 136–141.
[67] McKinley, "Emancipation Politics," 113–119; Oquendo, "The Solitude," Sagüés "Evolución institucional Argentina," 44; Uprimny, "The Recent Transformation," 1592.

its original text, provisions for the state of exception have been limited and the presidential term has been reduced from the original eight years, to six years, and to four. Life senators have been abolished, and there are new mechanisms for constitutional reform and judicial appointments.[68] Improvements have also been made in the National Security Council. This process of gradual constitutional change from a military regime in Chile is noteworthy. Peru's constitutional changes since Fujimori's rule ended in 2000 provide another example of this approach.[69] Other countries have made similar steps to limit the power of the executive in light of national and international recognition of human rights abuses and in response to documented atrocities, although the gradual reformation of a military regime's constitution remains a less common approach. When the Batista period ended in Cuba, its *Ley Fundamental de la República*, decreed in February, 1959, served as a constitutional document until 1976, when the Constitution of that date was put into effect. The Cuban Constitution of 1976 has served as a model of socialist legality in the region since then.[70]

These advances did not necessarily occur within a context of greater democracy and limitations on executive authority. Pushback from the limitation of presidential authority came in the form of reasserting executive authority to respond to economic crises. Neoliberal reforms, often implemented at the behest of international lenders, foreign investors, and those driving international economic policy, were often the direct product of the executive. Important steps in this direction in the 1990s were taken in Colombia under Andrés Pastrana, in Mexico under Vicente Fox, in Peru under Alberto Fujimori, and in Argentina under Carlos Menem.

Responding to the slow pace of benefits flowing from neoliberal policies, those lost in the process – workers, peasants, indigenous people, and the poor –mobilized in recent decades against such policies and practices. Presidents associated with these policies were impeached, threatened with impeachment, or driven from office through resignation or election. Presidents with substantially different agendas such as Evo Morales and Hugo Chávez were elected.[71]

---

[68] Gargarella, *Latin American Constitutionalism*, 149.

[69] Fuentes, "A Matter of the Few," 1742–1743, 1749.

[70] Rojas, "La Soledad Constitucional," 1–10.

[71] Gargarella, *Latin American Constitutionalism*, 151–154. There was a corresponding rise in the importance of professional economists in politics and goverment. See, for example, Dezalay and Garth, *The Internationalization*; Palacios, "De populistas," 99–158. For this phenomenon in mid-twentieth-century Colombia, see Palacios, *Between Legitimacy*, 174–178.

Constitutional Tribunals

Within the realm of institutional restructuring for modern constitutional states, courts or tribunals with some sort of constitutional jurisdiction have developed over the recent decades. An underlying principle of specialized constitutional tribunals is constitutional supremacy, the idea that a country's legal and political system is controlled by a constitutional system that can subject individual and state action to constitutional scrutiny. Constitutional tribunals and forms of constitutional actions are products of recognizing the constitution as a supreme guide to and check on governmental action.[72]

The region has witnessed an increase in the creation of constitutional tribunals that are accorded respect and effective enforcement of their sentences. And in some countries, such as Argentina, Colombia, and Mexico, supreme courts or constitutional courts have become important political actors.[73] Writing in 2012, Barker observed the growth and these tribunals this way:

In recent years, specialized tribunals for the adjudication of constitutional questions have been created in Ecuador, Guatemala, Chile, Peru, Colombia, and Bolivia, and specialized chambers have been established within the Supreme Courts of El Salvador, Costa Rica, Honduras, Paraguay, and Venezuela. In Costa Rica, El Salvador, Bolivia, Chile, Honduras, and Paraguay, constitutional adjudication is concentrated in the country's constitutional tribunals or chambers. In other countries, such as Colombia, Venezuela, Ecuador, Guatemala, and Peru, the constitutional tribunals or chambers have exclusive jurisdiction over some matters – typically "actions of unconstitutionality," in which the constitutionality of a state is challenged and where a declaration of unconstitutionality with *erga omnes* effect is sought – but the ordinary courts have power to protect litigants in particular cases, generally with the possibility of review by the constitutional tribunal or chamber.[74]

Thus, some constitutional tribunals have the power to declare a law inapplicable to the parties of an individual case, and others may examine the constitutionality of legislative acts outside the requirements of a particular case and controversy. The two processes can be combined, so that since the 1980s depending on their constitutional reforms, countries such as Argentina, Bolivia, Colombia, Costa Rica, the Dominican Republic, El Salvador, Guatemala, Honduras, Nicaragua, Panama, Paraguay, and

---

[72] Oquendo, *Latin American Law*, 196–200.
[73] Sagüés, "Evolución institucional Argentina," 51–52; Schor, "An Essay."
[74] Barker, "Latin American Constitutionalism," 11 citing Brewer-Carías, *Constitutional Protection*, 92–162, 397–412.

Venezuela have permitted individuals to initiate separate actions to determine constitutionality with an *erga omnes* effect.[75] Oquendo has correctly observed, "This development represents a paradigm shift, displacing, in practice, the notion that Latin American courts lack the power permanently to invalidate unconstitutional laws upon individual complaints."[76]

Under new constitutions or through other reform initiatives, countries have created new tribunals to handle constitutional cases. These can be extensions or modifications of existing judicial structures. For example, in 1989, Costa Rica created a Fourth Chamber (*Sala IV*) of the Supreme Court to handle constitutional questions. By relaxing standing and filing requirements, the activity of the court increased dramatically and, on the part of the other institutions of government, unexpectedly. Thus, by the end of the first decade of this century, the court had more than 200,000 cases, mostly *amparo* actions to protect constitutional rights, actions that were relatively nonexistent before the creation of the Chamber.[77]

Carving out powerful places in the political and constitutional landscape of countries can be daunting tasks as constitutional courts battle entrenched interests and institutions. The region has witnessed brave constitutional judges issuing bold holdings directed toward the executive, legislative, and military branches, indicating that the Cádiz effect is not necessarily a permanent fixture of Latin American constitutionalism. The case of rivalry between the recent Colombian Constitutional Court, created by the Colombian Constitution of 1991, and the Colombian Supreme Court has been well documented as the two courts have battled over jurisdiction and power.[78] More recently, the Colombian Supreme Court has served as an example in the region as a court active in defining and securing social and economic rights. Its decisions regarding the rights of internally displaced persons due to violence and insecurity in the country are noteworthy.[79]

Constitutional reforms in 1994 led to a much more active Mexican Supreme Court when they established two new forms of constitutional review, the action of unconstitutionality and a constitutional controversies jurisdiction. In the past twenty years, the Court has risen in political and popular stature while addressing a wide range of topics including

[75] Oquendo, *Latin American Law*, 125–126, 201.
[76] Ibid., 201–202.
[77] Gargarella, *Latin American Constitutionalism*, 188.
[78] Ibid., 135.
[79] Cepeda-Espinosa, "Transcript," 1699–1705; Rodríguez-Garavito, "Beyond the Courtroom," 1669–1698.

sexual and reproductive liberties.[80] A similar expansion of review in 1989 led Costa Rica to enter a new era of concentrated constitutional review that continues today.[81]

In Venezuela, President Chávez ensured that the Supreme Court would not block his agenda leading to, in Oquendo's words, "Venezuela's most serious constitutional crisis" when the constituent assembly in 1999 sought to sweep judicial and legislative opposition out of the way.[82] The assembly brushed the legislature aside and removed the legislature's right to make laws and to hold sessions.[83] Justices of the Supreme Court, the Judicial Council, and more than 1,000 judges were to be confirmed or dismissed for corruption by a commission of the assembly appointed to address a "judicial emergency."[84] The Supreme Court validated the action by a vote of eight to six. Declaring the death of the court and the loss of democracy, Chief Justice Cecilia Sosa Gómez resigned. The assembly removed all the justices and created a new court, the Supreme Tribunal of Justice in December, 1999. The Constitutional Chamber of the Supreme Tribunal of Justice is charged with its constitutional jurisdiction under the Constitution of 1999.[85]

The feud between the Supreme Court and President Duhalde in Argentina in 2002 provides another example of the increasing role and associated risks of the courts in effecting constitutional rule. Duhalde inherited significant economic problems from President de la Rúa, who had limited weekly cash withdrawal from bank accounts, the "*corralito*" put into effect in December, 2001. In a 6–0 decision with three abstentions and basing its determination on property rights, the Supreme Court held the limitation unconstitutional in February, 2002, and was almost immediately subjected to impeachment proceedings by the House of Deputies, who raised additional concerns about the political content of other decisions by the Court. The six justices appointed by Menem in 1990 to advance his reforms were the primary focus of the action. In October, 2002, Congress decided not to prosecute the impeachment actions, but in the following year the Chief Justice and another justice resigned while the Senate dismissed a third. Replacements were recognized as judges of high quality.[86] Garro has suggested that the court's activities may be improved

---

[80] Madrazo and Vela, "The Mexican Supreme Court's," 1862–1893.
[81] Barker, *Constitutional Adjudication*, 33–176.
[82] Oquendo, *Latin American Law*, 172.
[83] Ibid., 188.
[84] Ibid., 172.
[85] Ibid., 172–183, 187–188.
[86] Ibid., 168–170.

through oral arguments and greater transparency in the appointment of justices.[87]

Similarly for much of its existence, the Chilean Constitutional Court, founded in 1970 shortly before Pinochet's takeover, was an institution mostly charged with maintaining the structures of government and property rights as established in the Constitution of 1980. It was expected to maintain continuity from the period during Pinochet's rule and into the transition to democracy. Even in the first fifteen years of democracy, the Court was deferential to the legislature because of the general norms of Chilean legal culture and the regard the legislature and administrative actors had for their constitutional limitations. Since around 2005, Chile began to embrace notions of "neoconstitutionalism" in which constitutional courts actively scrutinize the other branches and vociferously defend human rights as found in constitutions and international norms. From that date, the court has been active in finding legislation unconstitutional leading to its political and popular recognition as an important constitutional institution.[88] Similarly, in several countries, high courts and constitutional tribunals are often granted jurisdiction to consider disputes arising from questions of vertical power between, say, municipalities and national authorities, and of horizontal power between states of federal countries, such as those of Argentina, Mexico, and Venezuela.[89]

Such tribunals do not always run counter to executive desires. Basing its decision on the exercise of unconditional political rights, the Constitutional Chamber of the Nicaraguan Supreme Court permitted the sitting president to run again despite language in a constitutional amendment to the contrary.[90] Nonetheless, some courts have established a practice of close scrutiny of executive action and decrees emitted under states of siege or emergency. For example, Rosenkrantz has surveyed the Argentine Supreme Court's jurisprudence since the 1980s and found a court carefully considering and reacting to various executive actions under such conditions.[91] And Miller has cautioned that the nature of judicial review by courts in Latin America is subject to the political circumstances in which they make decisions; the responsive rulemaking of such courts may be fragile.[92]

[87] Garro, "Judicial Review," 409–429.
[88] Couso, "Models of Democracy," 1530–1535.
[89] Oquendo, *Latin American Law*, 234–235.
[90] Figueroa, "Current Constitutional Developments," 13.
[91] Rosenkrantz, "Constitutional Emergencies," 1562–1567.
[92] Miller, "Judicial Review," 77–176.

Constitutional Actions

On the procedural level, new methods of bringing constitutional claims have developed. As noted, these include an increasing ability to question the constitutionality of legislation and even a growing acceptance of constitutional cases having a general or *erga omnes* effect so that their holdings are applicable to similarly situated individuals who were not parties to the original litigation. Many of these developments are related to the constitutional action of *amparo*.[93] Oquendo describes this procedure this way, "Virtually all Latin American constitutions establish a special judicial procedure through which people may vindicate their rights. They typically denominate this action '*amparo*,' a word that means protection or shelter. The Colombian Constitution uses instead the term '*tutela*,' which translates into guardianship or defense, while the Chilean charter opts for the concept of '*recurso de protección*, or (literally) 'protection recourse.'"[94] Such actions typically lower the procedural barriers and permit petitioners to make their claim with brief statements and informal writings. They often provide for maintaining the status quo through preliminary injunctions and other forms of temporary relief pending determination of the *amparo*.[95] For example, the Dominican Constitution of 2010 provides, "Under the law, the procedure shall take place preferentially, summarily, orally, publicly, gratuitously, and informally."[96]

For the origins of these specific actions protecting constitutional rights, we must turn again to Mexico, which gave birth to the modern action of *amparo*. The *amparo* is historically linked to the development of judicial review in Mexico and the use of binding cases (*jurisprudencia*) in Mexican constitutional practice.[97] From colonial antecedents, the *amparo* found its first modern expression in the 1840s in the Yucatán Constitution and amendments to the Mexican Constitution of 1824.[98] There were important successive Amparo Acts in the nineteenth century in 1861, 1869, and 1882. The Amparo Act of 1882, drafted by Ignacio Luis Vallarta, made judicial decisions obligatory and stated that five decisions create a "jurisprudence of repetition" (*jurisprudencia por reiteración*) that must be followed by judges. Subsequent codes of civil

---

[93] See generally Brewer-Carías, *Constitutional Protection*.
[94] Oquendo, *Latin American Law*, 277.
[95] Ibid., 329.
[96] Dominican Constitution of 2010, Art. 72 as translated in Oquendo, *Latin American Law*, 335.
[97] Mirow, "*Marbury* in Mexico;" Mirow, "Case Law in Mexico."
[98] Oquendo, *Latin American Law*, 279 citing Fix-Zamudio, *Ensayos*, 22–25.

procedure rejected or accepted this notion of jurisprudence of repetition for constitutional cases.[99] As might be expected, Vallarta was greatly influenced by United States law and practice in the area, as demonstrated by his reports of Mexican Supreme Court cases, and his comparative study of *amparo* and habeas corpus reveals the importance of U.S. law and practice in the area.[100] Emilio Rabasa, founder of the Escuela Libre de Derecho and who had lived in the United States from 1913 to 1920, criticized these developments, stating, "A complete submission to final judgments, despite the great advantages that it has produced in the Anglo-Saxon people, chokes the scientific spirit, because above the science of law one definitively places the opinion of the court."[101] In his book, *El Juicio Constitucional*, Rabasa also made it clear that the *erga omnes* effect of constitutional decisions would not be recognized when he read a provision of the Mexican Constitution of 1857 to prohibit such action.[102] Referring to *amparo* actions, Article 102 contained the well-known "Otero Formula" initially introduced by the Reform Act of 1847 by Mariano Otero.[103] It reads:

All cases addressed in the preceding article shall be brought by petition of the aggrieved party by means of procedures and methods of the judicial order as set forth in a law. The judgments shall always be such that concerns only the particular individuals, limiting itself to protect and guard them upon which the proceedings is brought, without making any general declaration respecting the law or act that motivated it.[104]

Rabasa was effective in pulling back Vallarta's sweeping notions of judicial review, constitutional jurisprudence, and *erga omnes* application. Today, the general prohibition of *erga omnes* effect continues in Mexico but with the exception that five consecutive, uninterrupted decisions under certain circumstances can create binding case law. Other high courts or constitutional courts in Bolivia, Costa Rica, Dominican Republic, Ecuador, Guatemala, and Venezuela have the power to create binding case law on other courts within the country under particular circumstances. As mentioned earlier, since the 1980s there has been an

[99] Mirow, "Case Law in Mexico," 227–232.

[100] Ibid., 232–245; Mirow, "*Marbury* in Mexico."

[101] Mirow, "Case Law in Mexico," 232 citing Carbonell y Sánchez, "Una Aproximación," 79; Mirow, "*Marbury* in Mexico," 68.

[102] Mirow, "*Marbury* in Mexico," 69.

[103] Oquendo, *Latin American Law*, 280.

[104] Mexican Constitution of 1857, Art. 102 as translated in Mirow, "*Marbury* in Mexico," 69.

increase in the possibility of obtaining constitutional decisions with an *erga omnes* effect.[105]

The scope of *amparo* actions can be unexpectedly wide compared to the constitutional review offered by courts such as the Supreme Court of the United States or constitutional tribunals in Europe. In Mexico, for example, *amparo* can be employed not only against the administrative and legislative actions of the state, but also against judicial actions. This has created massive recourse to *amparo* as a means of appealing first-instance sentences that are unfavorable to the petitioner.[106] Having a case wrongly decided against someone has become an unconstitutional action by the state that permits an *amparo*.

Similarly, the Colombian Constitutional Court established under the Constitution of 1991 has greatly expanded access through its *tutela* action (*acción de tutela*), which also does not require many formalities. It too has witnessed a tremendous increase in business with, for example, more than 100,000 *tutela* actions in the year 2001. From 1992 to 2005, slightly more than one-half of its cases concerned social rights, with the rest dealing with civil and political rights under the constitution. It sided with the plaintiff in about two-thirds of the cases.[107]

Although *amparo* actions are usually the product of legislation or a combination of legislative and constitutional provisions, some countries of the region have developed these actions to protect constitutional rights through the judiciary. The prime example is Argentina, which developed a judicially created writ of *amparo* though several decisions of the Supreme Court in 1957 and 1958. The idea was then placed into legislation in 1966 and gained constitutional recognition in the Argentine Constitution of 1994. A similar development occurred in the Dominican Republic in 1999 when the Supreme Court there drew upon international law to create the action. Although the Dominican Constitution of 2002 did not incorporate the *amparo*, the Constitution of 2010 provides for the action.[108]

Courts enforcing constitutions are uncovering excellent language and theory available to them in the new constitutions of the region. European models of constitutional concepts and interpretation are informing new constitutional courts and tribunals. For example, Néstor Pedro Sagüés has fully described the constitutional changes in Argentina after the country

---

[105] Oquendo, *Latin American Law*, 201–202, 280–281.
[106] Ibid., 285–293.
[107] Gargarella, *Latin American Constitutionalism*, 189–190.
[108] Oquendo, *Latin American Law*, 310–327, 335.

abandoned military dictatorship in 1983, leading to the Constitution of 1994. In these processes, one uncovers discussions and final constitutional texts addressing political rights, civil rights, ecological rights, consumer rights, equality rights, rights for children and women, workers' rights, indigenous rights, education rights, and international rights. Some rights may be enforced through writs of protection (*amparo*), judicial review, habeas corpus, and its recent cousin, habeas data, the right to knowledge of information held about oneself.[109] Nonetheless, progress is never linear. For example, as mentioned earlier, in 2002 and 2003, the Supreme Court in Argentina was placed under extreme political pressure, and several members resigned or were dismissed for upholding private property rights against government regulation during a freeze of bank accounts and other activities. Venezuela under Hugo Chávez provides another telling example of the relationship among the executive, the constitution, and the bench.

New Rights

The Mexican Constitution of 1917 was a watershed that led Latin America to create and to recognize constitutional rights that moved well beyond the traditional liberal constructs of the nineteenth century. The text of the constitution showed that it was possible to enshrine positive rights that encouraged or forced the state to provide a wide variety of social welfare protections and entitlements. Its text has been amended to expand these rights over time so that today it provides not only individual civil and political rights but also economic and social rights including rights to education, health, housing, and work. Moving into even newer territory, the Constitution now provides for environmental, developmental, and cultural rights. These newer rights are sometimes labeled "second- and third-generation rights" where second-generation rights relate to social-welfare rights and third-generation rights relate to culture, development, the environment, and information. There is a shift from rights that prohibit the state from acting against an individual toward the creation of rights that require the positive action of the state to enable the enjoyment of rights, such as health, housing, work, consumer protection, environmental protection and sustainability, and self-determination over one's cultural practices and one's information held by the state or others.[110] In the realm of health, the treatment of

---

[109] Oquendo, *Latin American Law*, 160-164 citing Sagüés, "An Introduction."
[110] Ibid., 127, 128, 350–351.

HIV/AIDS by Latin American health services in the past two decades has come before constitutional tribunals, and in the case of Chilean remedies, before the Inter-American Commission on Human Rights.[111]

In 2011, Gargarella, Filippini, and Cavana surveyed such new and amended constitutions in the region and found constitutions expressing a panoply of these rights that have come to guide contemporary practice in Latin American courts. They found that present Latin American constitutions protect affirmative action (nine countries), clothing (four countries), culture (seventeen countries), education (eighteen countries), environment (eighteen countries), food (fifteen countries), health (seventeen countries), housing (sixteen countries), and work (eighteen countries). They also found that such constitutions promote related rights-based notions of democracy (fifteen countries), gender equality (nine countries), multiculturalism (eight countries), popular control of policies (eight countries), popular consultation (sixteen countries), special status for human rights treaties (thirteen countries), and city councils (six countries).[112] For example, in addition to permitting the reelection of the president, the Argentine Constitution of 1994 expanded the base of rights in Argentina by calling for equality of opportunity for women in political offices and political parties, and establishing rights related to ecology; consumer protection; women, children, and mothers; workers, indigenous peoples, education, intellectual property, and international law. The new constitutional text provided actions for *amparo*, habeas data, and habeas corpus.[113]

The increase in the stature of international law has been an important factor in this development.[114] The 1980s and 1990s also brought greater recognition of international rights, particularly those related to human rights, into the sphere of domestic constitutional law. Many constitutions of the region recognize treaties, without additional legislative action, as the supreme law of the land. Bolivia and Peru require that their bills of rights be interpreted in light of international human rights, and the Inter-American Commission on Human Rights and the Inter-American Court of Human Rights have become important

---

[111] Bergallo, "Courts and Social Change," 1611–1641; Oquendo, *Latin American Law*, 363–386.

[112] Gargarella, *Latin American Constitutionalism*, 241–242 n. 8 citing Gargarella, Filippini, and Cavana, *Recientes reformas*.

[113] Oquendo, *Latin American Law*, 162–164 citing Sagüés, "An Introduction," 41.

[114] Gargarella, *Latin American Constitutionalism*, 150–151; Uprimny, "The Recent Transformation," 1592.

regional actors in human rights compliance.[115] The Inter-American Court has had to tackle difficult questions of domestic amnesties and the rights of truth, justice, recourse, and reparations accorded victims of human rights violations as well as general issues of nondiscrimination and indigenous rights.[116] Argentina and Bolivia have raised human rights treaties to a constitutional level, and Costa Rica and El Salvador have assigned them a status above national law. Peru and Colombia have incorporated international human rights standards into their constitutions.[117] Other countries, such as Argentina, have recognized a right of individual reply to publications that are counter to one's views based on regional international law.[118]

In response to criticism for the conduct of its military, particularly in the context of its war against drugs, Mexico undertook substantial constitutional reforms in the past decade that have made the country more responsive to international human rights law. These reforms include the country's assumption of a positive duty to investigate and to punish human rights abuses as well as the transfer of substantial jurisdiction over these matters to the National Commission of Human Rights.[119] Mexico is not alone in these practices, but merely serves as an example of a regional trend. Studying how courts have responded to such international norms, Rossi and Filippini have noted that courts have applied such international law as directly controlling the legal issue, consulted international law as interpretive tools to understand domestic law, supplemented domestic law with international norms, consulted decisions by international tribunals and organs to construct and to interpret domestic law, and applied decisions of such international organs to domestic cases.[120] Thus, countries of the region have experienced a noteworthy incorporation of international human rights law into domestic human rights interpretation and practice.

International trials of former presidents, since the trial of Augusto Pinochet, have put regional leaders on notice that the world is watching and willing to prosecute violations of human rights. International courts with jurisdiction over human rights abuses, such as the Inter-American Court of

---

[115] Oquendo, *Latin American Law*, 249–251.
[116] García-Sayán, "The Inter-American Court," 1835–1862.
[117] Gargarella, *Latin American Constitutionalism*, 169.
[118] Oquendo, *Latin American Law*, 251–276.
[119] Gargarella, *Latin American Constitutionalism*, 154–155.
[120] Ibid., 244 n. 29 citing Rossi and Filippini, "El derecho internacional."

Human Rights, have even indicated their willingness to set aside provisions of domestic law pardoning human rights abuses.[121] Domestic powers may withdraw amnesty after its grant, as a decision of the Uruguayan Congress did in 2011. Such domestic agreements are often the product of significant international outcry and national soul-searching and compromise.[122]

Since the 1980s and with attempts to strengthen democratic governance, many Latin American countries have developed the right of habeas data, giving petitioners information held by the state about them and sometimes giving them access to data about others. These provisions have increased greatly in the first decade of the twenty-first century, with Bolivia, the Dominican Republic, Ecuador, and Panama establishing such protections. The right to habeas data was judicially created by the Costa Rican Supreme Court in 1997.[123] As an example, Article 43 of the Argentine Constitution of 1994 provides:

Any person may commence [a writ of protection] action to obtain personal information stored in public as well as private registers and databases and to inquire into the purpose of keeping such files. If there is any falsehood or discrimination, the claimant may demand the suppression, rectification, confidentiality, or updating of the data.[124]

Two manifestations of the law of habeas data have developed in Latin American. One, a narrow form, is related to the ability of a person to control his or her information held by others and to correct it; the other, a broader form, is related the right of any person to obtain public information. Panama's application of the law has followed the former form while Peru, for example, has interpreted its provisions in the direction of the latter.[125]

Supplementing new rights provisions in constitutions, the phenomenon of "dormant clauses" in constitutions being awakened at a later date, often by more effective or more active constitutional tribunals, is an important aspect of this promise. Here, language long ignored or misinterpreted is rediscovered, reactivated, and brought to life in the constitutional thought of the nation. There is, of course, the debate over whether such aspirational language that sits dormant in the constitution actually undermines constitutional validity because it is not put into play from

---

[121] García-Sayán, "The Inter-American Court," 1841–1847; Gargarella, *Latin American Constitutionalism*, 170.

[122] Gargarella, *Latin American Constitutionalism*, 170.

[123] Oquendo, *Latin American Law*, 126–126, 396, 399–400.

[124] Argentine Constitution of 1994, Art. 43 as translated in Oquendo, *Latin American Law*, 397.

[125] Oquendo, *Latin American Law*, 400–415.

its enactment.[126] Language that has been perceived as purely symbolic or aspirational can take root and provide constitutional remedy, and can become, in the terminology of García-Villegas, protective.[127] Similarly, others have written about "latent" rights becoming "activated."[128] Gargarella has uncovered several reasons for activating these clauses, many related to the aspects just mentioned: legal internationalization, the impact of international human rights, academic criticism of the status quo related to these issues, and legal reforms, particularly those related to adjustments in constitutional standing. Thus, judges are now generally more open to cases that raise constitutional social rights with more empowered constitutional tribunals.[129]

Indigenous Rights and Afro-Latins

A notable regional development has been the incorporation of indigenous social, political, economic, and environmental rights into new constitutions. Gargarella has seen this as the second important wave of rights developments in Latin American constitutionalism; in his view the first was the general incorporation of social rights starting around the turn of the last century.[130] While the social and political aspects of constitutional equality still seek to be fulfilled in many countries, the question of indigenous land and its political and constitutional treatment was closely related to the communities themselves. For example, in nineteenth-century Mexico, despite a majority indigenous population, political and constitutional structures did little to pull indigenous communities into the state and its activities. Indeed, it appears that liberal programs were viewed as hindering the rights and privileges that these communities had under colonial and conservative regimes.[131] According to Hale, "There was a growing perception among late nineteenth-century observers that Indians were a major component of the population who could not be ignored."[132] Debates in Mexico during this period centered on questions of the educability of native populations and the role

---

[126] Gargarella, *Latin American Constitutionalism*, 144, 240 n. 21 citing Scheppele, "Aspirational and Adversive Constitutions."

[127] García Villegas, *La eficacia simbólica del derecho*; García-Villegas, "Law as Hope."

[128] Gargarella, *Latin American Constitutionalism*, 239 n. 13 citing Awarapa, "Despacio se llega lejos."

[129] Ibid., 145–146.

[130] Ibid., 179.

[131] Hale, *Mexican Liberalism*, 215–247.

[132] Hale, *The Transformation*, 220.

of public education.[133] Similarly, the territory successfully held by the Mapuche in Chile during most of the nineteenth century reminded the government of the region's separate population.[134]

Throughout the twentieth century Mexico has struggled with political and constitutional recognition of the *ejido*, or communally owned land of indigenous groups. At times, Mexico has sought to carve such land up into small parcels of individual ownership, and at other times it has sought to recognize communal exploitation and ownership as a cornerstone of indigenous life, as under Article 27 of the Constitution of 1917.[135] Nonetheless, as Aguilar Rivera has noted, attempts to promote equality by removing racial definitions in Mexico can be seen as incongruous with projects that are specifically protective of indigenous rights.[136] Thus, neoindigenism celebrating tradition and difference is an odd partner of the left; "Neoindigenism is taken by indigenous peoples as members of a culture that seeks to conserve its traditional social order, as oppressed individuals of an unjust order. It must be repeated: the left is committed to the idea of the essential equality of all human being."[137]

Indigenous rights have found expression in the constitutions of Nicaragua and Guatemala where, for example, indigenous land holding, languages, and traditions are mentioned, in addition to a prohibition of discrimination based on indigenous status. New constitutions and amendments in the 1990s in Argentina (1994), Bolivia (1994), Colombia (1991), Ecuador (1996 and 1998), Mexico (1992), Paraguay (1994), and Venezuela (1999) have incorporated substantial protections for indigenous peoples, property, and customs.[138] Such proposals and the concomitant advancement of multiculturalism have not been without considered criticism. Furthermore, collective and indigenous practices may run afoul of contemporary human rights norms.[139]

Protections for indigenous property have included transfer rights to natural resources, establishing participatory rights in exploitation, and consultation in the exploitation process.[140] Demands for political recognition and increased rights under these provisions are not always

---

[133] Ibid., 220–234.
[134] Collier, *The Making*, 161–166.
[135] Velasco Ibarra, *Expresión política*, 98–102.
[136] Aguilar Rivera, *El fin*, 29, 33.
[137] Ibid., 37–38.
[138] Gargarella, *Latin American Constitutionalism*, 181–182.
[139] Aguilar Rivera, *El fin*, 60–64, 88.
[140] Gargarella, *Latin American Constitutionalism*, 247 n. 22.

successful. Gargarella notes the slow process by which the San Andrés Agreements (*Acuerdos de San Andrés*) were gradually reduced in their substance and effectiveness in Mexico during the 1990s. The Agreements were signed in 1996 between the Mexican government and the EZLN (*Ejército Zapatista de Liberación Nacional*), a representative of indigenous groups in southern Mexico, Chiapas, who did not benefit from projected land reforms and who were shut out by the economic reforms of the early 1990s. An outgrowth of the Agreements was a special commission composed of national and regional authorities to propose constitutional amendments furthering the social and political rights of indigenous people. The distance between the positions of the two groups was too great, and the government appeared to have effectively whittled away at the demands of the indigenous people, particularly their assertions for autonomy. In what seems like a concerted effort, the branches of the Mexican national government eroded the Agreements. The legislature did not act as expected, and the Mexican Supreme Court rejected hundreds of thousands indigenous *amparo* claims questioning the reform process. In the end, the Zapatistas stopped negotiating. Confidence has not returned between the parties.[141]

There were important textual changes to the Mexican Constitution. Mexico expanded these rights substantially in 2001 by amending its Constitution.[142] These amendments, importantly at the beginning of the Constitution in the article addressing the Mexican nation, embraced multiculturalism with its indigenous peoples in pride of place. The Constitution sought to preserve indigenous social, economic, cultural, political, historical, and linguistic practices, beliefs, and institutions.[143]

Apart from Mexico, the recognition of indigenous rights has expanded since the 1990s. Bolivia, in 2009, constitutionally recognized thirty-two languages as official languages of the state. Venezuela and Bolivia have also recognized indigenous medical practices as part of their constitutional provisions related to indigenous peoples.[144] Some quite recent constitutions have moved beyond a traditional European framework of constitutionalism. Barker notes that the preamble of the Bolivian Constitution of 2009 states that the people of Bolivia have "left behind our colonial,

---

[141] Ibid., 177–179, 246 n. 16.

[142] Mirow, *Latin American Law*, 222; Oquendo, *Latin American Law*, 129. See generally Azuela, "Property in the Post-post-revolution," 1915–1942.

[143] Mexican Constitution of 1917, Art. 2 as amended; Oquendo, *Latin American Law*, 130–131.

[144] Figueroa, "Current Constitutional Developments," 11.

republican, and neoliberal past," and both the most recent Bolivian and Ecuadorean Constitutions refer to ideas of *Pacha Mama*, Mother Earth, as an aspect of constitutionalism.[145] These countries have expanded this arena to the idea of a right to *buen vivir*, which has been construed by some to shelter nature from any form of interference from human modification.[146] Such recent constitutional language has been seen as a rejection of colonial frameworks and an attempt to re-found countries based on a new set of ideals. While constitutions abandon ideas of state religion to recognize all beliefs, such as the Ecuadorian Constitution of 2008 and the Venezuelan Constitution of 1999, they nonetheless seek to import new moral goals of social integration, harmony, and goodness.[147] Thus, modern Latin American constitutions have embraced a multiethnic and multicultural polity.[148]

Many of the provisions related to indigenous people were the result of influences in international law. Convention 169 of the International Labor Organization spurred progress from international law and was the basis for many of these shifts. Recent constitutions of Bolivia (2009) and Ecuador (2008) were heavily influenced by a comprehensive document in international law, the U.N. Declaration of Rights of the Indigenous Peoples (2007), which spells out in detail a panoply of rights related to indigenous pluralism, languages, identity, and education. The Bolivian Constitution has been singled out as a document with particularly important innovations in the areas of protection of indigenous property. During ratification of the constitution in 2009, the country was asked to support sweeping changes to property through Article 398, which was approved by a large majority and limited the size of large estates based on productivity, social function, labor and its exploitative quality on an estate, and a general size restriction of 5,000 hectares. Nonetheless, the final text of the Constitution was somewhat more conservative in nature than earlier proposals, so that the indigenous aspects were diluted, agrarian reform could not act retroactively, and an important plural judicial tribunal was restricted to judges having a traditional academic training. As Gargarella notes, these developments as a whole have raised more questions about implementation than practical steps. The rights asserted often find their way into more receptive courts, but the judicialization of

[145] Barker, *Latin American Constitutionalism*, 16.
[146] Gargarella, *Latin American Constitutionalism*, 247 n. 23.
[147] Figueroa, "Current Constitutional Developments," 9–10, 18.
[148] Uprimny, "The Recent Transformation," 1589–1592.

such claims often reveals that solutions are better left for political and cultural action.[149]

There is also the question of costs where indigenous religious beliefs or practices may conflict with the fullest economic exploitation of lands, mines, rivers, mountains, and the like. A final question relates to reparations for past poor treatment by the state: What are the appropriate remedies under such circumstances? Exacerbating the solutions to such questions is, according to Gargarella, a lack of traditional legal scholarship on these topics in the region.[150] Indeed, provisions related to indigenous rights may be new areas for aspirational constitutionalism and dormant clauses.

Central authority in countries with new constitutions recognizing indigenous rights have repeatedly sided with economic exploitation rather than with the protection of natural resources as bases of indigenous life. For example, the case of the U'wa people in Colombia in their battle against oil companies and the unsatisfactory outcomes for them has been particularly well documented and studied. When there is lack of success with new institutions or constitutional provisions for indigenous rights, indigenous groups have turned to protest to assert their rights and gain notoriety in the public eye.[151] This has led to the practice of indigenous social protests.

The constitutional status of America's indigenous population was a primary political concern in the Cortes and the Constitution of Cádiz. The region continues to struggle with this central question. It was a bold and remarkable, although politically driven, step to include America's indigenous population as citizens within the Constitution of 1812. The questions raised by this constitutionalization of indigenous populations were a lasting legacy of this action and continue at the forefront of Latin American constitutionalism today. Indigenous rights, and their recognition on the constitutional level and their enforcement in domestic and international tribunals, are an example of the broader seriousness with which a range of social and economic rights are being asserted in the region.

Similarly, the expansion of the polity and the recognition of multiculturalism have also increased recognition of blacks in Latin America. Movements for equal treatment for blacks in Latin America were

[149] Gargarella, *Latin American Constitutionalism*, 180–182, 193–194.
[150] Ibid., 180–181.
[151] Ibid., 183, 190–192.

historically and socially hampered by the legacy of the Constitution of Cádiz's construction of citizenship and nineteenth- and twentieth-century policies and laws favoring European immigration, in an attempt to "whiten" the populations of Latin American countries (*blanqueamiento*).[152] Although some countries such as Cuba and Venezuela had antidiscrimination laws from the 1940s on, it was not until the 1980s that social and political change made substantial gains. Even more recently, notions of indigenous communities and their legal and constitutional protection have been extended to Afro-Latins.[153] Afro-Latins continue to be subject to societal and economic discrimination, but countries such as Colombia and Peru have taken steps toward enforcing antidiscrimination laws and affirmative action in political and educational spheres.[154] There has been an increase in antidiscrimination laws and their enforcement, particularly as these activities reflect the incorporation of international systems and institutions to combat racism.[155]

Elections

Since the 1970s, developments in electoral rights studied by Negretto indicate that constitutional reforms have often incorporated new approaches to regulating elections that have led to increases in electoral competition and expanded political representation.[156] Strong party systems have splintered in the past forty years, but they are not beyond influencing constitutional change. This is particularly true when considering electoral mechanisms.[157] Negretto notes, for example:

The constitutions of Nicaragua in 1987, Paraguay in 1992, and Venezuela in 1999, all made under the influence of a dominant incumbent party, have maintained restrictive electoral formulas, such as plurality, for electing presidents. With the exception of Paraguay in 1992, all recent constituent assemblies in which a single party had control over constitutional choice (Nicaragua 1987, Peru 1993, Venezuela 1999, Ecuador 2008) have made presidential reelection rules more permissive.[158]

[152] Cottrol, *The Long, Lingering Shadow*, 113–142; Hernández, *Racial Subordination*, 19–44.
[153] Cottrol, *The Long, Lingering Shadow*, 266–291.
[154] Cottrol, *The Long, Lingering Shadow*, 266–299; Hernández, *Racial Subordination*, 73–147.
[155] Hernández, *Racial Subordination*, 129–147.
[156] Negretto, *Making Constitutions*, 17, 29; Negretto, "Shifting Constitutional Designs," 1780–1785.
[157] Negretto, *Making Constitutions*, 136.
[158] Ibid., 136.

Presidential reelection was recently permitted in the Bolivian Constitution of 2009. Thus, the limits of having the same person hold the presidency are present and contested, but when presidents reveal their effectiveness in improving the economy, in stemming violence and unrest, and in improving the lot of the electorate, they appear to be frequently rewarded with reelection provisions and increased policymaking powers.[159] Modern Latin American constitutions have sought to strengthen elections and the representative nature of the franchise. For example, in Chile and Ecuador, autonomous electoral institutions have been created to ensure the transparency and accuracy of the process.[160]

Women gained the right to vote in Latin American countries during the twentieth century. For example, Argentina and Chile opened their polls to women in the 1940s and Mexico in the 1950s.[161] The struggle for equal civil status for women was also advanced in this period, usually through amendments of civil codes, rather than through constitutionally based changes. Nonetheless, constitutional principles in some instances informed such legislative action.[162] An increasingly powerful voice in Latin American politics, women have sought a greater role in constitutional drafting and the provisions that affect their lives and opportunities in society. In such processes they continue to be for the most part underrepresented.[163]

Conclusion

Modern constitutions with a panoply of political, social, economic, and cultural rights run the risk of containing language and guarantees that far outstrip the ability of the state to make good on these promises. García Villegas has noted that such "aspirational" constitutions that look toward the future, rather than concretizing past gains, have both their risks and benefits. By reaching quite far, these constitutions often lack the social and political buy-in needed for effective constitutional entrenchment and can produce significant gaps between the promised constitutional norms and the society in which they function. These unmet expectations and high hopes run the risks of constant legal reformism and of undermining the development of a belief in the rule of law. Nonetheless, such constitutions

---

[159] Ibid., 228–231.
[160] Uprimny, "The Recent Transformation," 1595.
[161] Mirow, *Latin American Law*, 203.
[162] Giordana, "La sanción," 25–42.
[163] Morgan and Alzate Buitrago, "Constitution Making," Morgan, "Founding Mothers."

also keep alive the idea that constitutional texts can instill social change, at times reinvigorate the polity, and sometimes connect change to political leaders who carry the mantle of such new constitutional provisions.[164]

The immediate politicization of constitutionalism resulting from the Constitution of Cádiz's promulgation, retraction, repromulgation, and retraction based on purely political considerations created deep-seated assumptions about constitutions that have continued to guide constitutional thought until today. Presidents in the region still promise reform through new constitutions and still legitimate their power through new constitutions once elected to office.

Although patterns of exceptional exercises of concentrated executive power appear frequently in the region, they are challenged more often and more fully by courts protecting constitutional rights. Such challenges are often unsuccessful, as the executive power cracks down on noncompliant judges, but at least they indicate an increase in judicial institutions' willingness to judicialize constitutional questions. There is promise in the region.

[164] García Villegas, "Law as Hope," 355–362.

Conclusion

The Constitution of Cádiz has shaped Latin American constitutionalism from the independence period to the present day. The first part of this book describes the state of constitutional limbo present at the origin of the Constitution of Cádiz. Individuals and groups in a kingless monarchy attempted to find and establish manifestations of sovereignty to maintain a massive and complex empire. Thought and actions related to independence were already present in the Americas as the political and economic needs of the peninsula beckoned for American support in the fight against the French.

American deputies at the Cortes fought for their positions regarding representation, America's diverse population, the power of the executive branch, the structure of government, and political and civil rights. Compromises reached in Cádiz would have lasting effects on local power, the role of the church, the construction of citizenship, the equal application of the law, and rights of the criminally accused. The Constitution contained an unusual mix of liberal and conservative views produced in an attempt to maintain an empire under an empty throne. It was the product of war, occupation, and financial crisis. Without these threatening aspects, it is unlikely Americans would have had much say in the process and the outcome of the debates. The Constitution perpetuated slavery and excluded people of African descent from citizenship. Indigenous people were citizens under the Constitution and counted for the purposes of representation.

The text of the Constitution and the American deputies arrived to America after the Cortes when the Americas themselves were in a state of constitutional uncertainty created mostly by the political crisis on the peninsula. The text of the Constitution and the experiences of deputies were brought to play in the independence process and in the text of the resulting independence constitutions. Because these texts moved in and out of application, the region learned that constitutions were not above politics, but rather were tools to be employed in the political process as ways of legitimizing changes in power and of erasing a political past and promising a better future.

The second part of this book describes and analyzes the legacy of the Constitution of Cádiz and constitutional change after independence and in the following two centuries. It sets out a general history of Latin American constitutions to the present day and focuses on the particular institutional and substantive challenges that shaped the path of constitutionalism in the region. The effects of the Constitution of Cádiz were felt around the region in the nineteenth century. Mexican political structure and constitutional institutions, for example, were strongly influenced by its text. The development of local and regional representative institutions under the Constitution served as models for local and regional government after independence. The Constitution's adoption of separation of powers became an accepted constitutional structure throughout the region. Its privileging of the Roman Catholic church was followed by newly independent countries.

For much of the nineteenth and twentieth centuries, constitutions emanated from political victories. Strong executives, with the military and states of exception, forced their wills upon countries often under the guise of constitutional rule. Legislative bodies yielded to executive decree-law, and courts frequently lacked the political independence and power to challenge executive action. Presidents often sought to improve political stability and economic development through new constitutional orders that would legitimize their rule and instill progress and prosperity. Constitutions also set out political and civil rights and legal thinkers developed constitutional remedies such as the *amparo* to enforce them. These were often conflicting developments.

The Mexican Constitution of 1917 and specifically its social rights related to property and labor in Articles 27 and 123 mark an important milestone in Latin American constitutionalism. Constitutions no longer set out a structure for government and a set of negative rights; they now expanded into a world of positive rights that has grown substantially in the last hundred years to include health, education, labor, and housing. Since the 1990s, cultural rights, particularly as they relate to indigenous communities; environmental rights; and informational rights have been the most recent additions. These substantive rights have been coupled with more effective constitutional institutions, such as constitutional courts, and improvements in constitutional actions that have come about in the past few decades. These developments have been strengthened by the incorporation of international norms into domestic constitutional law.

These changes have not wiped out lasting constitutional difficulties in the region. Autocratic rule may still wield its power over the judicial and legislative branches. In some countries, presidents exert tremendous control. The military is still an important political actor in countries of the regions. And disparities in wealth, political voice, and treatment are still legion. These are not all problems that can be immediately solved through constitutions. In some countries, constitutions are still the playthings of presidents and military rulers, but they are playthings that sometimes come to life unexpectedly and snap back.

The origins of present-day challenges to Latin American constitutionalism can be seen in the Constitution of Cádiz and its subsequent history in the region. The Constitution of Cádiz failed to take root in any meaningful way because of its immediate repeal by Fernando VII in 1814 and because by 1820, Latin American countries were already well on the road to independence. The pattern for Latin American constitutionalism was initiated.

Following the work of Schor, the Latin American experience with the Constitution of Cádiz provides, perhaps, the first important regional experience of a lack of "constitutional entrenchment."[1] The inability of the Constitution of Cádiz to attain any manner of entrenchment led to the constitutionally debilitating conclusion that constitutional politics were coextensive with ordinary politics, a lasting characteristic of Latin American constitutionalism. The Constitution of Cádiz also served to establish the idea of the malleability of constitutions in the face of political change; Schor correctly observed that if rules could be so easily changed by rulers, there was no reason for citizens to invest politically or legally in the rules.[2] Fernando VII said a few words, and the document his defenders so ardently created to support him disappeared. A few years later, with the shift of political tides, it was back again. After less than two year, it was repealed. This social understanding of constitutionalism has been matched with the frequent replacement of constitutions on the

[1] Schor, "Constitutionalism through the Looking Glass," 27–34.
[2] Ibid., 7.

level of regular politics in the region.[3] Fernando VII taught his American subjects all they would need to know about constitutions for centuries to come.

As noted earlier, the Constitution of Cádiz was not the only Latin American constitution to go into and out of effect as a result of political shifts. On November 27, 1811, the Congress of Nueva Granada (Colombia) enacted the Federal Act of the United Provinces of Nueva Granada, and the federal provinces also drafted their own constitutions over the next couple of years. The autonomous Venezuelan Congress drafted a constitution on December 21, 1811. The autonomous Congress of Quito enacted Quito Constitution of 1812 that shared much in spirit with the Constitution of Cádiz.[4] These constitutions of early independence movements in Latin America suffered similar fates as Spain regained control and the nascent constitutional republics dissolved. Again, the lesson was learned that constitutions were subject to political power and the ordinary course of political and military action.

The Constitution of Cádiz of 1812 was never in force for more than three consecutive years in Spain or its colonies. The provisions of the Constitution of Cádiz never formed an effective, lasting constitutional order in Spain or Latin America. The Constitution's immediate suspension and lack of long-standing force left fundamental fissures in Latin American constitutionalism from which the region still suffers. By linking constitutions to political change, the suspension of the Constitution of Cádiz politicized constitutional law and constitutionalism. In other words, constitutions became part of the tool bag employed by politicians to work political change, reform, or restoration. This hindered the ability of constitutions to transcend the political sphere in Latin America and led to patterns and difficulties found in modern Latin American constitutionalism.

The Constitution of Cádiz heralded liberal constitutionalism in Europe and Latin America. Its provisions shaped constitutions that were to come after it. It served as a model for structuring elections not only for Spain but also for several countries in Latin America, even after their independence from Spain. Experience in Cádiz and at the Cortes contributed to the political and constitutional savvy of constitutional drafters in America. The Constitution of Cádiz can be properly viewed as an important document in the history of national sovereignty, popular

---

[3] Ibid., 6–7.
[4] Rodríguez, *The Independence*, 115–116, 149, 155–156.

representation, liberal constitutionalism, constitutional rights, and Latin American independence. The use of historical justification in the debates of its drafters is noteworthy.

The immediate repeal of the Constitution of Cádiz and its resultant lack of entrenchment established a pattern detrimental to effective and lasting constitutionalism in Latin America. The Constitution of Cádiz and its subsequent history can be seen as the origin of many of the constitutional challenges facing the region today. In abolishing the Constitution of Cádiz and the work of the Cortes, Fernando VII sent a message that had lasting constitutional implications. His actions demonstrated that there was nothing special about the Constitution of Cádiz, constitutions, or constitutional law. It was, unfortunately, a lesson learned. Such practices and messages would be repeated over and over again.

Appendix

Selected Provisions of the Constitution of Cádiz of 1812*

DON FERNANDO VII, by the grace of God and the Constitution of the Spanish Monarchy, King of the Spains, and in his absence and captivity, the Regency of the kingdom, named by the general and extraordinary Cortes, to all to whom these presents may come: That the same Cortes have decreed and sanctioned the following POLITICAL CONSTITUTION OF THE SPANISH MONARCHY.

In the name of almighty God, Father, Son and Holy Spirit author and supreme legislator of society.

The general and extraordinary Cortes of the Spanish Nation, well convinced, after the most careful examination and mature deliberation, of the former fundamental laws of this Monarchy, accompanied by fortunate providence and precautions, that ensure their complete fulfillment in a stable and permanent way, shall be able to reach dutifully the great goal of promoting the glory, prosperity and the well-being of the entire Nation, decrees the following political Constitution for the good governance and proper administration of the State.

Article 1. The Spanish Nation is the reunion of all Spaniards of both hemispheres.

Article 2. The Spanish Nation is free and independent, and is not able to be the patrimony of any family or person.

Article 3. Sovereignty resides essentially in the Nation, and by the same, the right to establish its fundamental laws belongs exclusively to it.

* Reprinted with permission from M.C. Mirow, Florida's First Constitution, The Constitution of Cádiz: Introduction, Translation and Text. Durham, North Carolina: Carolina Academic Press, 2012.

Article 4. The Nation is obliged to preserve and protect by wise and just laws, civil liberty, property, and the other legitimate rights of all the individuals who make up the Nation.

Article 5. Spaniards are:

First. All free men born and legal residents (*avecindados*) and their children in the dominion of the Spains.

Second. Foreigners who have obtained a letter of naturalization from the Cortes.

Third. Those who without such letter have lived ten years as legal residents (*de vecindad*), spent according to law, in any town of the Monarchy.

Fourth. Freed blacks once they have obtained liberty in the Spains.

Article 6. The love of Country is one of the principal obligations of all Spaniards, as well as to be just and to be charitable.

Article 7. Every Spaniard is obligated to be faithful to the Constitution, to obey the laws, and to respect the established authorities.

Article 10. The Spanish territory includes in the Peninsula with its possessions and adjacent islands: Aragón, Asturias, Castilla la Vieja, Castilla la Nueva, Catalonia, Córdoba, Extremadura, Galicia, Granada, Jaén, León, Molina, Murcia, Navarra, the Basque Provinces, Sevilla y Valencia, the Balearic Islands, the Canaries with the other possessions of Africa. In Northern America: New Spain with New Galicia and the peninsula of Yucatán, Guatemala, the internal provinces of the East, the internal provinces of the West, the Island of Cuba with the Two Floridas, the Spanish part of the Island of Santo Domingo, and the Island of Puerto Rico with the other islands adjacent thereto and to the continent in both seas. In Southern America: New Granada, Venezuela, Perú, Chile, the provinces of the Río de la Plata, and all adjacent islands in the Pacific and Atlantic Ocean. In Asia, the Philippine Islands and those that depend on its government.

Article 12. The religion of the Spanish Nation is and shall always be the Catholic, apostolic, Roman, the only true religion. The Nation protects it by wise and just laws and prohibits the exercise of any other religion.

Article 13. The purpose of the Government is the happiness of the Nation, since the end of all political society is no other than the well-being of the individuals who make up the Nation.

Article 14. The Government of the Spanish Nation is a moderate hereditary Monarchy.

Article 15. The power to make law belongs to the Cortes with the King.

Article 16. The power to execute the law belongs to the King.

Article 17. The power to apply the law in civil and criminal cases belongs to the courts established by law.

Article 18. Citizens are those Spaniards who by both blood lines trace their origin from the Spanish dominions of both hemispheres and are legal residents (*avecindados*) in any town of the same dominions.

Article 21. Citizens are also the legitimate sons of foreigners domiciled in the Spains, who having been born in the Spanish dominions, have never left without license of the Government, and having reached 21 years of age, have been legal residents (*avecindado*) in a town of the same dominions, exercising in it some profession, office of useful industry.

Article 22. For Spaniards who by whatever bloodline have or are reputed to have their origins in Africa, the door to the virtue and merit of being citizens is left open: consequently the Cortes shall give a letter of citizenship to those who have performed proven services to the Country, or to those who have distinguished themselves by their talent, force and conduct, with the condition that they are children of a legitimate marriage of free parents (*padres ingenuos*), that they are married with a free woman (*mujer ingenua*), and legal residents (*avecindados*) in the Spanish dominions, and that they exercise some profession, office, or useful industry with their own capital.

Article 27. The Cortes are the reunion of all the deputies who represent the Nation, elected by citizens in a given manner.

Article 28. The basis for national representation is the same in both hemispheres.

Article 29. This basis is the population consisting of the natives (*naturales*) who by both bloodlines are of origin of the Spanish dominions, and of those who have obtained a letter of citizenship from the Cortes, as is also described in Article 21.

Article 34. For the election of the deputies of the Cortes, electoral meeting of the parish (*parroquia*), the district (*partido*), and the province shall be held.

Article 35. The electoral meetings of the parish shall be composed of all the citizen who are legal residents (*ciudadanos avecindados*) and residents (*residentes*) in the territory of the respective parish, among whom are included the secular ecclesiastics.

Article 59. The electoral meetings of the district are composed of the parish electors who are gathered at the chief town of each district, in order to elect the elector or electors who have to proceed to the capital of the province to elect the deputies of the Cortes.

Article 78. The electoral meetings of the province shall be composed of the electors of all the districts in it, that shall gather in the capital to elect the deputies that correspond to it to attend the Cortes, as representatives of the Nation.

Article 88. The electors that are present shall immediately proceed to the election of the deputy or deputies, who are to be elected one by one, drawing themselves to the table where the president, inspectors and secretary are seated, and the secretary shall write in a list in their presence the name of the person whom each one elects. The secretary and the inspectors shall be the first who vote.

Article 104. The Cortes shall gather every year in the capital of the kingdom, in a building assigned for only this purpose.

Article 121. The King shall attend by himself the opening of the Cortes; and if there be an impediment, the president shall do so on the scheduled day, so that for no reason it may be postponed to another day. The same formalities shall be observed in the act of closing the Cortes.

Article 124. The Cortes may not deliberate in the presence of the King.

Article 126. The sessions of the Cortes shall be public, and only in the cases that demand it may secret sessions be held.

Article 131. The powers of the Cortes are:

First. To propose and to decree laws, and to interpret them and repeal them in necessary cases.

Article 170. The power to execute laws resides exclusively in the King, and his authority extends to everything leading to the conservation of public order in the interior and the security of the State in the exterior, in accordance with the Constitution and the laws.

Article 171. In addition to the prerogative that the King has to sanction and promulgate laws, the following principal powers belong to him:

First. To issue decrees, regulations and instructions that he believes conducive to the execution of the laws.

Second. To ensure the speedy and full administration of justice in the entire kingdom.

Fourth. To name the magistrates of all civil and criminal courts, at the proposal of the Council of State.

Fifth. To fill all civil and military offices.

Sixth. To present all bishoprics and all ecclesiastical dignitaries and benefices under the royal patronage of the Church, at the proposal of the Council of States.

Article 172. The restrictions on the authority of the King are the following:

First. The King may not impair under any pretext the celebration of the Cortes in their times and cases set by the Constitution, nor suspend or dissolve them, nor in any manner impede their sessions and deliberations. Those who council or help in any tentative plan for these acts are declared traitors and shall be punished as such.

Tenth. The King may not take the property of any individual or corporation or disturb them in possession, use or enjoyment of it; and if in any case it is necessary for the goal of known common utility to take the property of an individual, without at the same time being compensated, he shall be given a good sum in the good judgment of good men.

Eleventh. The King may not deprive anyone of his liberty nor impose by himself any penalty. The secretary of the office who signs the order and the judge who executes it shall be responsible to the Nation and punished as criminals of attempt again individual liberty. Only for the good and security of the State requiring the arrest of any person, may the King issue orders to this effect; but with the condition that within 48 hours he ought to be brought for disposition before a competent court or judge.

Article 242. The power to apply the laws in civil and criminal cases belongs exclusively to the courts.

Article 243. Neither the Cortes nor the King shall be able to exercise in any case judicial functions, or to remove pending cases, or to order cases that have been closed to be opened.

Article 244. Laws shall set out the order and formalities of procedure that shall be uniform in all courts; and neither the Cortes nor the King shall be able to set them aside.

Article 245. The courts may not exercise other functions than those of judging and ensuring that the judgment is executed.

Article 248. In ordinary civil and criminal matters, there shall not be more than one single law (*un solo fuero*) for all classes of people.

Article 249. The church shall continue to enjoy the special laws (*fuero*) of its status in the terms provided by law or as provided in the future.

Article 250. The military shall also enjoy its particular special laws (*fuero*) in the terms provided by ordinance or as provided in the future.

Article 258. Civil, criminal, and commercial codes shall be the same for all of the Monarchy, without prejudicing variations that the Cortes shall make in particular circumstances.

Article 259. There shall be in the Cortes a court that shall be called the Supreme Tribunal of Justice.

Article 286. Laws shall determine the administration of criminal justice, so that procedure is carried out quickly, and without error, with the end that crimes are promptly punished.

Article 287. No Spaniard may be imprisoned without a preceding summary information of the deed, for him who deserves to be punished with corporal punishment according to law, and also an order of the judge in writing, which notifies him and the prison in the same order.

Article 290. The arrested, before being placed in prison, shall be presented to the judge, as long as there is nothing that obstructs it, so that he receives a declaration; but if this is not able to take place, he shall be brought to the prison as a detained person, and the judge shall receive the declaration within 24 hours.

Article 293. If it is resolved that the arrested should be placed in prison, or that he remain there as a prisoner, there shall be provided an order of detention, and a copy shall be given to the jailer, so that he inserts it in the book of prisoners, without this requirement the jailer shall not admit any prisoner as such, under the most strict responsibility.

Article 297. Prisons shall be arranged in a manner that serves to hold and not to disturb prisoners: so that the jailer shall have those the judge orders to be without communication in good and separate custody, but never in unhealthy or underground cells.

Article 300. Within 24 hours the accused (*tratado como reo*) shall be shown the reason for his imprisonment, and the name of his accuser, if there is one.

Article 302. Proceedings from now on shall be public in the manner and form determined by law.

Article 303. Torture or pressure (*apremios*) shall not be used.

Article 304. Neither shall the punishment of confiscation of goods be imposed.

Article 306. The house of any Spaniard may not be searched unless in cases determined by law for the good order and security of the State.

Article 308. If in extraordinary circumstances the security of the State demands it, in the entire Monarchy or in part of it, the Cortes may decree for a fixed time the suspension of some of the formalities provided in this Chapter for the arrest of criminals.

Article 371. All Spaniards have the freedom to write, print, and publish their political ideas without necessity of any license, revision, or approval before their publication, under the restrictions and responsibilities that laws establish.

Article 373. Every Spaniard has the right to petition the Cortes or the King to demand that the Constitution is observed.

Article 375. Until eight years have passed since the Constitution in all its parts has been put in practice, no alteration, addition, or amendment shall be proposed to any of its articles.

Cádiz, March 18, 1812.

Bibliography

Abreu y Abreu, Juan Carlos. "Las ideas constitucionales en México, en el marco de las cortes gaditanas." *Anuario Mexicano de Historia del Derecho* 22 (2010): 1–55.

Adame Goddard, Jorge. "Asimilación y rechazo en México del sistema de relaciones entre la iglesia y el estado contemplado en la Constitución de Cádiz." *Anuario Mexicano de Historia del Derecho* 22 (2010): 57–74.

Adelman, Jeremy. "An Age of Imperial Revolutions." *American Historical Review* 113 (2008): 319–340.

"Between Order and Liberty: Juan Bautista Alberdi and the Intellectual Origins of Argentine Constitutionalism." *Latin American Research Review* 42 (2007): 86–110.

Republic of Capital: Buenos Aires and the Legal Transformation of the Atlantic World. Stanford: Stanford University Press, 1999.

"What's in a Revolution?" *Latin American Research Review* 47 (2012): 187–195.

Aguilar Rivera, José Antonio, comp. *La espada y la pluma: Libertad y liberalismo en México 1821–2005*. México: Fondo de Cultura Económica, 2011.

Aguilar Rivera, José Antonio, coord. *Las elecciones y el gobierno representativo en México (1810–1910)*. México: Fondo de Cultura Económica, Instituto Federal Electoral, 2010.

Aguilar Rivera, José Antonio. *El fin de la raza cósmica: Consideraciones sobre el esplendor y decadencia del liberalismo en México*. México: Oceano, 2001.

El manto liberal: Los poderes de emergencia en México 1821–1876. México: Universidad Nacional Autónoma de México, 2001.

"El veredicto del pueblo: El gobierno representivo y las elecciones en México, 1809–1846." In *Las elecciones y el gobierno representativo en México (1810–1910)*, coord. José Antonio Aguilar Rivera, 123–163. México: Fondo de Cultura Económica, Instituto Federal Electoral, 2010.

"Introduction." In *Liberty in Mexico: Writings on Liberalism from the Early Republican Period to the Second Half of the Twentieth Century*. José Antonio Aguilar Rivera, ed., ix–xxix. Indianapolis, IN: Liberty Fund, 2012.

La geometría y el mito: Un ensayo sobre la libertad y el liberalismo en México, 1821–1970. México: Fondo de Cultura Económica, 2010.

ed. *Liberty in Mexico: Writings on Liberalism from the Early Republican Period to the Second Half of the Twentieth Century.* Trans. Janet M. Burke and Ted Humphrey. Indianapolis, IN: Liberty Fund, 2012.

Aguilar Rivera, José Antonio, and Rafael Rojas, coords. *El republicanismo en Hispanoamérica: Ensayos de historia intelectual y política.* México: Fondo de Cultura Económica, Centro de Investigación y Docencia Económicas, 2001.

Alberdi, Juan Bautista. *Bases y puntos de partida para la organización política de la República Argentina.* Buenos Aires: Ciudad Argentina, 1998 [1852].

Bases y puntos de partida para la organización política de la República Arjentina: Derivados de la lei que Preside al Desarrollo de la civilización en la América del Sud. Valparaíso: Mercurio, 1852.

Alvarado, Javier. *Constitucionalismo y codificación en las provincias de ultramar: La supervivencia del antiguo régimen en la españa del XIX.* Madrid: Centro de Estudios Políticos y Constitucionales, 2001.

Álvarez Cuartero, Izaskun, and Julio Sánchez Gómez, eds. *Visiones y revisiones de la independencia americana: La independencia de América: la Constitución de Cádiz y las constituciones iberoamericanas.* Salamanca: Ediciones Universidad de Salamanca, 2003.

Alvárez Junco, José, and Javier Moreno Luzón, eds. *La Constitución de Cádiz: Historiografía y conmemoración: Homenaje a Francisco Tomás y Valiente.* Madrid: Centro de Estudios Políticos y Constitucionales, 2006.

Alviar García, Helena. "The Unending Quest for Land: The Tale of Broken Constitutional Promises." *Texas Law Review* 89 (2011): 1895–1914.

Andalucía, Junta de. *Los orígenes del constitucionalismo liberal en España e Iberoamérica: Un estudio comparado.* Sevilla: Junta de Andalucía, 1993.

Andrés Gallego, José, coord. *Nuevas aportaciones a la historia jurídica de Iberoamérica.* Madrid: Digibus, 2000.

Anna, Timothy. *Spain and the Loss of America.* Lincoln: University of Nebraska Press, 1983.

Annino, Antonio, coord. *La revolución novohispana 1808–1821.* México: Fondo de Cultura Económica, 2010.

Annino, Antonio. "Cádiz y la revolución territorial de los pueblos mexicanos. 1812–1821." In *La Revolución Novohispana 1808–1821,* coord. Antonio Annino, 143–176. México: Fondo de Cultura Económica, 2010.

Historia de las elecciones en Iberoamérica, Siglo xix: De la formación del espacio político nacional. México: Fondo de Cultura Económica, 1995.

"La ruralización de lo político." In *La revolución novohispana 1808–1821,* coord. Antonio Annino, 384–464. México: Fondo de Cultura Económica, 2010.

Annino, Antonio, and François-Xavier Guerra. *Inventando la nación: Iberoamérica siglo XIX.* México: Fondo de Cultura Económica, 2003.

Arboleda, Sergio. *La constitución política.* Bogotá: Biblioteca de Autores Colombianos, 1952.

Arcidiácono, Pilar, Nicolás Espejo Yaksic, and César Rodríguez Garavito, coords., *Derechos sociales: Justicia, política y economía en América Latina.* Bogotá: Siglo del Hombre, 2010.

Arnold, Linda. *Bureaucracy and Bureaucrats in Mexico City 1742–1835.* Tucson: University of Arizona Press, 1988.

Artola, Miguel. *Constitucionalismo en la historia.* Barcelona: Crítica, 2005.

"Estudio preliminar." In *II La Constitución de 1812,* eds. Miguel Artola and Rafael Flaquer Montequi, 15–74. Madrid: Iustel, 2008.

"La Monarquía parlamentaria." In *Las Cortes de Cádiz,* ed. Miguel Artola, 105–123. Madrid: Marcial Pons, 2003.

Los afrancesados, 2nd ed. Madrid: Alianza Editorial, 2008.

ed. *Las Cortes de Cádiz.* Madrid: Marcial Pons, 2003.

Artola, Miguel, and Rafael Flaquer Montequi, eds. *II La Constitución de 1812.* Madrid: Iustel, 2008.

Asdrúbal Silva, Hernán. "La Revolución, independencia y constitucionalismo venezolano en la prensa rioplatense." *Boletín de la Academia Nacional de la Historia* (Venezuela) 79: 314 (April–June 1996): 55–62.

Awarapa, O. "Despacio se llega lejos: Cambio institucional, instituciones latentes y el caso de la Presidencia del Consejo de Ministros." *Apuntes* 67(2) (2010): 5–36.

Ayala Corao, Carlos, and Jesús M. Casal. La evolución político-institucional de Venezuela 1975–2005. In *La evolución político-constitucional de América del Sur 1976–2005,* ed. Humberto Nogueira Alcalá, 551–647. Santiago: Librotecnia, 2009.

Azuela, Antonio. "Property in the Post-post-revolution: Notes on the Crisis of the Constitutional Idea of Property in Contemporary Mexico." *Texas Law Review* 89 (2011): 1915–1942.

Bahamonde Rodríguez, Santiago. "Cuba y la Constitución de 1812." In *De Cádiz (1812) a La Habana (2012): Escritos con motivo del bicentenario de la Constitución española de 1812,* eds. Andry Matilla Correa and Marcos Francisco Massó Garrote, 73–90. Havana: Organización Nacional de Bufetes Colectivos, 2011.

Barker, Robert S. *Constitutional Adjudication: The Costa Rican Experience.* Lake Mary, FL: Vandeplas Publishing, 2008.

"Latin American Constitutionalism: An Overview." *Willamette Journal of International Law and Dispute Resolution* 20 (2012): 1–20.

Barrios, Feliciano. "Las secretarías del despacho gaditano." *Anuario Mexicano de Historia del Derecho* 22 (2010): 81–97.

Barrón, Luis. "La tradición republicana y el nacimiento del liberalismo en Hispanoamérica después de la independencia: Bolívar, Lucas Alamán y el 'Poder Conservador.'" In *El republicanismo en Hispanoamérica: Ensayos de historia intelectual y política,* coords. José Antonio Aguilar and Rafael Rojas, 244–288. México: Fondo de Cultura Económica, Centro de Investigación y Docencia Económicas, 2001.

Barros, Robert. *Constitutionalism and Dictatorship: Pinochet, the Junta, and the 1980 Constitution.* Cambridge: Cambridge University Press, 2002.

Bastian, Jean-Pierre. "Los propagandistas del constitucionalismo en México (1910–1920)" *Revista Mexicana de Sociología* 45: 2 (April–June 1983), 321–351.

Belaúnde, Victor Andrés. *Bolívar and the Political Thought of the Spanish American Revolution.* Baltimore: Johns Hopkins University Press, 1938.

Bellingeri, Marco, coord. *Dinámicas de Antiguo Régimen y orden constitucional: Representación, justicia y administración en Iberoamérica. Siglos xviii–xix.* Torino: Otto Editore, 2000.

Bellingeri, Marco. "Introducción." In *Dinámicas de Antiguo Régimen y orden constitucional: Representación, justicia y administración en Iberoamérica, siglos xviii–xix,* coord. Marco Bellingeri, 1–13. Torino: Otto Editore, 2000.

Benson, Nettie Lee. *Mexico and the Spanish Cortes 1810–1822.* Austin: University of Texas Press, 1966.

——— *The Provincial Deputation in Mexico: Harbinger of Provincial Autonomy, Independence and Federalism.* Austin: University of Texas Press, 1992.

Benton, Lauren. "Constitutions and Empires." *Law & Social Inquiry* 31, no. 1 (2006): 177–198.

——— *Law and Colonial Cultures: Legal Regimes in World History, 1400–1900.* Cambridge: Cambridge University Press, 2002.

——— "The Legal Regime of the South Atlantic World, 1400–1750: Jurisdictional Complexity as Order." *Journal of World History* 11 (2000): 27–56.

——— *A Search for Sovereignty: Law and Geography in European Empires, 1400–1900.* Cambridge: Cambridge University Press, 2010.

Benton, Lauren, and Richard J. Ross. "Empires and Legal Pluralism: Jurisdiction, Sovereignty, and Political Imagination in the Early Modern World." In *Legal Pluralism and Empires, 1500–1850,* eds. Lauren Benton and Richard J. Ross, 1–17. New York: NYU Press, 2013.

Benton, Lauren, and Richard J. Ross, eds. *Legal Pluralism and Empires, 1500–1850.* New York: NYU Press, 2013.

Bergallo, Paola. "Courts and Social Change: Lessons from the Struggle to Universalize Access to HIV/AIDS Treatment in Argentina." *Texas Law Review* 89 (2011): 1611–1641.

Berruezo, María Teresa. *La participación americana en las Cortes de Cádiz (1810–1814).* Madrid: Centro de Estudios Constitucionales, 1986.

Bethell, Leslie, ed. *The Cambridge History of Latin America.* Cambridge: Cambridge University Press, 1985.

Billias, George Athan. *American Constitutionalism Heard Round the World, 1776–1989: A Global Perspective.* New York: NYU Press, 2009.

Blanco Valdéz, Robert L. *El "problema americano" en las primeras Cortes Liberales Españolas 1810–1814.* México: Universidad Nacional Autónoma de México, 1995.

Bonilla, Daniel, and Manuel Iturralde, eds. *Hacia un nuevo derecho constitucional.* Bogotá: Universidad de los Andes, 2005.

Bonillo, Heraclio, ed. *La Constitución de 1812 en Hispanoamérica y España.* Bogotá: Alcaldía Mayor de Bogotá, 2012.

Borah, Woodrow. *Justice by Insurance: The General Indian Court of Colonial Mexico and the Legal Aides of the Half-Real*. Berkeley: University of California Press, 1983.

Botana, Natalio R. "El primer republicanismo en el Río de la Plata, 1810–1826." In *Visiones y revisiones de la independencia americana: La independencia de América: la Constitución de Cádiz y las constituciones iberoamericanas*, eds. Izaskun Álvarez Cuartero and Julio Sánchez Gómez, 157–170. Salamanca: Ediciones Universidad de Salamanca, 2003.

——. *La tradición republicana: Alberdi, Sarmiento y las ideas políticas de su tiempo*. Buenos Aires: Editorial Sudamericana, 1997.

Botana, Natalio R., and Ezequiel Gallo. "Introduction." In *Liberal Thought in Argentina, 1837–1940*. Natalio R. Botana and Ezequiel Gallo, eds., ix–xxxii. Indianapolis, IN: Liberty Fund, 2013.

——. eds. *Liberal Thought in Argentina, 1837–1940*. Trans. Ian Barnett. Indianapolis, IN: Liberty Fund, 2013.

——. *De la República posible a la República verdadera (1880–1910)*. Buenos Aires: Ariel Historia, 1997.

Botero Bernal, Andrés. "Algunas influencias del primer proceso constitucional neogranadino: El constitucionalismo gaditano, las revoluciones, las ilustraciones y los liberalismos." *Ambiente Jurídico* 10 (2008): 167–210.

——. "La visión del derecho y los rastros del derecho indiano en las constituciones independistas neogranadinas de entre 1811 y 1815." In *Actas del Decimosexto Congreso del Instituto Internacional de Historia del Derecho Indiano*, ed. Alejandro Guzmán Brito, Vol. 2, 783–807. Valparaíso: Ediciones Universitarias de Valparaíso, 2010.

Boza, Beatriz, ed. *Doing Business in Peru: The New Legal Framework*, 2nd ed. Lima: PromPerú, 1994.

Brading, David A. "A Recusant Abroad." In *Mexican Soundings: Essays in Honour of David A. Brading*, eds. Susan Deans-Smith and Eric Van Young, 13–37. London: Institute for the Study of the Americas, 2007.

Bravo Lira, Bernardino. "El absolutismo ilustrado en España e Indias bajo Carlos III (1759–1788): De la visión judicial a la visión administrativa del gobierno con motivo de un bicentenario." *Revista Chilena de Historia del Derecho* 14 (1991): 11–33.

——. *El estado constitucional en Hispanoamérica 1811–1991: Ventura y desventura de un ideal Europeo de gobierno en el Nuevo Mundo*. México: Escuela Libre de Derecho, 1992.

——. "Protección jurídica de los gobernados en el Nuevo Mundo (1492–1992). Del absolutismo al constitucionalismo." *Revista Chilena de Historia del Derecho* 16 (1990–1991): 315–341.

Breña, Roberto. *El imperio de las circunstancias: Las independencias hispanoamericanas y la revolución liberal española*. México: El Colegio de México, 2012.

——. *El primer liberalismo español y los procesos de emancipación de América, 1808–1824. Una revisión historiográfica del liberalismo hispánico*. México: Colmex, 2006.

Brewer-Carías, Allan R. *Constitutonal Protection of Human Rights in Latin America: A Comparative Study of Amparo Proceedings*, Cambridge: Cambridge University Press, 2009.

Bryson, W. Hamilton, and Serge Dauchy, eds. *Ratio Decidendi: Guiding Principles of Judicial Decisions*, Vol. 1: *Case Law*. Berlin: Duncker & Humblot, 2006.

Buergenthal, Thomas, Jorge Mario García Laguardia, and Rodolfo Piza Rocafort. *La constitución norteamericana y su influencia en latinoamerica (200 años 1787–1987)*. San José: CAPEL, 1987.

Busaall, Jean-Baptiste. "Constitution et culture constitutionnelle. La Constitution de Bayonne dans la monarchie espagnole." *Revista Internacional de los Estudios Vascos* 4 (2009): 73–96.

Busaall, Jean-Baptiste. *Le spectre du jacobinisme: L'expérience constitutionnelle française et le premier libéralisme espagnol*. Madrid: Casa de Velázquez, 2012.

Bushnell, David. *The Making of Modern Colombia: A Nation in Spite of Itself*. Berkeley: University of California Press, 1993.

The Santander Regime in Gran Colombia. Westport, CT: Greenwood Press, 1970.

Bushnell, David, and Neill Macaulay. *The Emergence of Latin America in the Nineteenth Century*, 2nd ed. Oxford: Oxford University Press, 1994.

Carbonell y Sanchéz, Miguel. "Una aproximación al surgimiento histórico de la jurisprudencia en México." *Revista de la Facultad de Derecho de México* 45 (1995): 63–94.

Carbonell, Miguel, and Pedro Salazar, coords. *La reforma constitucional de derechos humanos: Un nuevo paradigma*. México: Universidad Nacional Autónoma de México, 2011.

Carmagnani, Marcello, coord. *Constitucionalismo y orden liberal: América Latina, 1850–1920*. Torino: Otto Editore, 2000.

Carpizo, Jorge. *La Constitución Mexicana de 1917*, 12th ed. México: Editorial Porrúa, 2000.

"Presentación." In *La evolución político-constitucional de América del Sur 1976–2005*, ed. Humberto Nogueira Alcalá, 15–19. Santiago: Librotecnia, 2009.

Carrasco Delgado, Sergio. "La evolución político-constitucional de Chile." In *La evolución político-constitucional de América del Sur 1976–2005*, ed. Humberto Nogueira Alcalá, 303–336. Santiago: Librotecnia, 2009.

Casar, María Amparo, and Ignacio Marván, coords. *Governar sin mayoría: México 1867–1997*. México: Taurus, 2002.

Castagno, Antonio. "El pensamiento político de Bolívar y el constitucional-ismo hispanoamericano." *Boletín de la Academia Nacional de la Historia* (Venezuela) 68: 271 (July–September 1985): 735–756.

Cepeda-Espinosa, Manuel José. "Judicial Activism in a Violent Context: The Origin, Role and Impact of the Colombian Constitutional Court." *Washington University Global Studies Law Review* 3 (2004): 529–700.

"Transcript: Social and Economic Rights and the Colombian Constitutional Court." *Texas Law Review* 89 (2011): 1699–1705.

Chasteen, John Charles. *Americanos: Latin America's Struggle for Independence*. Oxford: Oxford University Press, 2008.

Cheibub, José Antonio, Zachary Elkins, and Tom Ginsburg. "Latin American Presidentialism in Comparative and Historical Perspective." *Texas Law Review* 89 (2011): 1707–1739.

Chiaramonte, José Carlos. "The 'Ancient Constitution' after Independence (1800–1852)." *Hispanic American Historical Review* 90 (2010): 455–488.

Nación y Estado en Iberoamérica. El leguaje político en tiempos de las independencias. Buenos Aires: Editorial Sudamericana, 2004.

Chust, Manuel, coord. *Doceañismo, constituciones e independencias: La Constitución de 1812 y América.* Madrid: Mapfre, 2006.

Chust, Manuel. *América en las Cortes de Cádiz.* Madrid: Fundación Mapfre, 2010.

"De rebeliones, independencias, y, si acaso, revoluciones." In *La Revolución Novohispana 1808–1821*, coord. Annino, 465–491. México: Fondo de Cultura Económica, 2010.

"El poder municipal, vértice de la revolución gaditana." In *Visiones y revisiones de la independencia americana: La independencia de América: La Constitución de Cádiz y las constituciones iberoamericanas*, eds. Izaskun Álvarez Cuartero and Julio Sánchez Gómez, 109–131. Salamanca: Ediciones Universidad de Salamanca, 2003.

La cuestión nacional americana en las Cortes de Cádiz. Alzira: Centro Francisco Tomás y Valiente, 1999.

Chust, Manuel, and Ivana Frasquet, eds. *Los colores de las independencias iberamericanas: Liberalismo, etnia y raza.* Madrid: Consejo Superior de Investigaciones Científicas, 2009.

Clark, David S. "Judicial Protection of the Constitution in Latin America." *Hastings Constitutional Law Quarterly* 2 (1975): 405–442.

Clavero, Bartolomé. "Hemisferios de ciudadanía: Constitución española en la América indígena." In *La Constitución de Cádiz: Historiografía y conmemoración*, eds. José Alvárez Junco and Javier Moreno Luzón, 101–142. Madrid: Centro de Estudios Políticos y Constitucionales, 2006.

Manual de historia constitucional de España. Madrid: Alianza, 1989.

Collier, Simon. *Chile: The Making of a Republic, 1830–1865: Politics and Ideas.* Cambridge: Cambridge University Press, 2003.

Ideas and Politics of Chilean Independence, 1808–1833. Cambridge: Cambridge University Press, 1968.

Collier, Simon, and William F. Sater. *A History of Chile, 1808–1994.* Cambridge: Cambridge University Press, 1994.

Colomer Viadel, A. *Introducción al constitucionalismo iberoamericano.* Madrid: Ediciones de Cultura Hispánica, 1990.

Constantini, Laurent. "Les projets constitutionnels sud-américains de Francisco de Miranda: La fondation d'une nouvelle société politique sur la vertu et les institutions." *Revue historique de droit français et étranger* 90, no. 4 (2012): 571–598.

Corfield, Isabel. "Constitucionalismo ilustrado en la experiencia poscolonial hispano-americana." *Todo es Historia.* 26, no. 307 (1993): 79–83.

Coronas, Santos M. "*De las leyes fundamentales a la constitución política de la monarquía española* (1713–1812)." *Anuario de Historia del Derecho Español* 81 (2011): 11–82.

Cottrol, Robert J. *The Long, Lingering Shadow: Slavery, Race, and Law in the American Hemisphere.* Athens: University of Georgia Press, 2013.

Couso, Javier. "Models of Democracy and Models of Constitutionalism; The Case of Chile's Constitutional Court." *Texas Law Review* 89 (2011): 1517–1536.

"The Politics of Judicial Review in Chile in the Era of Democratic Transition, 1990–2002," In *Democratization and the judiciary: The Accountability Function of Courts in New Democracies*, eds. Siri Gloppen, Roberto Gargarella, and Elin Skaar, 70. London: Frank Cass, 2004.

Couso, Javier, Alexandra Huneeus, and Rachel Sieder, eds. *Cultures of Legality: Judicialization and Political Activism in Latin America.* Cambridge: Cambridge University Press, 2010.

Cutter, Charles R. *The Legal Culture of Northern New Spain, 1700–1810.* Albuquerque: University of New Mexico Press, 1995.

"The Legal Culture of Spanish America on the Eve of Independence." In *Judicial Institutions in Nineteenth-Century Latin America*, ed. Eduardo Zimmermann, 8–24. London: Institute of Latin American Studies, 1999.

De Armellada, Fray Cesáreo. *La causa indígena americana en las Cortes de Cádiz.* Madrid: Ediciones Cultura Hispánica, 1959.

De Galíndez, Jesús. "La inestabilidad constitucional en el derecho comparado de Latinoamérica." *Boletín del Instituto de Derecho Comparado de México.* 5(14) (May–August 1952), 3–23.

De la Madrid Hurtado, Miguel. *Estudios de Derecho Constitucional.* México: Universidad Nacional Autónoma de México, 1977.

De la Torre Villar, Ernesto, and Jorge Mario Garcia Laguardia. *Desarrollo histórico del constitucionalismo hispanoamericano.* México: Universidad Nacional Autónoma de México, 1976.

Deans-Smith, Susan, and Eric Van Young, eds., *Mexican Soundings: Essays in Honour of David A. Brading.* London: Institute for the Study of the Americas, 2007.

Dezalay, Yves, and Bryant G. Garth. *The Internationalization of Palace Wars: Lawyers, Economists, and the Contest to Transform Latin American States.* Chicago: University of Chicago Press, 2002.

Domínguez Nafria, Juan Carlos. "La codificación del derecho entre Bayona y Cádiz: El código de Napoleón." *Anuario Mexicano de Historia del Derecho* 22 (2010): 149–175.

Dougnac Rodríguez, Antonio. *Manual de historia del Derecho Indiano.* México: Universidad Nacional Autónoma de México, 1994.

Durand Florez, Guillermo. *El Perú en las Cortes de Cádiz*, Vols. 1 and 2. Lima: Comisión Nacional del Sesquicentenario de la Independencia del Perú, 1974. Eastman, Scott, and Natalia Sobrevilla Perea, eds. *The Rise of Constitutional Government in the Iberian Atlantic World: The Impact of the Cádiz Constitution of 1812.* Tuscaloosa, AL: University of Alabama Press, 2015.

Echeverri, Marcela. "Popular Royalists, Empire and Politics in Southwestern New Granada, 1809–1819." *Hispanic American Historical Review*, 91 (2011): 237–269.

Elkins, Zachary, Tom Ginsburg, and James Melton. *The Endurance of National Constitutions*. Cambridge: Cambridge University Press, 2009.

Enciso Contreras, José. "Correspondencia de don José Miguel Gordoa, diputado a las Cortes de Cádiz, con la provincia de Zacatecas, 1811–1814." *Anuario Mexicano de Historia del Derecho* 22 (2010): 177–199.

Escudero, José Antonio. "Martínez Marina y la Teoría de las Cortes." *Anuario Mexicano de Historia del Derecho* 22 (2010): 201–208.

Estrada Michel, Rafael. *Monarquía y nación entre Cádiz y Nueva España: El problema de la articulación política de las Españas ante la revolución liberal y la emancipación americana*. México: Editorial Porrúa, 2006.

"Regnícolas contra provincialistas: Un nuevo acercamiento a Cádiz con referencia al caso de la Nueva España." *Revista Electrónica de Historia Constitucional* 6 (2005): 1–42.

"Los reinos de Indias y la nueva nación Española." *Anuario Mexicano de Historia del Derecho* 22 (2010): 209–236.

Feitlowitz, Marguerite. *A Lexicon of Terror: Argentina and the Legacies of Torture*. Oxford: Oxford University Press, 2011.

Fernández Estrada, Julio Antonio. "Cádiz en Félix Varela. El laicismo y Cuba." In *De Cádiz (1812) a La Habana (2012): Escritos con motivo del bicentenario de la Constitución española de 1812*, eds. Andry Matilla Correa and Marcos Francisco Massó Garrote, 157–170. Havana: Organización Nacional de Bufetes Colectivos, 2011.

Fernández Giménez, María del Camino. "El senado en el Estatuto de Bayona: Origen del debate parlamentario en las Cortes de Cádiz." *Anuario Mexicano de Historia del Derecho* 22 (2010): 237–250.

Fernández Sarasola, Ignacio. *La Constitución española de 1812 y su proyección europea e iberoamericana*. Alicante: Biblioteca Virtual Miguel de Cervantes, 2004. http://www.cervantesvirtual.com/FichaObra.html?Ref=12956&portal=56

Fernández Segado, Francisco, coord. *La Constitución de 1978 y el Constitucionalismo iberoamericano*. Madrid: Centro de Estudios Políticos y Constitucionales, 2003.

Ferrando Badía, Juan. "Proyección exterior de la Constitución de 1812." In *Las Cortes de Cádiz*, ed. Miguel Artola, 207–248. Madrid: Marcial Pons, 2003.

Ferrer, Ada. "Haiti, Free Soil, and Antislavery in the Revolutionary Atlantic." *American Historical Review* 117 (2012): 40–66.

Figueroa, Dante. "Current Constitutional Developments in Latin America." *International Legal Research Informer*. American Society of International Law. Summer 2011: 8–18.

Fix-Zamudio, Hector. *Ensayos sobre el derecho de amparo*. México: Porrúa, 1999.

Latinoamérica: Constitución, proceso y derechos humanos. México: Porrúa, 1988.

Flaquer Montequi, Rafael. "'Las Cortes de Cádiz' " diez años después: historiografía y balance." In *Las Cortes de Cádiz*, ed. Miguel Artola, 249–272. Madrid: Marcial Pons, 2003.

"El Ejecutivo en la revolución liberal." In *Las Cortes de Cádiz*, ed. Miguel Artola, 37–65. Madrid: Marcial Pons, 2003.

Franco, Antonio-Filiu. *Cuba en los orígenes del constitucionalismo Español: La alternativa descentralizadora (1808–1837)*. Zaragoza: Fundación Manuel Giménez Abad, 2011.

Frasquet, Ivana. "Cádiz en América: Liberalismo y Constitución." *Mexican Studies /Estudios Mexicanos* 20(1) (2004): 21–46.

Las caras del águila: Del liberalismo gaditano a la república Federal Mexicana (1820–1824). Castelló de la Plana: Publicacions de la Universitat Jaume I, 2008.

"'Se obedece y se cumple': La jura de la Constitución de Cádiz en México en 1820." In *Visiones y revisiones de la independencia americana: La independencia de América: la Constitución de Cádiz y las constituciones iberoamericanas*, eds. Izaskun Álvarez Cuartero and Julio Sánchez Gómez, 217–245. Salamanca: Ediciones Universidad de Salamanca, 2003.

Friedman, Lawrence M., and Rogelio Pérez-Perdomo, eds. *Legal Culture in the Age of Globalization: Latin America and Latin Europe*. Stanford: Stanford University Press, 2003.

Fuentes, Claudio A. "A Matter of the Few: Dynamics of Constitutional Change in Chile, 1990–2010." *Texas Law Review* 89 (2011): 1741–1775.

Galdames, Luis. *Historia de Chile, la Evolución Constitucional*. Santiago: Editorial Universitaria, 1925.

Galeana de Valadés, Patricia, coord. *El constitucionalismo mexicano: Influencias continentales y trasatlánticas*. México: Senado de la República, LXI Legislatura: Siglo XXI Editores, 2010.

Gallego Anabitarte, Alfredo. "España 1812: Cádiz, Estado unitario, en perspectiva histórica." In *Las Cortes de Cádiz*, ed. Miguel Artola, 125–166. Madrid: Marcial Pons, 2003.

Galván Rodríguez, Eduardo. "El Inquisidor General y la Constitución de Cádiz." *Anuario Mexicano de Historia del Derecho* 22 (2010): 251–255.

Garay Montañez, Nilda. "La idea de igualdad en el constitucionalismo liberal español: Lo racial, las castas, y lo indígena en la Constitución de 1812." *Cuadernos Constitucionales de la Cátedra Funió Ceriol* 69/70 (2012): 129–158.

García Belaunde, Domingo, and Francisco José Eguiguren Praeli. La evolución político-constitucional del Perú 1976–2005. In *La evolución político-constitucional de América del Sur 1976–2005*, ed. Humberto Nogueira Alcalá, 463–501. Santiago: Librotecnia, 2009.

García Gallo, A. "El derecho indiano y la independencia de América." *Revista de Estudios Políticos* 60 (1951): 157–180.

García Laguardia, Jorge Mario. *Centroamérica en las Cortes de Cádiz*. México: Fondo de Cultura Económica, 1994.

"Las Cortes de Cádiz y la constitución de 1812. Un aporte americano." In *La Constitución de Cádiz y su influencia en América (175 años 1812–1987)*, eds. Jorge Mario García Laguardia, Carlos Meléndez Chaverri, and Marina Volio, 11–23. San José, Costa Rica: Centro Interamericano de Asesoría y Promoción Electoral, 1987.

García Laguardia, Jorge Mario, Carlos Meléndez Chaverri, and Marina Volio. *La Constitución de Cádiz y su influencia en América (175 años 1812–1987)*.

San José, Costa Rica: Centro Interamericano de Asesoría y Promoción Electoral, 1987.

García Villegas, Mauricio. *La eficacia simbólica del derecho.* Bogotá: Uniandes, 1993.

"Law as Hope: Constitutions and Social Change in Latin America." *Wisconsin International Law Journal* 20 (2002): 353–369.

García-Sayán, Diego. "The Inter-American Court and Constitutionalism in Latin America." *Texas Law Review* 89 (2011): 1835–1862.

Gardner, James A. *Legal Imperialism: American Lawyers and Foreign Aid in Latin America.* Madison: University of Wisconsin Press, 1980.

Gargarella, Roberto. *Los fundamentos legales de la desigualdad: El constitucionalismo en América 1776–1860.* Buenos Aires: Siglo XXI, 2008.

"Grafting Social Rights onto Hostile Constitutions." *Texas Law Review* 89 (2011): 1537–1555.

Latin American Constitutionalism, 1810–2010. Oxford: Oxford University Press, 2013.

The Legal Foundations of Inequality: Constitutionalism in the Americas 1776–1860. Cambridge: Cambridge University Press, 2010.

Gargarella, R., L. Filippini, and A. Cavana. *Recientes reformas constitucionales en América Latina.* New York: United Nations Development Programme, 2011.

Garriga, Carlos, coord. *Historia y constitución: Trayectos del constitucionalismo hispano.* México: Instituto Mora, 2010.

Garriga, Carlos. "Cabeza moderna, cuerpo gótico: La Constitución de Cádiz en el orden jurídico." *Anuario de Historia del Derecho Español* 81 (2011): 99–162.

"Orden jurídico e independencia política: Nueva España, 1808–México, 1821." In *La revolución Novohispana 1808–1821*, ed. Antonio Annino, 35–124. México: Fondo de Cultura Económica, 2010.

Garriga, Carlos, and Marta Lorente. *Cádiz, 1812: La constitución jurisdiccional.* Madrid: Centro de Estudios Políticos y Constitucionales, 2007.

Garro, Alejandro. "Judicial Review and Constitutionality in Argentina: Background Notes and Constitutional Provisions." *Duquesne Law Review* 2007: 409–429.

Giordano, Verónica. "La sanción de la capacidad civil plena de la mujer en los países del cono Sur, 1945-199: Una propuesta de análisis del fenómeno legal." *Latin American Research Review* 48 (2013): 25–43.

Gloppen, Siri, Roberto Gargarella, and Elin Skaar, eds. *Democratization and the judiciary: The accountability function of courts in new democracies.* London: Frank Cass, 2004.

Gómez, Manuel A. "Political Activism and the Practice of Law in Venezuela." In *Cultures of Legality: Judicialization and Political Activism in Latin America*, eds. Javier Couso, Alexandra Huneeus, and Rachel Sieder, 182–206. Cambridge: Cambridge University Press, 2010.

González Marcos, Miguel. "Comparative Law at the Service of Democracy: A Reading of Arosemena's Constitutional Studies of the Latin American Governments." *Boston University International Law Journal* 21 (2003): 259–323.

Grafe, Regina. *Distant Tyranny: Markets, Power, and Backwardness in Spain, 1600–1800*. Princeton, NJ: Princeton University Press, 2012.

Grafe, Regina, and Maria Alejandra Irigoin. "The Spanish Empire and Its Legacy: Fiscal Redistribution and Political Conflict in Colonial and Post-colonial Spanish America." *Journal of Global History* 1 (2006): 241–267.

Guerra, François-Xavier. *Modernidad e independencias: Ensayos sobre las revoluciones Hispánicas*. Madrid: Editorial Mapfre, 1992.

"El soberano y su reino: Reflexiones sobre la génesis del ciudadano en América Latina." In *Ciudadanía política y formación de las naciones: Perspectivas históricas*, ed. Hilda Sabato, 33–93. México: Colegio de México, 1999; Biblioteca Virtual de Ciencias Sociales, www.cholnautas.edu.pe, 1–28.

Guzmán Brito, Alejandro. *Andrés Bello codificador: Historia de la fijación y codificación del derecho civil en Chile*. 2 vols. Santiago: Universidad de Chile, 1982.

Vida y obra de Andrés Bello. Santiago: Globo Editores, 2009.

Guzmán Brito, Alejandro, ed. *Actas del Decimosexto Congreso del Instituto Internacional de Historia del Derecho Indiano*. Valparaíso: Ediciones Universitarias de Valparaíso, 2010.

Hale, Charles A. *Emilio Rabasa and the Survival of Porfirian Liberalism: The Man, His Career, and His Ideas, 1856–1930*. Stanford: Stanford University Press, 2008.

Mexican Liberalism in the Age of Mora, 1821–1853. New Haven, CT: Yale University Press, 1968.

The Transformation of Liberalism in Late Nineteenth-Century Mexico. Princeton, NJ: Princeton University Press, 1989.

Haley, John O. "Foundations of Governance and Law: An Essay on Law's Evolution in Colonial Spanish America." *Diakion* 18 (2009), 164–203.

Halperín Donghi, Tulio, ed. *Proyecto y construcción de una nación (1846–1880)*. Buenos Aires: Ariel Historia, 1995.

Hampe Martínez, Teodoro, and José F. Gálvez Montero, "De la intendencia al departamento (1810–1830): Los cambios en la administración pública regional del Perú." In *Dinámicas de Antiguo Régimen y orden constitucional: Representación, justicia y administración en Iberoamérica, siglos xviii–xix*, coord. Marco Bellingeri, 339–368. Torino: Otto Editore, 2000.

Hernández, Tanya Katerí. *Racial Subordination in Latin America: The Role of the State, Customary Law, and the New Civil Rights Response*. Cambridge: Cambridge University Press, 2013.

Hernández Campos, Jorge. "El constitucionalismo: Ensayo sobre los orígenes de la paradoja del poder." *Nueva Política* 1, no. 2 (April–June 1976): 143–180.

Herrera Andrade, Eduardo. *Miguel Antonio Caro: Pensamiento y Acción*. Cochabamba: Editorial Javeriana, 2011.

Herzog, Tamar. "Citizenship and Empire: Communal Definition in Eighteenth-Century Spain and Spainsh America." In *Privileges and Rights of Citizenship: Law and the Juridical Constitution of Civil Society*, eds. Julius Kirshner and Laurent Mayali, 147–167. Berkeley: Robbins Collection, 2002.

Defining Nations. Immigrants and Citizens in Early Modern Spain and Spanish America. New Haven, CT: Yale University Press, 2003.

"'¡Viva el rey, muera el mal gobierno!' y la administración de justicia quiteña, Siglos xvii y xviii." In *Dinámicas de Antiguo Régimen y orden constitucional: Representación, justicia y administración en Iberoamérica, siglos xviii–xix*, coord. Marco Bellingeri, 77–95. Torino: Otto Editore, 2000.

Hilbink, Lisa. *Judges beyond Politics in Democracy and Dictatorship: Lessons from Chile*. Cambridge: Cambridge University Press, 2007.

Infante, Javier. *Autonomía, Independencia y República en Chile 1810–1828*. Santiago: Ediciones Centro de Estudios Bicentenario, 2014.

"La historiografía constitucional en la formación nacional de Chile: 1810–1833. Enfoques y discusiones." *Revista Chilena de Derecho* 41 (2014): 747–764.

Jaksić, Iván. *Andrés Bello: Scholarship and Nation-Building in Nineteenth-Century Latin America*. Cambridge: Cambridge University Press, 2001.

ed. *Selected Writings of Andrés Bello*. Trans. Frances M. López-Morillas. New York: Oxford University Press, 1997.

Jamanca Vega, Marco. "El liberalismo peruano y el impacto de las ideas y de los modelos constitucionales a inicios del siglo xix." *Historia Constitucional* 8 (2007): 1–30.

James, Timothy M. *Mexico's Supreme Court: Between Liberal Individual and Revolutionary Social Rights, 1867–1934*. Albuquerque: University of New Mexico Press, 2013.

Kennedy, Duncan. "Two Globalizations of Law & Legal Thought: 1850–1968." *Suffolk University Law Review* 36 (2003): 631–679.

Kirshner, Julius, and Laurent Mayali, eds. *Privileges and Rights of Citizenship: Law and the Juridical Constitution of Civil Society*. Berkeley: Robbins Collection, 2002.

Knight, Alan. *The Mexican Revolution*, Vol. 1: *Porfirians, Liberals and Peasants*. Cambridge: Cambridge University Press, 1986.

The Mexican Revolution, Vol. 2: *Counter-Revolution and Reconstruction*. Cambridge: Cambridge University Press, 1986.

Labra y Cadrara, Rafael María de. *América y la Constitución Española de 1812*. Madrid: Tipografía Sindicato de Publicidad, 1912.

Langford, Malcolm. *Social Rights Jurisprudence: Emerging Trends in International and Comparative Law*. Cambridge: Cambridge University Press, 2008.

Langue, Frédérique. "La representación venezolana en las Cortes de Cádiz: Jose Domingo Rus." *Nuevo Mundo Mundos Nuevos* [online] BAC – Biblioteca de Autores del Centro, Langue, Frédérique, online November 12, 2003. http://nuevomundo.revues.org/index1153.html

Lara Hernández, Eduardo. "Influencia de la Constitución de 1812 en el constitucionalismo cubano: El padre Félix Varela, 'patriota entero', y su divulgación." In *De Cádiz (1812) a La Habana (2012): Escritos con motivo del bicentenario de la Constitución Española de 1812*, eds. Andry Matilla Correa and Marcos Francisco Massó Garrote, 138–145. Havana: Organización Nacional de Bufetes Colectivos, 2011.

Lasarte, Javier. *Las Cortes de Cádiz: Soberanía, Separación de Poderes, Hacienda, 1810–1811*. Madrid: Marcial Pons, 2009.

Lasso, Marixa. *Myths of Harmony: Race and Republicanism during the Age of Revolution, Colombia 1795–1831*. Pittsburgh: University of Pittsburgh Press, 2007.

Lempérière, Annik. "La representación política en el imperio español a finales del antiguo régimen." In *Dinámicas de Antiguo Régimen y orden constitucional: Representación, justicia y administración en Iberoamérica, siglos xviii–xix*, coord. Marco Bellingeri, 55–75. Torino: Otto Editore, 2000.

Levaggi, Abelardo. "La constitución Española de 1812 e Hispanoamérica." *Iushistoria Investigaciones* 2 (2009): 7–30.

"Three Matters Concerning Argentine Constitutional History." *Rechtsgeschichte* 16 (2010): 82–84.

Levene, Ricardo. *Las indias no eran colonias*, 3rd ed. Madrid: Espasa-Calpe, 1973.

López Monroy, José de Jesús. "El concepto de 'provincias' y 'pueblos', y su régimen de gobierno interior en la Constitución de Cádiz." *Anuario Mexicano de Historia del Derecho* 22 (2010): 271–281.

Lorente Sariñera, Marta. "América en Cádiz." In *Los orígenes del constitucionalismo liberal en España e Hispanoaméricana: Un estudio comparado*, ed. Junta de Andalucia, 17–47. Sevilla: Junta de Andalucia, 1993.

"El juramento constitucional." In *Anuario de Historia del Derecho Español* 65 (1995): 584–632.

"Esencia y valor del constitucionalismo gaditano (Nueva España, 1808–1821)." In *La Revolución Novohispana 1808–1821*, ed. Antonio Annino, 293–383. México: Fondo de Cultura Económica, 2010.

La Nación y Las Españas: Representación y territorio en el constitucionalismo Gaditano. Madrid: Universidad Autónoma de Madrid, 2010.

Loveman, Brian. *The Constitution of Tyranny: Regimes of Exception in Spanish America*. Pittsburgh: University of Pittsburgh Press, 1993.

Loyda Zaldívar Abad, Martha. "El obispo Espada: Génesis del sentimiento constitucional por Cádiz en Cuba." In *De Cádiz (1812) a la Habana (2012): Escritos con motivo del bicentenario de la Constitución española de 1812*, eds. Andry Matilla Correa and Marcos Francisco Massó Garrote, 124–138. Havana: Organización Nacional de Bufetes Colectivos, 2011.

Lujambio, Alonso. *La influencia del constitucionalismo anglosajón en el pensamiento de Emilio Rabasa*. México: Escuela Libre de Derecho: Instituto de Investigaciones Jurídicas, Universidad Nacional Autónoma de México, 2009.

Lynch, John. *Caudillos in Spanish America, 1800–1850*. Oxford: Oxford University Press, 1992.

The Spanish American Revolutions: 1808–1826. New York: W. W. Norton, 1986.

Spanish Colonial Administration, 1782–1810: The Intendant System in the Viceroyalty of the Rio de la Plata. New York: Greenwood, 1969 (London: The Athlone Press, 1958).

Madrazo, Alejandro, and Estefanía Vela. "The Mexican Supreme Court's (Sexual) Revolution?" *Texas Law Review* 89 (2011): 1863–1893.

Maladona Polo, J. Luis. "Científicos americanos en las Cortes Constituyentes: La cuestión ultramarina." *Revista de Indias* 63, no. 227 (2003): 275–302.

Marchena Fernández, Juan. "El día que los negros cantaron la marsellesa: El fracaso del liberalismo español en América. 1790–1823." In *Visiones y revisiones de la independencia americana: La independencia de América: la*

Constitución de Cádiz y las constituciones iberoamericanas, eds. Izaskun Álvarez Cuartero and Julio Sánchez Gómez, 145–181. Salamanca: Ediciones Universidad de Salamanca, 2003.

"Revolución, representación y elecciones: El impacto de Cádiz en el mundo andino." *Procesos* 19 (2002–2003): 237–266.

Marcuello Benedicto, Juan Ignacio. "Las Cortes Generales y Extraordinarias: Organización y poderes para un gobierno de Asamblea." In *Las Cortes de Cádiz*, ed. Miguel Artola, 67–104. Madrid: Marcial Pons, 2003.

Marino, Daniela. "Indios, pueblos y la construcción de la Nación: La modernización del espacio rural en el centro de México, 1812–1900." In *Nación, Constitución, y Reforma, 1821–1908*, ed. Erika Pani, 163–204. México: Fondo de Cultura Económica, 2010.

Martiré, Eduardo. "Algo más sobre la Constitución de Bayona." *Anuario de Historia del Derecho Español* 81 (2011): 82–98.

Dos lecciones de historia del derecho argentino: Los derechos de las personas en Indias. Buenos Aires: Editorial Perrot, 1989.

1808: La clave de la emancipación hispanoamericana, ensayo histórico-jurídico. Buenos Aires: Elefante Blanco, 2002.

Massó Garrote, Marcos Francisco. "Significado y aportes de la Constitución de Cádiz de 1812 en el constitucionalismo español e iberoamericano." In *De Cádiz (1812) a la Habana (2012): Escritos con motivo del bicentenario de la Constitución Española de 1812*, eds. Andry Matilla Correa and Marcos Francisco Massó Garrote, 1–28. Havana: Organización Nacional de Bufetes Colectivos, 2011.

Matilla Correa, Andry. "Glosas sobre la Constitución Española de 1812 en Cuba." In *De Cádiz (1812) a la Habana (2012): Escritos con motivo del bicentenario de la Constitución Española de 1812*, eds. Andry Matilla Correa and Marcos Francisco Massó Garrote, 91–123. Havana: Organización Nacional de Bufetes Colectivos, 2011.

Matilla Correa, Andry, and Marcos Francisco Massó Garrote, eds. *De Cádiz (1812) a la Habana (2012): Escritos con motivo del bicentenario de la Constitución española de 1812*. Havana: Organización Nacional de Bufetes Colectivos, 2011.

McKinley, Michelle A. "Emancipatory Politics and Rebellious Practices: Incorporating Global Human Rights in Family Violence Laws in Peru." *New York University Journal of International Law and Politics* 39 (2006): 75–139.

Meléndez Chaverri, Carlos. "Las Cortes de Cádiz en sus circunstancias históricas: Origenes de la Constitución de 1812." In *La Constitución de Cádiz y su influencia en América (175 años 1812–1987)*, eds. Jorge Mario García Laguardia, Carlos Meléndez Chaverria, and Marina Volio, 27–45. San José, Costa Rica: Centro Interamericano de Asesoría y Promoción Electoral, 1987.

Méndez, Juan E., Guillermo O'Donnell, and Paulo Sérgio Pinheiro, eds. *The (Un)Rule of Law and the Underprivileged in Latin America*. Notre Dame, IN: University of Notre Dame Press, 1999.

Miller, Jonathan M. "The Authority of a Foreign Talisman: A Study of U.S. Constitutional Practice as Authority in Nineteenth-Century Argentina and the Argentine Elite's Leap of Faith." *American University Law Review* 46 (1997): 1483–1572.

"Evaluating the Argentine Supreme Court under Presidents Alfonsín and Menem (1983–1999)." *Southwestern Journal of Law and Trade in the Americas* 7 (2000): 369–433.

"Judicial Review and Constitutional Stability: A Sociology of the U.S. Model and Its Collapse in Argentina." *Hastings International and Comparative Law Review* 21 (1997): 77–176.

Mirow, M.C. "The Age of Constitutions in the Americas." *Law and History Review* 32(2) (2014): 229–235.

"Borrowing Private law in Latin America: Andrés Bello's Use of the *Code Napoléon* in Drafting the Chilean Civil Code. *Louisiana Law Review* 61 (2001): 291–329.

"Case Law in Mexico 1861–1919: The Work of Ignacio Luis Vallarta." In *Ratio Decidendi: Guiding Principles of Judicial Decisions*, Vol. 1: *Case Law*. W. Hamilton Bryson and Serge Dauchy, eds., 223–245. Berlin: Duncker & Humblot, 2006.

"Codification and the Constitution of Cádiz." In *Estudios Jurídicos en Homenaje al Profesor Alejandro Guzmán Brito*. Patricio-Ignacio Carvajal and Massimo Miglietta eds., Vol. 3, 343-361. Trento, Italy: Edizioni dell'Orso, 2014.

Florida's First Constitution, The Constitution of Cádiz: Introduction, Translation, and Text. Durham, NC: Carolina Academic Press, 2012.

"La contribución de Ignacio Vallarta al constitucionalismo Mexicano: Algunos aspectos estadounidenses." In *El constitucionalismo mexicano: Influencias continentales y trasatlánticas*, ed. Galeana de Valadés, 47–61. México: Senado de la República, LXI Legislatura: Siglo XXI Editores, 2010.

Latin American Law: A History of Private Law and Institutions in Spanish America. Austin: University of Texas Press, 2004.

"*Marbury* in Mexico: Judicial Review's Precocious Southern Migration." *Hastings Constitutional Law Quarterly* 35 (2007): 41–117.

"Origins of the Social Function of Property in Chile." *Fordham Law Review* 80 (2011): 1183–1217.

"The Power of Codification in Latin America: Simón Bolívar and the *Code Napoléon.*" *Tulane Journal of International and Comparative Law* 8 (2000): 83–116.

"Pre-constitutional Law and Constitutions: Spanish Colonial Law and the Constitution of Cádiz." *Washington University Global Studies Law Review* 12:2 (2013): 313–337.

"The Social-Obligation Norm of Property: Duguit, Hayem, and Others." *Florida Journal of International Law* 22 (2010): 191–226.

"Visions of Cádiz: The Constitution of Cádiz in Historical and Constitutional Thought." *Studies in Law, Politics, and Society* 53 (2010): 59–88.

Molina Martínez, Miguel. "De cabildos a ayuntamientos: Las Cortes de Cádiz en América." In *Visiones y revisiones de la independencia americana: La independencia de América: la Constitución de Cádiz y las constituciones iberoamericanas*, eds. Izaskun Álvarez Cuartero and Julio Sánchez Gómez, 133–155. Salamanca: Ediciones Universidad de Salamanca, 2003.

Mondelo García, Walter. "Félix Varela y los inicios del constitucionalismo cubano," In *De Cádiz (1812) a la Habana (2012): Escritos con motivo del bicentenario de la Constitución Española de 1812*, eds. Andry Matilla Correa and Marcos Francisco Massó Garrote, 146–156. Havana: Organización Nacional de Bufetes Colectivos, 2011.

Morán Orti, Manuel. "La formación de las Cortes (1808–1810)." In *Las Cortes de Cádiz*, ed. Miguel Artola, 13–36. Madrid: Marcial Pons, 2003.

Morelli, Federica. "El espacio municipal: Cambios en la jurisdicción territorial del cabildo de Quito, 1765–1830." In *Dinámicas de Antiguo Régimen y orden constitucional: Representación, justicia y administración en Iberoamérica, siglos xviii–xix*, coord. Marco Bellingeri, 17–54. Torino: Otto Editore, 2000.

Morgan, Martha I. "Founding Mothers: Women's Voices and Stories in the 1987 Nicaraguan Constitution." *Boston University Law Review* 70 (1990), 1–107.

Morgan, Martha I., and Monica María Alzate Buitrago. "Constitution-making in a Time of Cholera: Women and the 1991 Colombian Constitution." *Yale Journal of Law and Feminism* 4 (1992): 354–413.

Narváez H., José Ramón. "Cádiz: Su proyección en el trienio liberal mexicano." *Anuario Mexicano de Historia del Derecho* 22 (2010): 305–313.

Negretto, Gabriel L. *Making Constitutions: Presidents, Parties, and Institutional Choice in Latin America*. Cambridge: Cambridge University Press, 2013.

"Repensando el republicanismo liberal en América Latina: Alberdi y la Constitución de 1853." In *El republicanismo en Hispanoamérica: Ensayos de historia intelectual y política*, coords. José Antonio Aguilar and Rafael Rojas, 210–243. México: Fondo de Cultura Económica, Centro de Investigación y Docencia Económicas, 2001.

"Shifting Constitutional Designs in Latin America: A Two-Level Explanation. *Texas Law Review* 89 (2011): 1777–1806.

Nogueira Alcalá, Humberto, coord. *La evolución político-constitucional de América del Sur 1976–2005*. Santiago: Librotecnia, 2009.

Nogueira Alcalá, Humberto. "La evolución político-constitucional de Chile 1976–2005." In *La evolución político-constitucional de América del Sur 1976–2005*, ed. Humberto Nogueira Alcalá, 337–398. Santiago: Librotecnia, 2009.

"Preámbulo." In *La evolución político-constitucional de América del Sur 1976–2005*, ed. Humberto Nogueira Alcalá, 11–14. Santiago: Librotecnia, 2009.

Novoa-Cain, Mauricio Alfredo. "The Protectors of Indians in the Royal Audiencia of Lima: History, Careers and Legal Culture, 1575–1775." Ph.D. diss., University of Cambridge, 2014.

Nunca Más: The Report of the Argentine Commission on the Disappeared, 1986.

Núñez Martínez, María. *Los orígenes del constitucionalismo hispanoamericano*. Madrid: Universitas Internacional, 2008.

Olano García, Hernán A. *Constitucionalismo histórico: La historia de Colombia a través de sus constituciones y reformas*, 2nd ed. Bogotá: Ediciones Doctrina y Ley, 2007.

Oquendo, Ángel R. *Latin American Law*, 2nd ed. New York: Foundation Press, 2011.

"The Solitude of Latin America: The Struggle for Rights South of the Border." *Texas International Law Journal* 43 (2008): 185–242.

Ortiz Gutiérrez, Julio C. "La evolución político-constitucional de la República de Colombia 1976–2005." In *La evolución político-constitucional de América del Sur 1976–2005*, ed. Humberto Nogueira Alcalá, 205–280. Santiago: Librotecnia, 2009.

Ortiz Treviño, Rigoberto Gerardo. "El pensamiento de Miguel Ramos Arizpe en el constituyente gaditano (1810–1812). *Anuario Mexicano de Historia del Derecho* 22 (2010): 315–325.

Ots Capdequí, José María. *España en América*, 2nd ed. Bogotá: Universidad Nacional de Colombia, 1952.

Owensby, Brian P. "Between Justice and Economics: 'Indians' and Reformism in Eighteenth-Century Spanish Imperial Thought." In *Legal Pluralism and Empires, 1500–1850*, eds. Lauren Benton and Richard J. Ross, 143–169. New York: NYU Press, 2013.

Empires of Law and Indian Justice in Colonial Mexico. Stanford: Stanford University Press, 2008.

Palacios, Marco. *Between Legitimacy and Violence: A History of Colombia, 1875–2002*. Trans. Richard Stoller. Durham, NC: Duke University Press, 2006.

De populistas, mandarines y violencias: Lucha por el poder. Bogotá: Editorial Planeta Colombiana, 2001.

Pampillo Baliño, Juan Pablo. "Fray Melchor de Talamantes, ideólogo de la independencia." *Terra* 7(2010): 123–141.

El primer constitucionalista de México: Talamantes, ideología y proyecto para la América Septentrional. México: Porrúa, 2010.

Pani, Erika, ed. *Nación, constitución, y reforma, 1821–1908*. México: Fondo de Cultura Económica, 2010.

Parry, John H. *The Spanish Seaborne Empire*. New York: Knopf, 1977.

Peralta Ruíz, V. "Elecciones, constitucionalismo, y revolución en el Cusco, 1809–1815." *Revista de Indias* 56, no. 206 (1996): 99–131.

Pérez Guilhou, Dardo. *La opinion pública española y las Cortes de Cádiz frente a la emancipación hispanoamericana 1808–1814*. Buenos Aires: Academia Nacional de la Historia, 1981.

Pérez Ledesma, Manuel. "Las Cortes de Cádiz y la sociedad Española." In *Las Cortes de Cádiz*, ed. Miguel Artola, 167–206. Madrid: Marcial Pons, 2003.

Phelan, John Leddy. "Authority and Flexibility in the Spanish Imperial Bureaucracy." *Administrative Sciences Quarterly* 5 (1960): 47–65.

Pietschmann, Horst. "El primer constitucionalismo en México o ¿Cómo configurar una realidad colonial de antiguo régimen para un futuro en el marco de una nación republicana? Introducción a un trabajo de seminario de investigación." *Jahrbuch für Geschichte Lateinamerikas* 42 (2005): 235–242.

"Justicia, discurso político y Reformismo Borbónico en la Nueva España del siglo xviii." In *Dinámicas de Antiguo Régimen y orden constitucional: Representación, justicia y administración en Iberoamérica, siglos xviii–xix*, coord. Marco Bellingeri, 17–54. Torino: Otto Editore, 2000.

Polk, William R. *Violent Politics: A History of Insurgency, Terrorism & Guerrilla War, from the American Revolution to Iraq.* New York: Harper Perennial, 2007.

Ponce Alcocer, María Eugenia. "Las elecciones presidenciales de 1877 a 1888: modalidades y tendencias." In *Las elecciones y el gobierno representativo en México (1810–1910)*, coord. José Antonio Aguilar Rivera, 282–307. México: Fondo de Cultura Económica, Instituto Federal Electoral, 2010.

Portillo Valdés, José María. *Crisis Atlántica: Autonomía e independencia en la crisis de la monarquía Hispana.* Madrid: Marcial Pons-Fundación Carolina, 2006.

"El problema de la identidad entre monarquía y nación en la crisis Hispana, 1808–1821." In *Visiones y revisiones de la independencia americana: La independencia de América: la Constitución de Cádiz y las constituciones iberoamericanas*, eds. Izaskun Álvarez Cuartero and Julio Sánchez Gómez, 53–69. Salamanca: Ediciones Universidad de Salamanca, 2003.

"La Constitución universal." In *La Constitución de Cádiz: Historiografía y conmemoración*, ed. José Alvárez Junco and Javier Moreno Luzón, 85–100. Madrid: Centro de Estudios Políticos y Constitucionales, 2006.

"Monarquía, imperio y nación: Experiencias políticas en el Atlántico hispano en el momento de la crisis hispana." In *La revolución Novohispana 1808–1821*, coord. Antonio Annino, 125–190. México: Fondo de Cultura Económica, 2010.

Revolución de nación: Orígenes de la cultural constitucional en España, 1780–1812. Madrid: Centro de Estudios Políticos y Constitucionales, 2000.

Portuondo Zúñiga, Olga. *Cuba: Constitución y liberalismo*, Vols. 1 and 2. Santiago de Cuba: Editorial Oriente, 2008.

Pozas-Loyo, Andrea, and Julio Ríos-Figueroa. "The Politics of Amendment Processes: Supreme Court Influence on the Design of Judicial Councils." *Texas Law Review* 89 (2011): 1807–1833.

Prieto Valdés, Martha. "La Constitución de Cádiz y el ideario criollo en el proceso de formación del constitucionalismo cubano." In *De Cádiz (1812) a la Habana (2012): Escritos con motivo del bicentenario de la Constitución española de 1812*, eds. Andry Matilla Correa and Marcos Francisco Massó Garrote, 191–207. Havana: Organización Nacional de Bufetes Colectivos, 2011.

Prillaman, William C. *The Judiciary and Democratic Decay in Latin America: Declining Confidence in the Rule of Law.* Westport: CT: Praeger, 2000.

Quintero, Inés. "La iniciativa gaditana y la provincia de Venezuela." In *Visiones y revisiones de la independencia americana: La independencia de América: La Constitución de Cádiz y las constituciones iberoamericanas*, eds. Izaskun Álvarez Cuartero and Julio Sánchez Gómez, 195–216. Salamanca: Ediciones Universidad de Salamanca, 2003.

Quiroga Fernández de Soto, Alejandro. "Military Liberalism on the East Florida 'Frontier': Implementation of the 1812 Constitution." *Florida Historical Quarterly* 70 (2001): 441–468.

Ramos Arizpe, José Miguel. *Presencia de Ramos Arizpe en las Cortes de Cádiz 1811*. Monterrey: Archivo General del Estado, 1988.

Ramos Garbiras, Alberto, and Héctor Alonso Moreno Parra. *Bolívar y el constitucionalismo*, 2nd ed. Santiago de Cali, Colombia: Editorial Universidad Santiago de Cali, 1999.

Ramos Núñez, Carlos. *Historia de la Corte Suprema de Justicia del Perú*. Lima: Fondo Editorial del Poder Judicial, 2008.

Ramos Santana, Alberto. "La Constitución de 1812 y los americanos." In *Visiones y revisiones de la independencia americana: La independencia de América: La Constitución de Cádiz y las constituciones iberoamericanas*, eds. Izaskun Álvarez Cuartero and Julio Sánchez Gómez, 87–108. Salamanca: Ediciones Universidad de Salamanca, 2003.

Rector, John L. *The History of Chile*. Westport, CT: Greenwood Press, 2003.

Reich, Peter Lester. *Mexico's Hidden Revolution: The Catholic Church in Law and Politics since 1929*. Notre Dame, IN: University of Notre Dame Press, 1995.

Reid, John Philip. *Constitutional History of the American Revolution: The Authority of Law*. Madison: University of Wisconsin Press, 1993.

Reid, Paul Joseph. "The Constitution of Cádiz and the Independence of Yucatán." *The Americas* 36, no. 1 (July 1979): 22–28.

Reinaldo Vanossi, Jorge. "La desconstitucionalización y la re-institucionalidad." In *La evolución político-constitucional de América del Sur 1976–2005*, ed. Humberto Nogueira Alcalá, 63–99. Santiago: Librotecnia, 2009.

Rieu-Millan, Marie Laure. *Los diputados americanos en las Cortes de Cádiz (Igualdad o Independencia)*. Madrid: Consejo Superior de Investigaciones Científicas, 1990.

Rivera S., José Antonio. "La evolución político-institucional en Bolivia entre 1975 a 2005." In *La evolución político-constitucional de América del Sur 1976–2005*, ed. Humberto Nogueira Alcalá, 101–150. Santiago: Librotecnia, 2009.

Roberts, Stephen G. H., and Adam Sharman. *1812 Echoes: The Cádiz Constitution in Hispanic History, Culture and Politics*. Newcastle upon Tyne: Cambridge Scholars Publishing, 2013.

Rock, David. *Argentina 1516–1987: From Spanish Colonization to Alfonsín*. Berkeley: Unversity of California Press, 1987.

Rodríguez, Mario. *The Cádiz Experiment in Central America, 1808–1826*. Berkeley: University of California Press, 1978.

Rodríguez O., Jaime E. *The Independence of Spanish America*. Cambridge: Cambridge University Press, 1998.

"We Are Now the True Spaniards:" Sovereignty, Revolution, Independence and the Emergence of the Federal Republic of Mexico, 1808–1824. Stanford: Standford University Press, 2012.

Rodríguez-Garavito, César. "Beyond the Courtroom: The Impact of Judicial Activism on Socioeconomic Rights in Latin America." *Texas Law Review* 89 (2011): 1669–1698.

Rojas, Rafael. "De reino a república: Traducciones del autonomismo gaditano." In *La revolución Novohispana 1808–1821*, ed. Antonio Annino, 191–220. Mexico: Fondo de Cultura Económica, 2010.

"La soledad constitucional del socialismo cubano." Presented August 10, 2011, Cuban Research Institute, Latin American and Caribbean Center, Florida International University, Miami, Florida.

Rosenkrantz, Carlos. "Constitutional Emergencies in Argentina: The Romans (not the Judges) Have the Solution." *Texas Law Review* 89 (2011): 1557–1586.

Rosenn, Keith S. "Judicial Review in Latin America." *Ohio State Law Journal* 35 (1974): 785–819.

"The Protection of Judicial Independence in Latin America." *University of Miami Law Review* 19 (1987): 1–35.

"The Success of Constitutionalism in the United States and Its Failure in Latin America." *University of Miami Inter-American Law Review* 22 (1990): 1–39.

Rossi, Julieta, and Leonardo Filippini. "El derecho internacional en la justiciabilidad de los derechos sociales." In *Derecho sociales: justicia, política y economía en América Latina*, coords. Pilar Arcidiácono, Nicolás Espejo Yaksic, and César Rodríguez Garavito, 195–234. Bogotá: Siglo del Hombre, 2010.

Safford, Frank. "Politics, Ideology and Society in Post-Independence Spanish America." In *The Cambridge History of Latin America*, ed. Leslie Bethell, Vol. 3, 347–421. Cambridge: Cambridge University Press, 1985.

Safford, Frank, and Marco Palacios. *Colombia: Fragmented Land, Divided Society*. Oxford: Oxford University Press, 2002.

Sagüés, Néstor Pedro. "Evolución institucional Argentina: Sistema de gobierno, poder judicial, derechos fundamentales (1975–2005)." In *La evolución político-constitucional de América del Sur 1976–2005*, ed. Humberto Nogueira Alcalá, 21–61. Santiago: Librotecnia, 2009.

"An Introduction and Commentary to the Reform of the Argentine National Constitution." Keith S. Rossen, trans. *University of Miami Inter-American Law Review* 28 (1996), 41.

Sala Vila, Nuria. "La Constitución de Cádiz y su impacto en el gobierno de las comunidades indígenas en el virreinato del Perú." *Boletín Americanista* 33, nos. 42–43 (1992–1993): 51–70.

Salazar Andreu, Juan Pablo. "Puebla de los Ángeles en el contexto de la Constitución Española de 1812." *Anuario Mexicano de Historia del Derecho* 22 (2010): 327–338.

Salgado Pesantes, Hernán. "Treinta años de democracia formal en el Ecuador (1978–2008)." In *La evolución político-constitucional de América del Sur 1976–2005*, ed. Humberto Nogueira Alcalá, 399–419. Santiago: Librotecnia, 2009.

Santana, Arturo. *José Álvarez de Toledo: El revolucionario Cubano en las Cortes de Cádiz y sus esfuerzos por la emancipación de las Antillas*. San Juan: Centro de Estudios Avanzados de Puerto Rico y el Caribe, 2006.

Sayeg Helú, Jorge. *El constitucionalismo social Mexicano: La integración constitucional de México (1808–1988)*. México: Fondo de Cultura Económica, 1991.

Scheppele, Kim Lane. "Aspirational and Adversive Constitutions: The Case for Studying Cross-constitutional Influence through Negative Models." *International Journal of Constitutional Law* 1 (2003): 296–324.

Schor, Miguel. "Constitutionalism through the Looking Glass of Latin America." *Texas International Law Journal* 41 (2006), 1–37.

"An Essay on the Emergence of Constitutional Courts: The Cases of Mexico and Colombia." *Indiana Journal of Global Legal Studies* 16, 173–194.

Scott, Rebecca J. *Slave Emancipation in Cuba: The Transition to Free Labor, 1860–1899*. Princeton, NJ: Princeton University Press, 1985.

Solórzano Pereyra, J. *Política Indiana*, Vols. 1–5. Reprinted in Biblioteca de Autores Españoles, Vols. 252–256. Madrid: Atlas, 1972.

Stozky, Irwin. P. ed. *Transition to Democracy in Latin America: The Role of the Judiciary*. Boulder, CO: Westview Press, 1993.

Suarez-Potts, William J. *The Making of Law: The Supreme Court and Labor Legislation in Mexico, 1875–1931*. Stanford: Stanford University Press, 2012.

Suárez Suárez, Reinaldo. "Repercusiones de la Constitución de Cádiz: Guridi y Alcocer y la esclavitud en Cuba." *Anuario Mexicano de Historia del Derecho* 22 (2010): 339–366.

Summerhill, William R. "Fiscal Bargains, Political Institutions, and Economic Performance." *Hispanic American Historical Review* 88 (2008): 219–233.

Tau Anzoátegui, Victor. *Las ideas jurídicas en la Argentina (Siglos XIX–XX)*. Buenos Aires: Perrot, 1977.

La ley en América Hispana del descubrimiento a la emancipación. Buenos Aires: Academica Nacional de la Historia, 1992.

"Las observaciones de Benito de la Mata Linares a la Constitución de Bayona." *Boletín de la Real Academia de la Historia* 178 (1981): 243–266.

Tena Ramírez, Felipe. *Derecho constitucional mexicano*, 33rd ed. México: Porrúa, 2000.

Ternavasio, Marcela. "Entre el cabildo colonial y el municipio moderno: Los juzgados de paz de Campaña en el estado de Buenos Aires, 1821–1855." In *Dinámicas de Antiguo Régimen y orden constitucional: Representación, justicia y administración en Iberoamérica, siglos xviii-xix*, coord. Marco Bellingeri, 295–336. Torino: Otto Editore, 2000.

Tío Vallejo, Gabriela. "Los 'vasallos más distantes.' Justicia y gobierno, la afirmación de la autonomía capitular en la época de la intendencia. San Miguel de Tucumán." In *Dinámicas de Antiguo Régimen y orden constitucional: Representación, justicia y administración en Iberoamérica, siglos xviii-xix*, coord. Marco Bellingeri, 217–260. Torino: Otto Editore, 2000.

Tomás y Valiente, Francisco. *Agustín de Argüelles, Discursos*. Bilbao: Junta General del Principado de Asturias, 1995.

Torres-Cuevas, E., J. Ibarra Cuesta, and M. García Rodríguez, eds. *Obras. Félix Varela: El primero que nos enseñó en pensar*. Habana: Editorial Cultura Popular y Ediciones Imagen Contemporánea, 1997.

Uprimny, Rodrigo. "The Recent Transformation of Constitutional Law Latin America: Trends and Challenges." *Texas Law Review* 89 (2011): 1587–1610.

Uribe-Urán, Victor M. "La Constitución de Cádiz en la Nueva Granada, teoría y realidad, 1812–1821." In *La Constitución de 1812 en Hispanoamérica y España*, ed. Heraclio Bonillo, 272–303. Botogá: Alcaldía Mayor de Bogotá, 2012.

Honorable Lives: Lawyers, Family, and Politics in Colombia, 1780–1850. Pittsburgh: University of Pittsburgh Press, 2000.

Valadés, Diego. *La dictadura constitucional en América Latina*. México: Universidad Nacional Autónoma de México, 1974.

Valcárcel, C. D. "Bayona, constitución determinante de la de Cádiz." *Cuadernos Americanos* 186, no. 1 (January–February 1972): 137–145.

Valdés Domínguez, Eusebio. *Los antigüos diputados de Cuba y apuntes para la historia constitucional de esta isla.* Habana: Imprenta El Telegrafo, 1879.

Van Young, Eric. "El momento antimoderno: Localismo e insurgencia en México, 1810–1821." In *La revolución Novohispana 1808–1821,* ed. Antonio Annino, 221–292. México: Fondo de Cultura Económica, 2010.

Varela y Morales, Félix. *Observaciones sobre la Constitución Política de la Monarquía Española.* Habana: 1821; Madrid: Centro de Estudios Políticos y Constitucionales, 2008.

Varela Suanzes-Carpegna, Joaquín. "El constitucionalismo español y portugués durante la primera mitad del Siglo xix (un estudio comparado)." In *Visiones y revisiones de la independencia americana: La independencia de América: la Constitución de Cádiz y las constituciones iberoamericanas,* eds. Izaskun Álvarez Cuartero and Julio Sánchez Gómez, 13–51. Salamanca: Ediciones Universidad de Salamanca, 2003.

Velasco Ibarra, J. M. *Expresión política hispanoamericana: Ensayo sobre derecho constitucional hispanoamericano.* Santiago: Zig Zag, 1943.

Villabella Armengol, Carlos Manuel. "El constitucionalismo español en Cuba. La Constitución de Cádiz de 1812 y su repercusión en la Isla," In *De Cádiz (1812) a la Habana (2012): Escritos con motivo del bicentenario de la Constitución española de 1812,* eds. Andry Matilla Correa and Marcos Francisco Massó Garrote, 208–241. Havana: Organización Nacional de Bufetes Colectivos, 2011.

Villalonga, Cristián. *Revolución y Ley: La teoría crítica del derecho en Eduardo Novoa Monreal.* Santiago: Colección Derecho y Sociedad, 2008.

Volio, Marina. *Costa Rica en las Cortes de Cádiz.* San José: Editorial Juricentro, 1980.

Williford, Miriam. *Jeremy Bentham on Spanish America; An Account of His Letters and Proposals to the New World.* Baton Rouge: Louisiana State University Press, 1980.

Zamora, Stephen, José Ramón Cossío, Leonel Pereznieto, José Roldán-Xopa, and David Lopez. *Mexican Law.* Oxford: Oxford University Press, 2004.

Zavala, Silvio A. *Las instituciones jurídicas en la conquista de América.* México: Porrúa, 1971.

Zimmermann, Eduardo, ed. *Judicial Institutions in Nineteenth-Century Latin America.* London: Institute of Latin American Studies, 1999.

Index

Abascal y Sousa, José Fernando de, 77,
    101, 110
absolutism, 42, 71
accidents, 211
*Acta de la Federación de las Provincias
    Unidas de Nueva Granada of 1811*,
    25, 273
Adelman, Jeremy, 10
affirmative action, 259
afrancesados, 28, 33
Africa, 91, 98, 99, 120, 270, 276, 277
Afro-Latins, 267
Agar y Bustillo, Pedro, 36
agrarian reform, 187, 202, 241
    Bolivia, 228, 265
    Chile, 222
    Colombia, 217
    Cuba, 215
    Mexico, 5, 183, 204, 206, 213, 214, 237
Aguilar Rivera, José Antonio, 142,
    146, 180, 181, 182, 193, 194, 212,
    238, 263
Alamán, Lucas, 126, 179, 181, 188, 190
Alarcón, Fabián, 247
Alberdi, Juan Bautista, 159, 160, 161, 162,
    190, 199
Alessandri, Arturo, 220, 221
Alfonsín, Raúl, 225, 241, 242
*Alianza Popular Revolucionaria Americana
    (APRA)*, 226, 227, 231
Allen, Dr. John, 51, 70
Allende, Salvador, 222, 223, 234, 235
Álvarez de Toledo, José, 89, 90

amendment of constitution, prohibition,
    49, 107, 281
amnesty, 261
amparo, 14, 196, 197, 200, 204, 208, 211,
    233, 252, 255–258, 271
anarchy, 204
ancient constitution, 2, 9, 11, 50, 55, 56,
    57, 58, 73, 101, 102, 146
Andalucía, 92
Andes, 108
Anér, Felipe, 95
Angostura
    Constitution of 1819, 149, 150
    Discourse, 149
Angulo, José, 24
Annino, Antonio, 122
antidiscrimination laws, 267
Antioquia (Colombia)
    Constitution of 1812, 25
Apodaca, Juan Ruiz de, 136
Aragón, 33, 276
Aramburu, Pedro Eugenio, 225
Aranjuez, 33, 35
arbitration, 47, 65, 211
Arequipa, 88, 101
Argentina, 100, 127, 130, 133, 148,
    156–164, 165, 168, 198, 202, 215,
    224–226, 235, 250, 251, 254, 257
    abolition of slavery, 100
    amparo, 257
    Constitution of 1819, 133, 157,
        187, 199
    Constitution of 1826, 133, 158

307

Made in the USA
Coppell, TX
20 August 2021